Richard Owens
September 30, 2010.
Geneva.

Birmingham

PEVSNER ARCHITECTURAL GUIDES

Founding Editor: Nikolaus Pevsner

PEVSNER ARCHITECTURAL GUIDES

The Buildings of England series was created and largely written
by Sir Nikolaus Pevsner (1902–83). First editions of the county
volumes were published by Penguin Books between 1951 and 1974.
The continuing programme of revisions and new volumes has
been supported by research financed through the Buildings Books
Trust since 1994.

The Buildings Books Trust gratefully acknowledges
Grants towards the cost of research, writing and illustrations
for this volume from:

THE HERITAGE LOTTERY FUND

THE VICTORIAN SOCIETY MARY HEATH FUND

Assistance with photographs from:

ENGLISH HERITAGE
(photographer: James O. Davies)

Birmingham

ANDY FOSTER

with contributions by

GEORGE DEMIDOWICZ

IAN DUNGAVELL

OLIVER FAIRCLOUGH

ELAIN HARWOOD

PEVSNER ARCHITECTURAL GUIDES

YALE UNIVERSITY PRESS

NEW HAVEN & LONDON

In memory of my parents, Charles and Irene Foster
and also of David Bettelley, fellow churchcrawler of schooldays.

The publishers gratefully acknowledge help in
bringing the books to a wider readership from
ENGLISH HERITAGE

YALE UNIVERSITY PRESS
NEW HAVEN AND LONDON
302 Temple Street, New Haven CT06511
47 Bedford Square, London WC1B 3DP

www.pevsner.co.uk
www.lookingatbuildings.org
www.yalebooks.co.uk
www.yalebooks.com

Published 2005; reprinted with corrections 2007
10 9 8 7 6 5 4 3 2

Set in Adobe Minion by SNP Best-set Typesetter Ltd., Hong Kong
Printed in Singapore by CS Graphics

Library of Congress Cataloging-in-Publication Data

Foster, Andy.
Birmingham / Andy Foster ; with contributions by George Demidowicz . . .
[et al.].
  p. cm. – (Pevsner architectural guides)
  Includes bibliographical references and index.
  ISBN 978–0–300–10731–9 (pbk. : alk. paper)
  1. Architecture – England – Birmingham – Guidebooks. 2. Birmingham
(England) – Buildings, structures, etc. – Guidebooks. 3. Birmingham
(England) – Guidebooks. I. Demidowicz, George. II. Title. III. Series.
  NA971.B5F67 2005
  720´.9424´96–dc22
                              2004023814

Contents

RIVER TAME

N

M5

Excursion 2:
Soho House and
Soho Foundry

Exc
Aste
Aste

A456

EDGBASTON:
THE NINETEENTH-
CENTURY SUBURB

EDGBASTON:
THE UNIVERSITY
QUARTER

A456

A4040

BOURNVILLE

WORCESTER AND
BIRMINGHAM
CANAL

A38

1. Birmingham, showing areas covered by walks

Excursion 4:
St Mary, Pype Hayes

M6

A5127

B4148

A38

A38

A5127

nd
Church

RIVER COLE

GHAM
NTRE

Excursion 3:
St Agatha, Sparkbrook

A45 (Airport)

A41

GRAND UNION
CANAL

A34

A4040

HALL GREEN

0   4 km

0   2.6 miles

How to use this book

This book is designed as a practical architectural guide to inner Birmingham, and to a selection of outstanding areas and buildings in the suburbs. The divisions between the sections are shown on the map on pp. vi–vii. After a historical Introduction, the gazetteer begins on p. 39 with entries on eight Major Buildings in the centre. The area within the inner ring road is then described, with alphabetical street entries for the commercial centre followed by a separate section on the Newhall Estate area immediately to the north. Four Walks explore districts just outside the centre, and four further Walks cover selected suburbs: Edgbaston (two), Bournville, and Hall Green. Each Walk is provided with its own street map, and most are subdivided for ease of navigation. The final section suggests four excursions to buildings of outstanding interest elsewhere in the suburbs.

Other architectural highlights in the suburbs are mentioned briefly in the Introduction. A full re-survey of the suburbs, of the Black Country to the north, and of the surrounding counties of Staffordshire, Warwickshire and Worcestershire will be undertaken in future volumes in the *Buildings of England* hardback series.

Throughout the book, certain topics are singled out for special attention and presented in separate boxes:

Lost Buildings: Birmingham's Medieval Buildings p. 4, New Street Station p. 110

Birmingham Architects and Artists: William Hollins: The First Birmingham Architect? p. 8, William Bloye p. 65, J.H. Chamberlain p. 72, W.H. Bidlake p. 291

Building Types: Reformed Pubs p. 25, Arts and Crafts Churches p. 86

St Philip's Cathedral: The Stained Glass p. 45

Central Library: Shakespeare Memorial Room p. 80

Planning: The Civic Centre Schemes p. 144, Sir Herbert Manzoni p. 197, Madin's Edgbaston Plan of 1957 p. 214

Patrons and Manufacturers: George Cadbury and his Social Vision p. 257, The Soho Enterprises p. 287

Materials and Methods: Arts and Crafts Architects and brick bonding p. 295

Acknowledgements

My first debt is to Alexandra Wedgwood and the late Sir Nikolaus Pevsner, whose *Warwickshire* (1966) first made me look, as a schoolboy, at Birmingham's buildings. It is a particular pleasure, therefore, to thank Lady Wedgwood for help with Pugin and St Chad's for this book. Next come my thanks to the other contributors to this volume: George Demidowicz (Soho House and Soho Foundry), Ian Dungavell (Victoria Law Courts and the Webb & Bell buildings at Birmingham University), Oliver Fairclough (Aston Hall), and Elain Harwood (later C20 buildings at Birmingham University). Among the current staff of the Pevsner Architectural Guides my greatest debt is to Simon Bradley, who turned my rambling drafts into crisp and accurate descriptions. Many thanks also to Sally Salvesen; to Emily Winter, for her hard work in getting this book produced on time; to Emily Lees for her resourcefulness in dealing with illustrations; to Charlotte Chapman for copyediting; to Judith Wardman for the index; and to Touchmedia for the maps. I am particularly grateful to James O. Davies of English Heritage for his photographs, which make many points far better than any words. I am also grateful to Bridget Cherry, and to Gavin Watson for help with many administration matters. My thanks also to my fellow City Guide authors, especially Andrew Foyle, Clare Hartwell and Joseph Sharples, for much encouragement and support.

Several groups of people deserve special thanks. First, the staff of the Birmingham Central Library: Archives section, especially David Bishop, Rachel Macgregor, Zoe Rees, Angela Quinby, Chris Peers, and Alison Smith; and Local Studies section, particularly Richard Abbott, Patrick Baird, Joseph McKenna, and Paul Taylor. Fellow researchers in the Library gave much help and encouragement, especially John Bassindale, James Hyland, Peter Leather, and Ray Shill.

A few people gave expert help, including reading drafts, on particular topics: Alan Crawford (Arts and Crafts Movement), Michael Harrison (Bournville), Anthony Peers (Town Hall), Stephen Price (early buildings). Harry Harper walked round with some of the draft text, and made many helpful suggestions. Alan Brooks shared his knowledge of C19 stained glass and kindly came with me to check attributions. The staff of the Conservation group, Planning Department were endlessly helpful. My greatest debt here is to Toni Demidowicz for sharing her research into c18 and c19 building; also to her colleagues Chris Hargreaves, Richard Hudson, Stephen King and Nicola Coxon. Les Reynolds and his colleagues Justin Grace and Chantal Blair helped greatly with checking planning applications. Finally, friends in the Birmingham and West Midlands Group of the Victorian Society gave endless encouragement, especially Jim Berrow, Joe Holyoak, David Low, Stephen Hartland, Mary Worsfield and Barbara Shackley.

Several practising and retired architects gave me much help with their own or their firm's work: John Madin, John Ericsson, Derek Davis and Fred Mark (John Madin Design Group); Graham Winteringham and Bob Tolley (S.T. Walker & Partners); John Christophers and Walter Thomson (Associated Architects); Vernon Crofts (Seymour Harris Partnership); Peter Brownhill (Brownhill Hayward Brown); Martin Purdy (APEC).

For help of many kinds, including access to and information on individual buildings, I am grateful to: Laura Alden, the Rev. Jenny Arnold, Philip Aubury, Peter Baird, Phillada Ballard, David Blissett, Ann Brown, Anthony Collins, Chris Cronin, Michael Delaney, Fr Brian Doolan, Chris Eckersley, Edward Fellows, Alan Flight, Richard Gale, Andor Gomme, Stephen Grainger, Roger Hancox, Bill Harding, James Haworth, Peter Heath, Fr John Hervé, Michael Hodgetts, Julian Holder, Peter Howell, Michael Huxley-Evans, Chris Kirk, John Kirwan, Martin Lawton, Arthur Lockwood, Grace McCombie, George McHardy, Bernadette and Patrick Mellett, Roger Millward, Nick Molyneux, Ruth Mosley, Martin Mullaney, John Mullen, Fr Guy Nicholls, Dr and Mrs O'Neill, Steve Parsons, Elizabeth Perkins, Alan Powers, Audrey Price, the Rev. Tom Pyke, the Rev. Duncan Raynor, Michael Reardon, Colin Rodgers, John Sawkill, the Rev. David Senior, Fr John Sharp, Ron Singer, Alistair and Chloe Smith, Paul Spencer-Longhurst, the late Canon Ralph Stevens, the late John Surman, Jean Templeton, Canon Nicholas Thistlethwaite, the Rev. Nigel Traynor, Tony Trott, Dame Rachel Waterhouse, Stephen Wildman, David and Fiona Williams, Jeff and Gill Wilyman, Bill Wood, Stephen Wycherley, John Yates and Andy Yeo. Also to anyone I have forgotten, with my apologies.

Finally three slightly older personal thank-yous: to the late Douglas Hickman, who I have wished was there to consult on every day of writing this book; to teachers, in time order the late May Henry, Charles Blount, Michael Parslew, Bruce Hurn, Duncan Robinson, David Watkin, and Geoff Hoare; and to Dick (Sir Richard) Knowles and colleagues of all parties, for putting up with me on the city Planning Committee between 1981 and 1992.

The shortage of published sources on Birmingham architecture meant that this book involved much primary research. For this reason, and others, it will certainly have errors and omissions. May I appeal to readers to send corrections to me at the publishers.

Introduction

Introduction

From the Middle Ages to the Civil War

Birmingham is the largest city in Britain outside London (population 977,087 in 2001). Between the C16 and C19 it grew from a Midlands town into one of the greatest manufacturing centres in the world: the 'city of a thousand trades'. It did so without any natural advantage of geography. It is not on the sea, or a navigable river. The old town, a settlement in the ancient forest of Arden, lies on the w bank of the modest River Rea, on a slope leading to a modest ridge along the present Colmore Row. It gained a market charter in 1166 but in medieval times was never incorporated as a borough. This made it open to immigrant craftsmen and labourers, without the restraints a system of burgesses would have put upon trade.

What gave Birmingham its economic advantage was its location. It lies immediately SE, on the side nearer London, of the scatter of villages now linked into the conurbation of the Black Country, already in medieval times a centre of iron and coal working. Birmingham used these resources to make metal goods. A goldsmith is recorded as early as 1406. In 1511 the Clerk to the Ordnance ordered horseshoes and bits from Birmingham makers. In 1538 Leland found 'many smiths in the towne that use to make knives and all mannour of cutting tooles, and many lorimers that make bits, and a great many naylors. So that a great part of the towne is maintained by smithes . . .' There were ample streams, many with water mills. In 1643 Prince Rupert, Charles I's commander in the Civil War, sacked the unfortified town because its gunmakers were supplying Parliament's armies.

The late medieval town was overwhelmingly composed of timber-framed buildings. The cutting of New Street in the C14 suggests it was already a thriving market centre by then. It had a small hospital or priory, and two guilds: the Guild of the Holy Cross, re-founded at the Reformation as King Edward's School, and the Guild of St John the Baptist of Deritend, whose guildhall, now the Old Crown Inn, is the only complete medieval building to survive. As a complex of hall, school and master's accommodation it is comparable to e.g. the Guildhall in Stratford-on-Avon and that at Lavenham, Suffolk.

2. St Martin in the Bull Ring, left, and Selfridges, by Future Systems, 2001–3

Birmingham's Medieval Buildings

Early C19 guidebooks drew attention to Birmingham's wealth of timber-framed buildings, comparing it with Shrewsbury and Chester. Samuel Lines' drawings of *c.* 1800 show houses around St Martin's churchyard with jettied first floors and heavy curved angle braces, probably C15. C16 and C17 houses developed as tall, multi-gabled jettied structures. The wall framing was in distinctive West Midlands patterns: close studding, herringbone work and square panels with decorative braces forming quadrant patterns in the gables. The type was exemplified by Lamb House, Bull Street (dem. 1889) and the Golden Lion Inn, Deritend, of which the front survives, re-erected in Cannon Hill Park. Timber construction survived into the C17 and even the early C18, as the evidence of a timber structure at No. 137 Digbeth shows.

The local sandstone, used for medieval churches and for houses from the C16 at least, is easily worked but erodes badly. It survives inside the tower of St Martin, and the C15 tower of Aston church is also built of it. The sandy local soil, however, has been used to make excellent bricks since the C16. Brick, with sandstone dressings, is used for the single surviving building in the Jacobean style: Aston Hall, built from 1618 onwards from designs by *John Thorpe*. This is a major country house now within the city, comparable to e.g. Hatfield or Blickling, conservative in its **U**-shaped plan but progressive in its external symmetry (enhanced by mid-C17 alterations).

From the Restoration to the Mid Eighteenth Century

Birmingham grew rapidly in the century following the Civil War, from a population of 5,372 in 1650 to 15,032 in 1700, and around 35,000 by 1760. The town's first **planned development**, Old Square, was begun in 1697 by John Pemberton. Its two-storey brick houses had hipped roofs and end pilasters, late examples of a Restoration style deriving from Holland. Development of the Phillips (later Inge) and Walker lands started with Temple Street, laid out from 1709, and Temple Row from 1715. Cherry Street and Cannon Street were laid out in 1733, and the Colmore family's Newhall estate, NW of what is now Colmore Row, was started in 1747, following a private Act the previous year. Development was happening all round the town: Freeman Street, between Moor Street and Park Street, was laid out in 1728, and houses spread w up New Street and as far as Suffolk Street.

The most significant building of this period is **St Philip's** church (now cathedral), begun in 1709. It is exceptional, an early and sophisticated Baroque design by *Thomas Archer*, brother of a Warwickshire squire, and the only English architect of his day who knew the Italy of Bernini and Borromini. The Italian influence is most obvious in the contrasted convex and concave shapes of the tower, but the nave exterior, with its fully developed giant Doric order, is also progressive. Hall Green church of 1703 by *Sir William Wilson*, originally a country chapel, has a much more rustic Doric order, though still forward-looking for its date. The most important house of the period is also rural in origin: **Edgbaston Hall**, of 1717, perhaps by *Francis Smith* of Warwick. It is an extremely plain brick block with a parapet, its one progressive feature a *piano nobile*. The main staircase, of 1751–2 by *William & David Hiorn*, is a fine piece, though by then old-fashioned.

Early C18 **town houses** in the principal streets were of a provincial Baroque type, with parapets (some with swept-up ends), pedimented doorcases, and sometimes decorative lintels. A few doorcases had swan-neck pediments, e.g. in Temple Row. Colmore leases specified houses of three storeys with sash windows and stone dressings including a 'cornis' and 'stone arches over and stone walls and blocks under' the front windows. The last survivors disappeared in the 1960s.

Builders were mostly craftsmen. The carpenter *Samuel Avery* was active in Temple Street, Temple Row, Freeman Street and elsewhere. Another carpenter, *William Westley* (*Sen.*), the bricklayer *Richard Pinley*, and other workmen associated with St Philip's also appear. Away from the main streets, new buildings still had plain walls and steep roofs well into the C18; the Fox and Grapes, Freeman Street, completed by 1731, is a rare survivor.*

Birmingham *c.* 1760–*c.* 1830

The population of Birmingham (excluding Deritend, in Aston parish) grew from *c.* 35,000 in 1760 to 74,037 in 1811. The town continued to attract skilled and enterprising people from surrounding areas, which helped it survive the depressions due to the French wars after 1793. Small specialist trades flourished: toy-making (small metal articles), button-making, gunmaking. The town was also helped by better transport and by the development of the Black Country ironmaking. It became an important centre of canals, beginning with the Birmingham Canal of 1768–72. Banking began with Taylors and Lloyds in 1765, and insurance offices multiplied in the early C19.

Growth was continuous in all directions. The Colmore estate NW of Colmore Row started in 1746 and its NW part around St Paul's Square was developed from 1777. SW of the town were the Gough, Gooch and Inge estates, with surviving houses in Horse Fair of *c.* 1778 and in

*The best place now to appreciate Birmingham buildings of the early C18 is High Street, Sutton Coldfield. No. 20, of *c.* 1700 with hipped roof and giant end pilasters, is similar to the original houses in Old Square. No. 36 has a swept-up parapet and a doorcase with swan-neck pediment, like the first houses in Temple Row. Nos. 42–44 have stone lintels like the first Newhall Estate houses in Colmore Row.

Bromsgrove Street of 1792–3. A handsome and consistent Georgian townscape is recorded in old photographs of the main streets. The standard house type remained three-storeyed, of brick, with decoration confined to simple lintels and doorcases. A common lintel design from *c.* 1790 is segmental, with a thin continuous moulding, small end stops, and usually a similar keystone, e.g. Nos. 99–100 Bromsgrove Street and Nos. 55–63 Hurst Street. A design like a modest cornice, on consoles, appears by 1816 (Brewmaster's House, by the Convention Centre) and is used up to the mid C19. At the end of the C18 Wyatt-type windows appear, with a central light flanked by narrower ones in a single frame, e.g. at No. 64 Hagley Road of *c.* 1795 (cf. Samuel Wyatt's Theatre Royal [3]). Surviving doorcases of the 1780s in St Paul's Square show the common local type with open pediments and, sometimes, Doric half-columns. Formal schemes were rare: the Crescent, N of Broad Street, by *Charles Norton*, was started in 1795 but only a small section was completed (dem. *c.* 1960). Matthew Boulton's Soho House of 1796–9, perhaps by *Samuel Wyatt*, is exceptional as a grand Neoclassical design, though smaller early C19 villas survive at No. 3 Summer Hill Terrace and Heaton House, Camden Street. Sustained development of Edgbaston began in 1810, with typical Late Georgian houses. Most seem to be builders' designs, e.g. No. 60 Calthorpe Road of 1814–15. For the fine group at Nos. 97–109 Hagley Road we know that *Thomas* and *Joseph Bateman* were the surveyors, but it is not certain that they designed it.

All these houses, however, were exceptional. The great majority of development was in densely packed courtyards of back-to-back houses, with small workshops close by. The best surviving example is Nos. 55–63 Hurst Street and Court No. 15, Inge Street. Original details here are extremely simple: sashes of the plainest type and a characteristic oval serif-lettered court number plate. Slightly grander houses were passage-entry pairs or 'three-quarter' houses, e.g. Nos. 37–40 Lee Crescent of *c.* 1830, with fronts like a single three-bay house, but a passage behind the central entrance to houses at each end.

Expansion on such a scale brought other changes in its train. **Street Commissioners** were set up under an Act of 1765 with highway and lighting powers, and gained greater powers under an Improvement Act of 1801. Between 1806 and 1809 they cleared and redeveloped the old houses around the Bull Ring, and replanned the market space with a pump by *William Hollins* (who also designed the Commissioners' offices; *see* topic box, p. 8) and *Westmacott*'s Nelson monument.

The **Birmingham Churches Act** of 1772 meanwhile allowed the building of St Mary, by *Joseph Pickford* of Derby, 1773–4, with an octagonal nave (dem. 1925), and the surviving St Paul, by *Roger Eykyn* of Wolverhampton, 1777–9, a handsome but old-fashioned Gibbsian design. Christ Church (dem. 1899), by *Charles Norton* with *William Whitmore*, was begun in 1805 but went through several hands before completion in 1814, with a much-criticized spire replacing the proposed cupola. Of the new generation of churches after Waterloo, the exterior of *Francis Goodwin*'s Holy Trinity, Bordesley of 1822 survives – a Gothick box of King's College Chapel type, elegantly done. *Thomas Rickman*'s St George, 1819–22, was by contrast very forward-looking, a landmark of the early Gothic Revival; Charles Eastlake's *History of the Gothic Revival* (1872) praised its late Middle Pointed style, its fine tower, and lack of 'structural meanness' except for its iron windows. Rickman's St Peter, Dale End (dem.), 1825–7, and St Thomas, Bath Row, 1826–9, of which the tower survives, were impressive classical pieces, perhaps by his short-lived partner *Henry Hutchinson*. Rickman's last two Birmingham churches were less correct Gothic: All Saints of 1832–3 was octagonal, Bishop Ryder church, Gem Street, of 1838 had a very tall tower with octagonal belfry. The grandest Nonconformist meeting house, since replaced, was Carrs Lane chapel, as rebuilt in 1820 by *Thomas Stedman Whitwell*.

Other **public institutions** were modest architecturally. The General Hospital, opened in 1779 in Summer Lane, was plain with a pedimented centre, like a large villa. The Blue Coat School in St Philip's Place was rebuilt equally plainly by *John Rawstorne*, 1792. The Theatre Royal of 1773–4 was given a sophisticated new façade by *Samuel Wyatt* in 1780, exceptional in the town. The first floor had an open Ionic colonnade between end pavilions. The ground floor opened in segmental arches. Its influence is visible in the ground-floor elevation of the former New Meeting House of 1802, off Albert Street. Wyatt's elegant Neoclassicism can still be seen in his E window surround of 1791 at St Paul's church.

In **industrial architecture**, the Soho Manufactory of 1765–7 by *William Wyatt* was exceptional for size and pretension, if not sophistication. The Birmingham Canal Navigation offices of 1771 were an

3. Theatre Royal, New Street, façade by Samuel Wyatt, 1780. Engraving, 1783

Architects of the 1760s–70s often came from outside: Pickford of Derby, Eykyn of Wolverhampton. The local names which appear slightly later are builder-architects: Charles Norton, John Horton. *William Hollins* (1763–1843) is closer to an architect in the modern sense of one providing designs for others, even if no surviving building can definitely be attributed to him. He was trained as a stonemason, and worked all his life as a monumental sculptor, with a great liking for drooping laurels. As an architect he was self-taught: in the words of his obituary, 'he boldly forged a key to the temple of knowledge'. His Old Library of 1798 in Union Street had slightly fussy paired pilasters but an elegant bow containing the entrance. The Public Offices in Moor Street, 1805–7, were a competent reworking of the centre of Samuel Wyatt's Theatre Royal façade. His 1806 proposal for a memorial column to Nelson, 100 ft (30 metres) high, rising from 'an appropriate building with two fronts suitable for a dispensary and post office', was rejected in favour of Westmacott's design (*see* p. 86). In 1807 he designed a modest tapering 'Egyptian' pump for the Bull Ring, and in a public letter traced its ancestry back for 3,297 years to the worship of Osiris. St Austin (R.C.) church of 1808–9 was simple, with a Doric porch. The Union Mill of 1813 in Grosvenor Street West, with its crisp pedimented centre, looks like Hollins's work [5].

original but slightly incoherent group of octagonal centre linked by archways to quadrant side ranges, with prominent Diocletian windows. The surviving Brasshouse of 1781 in Broad Street has a charming but rather overloaded façade with a central Venetian window flanked by Wyatt triplets. The Gun Barrel Proof House of 1813–14 is a lovable piece of builder's Georgian by *John Horton*.

Birmingham, *c*. 1830–*c*. 1865

In the years around 1830 Birmingham was at the forefront of national politics. The Birmingham Political Union was founded in 1830 by Thomas Attwood and its huge public rallies helped secure the parliamentary Reform Act of 1832. A further campaign gained the town a Borough charter in 1838. This new self-confidence was reflected in a series of high quality **public buildings**, on a larger scale than anything existing in the town, and increasingly showing the stylistic pluralism of the C19.

The largest building yet seen in the town was *Charles Edge*'s Market Hall of 1831–5, a massive Greek Revival block with a spectacular iron roof structure and columns inside. *Hansom & Welch*'s Town Hall was begun in 1832. Its temple design raised on a high basement, based on the Temple of Castor and Pollux in the Roman Forum, marks the beginning of a Roman Revival in English architecture which Frank Salmon has acutely related to the admiration of Radicals such as Attwood for Roman republican ideals. In their brief career, before bankruptcy in 1834, its architects tried to ride the radical wave. They were early Socialists; Hansom brought Robert Owen to the town in 1833. At the Town Hall they recognized building unions (while Walthews, contractors at the Market Hall, dismissed union members). They were skilled in public relations: in 1833 the radical *Birmingham Journal* ran the first architectural features in a local newspaper, concentrating on Hansom & Welch's work.

King Edward's School in New Street was rebuilt in 1833–7 by *Charles Barry*, a great contrast to Hansom & Welch: a respectable and hugely successful C19 figure. His design was consciously scholastic, in Tudor Gothic, fashionable in the 1830s, but also referring to the foundation in 1552. The street front, with tall three-light windows and stepped buttresses, closely followed John Shaw Sen.'s Great Hall of 1829 at Christ's Hospital in London, but with gable-ends replacing Shaw's turrets. Its fanciful central spire was not built. Much of the stone carving and woodwork was executed from 1833 by the young *A.W.N. Pugin*. Its scholarship and confidence prefigure his greater collaboration with Barry at the Houses of Parliament.*

Pugin returned to Birmingham to design St Chad's Cathedral, built 1839–41. Its use of foreign sources is exceptional for its date, but the change of approach from Barry's work is immediately recognizable also in e.g. its reduction of window area compared to wall, and irregular but functional picturesque grouping. This was more prominent in *Pugin*'s Bishop's House of 1840 (dem.) opposite the cathedral, a pioneer of picturesque, functional domestic Gothic.

Pugin's influence was twofold. First, he encouraged quality manufacturers, especially *Hardmans*, whose stained glass is exceptionally important in the rediscovery of medieval design and colouring, but who also produced brassware of a new standard for the town. More immediately obvious was his effect on archaeologically accurate **church design**. It can be seen in the work of the Birmingham Church Building Society (the 'Ten Churches Fund'). This was an Anglican and Tory project, led by the Rev. John Garbett, vicar of St George's, John Taylor the banker and Daniel Ledsam. Its first church, St Matthew Duddeston, by *William Thomas*, 1838, is a simple brick box with lancet windows. St Luke, Bristol Street, by *Harvey Eginton*, 1839, was Neo-Norman; St Mark, Ladywood was an early design by *Gilbert Scott*, 1841, still with paired lancets (both dem.). Then comes a change. St Stephen, Newtown Row of 1843–4 and St Andrew, Bordesley of 1844–6 (both also dem.) were early works by the 'Anglican Pugin', *R.C. Carpenter*, in simple but confident Dec, with flowing tracery. *Hamilton & Medland*'s

---

*The upper corridor of the C19 building was re-erected within the school's new Edgbaston premises after its demolition in the 1930s.

chapel (dem.) and surviving lodge at Warstone Lane cemetery of 1847–8 are thoroughly Puginian. *S.S. Teulon*'s St James, Edgbaston of 1850–3 is picturesque mid-C19 'rogue' Gothic, with complex timber-work, big dormers, and involved window tracery. Significantly, his very un-Puginian Gothic was for an Evangelical patron, Lord Calthorpe.

Local architects become more numerous around 1830. *Charles Edge* followed the Market Hall with a Greek Doric chapel of 1836 at Key Hill Cemetery, a typical Nonconformist choice of style, contrasting with Anglican Gothic. Edge is difficult to assess because surviving drawings are mostly for demolished buildings, while similar survivors cannot certainly be attributed. But it is clear that he plays variations on two or three types. One has entrances at one or both ends, with the centre hardly stressed, in a way typical of early C19 Neoclassicism: the Bank of Birmingham of 1833, and a house of 1838 in Chad Road (both dem.). Another has the wall surface cut back in panels round the windows: Nos. 6–10 Bennetts Hill of *c.* 1829 where his father was lessee, a block of 1843 on the corner of New Street and Bennetts Hill (dem. *c.* 1950), and almost certainly the similar block of *c.* 1842 on the corner of New Street and Temple Street. The last and most frequent type has a narrow central feature, often with a porch with columns *in antis*, and topped by a small vestigial pediment: the E and W entrances of the Market Hall; the New Hall Coal Co. offices, Bennetts Hill 1832 (dem.); and probably also Hallfield, the Priory School, of 1829; No. 22 George Road, Edgbaston of *c.* 1833–6, Apsley House, Wellington Road of 1836, and No. 15 Chad Road of 1838. Factories attributable to Edge are noted below, p. 12.

Of other Birmingham architects, *John Fallows*'s work combines handsome proportions with picturesque, sometimes eccentric, detail: his trademark tapering 'Graeco-Egyptian' architraves appear on the N side of Waterloo Street of 1828–35, but the best place to assess him is the SW end of Calthorpe Road, with three houses of 1829–30: No. 31; No. 35, a cool Greek villa disrupted by wild details; and No. 36, which integrates his characteristic windows into a tight grid of columns and cornices. His Plough and Harrow Hotel, Hagley Road, of 1832–3, has excessively tall Tudor gables, perhaps derived from the work of Jeffry Wyatville, e.g. Lilleshall Hall of 1822. The short-lived *Richard Tutin* achieved scholarly Greek Revival in his Severn Street synagogue of 1827. Rickman's equally short-lived partner *Henry Hutchinson* applied the temple style effectively to the bank of 1831–2 on the corner of Waterloo Street and Bennetts Hill, on the Inge estate development started in 1818. *Bateman & Drury* developed a characteristic manner with round-arched doorways, seen in houses of 1836–41 in Yew Tree Road, Edgbaston.

Public building languished in the mid C19. The Town Hall was completed by *Edge* in 1847–51. In 1851 Town Council absorbed the Street Commissioners and gained their vigorous surveyor, John Pigott Smith. But the Council was increasingly controlled by 'economists', right-wing

Liberals averse to public spending, who frustrated Pigott Smith's highway and sewerage schemes, and in 1857 dismissed him.

Domestic and commercial architecture remained classical in the town well into the second half of the C19. *William Thomas*'s Warwick House, New Street of 1839 (dem.), the town's first department store, had a giant Corinthian order. *Edge & Avery*'s Norwich Union Fire Engine House of 1846 in Temple Street is still Cheltenham-Regency. *Samuel Hemming*'s Unity Insurance building of 1854 next door marks both an increase in scale and the arrival of a distinctively richer classicism, in this case an Italian palazzo style deriving from Charles Barry. Richer Italianate and rural villa styles were introduced in Edgbaston in the 1840s–50s, by *Hemming*, *F.W. Fiddian*, *J.J. Bateman* and others, in e.g. Wellington and Sir Harry's roads. The change is well seen in Carpenter Road. Tudor Revival, an Early Victorian alternative to Gothic, appears in the work of *J.J. Bateman* and the young *J.A. Chatwin* in Edgbaston from the early 1850s.

This context is necessary to understand the startling challenge of No. 12 Ampton Road, built in 1855 by the young *J.H. Chamberlain* (*see* topic box, p. 72). Its Italian sources and its polychromatic treatment, inspired by the writings of John Ruskin, mark it as distinctively **High Victorian**. Italian Gothic was used for commercial and industrial work in e.g. *Charles Edge*'s shop and works for the gunmaker William Powell in Carrs Lane of 1860–1, a late work. His contemporary Proof Hole at the

4. No. 12 Ampton Road, Edgbaston, by J.H. Chamberlain, 1855

Proof House [88], where Powell was Chairman of the Guardians, is chunky Romanesque. This 'Lombardic' Romanesque, with coloured brick patterns, was another mid-C19 fashion. *Yeoville Thomason* was using it from *c.* 1853, but with gentler, more conventional proportions. His Singers Hill Synagogue of 1855–6 is massive Italianate with both Romanesque and Renaissance references.

Some of the biggest changes in Birmingham during these years were due to the coming of the **railways**. The London & Birmingham Railway, opened in 1837, was the first main line in Britain. Its arrival was marked by *Philip Hardwick*'s terminal buildings, architecture of heroic classicism. His Euston Arch in London has gone, but its Birmingham counterpart, Curzon Street station of 1838, survives: here its Greek Ionic portico is attached to the block of entrance hall and offices. The original New Street station of 1849–54 by *John Livock* was Italianate; its spectacular train-shed roof, designed by *E.A. Cowper* of Fox, Henderson & Co., was the greatest expression of the iron and glass manner of the Crystal Palace in the town (dem.; *see* topic box, p. 110).

Railways apart, **industrial architecture** in the 1830s was still largely on a domestic scale, e.g. George Unite's house and factory at No. 65 Caroline Street of 1836, perhaps by *Fallows & Hart*, and Nos. 14–15 Regent Parade of *c.* 1840, probably by *Bateman & Drury*. A severer classical approach can be seen at Elliott's factory of 1837–8 in Vittoria Street, and a new scale is set by Joseph Gillott's Victoria Works pen factory of 1839–40, both probably by *Charles Edge*. Mid-Victorian fashion, and a yet grander scale, arrives with *J.G. Bland*'s huge Lombardic Romanesque pen works, now the Argent Centre, of 1862–3 [75].

5. Union Mill, Grosvenor Street West, perhaps by William Hollins, 1813

Later Victorian Birmingham: the Civic Gospel

Between 1865 and 1890 Birmingham went through such profound changes that it came to be seen, by historians such as G.M. Young, as epitomizing Late Victorian England, just as Manchester epitomized the earlier years of the Queen's reign. Nonconformist preachers such as George Dawson, H.W. Crosskey and R.W. Dale taught what became known as the **Civic Gospel**: in Dawson's words, 'A town is a solemn organism through which shall flow, and in which shall be shaped, all the highest, loftiest and truest ends of man's moral nature.' They taught a practical idealism: Dale preached that Christ would bless 'those who supported a municipal policy which lessened the miseries of the wretched'. Crosskey was probably the 'adventurous orator' recalled by Dale, who would dwell on 'the glories of Florence and of the other cities of Italy in the Middle Ages, and suggest that Birmingham, too, might become the home of a noble literature and art'. The Italian ideal was replaced, particularly after 1880, by an admiration for the Paris replanned by Haussmann for Napoleon III, and also for America: Dale lectured at Yale in 1877, and spoke of God having 'placed America in the van of progress'.

The man who put these principles into action was **Joseph Chamberlain** (1836–1914), a Unitarian screw-maker who was a councillor from 1869, Mayor in 1873–6, and leader of the city's Liberal caucus (arguably the first political party organized in the modern way). He was a member of Crosskey's congregation. His allies included the merchant George Dixon, chairman of the School Board, and the Quaker alderman William White.

Chamberlain and his friends first municipalized gas and water, improving both the services and the council's finances. Then they turned to development. The Council House was begun in 1874. Thirty Board Schools were built between 1871 and 1883, and the School of Art in 1883–5. The Free Library which had opened in 1865 was rebuilt, after a fire in 1879. The Art Gallery was built in 1881–5 above new offices for the gas service which paid for it. Corporation Street, started in 1878, was Birmingham's first municipal 'Improvement Scheme', followed by John Bright Street, cut in 1882. Projects like these increased the status of architects, and their local professional body, the Birmingham Architectural Association, was founded in 1868.

If the Birmingham Liberals followed an 'artistic' thinker, it was Ruskin. J.H. Chamberlain was both a devoted Ruskinian and a trusted member of Joseph Chamberlain's inner circle, a unique position for an architect in Birmingham history (*see* topic box, p. 72). The Pre-Raphaelites were exhibited at the Society of Artists from the early 1850s. Ruskin visited Birmingham in 1877. Benjamin Creswick, the Sheffield knife-grinder discovered as a sculptor by Ruskin, came to Birmingham in 1889 as Master of Modelling at the School of Art. J.H. Whitehouse, Ruskin's friend of later years, lived in Birmingham, and built a national memorial to him here (p. 258).

6. Board School (now Ikon Gallery), Oozells Square, by Martin & Chamberlain, 1877

The new **public buildings** reflect the major stylistic approaches of the later C19. *Yeoville Thomason*'s Council House, the most obvious monument of civic renewal, shows the strength of the classical tradition in the town. The fiasco of the competition, with the assessor Alfred Waterhouse's choice, *W. Henry Lynn* of Belfast, rejected by councillors in favour of the local architect Thomason, showed the power of small-town loyalties. Thomason's excellent planning is not quite matched by his Italo-French architecture, which is satisfyingly civic, but lacks the inspiration of Brodrick's Leeds City Hall or Waterhouse's Manchester Town Hall. The other major public building of the period, *W.H. Ward*'s Parish Offices in Edmund and Newhall streets of 1882–5, now only façades, shows his massive but well-articulated French Renaissance with crisp detail pointing up the whole design. For the Law Courts, *see* p. 17; for the University, p. 240.

In **educational architecture** the Liberals could control the process, and *J.H. Chamberlain*'s schools [6] are the clearest expression of their ideals (*see* topic box, p. 72). His School of Art of 1883–5 has national importance as the most direct major expression of Ruskinian Gothic after the Oxford Museum. His evolutionary view of architecture is perfectly shown in his development of Gothic with bold iron construction, already used on a smaller scale in his school assembly halls. *J.A. Cossins*, an equally committed Liberal, used Gothic for Mason College, the predecessor of Birmingham University, begun in 1875 (dem.).

By contrast, late C19 **commercial architecture** is dominated by rich and varied classicism. *Thomason* used Italianate for the Post and Mail buildings on New Street, from 1864, and in his clever transformation of *Rickman & Hutchinson*'s Birmingham Banking Co. in Waterloo Street of 1877. Perhaps his best design is the opulent and subtle Union Club [7] (1869 and 1885) in Colmore Row, part of the Colmore Estate redevelopment begun in 1869, where the landowner enforced design rules such as common cornice heights. But the finest local Victorian classicists were *J.A. Chatwin* and *W.H. Ward*. *Chatwin*'s early Birmingham Joint Stock Bank of 1864 in Temple Row West is a subtle and masterly palazzo design, showing his training by Charles Barry. His premises for Spurriers the silversmiths at Nos. 79–83 Colmore Row integrate varied functions successfully into a classical composition. *Ward* was a strong designer, as seen in the mutilated Gazette Buildings, Corporation Street, of 1885–6, with their scholarly handling of Italian Renaissance. His masterpiece was the Colonnade Building, New Street of 1882 (dem.), successfully integrating Italian and French Renaissance detail into powerful overall massing. *Edward Holmes* was another talented classicist; his Midland Bank of 1867–9 in New Street combines real urban presence with typically mid-Victorian mixed detail.

7. Union Club, Colmore Row, by Yeoville Thomason, 1869 and 1885

8. Gazette Buildings, Corporation Street, by W.H. Ward, 1885–6

A more eclectic picture is presented by the new **Corporation Street** [8], planned from 1875 by the council's Improvement Committee, chaired by William White. This was the first improvement scheme in England to use the Artisans' Dwellings Act of 1875 to demolish areas of unfit housing. As well as the new route running NE from New Street, the scheme included the shorter Martineau Street, running E from it to Dale End. Work began in 1878 at the s end, the first building plan was approved in 1879, and construction reached Old Square and Aston Street in 1882. The final section to Aston Road near the corner of Bagot Street was not started until 1902.

The completed street is a Parisian boulevard, 66 ft (20 metres) wide. It is clear that *J.H. Chamberlain*, whose firm *Martin & Chamberlain* were the street's surveyors, intended it as a challenge to the town's conservative and slightly comfortable classical tradition. Its architecture is, deliberately, a picturesque mixture. It starts with *Ward*'s French Renaissance blocks at the New Street end and his rich Chambord-style Central Arcade of 1881. *Martin & Chamberlain*'s Marris & Norton block of 1880–1 is a sharp contrast: Flemish, gabled and turreted, in bright pinky-red terracotta. *William Doubleday* used Gothic for the Cobden temperance hotel of 1883 (dem.). The young *J.L. Ball* used the Queen Anne style of Shaw, Nesfield, J.J. Stevenson and others, with its characteristic rubbed and moulded brick detail, just off the street at Nos. 13–14

*A surviving example of this manner is *Bateman & Corser*'s Christ Church, Tettenhall Wood, Wolverhampton, 1865–6.

Cannon Street of 1881–2. Even *Thomason* used a quirky gabled Flemish style in Corporation Street, where his classical Post and Mail buildings of 1879 in New Street run through. The street's picturesque skylines also suggest an affinity with the New York of Richard Morris Hunt and George B. Post. The trend reached Colmore Row in 1878, with *J.J. Bateman*'s No. 59.

The major public building of the later C19, and the focus of the N part of Corporation Street, the **Law Courts** [31], is best dealt with here. Alfred Waterhouse – the ghost architect of late C19 Birmingham – was again frustrated by local political pressure, and became the assessor. *Aston Webb & Ingress Bell*'s use of terracotta for their sophisticated and eclectic complex of 1887–91, and its picturesque composition, were calculated to appeal to both Waterhouse and to local Liberals with their taste schooled by J.H. Chamberlain. It gave Birmingham architecture a national profile: in 1897 *The Builder* called it 'one of the best planned modern buildings in England' and noticed that Birmingham was becoming 'a city of terra-cotta architecture'. The 'terracotta style', as contemporaries called it, was remarkably eclectic, mixing Flemish, Gothic, French Renaissance and even Indian motifs. The finest commercial

9. Birmingham Midshires (former Ocean Assurance), Temple Row West, by Mansell & Mansell, 1900–2; extended by Peter Hing & Jones, 1983–4, left

examples are the National Telephone Co. offices of 1896 in Newhall Street by *Frederick Martin* of *Martin & Chamberlain*, and *Ewen & J. Alfred Harper*'s Central Hall, Corporation Street of 1900–3. The group of the latter, the Law Courts opposite, and nearby offices of 1898–1901 by the *Harpers* and *J.W. Allen* is the best surviving expression of the increased stature of the late C19 town, which became a city in 1889.

The influence of Paris can also be seen in the large number of **shopping arcades** built in the later C19. 'Birmingham seems to be . . . quite an Arcadian town . . .', said the *Birmingham Post* in 1882. The Central Arcade has already been mentioned; better preserved are *W.H. Ward*'s Great Western Arcade of 1874–6 [49], significantly in French Renaissance style, a technical tour de force built over a railway cutting, and part of *Newton & Cheatle*'s Midland and City Arcades, Union Street [53], 'terracotta style' of 1900–1. Comparably exuberant are *Essex, Nicol & Goodman*'s asymmetrical pair of offices of 1896–1900 on the corners of Newhall Street and Cornwall Street, their block of 1898 in New Street, and their Louvre department store, High Street, of 1896 (dem.), described by *The Builder* as having tracery like lace curtains.

Below these leading firms were a large number of commercial architects and architect–surveyors, adept at picking up new styles. Cheap editions of Ruskin must lie behind *J.S. Davis*'s eccentric Gothic Nos. 31–51 Constitution Hill of 1881–2 and his Nos. 391–396 Summer Lane of 1883, as well as the obscure *Alfred T. Greening*'s delightful design of 1890, mixing tilework and Queen Anne, on the corner of Bristol Street and Essex Street. (Davis was probably a relative of H.H. Statham, editor of *The Builder*, which featured his work a lot.) *Thomson Plevins* left a large mark, with his blocks in New Street of 1867 to 1875, his work for Isaac Horton such as the Grand Hotel of 1876–8, his replanning of the Newhall Estate for William Barwick Cregoe Colmore from 1869, and similar work in the John Bright Street and Station Street area. The Grand Hotel and the New Street blocks show that he had a sense of urban scale, but his hotel elevations are additive, and his attempt at something grander at the Market Hotel, Station Street (1883, with *J.P. Norrington*) is loosely composed.

Later C19 **pub architecture** relied on architects like this. *Plevins*'s Victoria, John Bright Street of 1883, is cheerfully old-fashioned classical. More common was an eclectic mix of Gothic and Italian, often with bargeboarded gables: *William Hale*'s Albion, now the Old Contemptibles, Edmund Street of 1880, and his Big Bull's Head, Digbeth of 1885; *William Jenkins*'s Rose and Crown, Bromsgrove Street, of 1900 and *Joseph Wood*'s Queens Arms, Newhall Street of 1901. From about 1890, however, *James & Lister Lea* obtained a commanding position in this field. Their best work shows off effectively, mostly in Jacobean style, with big windows and much terracotta decoration outside and sumptuous, usually *Minton*, tiling within, e.g. the Woodman, Albert Street, 1897, and White Swan, Bradford Street, 1899–1900. At the

Wellington, Bristol Street, of 1890–1, they extended a genuine early C19 pub in wonderfully convincing imitation Regency.

Theatres and music halls of the C19 have almost entirely disappeared. Pub music halls were a notable feature of the town, but the only survivor is the shell of the London Museum Concert Hall in Park Street, Digbeth of 1863. The Hippodrome in Hurst Street and Inge Street retains some fabric of *Frederick W. Lloyd*'s 'Tower of Varieties' of 1899.

Church architecture from the 1860s is dominated by *J.A. Chatwin*. His early work, such as St Clement, Nechells (1858, dem.,) and Holy Trinity, Birchfield Road, Handsworth (1860) gained him a reputation for solid Gothic work at a reasonable price. He used very 'rogue' Gothic at St Lawrence, Dartmouth Street (1862, dem.). His rebuildings of, and extensions to, existing churches show remarkable tact and sensitivity even when much demolition was involved. At St Martin in the Bull Ring of 1872–5 he was constrained by the awkward site, but followed the Dec style of the retained NW tower, producing a solidly competent piece. At St Philip's his superb chancel of 1883–4 enriches the Baroque character of Archer's original; at St Bartholomew, Edgbaston in 1885–6 he produced fine work of a rather Northern character by following the low proportions of the old church and *Fiddian*'s arcade of 1854. At Aston the medieval W tower caused less interference, and his new church of 1879 etc. is a convincing re-creation of grand late medieval Midlands work. A popular style for churches in the 1860s was a very spiky Dec with cross-gabled aisles and apses, e.g. *Yeoville Thomason*'s St Asaph, Great Colmore Street of 1868 and *J.J. Bateman (Bateman & Corser)*'s St Cuthbert, Winson Green Road of 1872 (both dem.).* St Alban, Bordesley of 1879–81 is exceptional as a major work by a London architect of the first rank, *J.L. Pearson.* It is a fine example of his late style, with its austerity of detail, mastery of proportion (with the use of the Golden Section), and stone vaulting throughout.

Nonconformist chapels must be mentioned here, especially for the grand rebuildings for the preachers of the Civic Gospel, despite almost total loss in the later C20. George Dawson's Church of the Messiah, Broad Street, of 1860–2 was by *J.J. Bateman* in his much-gabled Gothic. Crosskey's Church of the Redeemer was rebuilt on the grandest scale in Hagley Road by *James Cubitt* in 1881–2, with a central octagon surmounted by a tower. *Yeoville Thomason* refronted Carrs Lane chapel for Dale in 1876 in rich Renaissance. *George Ingall*, a Congregationalist lay minister as well as an architect, built several chapels of which the simple Gothic former Unitarian Chapel in Fazeley Street of 1876–7 is a mutilated survivor.

Domestic architecture of the late C19 is largely outside the scope of this book. The city continued to expand, with working-class housing of

---

*A surviving example of this manner is *Bateman & Corser*'s Christ Church, Tettenhall Wood, Wolverhampton, 1865–6.

following industry in areas such as Saltley and Small Heath, large areas of 'tunnel-back' terraced houses for the skilled working class and lower middle class in e.g. Aston and Sparkhill, and middle- and upper-middle-class developments in Handsworth and Moseley. Much of this was outside the C19 boundaries. *J.H. Chamberlain* was as committed to Ruskinian Gothic for houses as in his educational work (*see* topic box, p. 72), though his lodge house of 1879 in Westbourne Road, Edgbaston is a rare example of Norman Shaw's Old English style in the town. *J.J. Bateman* designed Gothic villas of vigour and charm in St Augustine's Road, Edgbaston, 1872–4. The Queen Anne style was first fully applied in Birmingham by *J.A. Chatwin* in his Lench's Trust Almshouses, Conybere Street, of 1878–80. Perhaps its finest exponent was *J.A. Cossins* in his majestic No. 15 Westbourne Road of 1881–2 and his austere Nos. 8A–10 Bordesley Street of 1882–4.

The Queen Anne style was also used for several of the new **hospitals and medical buildings** of the late C19, perhaps for its friendly, domestic associations, e.g. *Payne & Talbot*'s Eye Hospital, Church Street, of 1883–4, and *James & Lister Lea*'s Skin Hospital, John Bright Street of 1887. The finest is *J.A. Cossins*'s massive but beautifully balanced Ear and Throat Hospital, Edmund Street of 1890, now façaded. *William Henman*'s General Hospital, Steelhouse Lane, of 1894–7, is deeply influenced by Alfred Waterhouse (for whom his later partner, Thomas Cooper, worked) in its planning and tough Romanesque terracotta style.

Late C19 **industrial architecture** is often by builders such as *James Moffat*, or commercial architects such as *W.T. Foulkes*. The Jewellery Quarter has early work by *Ewen Harper, T.W.F. Newton,* and *J.P. Osborne*.

Finally, Ruskin's influence saw the first stirrings of the **conservation** movement in the town. Toulmin Smith rescued the Old Crown, Deritend, in 1862 with J.H. Chamberlain's help, J.T. Bunce's *Old St Martin's* (1875) described the church before its demolition, with illustrations by *Anthony Everitt*, who recorded many old Birmingham buildings. J.A. Cossins was an early reporter for the S.P.A.B. (Society for the Protection of Ancient Buildings) after its foundation in 1877.

The Impact of the Arts and Crafts Movement, c. 1890–1914

A distinctive **Arts and Crafts** architecture appears in Birmingham in the 1890s. This was the manner pioneered by architects from the offices of Norman Shaw and J.D. Sedding, young men inspired by the work of Philip Webb, by the ideals of William Morris, and, further back, by the writings of Ruskin. W.R. Lethaby, the most important thinker and writer of the movement after Morris, had close links with the city.

The approach is unassuming and reticent. It is essentially rural and domestic, its ideal the country cottage. It uses simple materials, in Birmingham predominantly brick, sometimes contrasted with render or roughcast. It emphasizes craft techniques such as brick pointing and bonding (*see* topic box, p. 295), and other skills such as leadwork. It stresses honest construction and values straightforward building methods more than conscious 'architecture' and added features (a favourite term of abuse of Lethaby was 'stuck on'). Sometimes this leads to a calculated awkwardness of composition, a deliberate placing together of apparently incompatible parts, almost always signifying a difference of function: a rejection of the deliberate picturesqueness of Shaw and Nesfield. In Birmingham it is a deliberate reaction against the over-decoration of the terracotta style and of many local manufactured goods, and it avoids ornament so much as sometimes to appear austere [59]. Early work in the Queen Anne manner here in the 1880s already hints at the simplicity of the new approach: *J.L. Ball*'s offices in Cannon Street (*see* above) and *Arthur Harrison*'s remarkable premises in Albert Street of 1888 both might be mistaken at first sight for town houses.

The influence of Ruskin in the town, and its interest in craftsmanship, made Arts and Crafts ideas attractive. William Morris had many links: he and Burne-Jones were travelling to Birmingham as young men in 1855 when they decided to become architect and artist, and it was in Cornish's bookshop that they discovered Malory's *Morte d'Arthur*. Morris was President of the Birmingham Society of Arts in 1878–9 and lectured there on 'the proposed destruction of St Mark's, Venice'. The School of Art under E.R. Taylor produced decorative artists, stained-glass makers and metalworkers of high quality: Henry Payne, Joseph Southall, Arthur and Georgie Gaskin. The major local Arts and Crafts architects, many starting their careers in the late C19, had good contacts in London: *W.H. Bidlake* and *C.E. Bateman* were pupils there, and *A.S. Dixon* and, slightly later, *Holland W. Hobbiss* knew Norman Shaw. Perhaps most important is the example of Lethaby, who was a friend and collaborator of *J.L. Ball*, and a particular inspiration to *E.F. Reynolds*. Alan Crawford has also pointed out that over half of Lethaby's buildings are either in Birmingham and its neighbourhood, or for Birmingham clients.

Arts and Crafts figures started architectural education in the city. Bidlake taught at the School of Art from 1893, Lethaby lectured twice there in 1901 – the second lecture was his important account of 'Morris as a work-master'. In 1909 the School of Architecture was founded as a branch of the School of Art, with Ball as Director: a contrast with the Beaux-Arts approach of the Liverpool School of Architecture under Charles Reilly.

Arts and Crafts **domestic architecture** in the suburbs, near to its rural ideal, was inspired by Lethaby's The Hurst, Four Oaks, Sutton Coldfield, of 1892 (dem.). Its simple massive treatment, and details such as its rounded-off gables and canted bays rising clear of the eaves, recur in much later Birmingham work. *J.L. Ball*'s Edgbaston houses, starting with his own Nos. 17–19 Rotton Park Road of 1895, are exceptionally simple, with typical long roof-lines. *W.H. Bidlake*'s Garth House, Edgbaston Park Road, 1901, has a markedly progressive feel with its

10. Former Methodist Central Hall, Corporation Street. Lamp by Ewen Harper & Brother & Co., 1928

cool roughcast elevations, and its apparent gentleness and almost random composition mask its careful balance and hidden power. Also important are *Buckland & Haywood-Farmer*'s houses in Yateley Road, Edgbaston of 1901 etc. *Cossins, Peacock & Bewlay*'s No. 9 Pritchatts Road, Edgbaston of 1905–6 shows a comfortable version of this manner which never challenges middle-class assumptions.*

Perhaps the fullest expression of Arts and Crafts ideals is the pioneering model village of Bournville three miles sw of the centre, developed by George Cadbury from 1894. Nationally it marks an advance beyond the company village of Port Sunlight (1888 etc.) towards the Garden Cities of the early c20. Cadbury's architect, the very

*Much Arts and Crafts work is outside the scope of this book: *Bidlake*'s houses and churches (*see* topic box, p. 291); *Bateman*'s Redlands, Four Oaks, Sutton Coldfield, of 1903; also *Reynolds*'s early All Saints, Four Oaks (1908) and St Germain, Edgbaston (1915–17), and *Hobbiss*'s St Mark's Church House, Washwood Heath (1909–10).

young *W. Alexander Harvey*, designed delicately varied cottage-style houses in pairs and rows, in substantial gardens with fruit trees. Simple and handsome public buildings cluster round a village green. Bournville, together with other local Arts and Crafts houses, is described in Hermann Muthesius's *Das englische Haus* (1904–5), so is of more than national importance in the early C20.

Also domestic in its approach is *A.S. Dixon*'s Guild of Handicrafts, Great Charles Street, of 1897–8, a simple and influential radical statement. Its round-arched windows, later a leitmotif of Arts and Crafts work in Birmingham, are a deliberate rejection of the Gothic Revival – Dixon was an Anglo-Catholic Socialist who associated Gothic with establishment conservatism and dreary Evangelical piety. His St Basil, Heath Mill Lane, Deritend, of 1910–11 belongs with a group of Early Christian Revival **churches** associated with Charles Gore, the first Bishop of Birmingham, and his circle (*see* topic box, p. 186). Earlier Arts and Crafts church work is dominated by *Bidlake* (*see* topic box, p. 291), and especially by his superb St Agatha, Sparkbrook, of 1899–1901.

After 1890 a series of **urban buildings** combine Arts and Crafts simplicity and reticence with remarkably original composition, in the so-called Free Style. *Martin & Chamberlain*'s later schools, with very large windows and repetitive motifs, frankly express their structure, e.g. Floodgate Street school of 1890–1, and the School of Art extension of 1892–3. The next sign is the appearance of later Shaw influence. *Mansell & Mansell*'s former Ocean Assurance of 1900–2 in Temple Row West shows the late C19 terracotta style transformed by expressing the structural grid [9]. But incomparably the finest Arts and Crafts office building is *Lethaby & Ball*'s Eagle Insurance, Colmore Row [38], of 1900. Alexandra Wedgwood called it 'one of the most original buildings of its date in England'. Here, in an office building in a street context, the ideal of honest building leads to simple, direct structural expression, but combined with a complex personal symbolism, in such motifs as the bronze doors and crowning eagle.

The local firm who best rose to its challenge, in a short but brilliant career, were *Newton & Cheatle*. Their progress can be followed from the luscious terracotta No. 134 Newhall Street of 1897, through the much simpler Nos. 121–123 Edmund Street of 1898–9, with its quietly powerful relieving arch, and the refined Shavianism and complex balance of Nos. 125–131 Edmund Street of 1898–1900, to the extraordinary fantasy of Nos. 41–43 Church Street of 1900–1 [60]. Their Nos. 37–39, of 1901–2, returns to simplicity but also heralds the renewed national interest in classicism. For Arts and Crafts architects this is commonly expressed as **Neo-Georgian**. Locally this interest was sharpened by demolitions: J.L. Ball lamented the 'finely-conceived and solidly-built houses' of Old Square and elsewhere in the *Architectural Review* in 1907. The finest local examples of 1900s Neo-Georgian are in Cornwall Street: *Newton & Cheatle*'s Nos. 93 and 95 and *C.E. Bateman*'s Nos. 89–91. These are rare Birmingham instances of Victorian or Edwardian town houses, built here because they doubled as medical consulting rooms.

Industrial architecture is not normally associated with the Arts and Crafts Movement, but Birmingham has some fine examples. The impressive round arches of *Ernest C. Bewlay*'s cold store of 1899 in Digbeth probably owe something to A.S. Dixon as well as to H.H. Richardson's Marshall Field store in Chicago. *C.E. Bateman*'s Westley Richards gun factory in Bournbrook of 1902, outside the area covered by this book, also uses round arches, but in a deliberately simple brick range. *Buckland & Haywood-Farmer*'s No. 58 Oxford Street, 1911–12, was built for A.S. Dixon's relations, the Walker family. Its planning around a central double-height space links it to the firm's schools, which are outside the scope of this book.* *J.L. Ball*'s factory extensions of 1911 etc. in Sparkbrook for the pioneer car maker Frederick Lanchester are also noteworthy. The factory architect *George E. Pepper* uses Arts and Crafts motifs mixed with Baroque (for which *see* below) in his work of *c.* 1910 in the Jewellery Quarter.

Crouch, Butler & Savage's No. 32 Frederick Street of 1914, a good example of a progressive T-plan factory, uses the cream **faience** that became fashionable nationally *c.* 1910 because of its resistance to dirt and pollution. *Nicol & Nicol*'s Picture House, New Street, 1910, uses cream and green faience in a classical design with giant arch and Wren-style turrets, a largely Arts and Crafts and Neo-Georgian language; *Crouch & Butler*'s former Royal Birmingham Society of Artists across the street, of 1912, shows monumental classicism in its piled-up end towers.

The vein of austerity in the Birmingham Gothic and Arts and Crafts traditions may explain the lack of full-blown **Edwardian Baroque** examples in the city. Where they do appear, they may be by an outside architect, such as *Paul Waterhouse*'s Atlas Assurance of 1912 in Colmore Row. Its handling has something of Edwardian Mannerism, the type used by Holden and J.J. Joass, expressing the building's framed construction by using classical motifs unstructurally, e.g. paired pilasters over windows. *Marcus O. Type*, an eccentric original whose career starts with oddly handled Gothic and Jacobean in John Bright Street of 1900–1, uses this Mannerist approach at Avebury House, Newhall Street of 1905–6. *Arthur Harrison*'s Digbeth Institute of 1906–8 has Doric columns supporting nothing, and recessions in the façade above them. Edwardian Baroque gives way nationally after *c.* 1905 to a monumental classical manner, stirring in elements of French Beaux Arts and the America of McKim, Mead & White. This proved attractive to municipal clients: Birmingham's monument of this style is the Council House Extension of 1908–17 by *Ashley & Newman*, the major municipal building of this period. Its doorcases, based on Wren's St Mary-le-Bow, occur

---

*The most important are Handsworth New Road (1900–2) and George Dixon, City Road (1904–6).

Birmingham was in the forefront of the early c20 public-house reform movement, which was a reaction to concerns about heavy drinking, and Nonconformist campaigns for temperance and 'local option' – prohibition enforced by local councils. In place of small, disreputable street-corner pubs, with their ornate mass-produced detail, reformed pubs were idealized village inns, in restrained traditional styles deriving from the Arts and Crafts Movement, detailed by craftsmen in brick and stone. They were the pubs Bishop Gore wanted, 'on the lines of a German beer garden, where there was no reflection on a man or his wife and children if they were seen going in or going out'.

Birmingham started reform early, under Arthur Chamberlain, chair of the Licensing Justices from 1894. The architect *H.T. Buckland* was designing simple gabled pubs by 1897. Full-blown Brewer's Tudor – the only style Birmingham can claim to have invented – appears at *C.E. Bateman*'s Red Lion, King's Heath, 1905, in Cotswold stone and with a magnificent full-height bay window. *Holland W. Hobbiss*'s Fox and Goose, Washwood Heath, 1913, is already a typical timber-gabled road-house of the type we associate with 1930s by-pass roads.

The leaders of reform in Birmingham between the wars were George Bryson, chair of the Licensing Justices, devout Anglican and friend of Gore, and Sir William Waters Butler, chairman of the brewers Mitchells and Butlers. The best local architects were employed, especially the later Arts and Crafts figures.* The most spectacular result is the Black Horse, Northfield (1929), designed by *Batemans*' pub specialist *Francis Goldsbrough*: a huge Tudor range with timber gables and exquisite stonework on the garden front. *Edwin F. Reynolds* used massive Neo-Georgian at the Shaftmoor, Hall Green (1930), the Abbey, Bearwood (1931), and the Grant Arms, Cotteridge (1932). In 1935 he used slightly Spanish classical at The Towers, Walsall Road, and moderne for the Three Magpies, Hall Green. *Hobbiss*, eclectic as ever, ranged from grand but loose Baroque at the College Arms, College Road (1930, now a McDonald's) to Neo-Georgian at the Brookvale, Slade Road (1934), and timber-gabled Tudor at the Cottage, Yardley Wood (1935, dem.). *J.P. Osborne & Son* used very restrained Neo-Georgian and Tudor, e.g. the Dog and Partridge, Yardley Wood (1929 and 1938). *J.B. Surman* used a butterfly plan at the King George, Northfield (1935, now a Chinese restaurant). *F.W.B. Yorke* wrote a standard guide for architects, *The Planning and Equipment of Public Houses* (1949); his best surviving pub is the Journey's End, Clay Lane (1939). Many reformed pubs have been demolished in recent years. The best surviving interior is at *James & Lister Lea*'s British Oak, Stirchley (1923–4).

*Of the pubs mentioned, all but the Three Magpies lie outside the scope of this book.

again at *Ewen Harper, Brother & Co.*'s Phoenix Assurance in Colmore Row of 1915–17, where the treatment is smoother and American influence more obvious. *P.B. Chatwin*'s Lloyds Bank, Five Ways, of 1908–9 effectively uses English Baroque and Palladian models.

Municipal improvements lagged; Corporation Street and John Bright Street were still being built up until after 1900. The largest public project of the period is the University, at Edgbaston, by *Aston Webb & Ingress Bell*, 1900–9. Its Byzantine style owes something to Lethaby, its romantic skyline is unforgettable, but its hard treatment comes from an older tradition than the Arts and Crafts. Large boundary extensions of 1911 created the present outlines of the city (the only major addition is Sutton Coldfield, in 1974).

Between the Wars

The First World War gave the City Council an enhanced role, which in turn gave new impetus to **municipal improvements**. In 1917 the city's Public Works Committee approved lines for a network of arterial roads across the city. In 1918 the architect *William Haywood* published *The Development of Birmingham*, with a foreword by Neville Chamberlain, which created the development agenda of c20 Birmingham. He proposed a civic centre at the E end of Broad Street (*see* topic box, p. 144), culminating in a thirty-six-storey tower for the 'Municipal Buildings', and separated from Victoria Square by an extended Central Library. New Street Station was to be remodelled round a large concourse with a barrel-vaulted roof, an obvious crib from New York. A ring of boulevards was to surround the centre, with formal junctions at Lancaster Place and the end of Smallbrook Street (now Queensway), on the line of the post-war Inner Ring Road. This formal, American-influenced Beaux-Arts approach was an emphatic challenge to the local Arts and Crafts tradition, and the impressive list of subscribers significantly included only one architect, Haywood's partner *H.T. Buckland*.[*]

Further schemes for the end of Broad Street followed over the next twenty years (*see* topic box) but there was never the money and energy to carry them out. *Buckland & Haywood*'s educational work in this Beaux-Arts manner gained a national reputation, e.g. the Royal Hospital School, Holbrook, Suffolk, 1925–33. A small local example is their University entrance of 1930 in Pritchatts Road. Haywood also did much to popularize this formal approach as secretary of the Birmingham Civic Society. Beaux-Arts methods were introduced at the School of Architecture by *George Drysdale*, appointed Head in 1924. He taught, among others, Frederick Gibberd and F.R.S. Yorke.[†]

Public buildings appeared slowly at the E end of Broad Street, starting with the city's war memorial, the Hall of Memory, by *S.N.*

[*]Haywood succeeded as Buckland's partner his relative Edward Haywood-Farmer (d.1917).
[†]Drysdale practised in London as successor to Leonard Stokes. His finest building locally is Our Lady and St Hubert (R.C.), Warley, 1935.

Cooke and *W.N. Twist*, 1922–5. Its formula followed national trends and Haywood's schemes: stripped monumental classicism in Portland stone, more restrained than the pre-war kind, with the order mostly implied by a substantial cornice. The Hall set the pattern for *Rupert Savage*'s Masonic Hall, 1926–7, and *T. Cecil Howitt*'s Municipal Bank, 1931–3 and Baskerville House, 1938–40, all nearby. Howitt's buildings have an eye to the overall plans for the area – the elevation of Baskerville House is close to the podium of Haywood's proposed tower – but impress because of his sharp classical detail and effortless sense of urban scale. The most important public building of the 1930s, however,

11. Former Phoenix Assurance, Colmore Row, by Ewen Harper, Brother & Co., 1915–17

is in Edgbaston: the Queen Elizabeth Hospital by *Lanchester & Lodge*, 1934–8, severely stripped classical on a huge scale, the largest hospital development of its time in England. Civic buildings elsewhere are Neo-Georgian. The *City Engineer and Surveyor* produced the workaday Police Station, Steelhouse Lane, 1930, and Central Fire Station, Corporation Street (outside the Inner Ring), 1932. *Peacock & Bewlay*'s Juvenile and Coroner's Courts, 1930 and 1936–7, in Steelhouse Lane and Newton Street are better examples.

The most important interwar **commercial architecture** was produced by *S.N. Cooke & Partners*, though their work is difficult to assess. It starts with good stripped classical: No. 126 Colmore Row, 1926, and the Sun Building, Bennetts Hill, 1927–8. Smart Bros' furnishing store, Temple Street, 1931, combines streamlined moderne features with residual classical motifs in quite a sophisticated way. The Legal and General Assurance, Waterloo Street, 1931–2, a progressive cubic block, shows the influence of the emerging Modern Movement. But then their work goes rapidly downhill: Lombard House, Great Charles Street, 1933, and New Oxford House, Waterloo Street, 1934–5, are big lumpy classical jobs of little merit.* *Batemans'* interwar work was sophisticated and eclectic, e.g. their Neo-Grec transformation of the National Provincial Bank interior in Waterloo Street, 1927, and the soberly impressive Birmingham Law Society, Temple Street, 1933. *W.N. Twist*'s work combines solid massing with good detail, e.g. his streamlined Neville House, Waterloo Street, 1934, with hints of Art Deco. *Riley & Smith*'s No. 25 Bennetts Hill, 1926–7, is effective though rather loud. *Essex & Goodman*, however, show a sharp decline from their work of *c.* 1900. Essex House, Temple Street, 1924–5, and Waterloo House, New Street, 1926–7, are watered-down Edwardian in chilly faience, and King Edward House, New Street, 1936–7, is a bland classical lump. *W.T. Orton*'s Cavendish House, Waterloo Street, 1937, is notable for its grand scale, probably due to his consultant *T. Cecil Howitt*. **Cinemas** are mostly outside the scope of this book but must be mentioned because of Oscar Deutsch's Odeon chain and his architects *Harry W. Weedon & Partners*.† *W.T. Benslyn*'s cinemas included Gaumonts at Colmore Circus, 1931 (dem.) and Grove Lane, Smethwick, 1934.

Industrial architecture between the wars did not often have architectural pretensions. *Buckland & Haywood* used their massive classical style in e.g. the entrance block at the Soho Foundry, Smethwick, 1925. *Weedon* did the massive Typhoo tea factory of 1929 etc. in Bordesley

---

*Many of Cooke's buildings were designed in partnership, e.g. the Hall of Memory. Douglas Hickman, who probably had information now lost, ascribed the Legal and General building to Cooke's assistant, *E. Holman*. Cooke's success in the competition for the Hall of Memory created ill-feeling among Birmingham architects which lasted for many years.
†Odeons by *Weedons* in the Birmingham area include Kingstanding (1934–5) and Sutton Coldfield (1936).

Street, with details like triangular piers, hinting at his cinema work. The engineer and architect *C.F. Lawley Harrod* designed large blocks with streamlined window bands for the car-body makers Fisher & Ludlow including those in Bradford Street, 1931 and 1934, and Hurst Street, 1935.

In **houses, churches, and pubs** between the wars, the local Arts and Crafts school remained dominant. The two most important figures are *Edwin F. Reynolds* and *Holland W. Hobbiss*: Reynolds austere, massive, purifying his style down to a small range of decorative features, Hobbiss all spreading compositions, eclectic, allusive, and with the deliberate awkwardness of the Philip Webb tradition. Reynolds's best work, St Mary Pype Hayes, 1929–30, is a masterpiece of architectural logic, where the need for everyone to see the altar generates a complex plan marrying basilica and Latin cross, and spare details such as the tile-arched windows seem to grow naturally from the brick structure. Hobbiss's Guild of Students at the University, 1928–30, adapts the C17 Midlands manor house to C20 use, and his King Edward's Schools, 1937–47, slip without warning from Tudor splendour into domestic charm and unexpected grandeur in the s front. The Bournville tradition was continued by *J.R. Armstrong*, e.g. his Day Continuation School of 1925.

Later Arts and Crafts domestic architecture is well shown by *Harvey & Wicks*'s No. 12 Fox Hill, 1922–3, asymmetrically composed but with Neo-Georgian detailing, like late Baillie Scott. *Hobbiss* used gentle Tudor at e.g. No. 56 Wellington Road, 1936. Two Edgbaston houses of the 1930s stand out as differing attempts to break out of this tradition. Ravensbury, Westbourne Road [12, 108], 1935 by *T.M. Ashford*, combines Tudor revival with abstract patterning, neo-primitivism and Art Deco. No. 11 Church Road, 1936–7 by *Buckland & Haywood*, is a cool cubic brick block influenced by contemporary Scandinavia. **Mass housing** of the period, both public and private, also uses an essentially Arts and Crafts and Tudor Revival vocabulary. Birmingham is a city of delightful suburbs. The best commercial house builder was probably *H. Dare & Son* ('Dare to Build' on hoardings), who were particularly active in the archetypal middle-class suburb of Hall Green [132]. Birmingham's municipal housing programme was the largest in England apart from the London County Council's, reaching 50,000 houses in 1939. They were mostly plain brick cottage pairs and rows, in the Bournville tradition, occasionally varied by streamlined, rendered designs. The largest estate was Kingstanding, started in 1930. *Herbert Manzoni*, City Engineer from 1935, began to plan for slum clearance and high density flats (*see* topic box, p. 197).

Among public buildings, *Robert Atkinson*'s Barber Institute of 1936–9 [122] at the University is an exceptional, nationally important example of this style. Cool and sophisticated, with interior finishes in beautiful materials, it is a perfect place to contemplate works of art. Odeon cinemas, Dudok-style pubs, and cubic houses are close to the early Modern

12. Ravensbury, Westbourne Road, by T.M. Ashford, 1935

Movement, but this had little direct impact on Birmingham before the Second World War. It had enthusiastic admirers in Philip Sargent Florence, Professor of Commerce at Birmingham University, and his circle, which included progressive manufacturers such as Bob Best, and for a while the young Nikolaus Pevsner. Sargent Florence was a friend of *Walter Gropius* – the ghost architect of mid-c20 Birmingham as Waterhouse was in the later c19 – and there are unsubstantiated rumours of a Gropius building for him or one of his friends. When Gropius spoke in Birmingham in 1934, the chair of the meeting was the architect *W.T. Benslyn*. In the later 1930s his work moves from restrained moderne to the concrete structure, with deep canopies and flying staircases, of Brearley Street Nursery School, a radical statement not parallelled in the city for twenty years.

Second World War to New Birmingham: 1945–79

The centre and inner areas suffered heavily from **air raids** in 1940–1. The last and worst, on 9–10 April 1941, destroyed much of lower New Street and the E side of the Bull Ring. There was no large-scale **post-war plan** like Abercrombie's for London or Sharp's for Newcastle; the West Midlands Group's *Conurbation* (1948) was essentially a regional study. Manzoni's response was comprehensive redevelopment of older housing, and the Inner Ring Road (*see* topic box, p. 197). This road, the new Civic Centre (*see* topic box, p. 144), a rebuilt New Street station – essentially Haywood's 1918 ideas – were intended both to enlarge and revive the centre. This supplanted older civic and Arts and Crafts ideals, as can be seen in the enthusiastic welcome given by the Group's secretary, Paul Cadbury – Liberal councillor, Bournville trustee, owner of an E.F. Reynolds house – in his *Birmingham: Fifty Years On* (1952) [13]. The first section of the new road, Smallbrook Ringway (now Queensway) was built in 1957–60 as a wide boulevard lined with shops. But a municipal visit to America, changes in government road policy, and a strong attack in 1959 by Leslie Ginsburg, Professor of Planning at Birmingham University, helped change the remainder to the partly surviving urban motorway, completed 1971: separating cars and people was seen, ironically, as more human. Conservationists were ignored, and large-scale demolitions started with the bombed-out Market Hall, agreed in 1958.

The first City Architect, *A.G. Sheppard Fidler*, a distinguished pupil of Reilly in Liverpool, was appointed in 1953. His own housing schemes are outside the scope of this book. He also advised on planning decisions; Manzoni and the Public Works Committee made them. The results were mostly bland, e.g. the Big Top scheme, High Street, of 1956–61 by the prolific developer Jack Cotton and his in-house architects *Cotton, Ballard & Blow*. Sheppard Fidler lost his battles with Manzoni, and left in 1964.

13. New Street in 2002, from *Birmingham: Fifty Years On* (1952)

14. *Changing Weaman Street*, 1961. Watercolour by Frank Lockwood, showing the small scale of pre-1960s Birmingham; under construction, Lloyd House, Colmore Circus, by Kelly & Surman

Nevertheless, there is a scatter of good buildings up to the early 1960s. Earlier ones are **industrial**, due to building controls. No. 80 Wrentham Street by *Rudolf Frankel*, 1948, is a simple curtain walled factory (altered). *J. Seymour Harris & Partners'* furniture factory of 1954–5 in Blucher Street is a good example of 'Festival of Britain', contrasting curtain walling with brick punctuated by projecting headers. From about 1957, the property boom produced much **commercial** architecture. The most consistent early post-war townscape was, until 2004, Smallbrook Queensway, with *James Roberts's* sweeping E side of 1958–62, *Hurley Robinson's* Norfolk House of 1958–60, and formerly *John Madin's* A.E.U. building of 1960–1. *J. Seymour Harris & Partners'* Commercial Union development of 1959–65 in Corporation Street was the first slab-and-podium in the commercial centre; its surviving tower has tapering ends, an early derivative of Ponti's Pirelli Tower in Milan. This was the 'New Birmingham' hymned by Frank Price and Manzoni in the *Birmingham Mail* in 1959. The redevelopment of Edgbaston started in 1957 to *John Madin's* plan (*see* topic box, p. 214). His first building, No. 16 Frederick Road, reflects the fashionable 'Contemporary' manner in its characteristic control of bold materials, like his subtly composed Chamber of Commerce, Harborne Road, of 1959–60.

Madin's firm – *John H.D. Madin & Partners* (here *Madins*) from 1962, the *John Madin Design Group* (here *JMDG*), including planners and landscape architects, from 1968 – consistently produced the city's best architecture for the next thirty years. The best 1960s commercial building is *Madins'* Post and Mail development at Colmore Circus, an integrated office and printing works of 1963–6. It shows the gentle 1950s manner replaced by something tougher – here deriving from Skidmore, Owings & Merrill's Lever House, New York, 1951–2, and through it from Mies van der Rohe – and is of national interest as only the second example of this influential model in Britain. Madins' simpler blocks on Hagley Road were also excellent – the best survivor now is Hagley House of 1963–5. *Walter Gropius*'s huge proposal of 1962 for between New Street and Temple Row had intricate low-rise courtyard planning and a single tall block, which alone emerged to *Fitzroy Robinson & Partners*' executed design of 1969–72. *James Roberts* used mosaic cladding for his iconic Rotunda of 1964–5, which shows a decline from his Smallbrook work. *Holland W. Hobbiss* remained classical, e.g. Fountain Court, Steelhouse Lane, of 1963–4. The two largest 1960s schemes were also the worst: the Bull Ring Centre of 1961–7 by *Sydney Greenwood* and *T.J. Hirst*, notorious for its pedestrian subways, and the rebuilt New Street Station and mixed-use complex above, of 1964–70. The best purely **retail architecture** is *Frederick Gibberd*'s Corporation Square of 1963–6, with its cool podium, sculpted roofscape, and ingenious planning. Its slit windows are echoed in *Paul Bonham Associates*' former Thomas Woolf store, Priory Queensway, of 1972.

In the late 1960s and 1970s architectural fashions became grander and more romantic. *JMDG* were influenced by Louis Kahn, whose discrete staircase towers appear in their 1964 proposal for the National Westminster Bank, Colmore Row, and the firm's own offices, No. 123 Hagley Road, of 1965–7. The latter is faced in brick, Birmingham's local material, then becoming fashionable again. The most significant **church** of the period in the centre, Carrs Lane Chapel of 1968–71 by *Denys Hinton & Partners*, shows this trend, though its split gables show another pervasive influence: Alvar Aalto. *Harry Harper*'s gentle Cotteridge Friends' Meeting House, 1962–4, shows the enduring spirit of the Birmingham Arts and Crafts tradition.[*]

The culmination of romantic 1960s architecture was Brutalism. The city's best examples are the two finest post-war **public buildings**. *JMDG*'s Central Library [15, 32], designed 1964–6 and built 1969–74, a complete cultural centre including lecture hall and exhibition areas, was the first Birmingham building of European importance since the time of Bidlake. Its dramatic cantilevered construction, deriving from late Corbusier and early Denys Lasdun, allows magical spatial flow inside. *Graham Winteringham*'s Repertory Theatre of 1969–71 has an intriguingly assembled exterior of massive elegance. *JMDG* designed

[*]Fine churches outside the scope of this book include: St John Longbridge (1956–8) and St Boniface Quinton (1958–9) by *George While*; St Thomas, Garretts Green (1958–60) by *S.T. Walker* and *Graham Winteringham*; and two important examples of new liturgical planning, St Matthew, Perry Beeches by *Maguire & Murray*, 1962–4, and Our Lady Help of Christians, Tile Cross, by *Richard Gilbert Scott* of *Giles Scott, Son & Partner*, 1966–7.

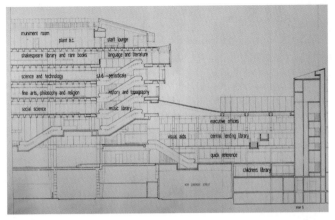

15. Central Library, Paradise Circus, by John Madin Design Group, 1969–74. Section

the Brutalist National Westminster Bank, Colmore Row of 1969–73. Related to Brutalism, but lighter and jazzier in effect, is the 'pop' architecture of *H. George Marsh* of *Richard Seifert & Partners*. The city has one of his best works, the ATV development of 1969–73, with external concrete framing worked in angular shapes, and a cranked tower. Against these trends, but of exceptional quality, is *Douglas Hickman* of *JMDG*'s Miesian Neville House, Harborne Road, of 1975–6.

In any account of the city in the 1960s, **Birmingham University** deserves a special place. The work there by *Casson, Conder & Partners*, *Howell, Killick, Partridge & Amis, Chamberlin, Powell & Bon, Arup Associates* and others, forms the finest complex of university buildings of the period outside Oxford and Cambridge (*see* p. 240).

1960s **housing** is seen at its best in *Madins'* work in Edgbaston. His care for materials, quietly sculptural hollowing-out behind façades, and fine landscaping can all be seen in flats (St George's Close, 1959–62), terraces (Cala Drive, 1962–3), and high blocks (Warwick Crest, 1962–3). Municipal housing under *Alan Maudsley*, City Architect from 1966, concentrated on simple terraces and high towers built quickly and cheaply.

Conservation first became an effective force in the 1970s. The Birmingham group of the Victorian Society was founded in 1967. The long campaign to preserve the Post Office in Victoria Square was the turning point. In 1973 the group forced a public inquiry into demolition; they lost, but in 1978, in alliance with community groups, finally succeeded in saving the building. The city's first, modest Conservation Areas were declared in 1969. The first façade retention scheme was *JMDG*'s Nos. 97–107 Hagley Road, *c.* 1971.

16. Alpha Tower (former ATV Tower), by Richard Seifert & Partners (H. George Marsh), 1969–73

Recession and Revivals: 1980–2000

The recession of 1980–2 hit the West Midlands worse than anywhere else in Britain. Manufacturing industry contracted sharply, and unemployment in the city rose from 7 per cent in 1979 to 20 per cent in 1982. **Planning** in the 1980s, under *Graham Shaylor*, the city's first Chief Planning Officer (1974–90), was mainly concerned to broaden the economic base. The largest project, the International Convention Centre and Hyatt Hotel of 1987–91, is architecturally disappointing, but improved the urban fabric by bridging the Inner Ring Road (Centenary Way, 1989) and creating Centenary Square. Commercial development was encouraged around Colmore Row and Edmund Street, designated the 'Primary Office Area'. It was affected, however, by increasing criticism of C20 Modernism. This began in the 1970s with attacks on municipal high-rise building, made stronger by the 1974 conviction of the City Architect, Alan Maudsley, for corruption. The Prince of Wales's Mansion House speech of 1984 increased the interest in conservation. A good example is the 1986 refurbishment and reconstruction at Nos. 168–170 Edmund Street, replacing earlier proposals for a ten-storey slab.

The appointment of Les Sparks as Director of Planning and Architecture in 1990 coincided with a new way of planning, encouraged by a lively community group, Birmingham For People. It was epitomized in Tibbalds Colbourne Karski Williams's *City Centre Study* of 1990, which stressed traditional streets, attractive vistas, and human scale. The resulting architecture can be labelled Postmodern, contextual, or both. The best is No. 2 Cornwall Street by the *Seymour Harris Partnership*, 1989–92, with warm brick and turrets recalling late C19 traditions. Pure Postmodern of e.g. the Terry Farrell type is rare in Birmingham, like Edwardian Baroque. Perhaps its showiness offended down-to-earth attitudes. A rare example is No. 36 Paradise Street of 1991 by *David Delaney-Hall* of *Sinclair Architects*. The façading of the Parish Offices block in Edmund Street and Newhall Street, 1984–6, was the first of many in the area.

The masterpiece of the contextual approach is the **Brindleyplace** development, begun in 1995. Its progressive planning created a new mixed-use neighbourhood of traditional streets and squares, including housing (the first of many city centre flat developments). Its architecture, unified by scale, materials and division into base, main storeys and attic, ranges from the full-blown Classical Revival of No. 3 by *Porphyrios Associates*, through the Postmodern inflections of No. 5 by *Sidell Gibson*, to the axial complexities of No. 1 by *Anthony Peake Associates*.

Stanton Williams's No. 4 Brindleyplace, 1997–9, shows the move to a consciously **revived Modernism** particularly associated with the American architect Richard Meier, its cool planar surfaces deriving from interwar Modernist sources such as Le Corbusier's Villa Savoie. This manner starts in Birmingham with No. 30 St Paul's Square of 1993 by *Associated Architects*, whose founder Walter Thomson worked for

17. Iron:Man, Victoria Square, by Antony Gormley, 1992

Gropius on the New Street scheme. The firm developed a Modernist manner capable of incorporating historic references, like those to Renaissance palazzi at The Mailbox conversion of 1999–2001, and with an instinctive feeling for urban scale. Their new front block of 2000–1 at the Birmingham Hippodrome, in association with *Law & Dunbar-Nasmith*, combines subtle historic allusions with excellent materials to produce the finest building of its time in the city. *Glenn Howells Architects* have also done outstanding work, notably their Custard Factory conversion in Deritend of 1994 and the adjoining new block of 1997–8, with its delicate suspended balconies. Recent works by two important national practices – *Nicholas Grimshaw & Partners'* Millennium Point (including a new science museum) and *Norman Foster & Partners'* Sealife Centre, Brindleyplace – show neither at their best.

Public art, especially sculpture, also flourished in the 1990s, e.g. at *Dhruva Mistry's* remodelling of Victoria Square (1991–3), which also includes *Antony Gormley's* Iron:Man [17]. *Tom Lomax's* Spirit of Enterprise, Centenary Square, 1991, also stands out.

Into the Twenty-first Century:
Another New Birmingham?

The distinguished planner Gordon Cherry characterized Birmingham as 'a city of process and dynamic change'. The C20 industrial city, driven by production engineers like Leonard Lord of Austin Motors, thought little of aesthetics, everything of achievement – delivering projects on time and to budget. Manzoni exemplified this perfectly: an engineer, ambivalent about town planning, indifferent to architecture, and contemptuous of history.

Production attitudes returned during the council leadership of Sir Albert Bore (1999–2004). Some developments have been positive: the removal of the Inner Ring Road continued with the demolition of Masshouse Circus, 2001–3 giving access to the new Eastside development area. Others are more mixed. The revival of city living is producing many large, anonymous apartment blocks. The new Bull Ring, cleverly planned and efficiently delivered, is architecturally little better than its rightly reviled predecessor. (The *Richard Rogers Partnership*'s proposal of 2001 for a new Central Library, seems to have been abandoned (March 2005).) It would involve the demolition of JMDG's library, one of many fine post-war buildings under threat: Madin's Chamber of Commerce and Post and Mail (all refused listing), and Gibberd's Corporation Square. Conservation, except for the Jewellery Quarter, is in retreat: losses and decay in John Bright Street, the new block on the corner of New Street and Temple Street, uncontrolled plastic windows in Hall Green and the Bournville Tenants' Estate.

The architecture of several **new developments** is fashionably freeform. The angular manner associated with Daniel Libeskind appears in the uncomfortably sited Welcome Centre, New Street, by the Council's *Urban Design* team, 2003. The alternative organic, waveform type is spectacularly visible in *Future Systems*' Selfridges store of 2001–3. In local estimation this is the centrepiece of an urban renaissance, with its 'voluptuous shape and shimmering façade'*; to the *Architectural Review* it is 'a blue blancmange with chicken-pox . . . scaleless, uninviting'. The café in the Bull Ring by *Marks Barfield*, 2004, elegantly combines waveforms and overlapping planes.

In 2002 the City Council produced 'High Places', planning guidance encouraging high buildings. The first, *Ian Simpson Architects*' Beetham Tower, Holloway Circus, is under construction (2005). The new policy allows high towers in Paradise Circus worryingly close to Victoria Square, to fund the new library. Birmingham will be 'a better place to live in, to look at, and in which to enjoy ourselves . . . the many magnificent building projects . . . (are) making Birmingham one of the most interesting cities in Europe.' But this was (Sir) Frank Price, writing in 1959. We know what happened next.

*Deborah Parsons, in Kennedy (ed.), *Remaking Birmingham*, 2002.

Major Buildings

St Philip's Cathedral

Colmore Row

By *Thomas Archer*, 1709–25, a building of national importance, exceptional in what was a modest C18 town. It is small for a cathedral, only 150 ft (45.7 metres) long, and was a parish church until the Diocese was created in 1905. But it is one of the earliest English town churches of the C18, and in Alexandra Wedgwood's words 'a most subtle example of the elusive English Baroque'.

Archer was a local man, whose brother Andrew owned Umberslade Hall in Warwickshire. But he was also the only English architect of the generation after Wren who knew Italian Baroque at first hand. He is known to have travelled in Europe in 1690–1, going via Holland to Italy, visiting Padua and almost certainly Rome, where he would have seen the work of Francesco Borromini. It is the Borromini-like treatment of details, and use of dramatically contrasted convex and concave shapes, which make St Philip's so remarkable. Also impressive is the late C19 enlargement by *J.A. Chatwin*, done with the building's new status already in mind.

History

The church was built by a Commission set up under an Act of Parliament of 1708, obtained by John Hough, Bishop of Lichfield and Coventry, because St Martin's was already inadequate for the growing town. The Commissioners were mostly local landowners, including Andrew Archer and his brother, Thomas. Thomas, significantly, signed the final accounts in 1718. A gentleman, holding the lucrative court position of Groom Porter, he must have given his design free.

St Philip's is also an estate church of the type familiar in C17–C18 London. The site was a field called the Horse Close, sold at favourable terms by William Inge and Elizabeth Phillips, who were developing Temple Street and Temple Row. Phillips is remembered by the dedication. Construction began in 1709 and the body of the church was completed in 1715. It cost £5073 13s. 10d., nearly all raised by small local subscriptions, though Sir Charles Holte gave £100, Bishop Hough £50, Lord Digby £40, and Lord Weymouth £20. The tower was completed between 1722 and 1725, when George I gave £600. We know the craftsmen's names: *Joseph Pedley*, stonemason, *William Davis*, who carved 'ye 4 Pediments and Windows over ye Doors'. *Richard Huss*, plasterer, and

18. St Philip's
Cathedral, by Thomas
Archer, 1709–25, east
elevation. Engraving
after Colen Campbell,
Vitruvius Britannicus
(1715–25)

carpenters and joiners including *William Westley*, *Thos Lane*, *Richard Perks*, *John Blun*, and *William Ashes* (or *Ashcroft*). *Richard Pinley* the bricklayer built two kilns on site. The original stone was from Andrew Archer's quarry at Umberslade, and nearby Rowington. It did not last, and refacing of the nave and aisles started in 1859 at the sw corner, supervised by the sculptor *Peter Hollins*. In 1860 the parish petitioned to remove memorials from the outside walls for recasing with stone: work completed by 1871, when *Yeoville Thomason* redecorated the interior. The church was re-pewed in 1814, with a central three-decker pulpit, and the pews were reconstructed conservatively, still as boxes, by *Orford & Nash* in 1850.

In 1883–4 *J.A. Chatwin* extended the church E with a full chancel, replacing the original small apse and the E nave bay, created NE and SE vestries, and opened out the ground floor of the tower, removing the W gallery. He was the intermediary between *Edward Burne-Jones* and Emma Villiers-Wilkes, the donor, for the superb stained-glass windows (*see* below). In 1905 *Philip Chatwin* refitted the chancel and replaced the pews with chairs. In 1940 an incendiary bomb burnt much of the roof off. *Philip* and *Anthony Chatwin* repaired the damage in 1947 and refaced the tower in 1958–9. *Michael Reardon & Partners* reordered the interior in 1980–2, built an ingenious underground meeting room and song school in the former burial vaults in 1989, and repaired the fabric again in the 1990s.

Exterior

A preliminary warning: every visible stone is C19 or C20, though details appear to have been very carefully reproduced. Hollington stone. Archer's **plan** is a simple aisled nave and w tower, with none of the complexity of his later churches at Deptford and Westminster. What distinguishes it from Wren's London churches is the use of a giant order to control the elevations all round: sober Doric pilasters, coupled on the w bay, and with a full entablature throughout. A controlling giant order appears only once before on an English church, at Dean Aldrich's All Saints, Oxford (1706–10), though Sir William Wilson's Hall Green church (*see* p. 269) has a naïve treatment without a proper base. Archer would have known both. The walls have channelled rustication, highlighting the plain pilasters and bases, and above the windows are raised blocks – a three-dimensional, plastic treatment. The doors and 'ye 4 Pediments' are particularly Borrominesque: the w ones have incised pilasters tilted outwards, enclosing a fluted architrave tilted inwards, and hugely extended triglyphs supporting a pediment broken forward in the middle and with its ends tilted backwards to mirror the pilasters. The E ones have plain panelled pilasters but extraordinary bulbous shapes above like table legs supporting big segmental pediments. The 'Windows over ye Doors' are oval, with scrolly surrounds growing into goggling masks at the tops. The urns were originally over alternate pilasters, though the full set was present by 1756. Chatwin's E end follows Archer's elevation closely, even to the quarter-rounds flanking the E window, which follow the design of the small C18 apse. Only the windows are taller, so the raised blocks are omitted.

The w end projects forward with a big segmental pediment; its sides have deep round-headed and circular niches. The **tower** above is where the Roman Baroque character is strongest. Above the convex shape of the pediment is a tremendous bell-stage with four deeply concave sides running to paired Corinthian piers set at the diagonals; then the clock stage with big paired volutes to the diagonal faces, supporting an elongated convex octagonal dome. The clock faces incorporated into the design are also a step beyond London churches of the period. Above, an open colonnaded lantern encircled by an ironwork balcony is topped by a boar's-head **weathervane**, the Gough crest. All the way up, convex and concave shapes succeed each other in dramatic contrast, but the result is perfectly unified.

Interior

Entrance is by the D-shaped sw porch, its curving gallery stair retaining the original dado and iron balustrade. The **nave** has five-bay arcades of square fluted Doric piers, the lower parts reeded. Arches with plain soffits, perhaps a C19 alteration as early illustrations show panelling and rosettes. Stepped keystones with big attached consoles. Deep entabla-

19. St Philip's Cathedral, nave and chancel

ture with four-part architrave, plain frieze, and cornice with alternating leaf consoles and rosettes; coved ceiling. The galleries are flush with the piers. Their fronts have simple fielded panels, of the 'Norway oak' supplied by *S. Fosbrook* in 1714. The original giant Corinthian order survives in the pilasters at the w end, their unusual low capitals with one big tier of leaves and flying volutes. The combination of two orders, a Baroque treatment deriving from Michelangelo's Capitoline palaces, is Archer's. The E vestries were extended into the aisles in 1905. The **floor** is by *Michael Reardon*, 1980, Hopton Wood stone, with black and white paving for the extended chancel.

Chatwin's tower arch tactfully follows the design of the arcades. But looking E the view is dominated by his magnificent chancel, enriching the Baroque character of the interior. Its three bays are divided by giant Corinthian columns and sections of entablature coming forward on each side, with answering pilasters behind. The inspiration must be Cockerell, who gave the young Chatwin a reference with Charles Barry. The capitals are grand but more conventional than Archer's. The marbling of the shafts is by *Michael Reardon*, 1979–80. The narrow setbacks of the coved ceiling between each bay faithfully follow the original E end treatment. The dramatic stroke is the omission of a chancel arch. The ceiling runs straight through, in the chancel coffered with rosettes.

Furnishings

Former **altar rail**, E end. A beautiful wrought-iron piece by *Robert Bakewell*, 1715, with rosettes, sprays of leaves, and religious symbols: flaming urns, and St James's cockleshells. – **Stalls** by *Chatwin*, 1884, rich Renaissance designs with his typical scrolled tops to the ends. – **Bishop's throne** and **canons' stalls** by *P.B. Chatwin*, 1905. – **Organ case**. Early C18, certainly pre-1733, probably by *Thomas Swarbrick*, who repaired it in 1748. Big putto heads, and towers with traditional crown and mitre finials. Facing the N gallery, a second **organ case** with beautiful carved trophies of instruments. Made for Dr Justinian Morse for Barnet church, Herts. before 1749; moved several times, latterly to St Chrysostom, Hockley; installed here *c.* 1980. – New forward **altar rail** by *Michael Reardon*, 1980–2. – **Pulpit**. A simple C20 wooden drum. – S aisle **altar**, heavy, with blind arcading, probably by *A.S. Dixon*, 1908. – **Sculpture**. N aisle. A crucified Christ carved from railway sleepers, and two standing figures, by *Peter Ball*, 1984. – **Box pews**. Two survivors, probably of 1850, at the W end. More in the galleries. – Bronze **door handles**, S aisle, E end door, finely fashioned as three-winged heads of a lion and bull, evangelical symbols (the other two on the inner face). By *David Wynne*, part of the Bishop Barnes memorial (*see* below). – **Dado** along the aisles and round the pier bases made from C18/C19 pews. – **Font** by *John Poole*, 1982. A lettered bronze-gilt bowl. – **Plaque**, SW porch, recording George I's donation 'upon the kind Application of Sr. Richard Gough to the Rt. Honourable Sr. Rob. Walpole', 1725. – Four **portraits** of early rectors, N gallery. – **Stained glass**: *see* topic box.

Monuments

Many small tablets, with much contrast of limestone and grey marble and many urns, the general quality reflecting the fashionable status of the church. Particularly appealing the ones with obelisk tops on the nave piers. These include: N side, Chief Justice Oliver of Massachusetts, d. 1791, the inscription stressing his 'love and loyalty to his SOVEREIGN'. – Francis Rogers M.D. d. 1804, by *P. Rouw*, oval tablet, snakes coiling round a club in the pediment; Girton Peake d. 1770, oval tablet with soul rising above, odd relief in the predella. – S side, William Higgs d. 1733, the first rector. With coat of arms, and foliage scrolls in the predella. – William Vyse d. 1770, stag's head and cross in the predella. – Rev. Charles Newling d. 1787, with an elegant low urn. – Edward Villers Wilkes d. 1835 by *P. Hollins*, urn and mourning woman, solid but with a calm expressive face. – Entrance to chancel, S side, Bishop Barnes d. 1953, small bronze portrait relief by *David Wynne*, 1954.

N aisle: N wall, Rebecca and William Grice d. 1781, 1790, by *William Thompson*. – Henry Perkins d. 1817, by *William Hollins* with his typical drooping foliage. – W wall, Sobieski Brookshaw d. 1811, by *Thompson*,

Chatwin always intended his new chancel for stained glass. His good luck was that the patron of the work, the heiress Emma Villiers-Wilkes, agreed also to meet most of the bills for three new E windows, and that the greatest stained-glass designer of the day, *Edward Burne-Jones*, agreed to design them. Burne-Jones was born close at hand in Bennetts Hill in 1833, and, like Chatwin himself, had been baptized in the church. By the mid 1880s he was at the height of his powers, and his long-time collaborators *[William] Morris & Co.* knew exactly how to translate his painterly designs into the bolder outlines and simpler colours the medium required. Even so, Burne-Jones grumbled about his 'pittance' of £200 per design – the Morris firm gave no special favours, even to their old colleague.

20. St Philip's Cathedral, west window, designed by Burne-Jones, 1897

The **subjects** are the Ascension (centre, E), 1885, and Nativity and Annunciation to the Shepherds (NE) and Crucifixion (SE), both 1887–8. The choices were the artist's own, overruling his patrons (though Emma did manage to exclude oxen from the NE window, saying, 'I wish the "Nativity of Our Lord" not a Cattle Show.') Colours are vibrant and exciting, with reds and blues predominant; designs are simple and dramatic, with a strong division between upper and lower zones, and with figures of an exceptional scale.

The **w window** of 1897 glows from within the tower. A separate commission, in memory of Bishop Bowlby of Coventry (d. 1894; rector here 1875–92), it shows the Last Judgment.

Simon Bradley

with scrolls above and a very severe urn. – Moses Haughton, 'an eminent artist', d. 1804, by *Rouw*. Impressive portrait medallion, books (one labelled 'Sketches') and palette below. – Sir Edward Thomason d. 1849. Small tomb-chest above, and a bird holding a twig, symbolizing hope. – Royal Warwickshire Regiment war memorial, 1920 by *A.S. Dixon*. An unusual and original arrangement of five tablets, central rectangle with top and bottom triangular projections surrounded by four diamonds. – s aisle, s wall. James Bayley d. 1834, William Taylor d. 1825, and Edward and Hannah Wilkes d. 1787, 1820, all three by *W. Hollins*. – w wall, Beatrix Outram d. 1810, by *Westmacott*. A rose in bud above, a rose broken off below. – Edward Outram, Archdeacon of Derby d. 1821, by *W. Hollins*. Draped tomb-chest. – William Westley Richards d. 1865 by *J. Gow*, still in the c18 tradition but more decorative.

In the tower, s side, G. Yeoville Thomason d. 1896, by *Roddis & Nourse*, alabaster. Then a group brought from Christ Church, demolished 1899: Rev. John George Breay d. 1839, with oval portrait medallion and pedestal tomb; Rev. Albert Workman d. 1881, by *T. Chaplin*; John Binnie d. 1856, Gothic. – Edward Palmer d. 1818, by *W. Hollins*, with draped urn, foliage and good lettering. – N side, Henry Price d. 1890, by *H. Lindley*. – sw lobby: David Owen d. 1823, by *W. Hollins*, with draped urn and more droopy foliage.

Churchyard

The grassed space was originally laid out with lime avenues for promenading. Burials ceased in 1848. Landscaped as a garden by the *City Council* in 1912, gently refurbished by the city's landscape architect *Mary Mitchell* in 1970 and again by the *Planning Department* in the 1980s. A Lottery-funded scheme of 1998–2003 included gross railings with gilded arrowheads and ironwork piers, paths of mechanical York stone and flagpoles interrupting the view from the se. – **Monuments**. w of the church, Bishop Gore by *Stirling Lee*, 1914. – s side, big obelisk to Col. Burnaby, killed in the Sudan, by *Robert Bridgeman* of Lichfield, 1885; smaller red granite obelisk to Lt-Col. Unett, killed at Sebastopol, by *Peter Hollins*, c. 1856. – Further e, John Heap and William Badger d. 1833, killed building the Town Hall. The base and lower part of a fluted column like those of the Hall, in Anglesey marble. – e again, a late c19 iron former **drinking fountain**. Brooding angel and shell-shaped bowl.

St Chad's Cathedral (R.C.)

St Chad's Queensway

A major work by *A.W.N. Pugin*, 1839–41, and a landmark in the Gothic Revival. It was built for Bishop Thomas Walsh, whom Pugin had met when working at Oscott College. Significantly in the revival of Gothic, Pugin replaced *Thomas Rickman*, who had produced designs in 1834. His builder was *George Myers*, an early collaboration. The first Catholic cathedral built in England since the Reformation, in a town with a long Catholic tradition. Services were held at the Masshouse in Pritchatts Road (*see* Edgbaston, p. 252) in the C18. St Peter's church, off Broad Street, was built in 1786 (dem.). Pugin's site is that of St Austin, the town's second Catholic church, a classical design by *William Hollins* of 1808–9.

St Chad's is early Pugin. It follows the programme suggested by his famous *Contrasts* (1836), creating a Catholic Gothic church in a heathenish industrial town whose medieval originals have been defaced, rather than recovering the logical structural Gothic tradition defined in his *True Principles of Pointed or Christian Architecture* (1841), and embodied in quintessentially C14 English forms at e.g. St Giles, Cheadle, Staffs., designed as St Chad's was being completed. When built it was tightly surrounded by the factories and workshops of the Gun Quarter. The w front, now diminished by the dual carriageway of the Inner Ring Road, originally faced the narrow Bath Street.*

The style of the building is North German C13, which Pugin, describing his first, smaller design of 1837, defended as 'cheap and effective and . . . totally different from any *protestant* errection' [sic]. In plan and elevation it is like a reduced version of St Elizabeth, Marburg: a tall church with aisles but no clerestory, and a centralizing E end of transepts and sanctuary. The tracery is influenced by English Geometrical and Decorated, but also has German parallels. Also German is the use of brick, but laid in English bond, with dressings of Bath stone. Eastlake admired the church while criticizing its economy: 'The walls are thin and poor, the roof timbers slight and weak looking.' But Pugin had to create a convincing cathedral, not just a parish

---

*It actually faces SE. 'Ritual' directions are used in this description. *Pugin*'s important brick courtyard Bishop's House of 1840–1 opposite the Cathedral was demolished in the 1960s, a major loss.

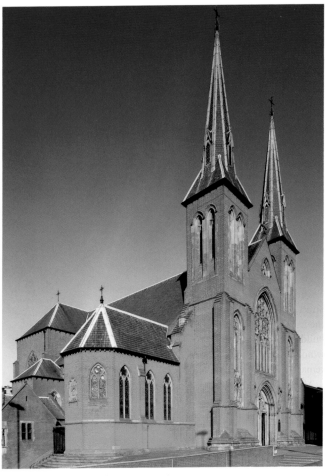

21. St Chad's Cathedral (R.C.), by A.W.N. Pugin, 1839–41

church, on a relatively small budget. Bishop Walsh contributed nearly £14,000 of the total cost of just under £20,000.

The sanctuary was rearranged by *E.W. Pugin*, 1854 incorporating the crossing. Otherwise the cathedral remained largely unaltered until 1966–8, when *Weightman & Bullen* drastically reordered the interior for Archbishop Dwyer, making it a single space. Some of its original character has been regained in further alterations since 1992 by *Duval Brownhill* (now *Brownhill Hayward Brown*).

Exterior

The w front immediately announces a cathedral, with its symmetrical pair of towers with spires flanking the gable of the nave. sw tower completed only in 1856 by *E.W. Pugin*. Central doorway divided by a stone pier. Tympanum with relief of the Virgin and Child with censing angels. Majestic six-light w window with spectacular Geometrical tracery: three large circles each containing seven small quatrefoiled ones. In the gable, a small spherical triangle window containing three small foiled ones. The towers are carefully designed to stress the height throughout: very tall two-light windows with statue niches below them treated integrally to increase the effect, very tall and thin paired lancets above. Their tops have spherical triangles echoing the main gable. More statues in niches flanking the doorway. The figures on the w front are all English saints: from the N, SS Augustine, Chad, Swithin, Wulstan, Thomas of Canterbury and Hugh of Lincoln. The spires have their main faces dying into very flattened broaches, which stress the upward push of the spires themselves. To the NW, St Edward's Chapel by *Sebastian Pugin Powell*, 1933. It has a three-sided apse echoing the main E one. Beyond, the nave has two-light nave windows with sexfoiled circles, cf. the Liebfrauenkirche at Trier. Then a well-grouped, rather domestic, forward extension, planned as a school, forms the entrance to the crypt. The former baptistery projects to its E, with a nicely corbelled angle. The transept has a tall six-light window including trefoiled circles and triangles. The E end groups most impressively above Shadwell Street, with the three-sided apse rising sheer out of offices to the s and the Lady Chapel to the N. The chapel was redesigned by Pugin during building, in English C14 style comparable to Cheadle. Its three-light E window has a spherical triangle in the head, and split-cusped tracery, remarkable for 1841 and looking like G.E. Street *c.* 1860.

Modern extensions for offices: **Cathedral House**, to the E, brick range with steep gables by *Gordon H. Foster*, 1992, and behind but at a lower level, six-storey block of 1963 by *Harrison & Cox*.

Interior

Entrance is through the main w door and inner side doors, so the first sight of the nave is from the w end of an aisle. This is the great surprise of the building. The **nave**, which appears from outside a single volume, has five-bay arcades, exceptionally tall and delicate. They define a space which is at once complex but more unified than the additive plans of later Pugin, e.g. Ramsgate. They have circular columns with four attached three-quarter rounds, a similar section to Marburg, and foliage capitals. The arches have a quite different, rather English, section with keeled rolls and hollows. The **crossing** has similar piers and arches. The N aisle is wider than the s, perhaps because of its special status as the Lady aisle. In the Lady Chapel a piscina with nodding ogee arch.

The roofs are of daringly thin timbers; anything heavier would overwhelm the arcades. They quietly delineate the different parts of the interior, as Pugin thought essential. The nave has a high queen-post truss with arched braces to an upper collar, supported by curved braces to wall posts, which are the continuation of stone shafts rising from the springing of the arcades. The aisles have plain purlin and rafter roofs supported by diagonal struts off the arcades. The crossing roof is flat, in nine panels; the chancel's moulded rafters and ridge purlin are supported by curved brackets, mirroring those in the nave. Encaustic tile floors of 1992 by *H. & R. Johnson*, in C19 style.

The **crypt** was first designed as a school but before completion became a burial place, for Pugin 'the first fully Catholic place of sepulture to be revived', with private chapels for donors. Staircase from the N aisle with a big moulded stone handrail in two sections, and foliated ends. Plain whitewashed brickwork and round arches; wooden chapel screens. **St Peter's Chapel** at the E end has an impressive Neo-Norman arch of two orders with massive roll mouldings, chunky columns and scalloped capitals. Imaginary history: but Pugin may be stressing the continuity of Catholic England. Painted Geometrical patterns of *c.* 1883. The **Hardman Chantry** at the NE has remains of painted decoration of 1877 (restored 1998).

Furnishings

Eastlake, in 1872, praised the fittings as 'correct in form as any antiquary could wish, and . . . wrought with marvellous refinement'. Significant items include important C15 and C16 German and Netherlandish work installed by Pugin, following his ideas of combining the Gothic and the Revival, a significant collection of *Pugin*-designed stained glass and later *Hardman* stained glass and recent work showing late C20 Gothic taste. The removal of Pugin's great rood screen in 1966 (now in Holy Trinity, Reading) altered the spatial qualities of the interior.

Nave. Pulpit. Against the NW crossing pier, moved from the s side in 1968, when it lost its sounding board. Given by the Earl of Shrewsbury in 1841; probably from the Abbey of St Gertrude, Leuven, whose furnishings were sold in 1798. Hexagonal, of oak. Elaborately carved decorative columns with small figures divide concave panels with seated figures, probably the four Latin Doctors, under rich layered canopy work. Plain moulded and panelled pendant vault. Probably early C16. Transitional in style between Gothic and Renaissance. Entrance stairs and door by *Pugin*. – **Organ case.** Spectacular but slightly thin Gothic of 1992 by *David Graebe*. Two tiers each with paired towers. – **Pews** of Japanese oak by *G.B. Cox*, 1940. – Wooden **statue** of St Chad, s side, C19, of before 1869 as he holds a model of Lichfield Cathedral before Scott's restoration. Expressive face in German late medieval style. – N **aisle. Font.** By *Pugin*, 1846. Octagonal, plain, with the evangelical symbols on the cardinal faces. – N **transept.** Elaborate canopied **monument** to Bishop Walsh by *Pugin*, made in 1850 by *George Myers* and shown at the Great Exhibition. Bath stone. English C14 style. Ogee arch with big cusps containing angels. Reclining effigy with mitre and crozier. Back patterned in squares containing four-petalled flowers. – Ledger **brass** to John Bernard Hardman d. 1903, surrounded by small tablets. – s **aisle.**

War memorial of 1921 by *Gerald J. Hardman* with relief of the Deposition. – Tablet to Archbishop Williams d. 1946, by *G.B. Cox*, with fine lettering. – Along both aisles, fourteen Netherlandish **Stations of the Cross** by *Albrecht Franz Lieven de Vriendt* of Antwerp, 1875, fully modelled but in very shallow perspective. – **Altar** in St Edward's Chapel by *Gerald J. Hardman*, 1933.

Chancel. High Altar by *Pugin*, 1841. An important, early, re-creation of medieval fittings, comparable with Pugin's thrones in the House of Lords. The dominating ciborium has a canopy with a large gable enclosing a cusped and sub-cusped pointed arch with foliage and angel stops. The original altar now has a **tabernacle** of 1878 by *J.H. Powell* with enamels of the doors depicting the Agony in the Garden. **Reredos** with seven two-light bays. Above it, a **relic chest** by *Pugin* with crowning spire, supported by angels, by *Gerald Hardman*, 1933. – Oak **choir stalls** of *c.* 1520. Five seats on the s, six on the N, with a detached seat, now the Provost's chair, to their E. Traditionally from St Mary-in-Capitol, Cologne, but probably Netherlands work, perhaps from western Belgium. Substantially restored, but with original linenfold on the backs and beasts on the arms. C19 desks with fine C15 or C16 ends with tracery and carvings. On the N side, a Pietà on the w end, one of the Magi presenting a chalice to the infant Christ on the E. On the s side, monks preparing food, and two laymen, one with clawed feet holding a shield with the Imperial eagle. The Provost's chair has a back board, probably reassembled, with a Virgin and Child crowned by angels and with praying monks, two flanking saints, and panels of vine foliage and grapes.

Lady Chapel. Altar by *Pugin*, 1841 with carvings of the Presentation in the Temple, the Nativity, and the Adoration of the Magi. Circular tower tabernacle. – Contemporary **reredos** with the Virgin and Child flanked by the Annunciation and Visitation. – Also by *Pugin* the w **screen** with sharply pointed arches and **parclose screen** with reticulated tracery. – C15 German **statue** of the Virgin and Child, given by Pugin. Heavily modelled faces; the Virgin memorably enduring and serene. – **Stencilling** on the walls in blue and gold. **Statue** of St Joseph with his carpenter's tools, by *Michael Clarke*, 1969; fibreglass. Calm, capable face.

Crypt. In the second s bay from the E, **monument** to Archbishop Ullathorne d. 1888, by *Peter Paul Pugin*, 1890. Four-centred arched canopy, reclining effigy in vestments. A relief on the back wall has a monk to the left and an angel to the right, who is pointing up from the head of the effigy to the Virgin and Child in the centre.

Stained Glass. An important C19 collection, mostly by *Hardmans.** Their early windows have bright reds and blues contrasted with quieter greens and browns, and grisaille. Nave, aisles and chancel are treated

---

*The family were prominent lay members of the church. John Hardman gave Pugin's rood screen. His son John Hardman Jun. founded the choir in 1854.

clockwise from the w end. N aisle. Second from w, the Glassworkers' window, 1865, given by Hardman employees. Under St Luke and St Andrew of Crete are scenes of glass-making. Then the Fitzherbert Brockholes window of 1851 with St Francis and St Thomas Apostle. Above, a small figure of St Cecilia playing a portative organ, given by Johann Benz, the first organist, in 1850. – Former baptistery. Three windows of 1843 designed by *Pugin* and made by *William Wailes* with characteristic dense colouring: w St Thomas, N St James, E St Patrick, quite expressive. Small figure scenes strongly contrasted with the dark backgrounds. – N transept. Immaculate Conception window, 1868 by *John Hardman Powell*. Six large scenes in ovals, many smaller panels. They include the Annunciation, and Pope Pius IX defining the doctrine in 1854. In memory of John Hardman, who kneels at bottom left in his choir cope; lines of Gregorian chant run along the bottom. In Alexandra Wedgwood's words 'astonishingly accomplished both in colour and design'. – Lady Chapel: N, Annunciation with small scenes of children by *Warrington*, the gift of St Chad's School, 1844; E, Our Lady, St Cuthbert and St Chad. – Chancel. Apse windows designed by *Pugin* and made by *Warrington*. Paid for by the Earl of Shrewsbury. N, St John the Evangelist and St Peter above St Michael and St Edmund: E, Our Lady and St Chad; s, St Paul and St Joseph above St Edward the Confessor and St Edward King & Martyr. Canopy work with heavily stressed verticals to add to the sense of height. On the s side two four-light windows, 1928. – s transept. Scenes from the life of St Thomas of Canterbury, 1865. – s aisle: first, First World War memorial, 1921, with darker, muted colours showing Kempe's influence; second, Our Lady and St George, given 1850. – St Edward's Chapel. The story of the relics of St Chad, all of 1933, by *Donald Taunton* of Hardmans.

St Martin in the Bull Ring

The ancient parish church of Birmingham, at the s end of the Bull Ring, now dramatically placed in an amphitheatre created by the shopping centre of 2000–3, with a fine view from its balcony. The new development has swallowed its churchyard, and the church now rises directly from the square to its N, with the slight feeling of a big ornament or art work [2, 22].

A church probably existed by the C12 and is documented in 1263. The late medieval building had an aisled nave, chancel, and NW tower. The arcades, with typical octagonal piers, and arches with roll mouldings and hollow chamfers, survived until the C19, but the outer walls and tower were encased in brick in 1690, a brick clerestory was added in 1733, and *William Hiorn* added a SE vestry in 1760. Medieval wall paintings were uncovered during the C19 rebuilding.

An attempt to restore the church in 1849 failed for lack of money. In 1853–5 *P.C. Hardwick* restored and recased the tower and rebuilt the spire. Then in 1872–5 the remainder was carefully demolished and rebuilt by *J.A. Chatwin*, slightly enlarging the medieval plan, and adding transepts and chancel aisles. This is the church we see today. In 1941 a bomb seriously damaged the w end and destroyed nearly all the glass. *Philip* and *Anthony Chatwin* repaired the church in 1950–3 and added the parish rooms on the s in 1954–7 and the sw octagon in 1960–1. In 2000–1 *APEC* reordered the interior, and in 2002–3 they repaired the exterior and extended the parish rooms and octagon to form a café and meeting spaces.

Looking at the N side from the new Bull Ring, the NW tower dominates the view. Hardwick's grey-brown sandstone, rough faced, with smooth quoins and details. The Dec style follows evidence discovered during the restoration: reticulated w window, petal forms in the belfry. On the N side two arched tomb recesses, restored from medieval remains, and the external **Miller pulpit**, under a little hood. Open trefoiled parapet. The spire is ashlar. It has three tiers of lucarnes alternating between cardinal and diagonal faces, following its predecessor.

J.A. Chatwin's rebuilding is typical of him in its tactful approach to existing work. Grinshill stone, again rough faced, a near match with

22. St Martin in the Bull Ring, medieval, 1853–5 and 1872–5, from the north west

the tower. Dec windows: reticulated in the transepts and the s aisle w, Geometrical shapes Lincs-style but with petals below in the great w window, a purer Geometrical ᴇ window, and a clerestory mixing Geometrical, intersecting and reticulated designs. Spherical triangles reserved for the transept gables. Wavy parapet on the nave, quatrefoiled on the chancel. Impressive, sharply gabled and pinnacled ᴇ end rising above Digbeth. The s side shows exquisite detail typical of Anthony Chatwin: rubble base merging into smooth stone above, the hall piers growing out of the rough work, and well-placed beasties on the cornice. His octagon now has a cantilevered upper floor in glass and lead cladding by *APEC*, with a similar gabled s porch to its ᴇ.

We enter by the w door, now with a glass inner porch of 2002. J.A. Chatwin's interior is faced in Codsall sandstone, deep rose pink with hints of grey. His arcade piers have four attached half-columns. Their arches have two chamfers, the outer with a wave moulding, the design developed from the c14 s arch of the tower into the nave, with its two heavy plain chamfers. The N arcade spandrels have a diaper pattern of flowers. Crossing piers more complex, with attached shafts. Rich timber roof: alternating hammerbeams and big arch braced trusses, both with angels. The aisle roofs have separate pitches and unexpected bowed trusses where they meet little cross-gables. Limestone floor of 2000–1. Medieval stonework survives in the ground floor of the tower. w door arch with two big chamfers, much restored. A narrow passage runs in front of the window above. Typical Chatwin chancel arch with shafts on corbels. Chancel arcades with boldly cusped arches. Boarded chancel roof with decorative wooden trusses on paired angel corbels. The chancel projects beyond the aisles, with arcaded **sedilia**. In the re-entrant angles, quarter-round linking passages. The 1954–7 link, down steps, from the s aisle to the café was modified by *APEC* for a disabled lift: an ingenious spatial effect.

Chatwin's **fittings** include characteristic **choir stalls** with scrolled tops to their traceried ends. – **Reredos** made by *Farmer & Brindley*, 1876, in 'scotch red sandstone'. Open arcade with serpentine shafts. Behind it, alabaster reliefs of scenes from the end of Christ's life: from the left, Entry into Jerusalem, Expulsion of the Traders, Last Supper, Agony in the Garden, Betrayal. – *Minton* **tiles**, with the arms of Clodeshall and de Birmingham, and borders with the Instruments of the Passion. – Big polygonal **pulpit** carved by *John Roddis* with open arches alternating with seated figures under canopies: Christ, flanked by Elijah and Moses, N, and St Peter and St Paul, s. – Brass eagle **lectern** by *Jones & Willis*. – *Chatwin*'s **pews** survive, re-stained, in the nave only. – N transept **organ screen** by *George Pace*, 1954. – N chapel **reredos** by *Pace*, 1956, with very attenuated gilded columns in his early post-Comper way. Also by *Pace* the **altar** and **rail**. – **Font**, w end, by *Jacqueline Gruber Stieger*, 2002, three shallow bowls cast in bronze by the lost wax method, with water flowing between them and into a shallow pool below.* – **Nave altar** and **reading desk** by *Toby Winteringham*, 2000–1.

Stained glass. s transept, a major work of *Burne-Jones*, made by *Morris & Co.*, 1876–7. In three tiers: at the top, Our Lord (the Salvator Mundi first designed by *Burne-Jones* in 1864) flanked by the Evangelists; in the middle Old Testament Prophets; at the bottom, small scenes in panels: Annunciation, Nativity, the Magi, Flagellation, Entombment. In the tracery angels playing instruments. Deeply autumnal colours, the large figures all brown, green and dark red, with blue clouds in the

*Chatwin's font was stolen. His tall octagonal hanging cover is in store.

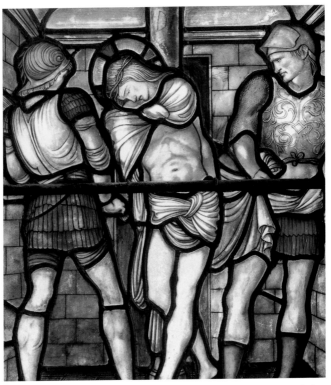

23. St Martin in the Bull Ring, detail of south transept window, by Burne-Jones, 1876–7

tracery and garments in the lower panels. Graceful, slightly serpentine figures, the aged Moses (middle left) particularly effective. The Flagellation and Entombment panels were new designs for this window, the former with angled standing figures hinting at *Burne-Jones's* later style (*see* St Philip's Cathedral), the latter with an expressive limp dead Christ. Other glass post-war: E and W windows by *Hardmans*, 1952–4, the latter partly following their original of 1875; N chapel E by *H.W. Harvey*, 1956, very like his master Harry Stammers with its bold yellow and orange, and angular figures; s aisle westernmost by *Laurence Lee*, 1980.

Monuments. Four medieval effigies, traditionally of members of the de Birmingham family. Between chancel and N chapel, going E, Sir William *c.* 1325, a cross-legged knight in soft red sandstone; Sir Fulk *c.* 1370, recumbent effigy in grey sandstone. N chapel, N side, Sir John *c.* 1390, alabaster effigy in armour, his feet on a lion, on a panelled Gothic tomb-chest designed by *M.H. Bloxam*, 1846, when all the effigies were 'restored'. Between chancel and s chapel, alabaster effigy of a priest in choir robes, C15. Original tomb-chest with angels under canopies, holding shields.

Town Hall

New Street and Paradise Street

A Roman temple on a high podium, begun in 1832 and designed by *Joseph Hansom & Edward Welch*, Birmingham's first large-scale civic building, and still an icon of the city [24]. Frank Salmon has emphasized its importance and originality as the first substantial C19 Roman Revival building in England, and a work of European importance.*

The Commissioners' choice reflected an interest in Roman learning and government among leading Birmingham citizens. Thomas Attwood, a former chairman of the Commissioners and active in commissioning the building, also led the Birmingham Political Union, which organized mass meetings in support of the Great Reform Bill in 1832, while the building was being planned. When it was new, it dominated by sheer size: in Joe Holyoak's words, like 'an ocean liner anchored in a fishing village'.

The Town Hall was the venue of the Birmingham Triennial Musical Festival, which raised money for the General Hospital, and saw the premieres of Mendelssohn's *Elijah* and Elgar's *Dream of Gerontius*. It was home to the City of Birmingham Symphony Orchestra from 1920. Dickens gave readings here; political rallies included a near riot in 1901 when Lloyd George spoke against the Boer War and had to escape disguised as a policeman.

The decline of big meetings reduced the need for the hall. In 1991 the orchestra moved to Symphony Hall (*see* p. 146), and in 1996 it closed. Refurbishment begun in 2004 by *Birmingham Design Services* with *Rodney Melville & Partners* will reconstruct the interior, reinstating the original single gallery.

History

In 1828 the Street Commissioners obtained an Act to erect a Town Hall to accommodate 3,000. It was to be used for 'ratepayers' and other public meetings, or for judicial activities', and the musical festivals. The Commissioners first tried to buy a plot at the corner of Waterloo Street and Bennetts Hill. In December 1830 a competition for the present site was advertised in *The Times*, which attracted seventy entrants including *Charles Barry* and *Thomas Rickman*. Despite a local feeling that

*In *Building on Ruins, the Rediscovery of Rome and English Architecture*, 2000.

Barry's Greek Revival design based on the Theseion at Athens would win, the three finalists were *Rickman & Hutchinson*, *John Fallows*, and *Joseph Hansom & Edward Welch*.

On 6 June 1831 *Hansom & Welch* were selected. Their radical politics may have helped. The Commissioners accepted a tender from *Thomas & Kendall* of £16,648, but required the architects to stand surety for excess above £17,000. The first brick was laid on 27 April 1832. Costs escalated, and Hansom was declared bankrupt in May 1834 and removed from the work, which was supervised to completion that December by *John Foster* of Liverpool. The actual cost was *c.* £25,000.

Hansom & Welch designed a free-standing temple, fourteen bays by seven (as it now exists). This proved too large for the site, and had to be cut down. The 1832–4 building was only twelve bays long, with a plain podium on the w where houses stood very close, and a blank n side. Almost immediately it was realized that there was no space for an orchestra for concerts, and in 1837 *Charles Edge* extended the n side with a large rectangular internal recess, and moved the organ into it. Then in 1849–51, when a new street was opened on the n and w sides, *Edge* completed the w podium to match that on the e, extended the building to fourteen bays, and built the n front with a pediment to match that on the s. At the same time he excavated the basement room below the Great Hall, and completed carving the twenty columns which had been left raw in 1834. The new n front had two internal columns flanking the organ recess, removed in 1889–91 when staircases designed by *Cossins & Peacock* were built to give access to the roof space. In 1995 the arcade at the s end of the podium, with its wonderful vistas through the arches, was infilled by the City Council's *Department of Planning & Architecture*, to increase the size of the foyer.

Exterior

The building is, in Welch's words, a 'simple Corinthian temple', closely modelled on the Temple of Castor and Pollux (then called Jupiter Stator) in the Roman Forum, which Hansom and Welch probably knew in detail from Taylor and Cresy's *Architectural Antiquities of Rome* (1821–2). It stands perfect and aloof, as a temple should. The stone is 'Anglesey marble', a white carboniferous limestone from Penmon, and the cost of quarrying and transport was a major cause of Hansom's bankruptcy.

The design follows the proportions of the Temple of Castor and Pollux almost exactly, scaled down to about three-quarters. It includes the Temple's most remarkable feature, its very tall podium, with rough rustication. In the original, this has column bases linked by round arches; Hansom and Welch transferred the arches to their window openings. The result was a completely new concept in England.

The Corinthian order also follows the Temple closely, but the entablature is simplified, with a plain architrave and dentil cornice. The

24. Town Hall, by Hansom & Welch, 1832–4; from the south east. Photograph *c.* 1895

capitals have rich acanthus leaves and distinctive interlocking spirals. Eroded by air pollution, they now have the haunting feel of an ancient ruin themselves. The cella is lit by large windows with eared architraves. At the N end it is set back, and the stair-towers of 1891 can be seen, flanking the organ recess of 1837. At the S end was an open entrance arcade two bays deep.

Interior

Originally, there was a single gallery with side balconies, a rich ceiling of three large roses with border panels, and deep coffered squares along the coving. Many efforts have been made to improve the defects of the original plan: the hidden entrance through the arcade, and the cramped entrance hall and subsidiary spaces. In 1875–6 *Martin & Chamberlain* proposed substantial alterations (including extensions in the middle of the long sides!) but built only the staircases to the cloakrooms and gallery at the S end. In 1891 *Cossins & Peacock* constructed the present entrance hall within the S end, shortening the Great Hall by 7 feet (2.1 metres), and created a crush hall above. Redecorations were by *J.G. Crace*, 1840s, Mr *Ingram*, 1855, and *John Taylor*, 1891, when panel paintings of scenes from Birmingham's history by *Henry Payne, Charles Gere* and other students of the School of Art were placed below the windows. Then in 1927 *Sir Charles Allom* of *White Allom & Co.*, decorators of London and New York best known for their work on ocean liners, replaced the single gallery with separate upper and lower ones, to increase capacity for concerts, removed the paintings, and replaced the ceiling and nearly all the internal decoration.

The **entrance** is still at the S end through the arcade, glazed in 1995 behind the arches, painful in this emphatically classical context. *Cossins*

& *Peacock*'s **entrance hall** beyond has opulent brown marble for its fluted pilasters and high dado. Square coffered ceiling. Two bronze plaques of 1934, probably by the *Birmingham Guild*. N and S lobbies lead to **side passages** running the length of the building, with original plain pilasters supporting cross-beams. They lead to offices and performers' rooms in the podium.

The **Hall** itself is a surprise.* The exterior suggests a hall raised above subsidiary rooms, but a single Great Hall rises the whole height of the building. This places the windows high up, impressive visually and useful for noise insulation. The shape and structure, including the cove of the ceiling, are of 1834, and the N organ recess of 1837. The fluted Corinthian pilasters and the cornice are also of 1834. The band of leaf decoration below the pilasters seems later C19. Everything else is *Allom*'s 1927 attempt at a rich Early Victorian interior. The best piece is the ceiling, with a restrained Baroque starburst in the centre, and richly modelled city arms with appropriately Roman trophies in the corners of the coving. The gallery fronts are treated as balustrades in relief, with bulbous little balusters. More of these underneath the windows, which have coffering in the reveals, helmets on top, and panels of not-quite-Greek-key ornament below. More of this on top of the gallery columns. The original roof largely survives.

The **organ** was built in 1834 by *William Hill*, moved back into the recess in 1837. The designer was probably either Neukomm of Austria, or Vincent Novello. The spectacular case was designed by Mr *Mackenzie* of London, who did others for Hill. Five crowned towers of large diameter pipes, linked by arrays of smaller ones. The decoration with large acanthus patterns is of 1890 but appears to follow *J.H. Chamberlain*'s designs of 1880. *Allom* could not resist altering the tops of the towers, and adding garlands and a portrait medallion of Queen Victoria.

*This description is of the interior as at 2002.

Council House

With the Museum and Art Gallery, and Council House Extension
Victoria Square and Chamberlain Square

The city's principal municipal building, and a major architectural monument of the reinvigoration led by Joseph Chamberlain; a large and richly detailed classical composition by *Yeoville Thomason*, 1874–9, extended in 1881–5. The Council House Extension to the N, linked by a bridge across Edmund Street (now called Chamberlain Square), was added by *Ashley & Newman* in 1908–12, its N range completed 1912–17.

History

The site was bought in 1853, but mid-C19 concern for economy meant that proposals of 1858 and 1868 were frustrated. In 1870 a competition was held for council buildings and assize courts, with Alfred Waterhouse as assessor. What followed was a farcical intrigue; designs were supposed to be anonymous, but competitors' names were well known. Waterhouse recommended two designs in turn by outside architects, the first by *W. Henry Lynn* of Belfast, and the Council substituted ones by local architects, with *Thomason*'s placed first. His scheme placed the council buildings on the s half of the site and the courts on the N. The elevations were in an expanded version of his Italianate commercial manner, with round-headed windows separated by paired Corinthian columns (cf. his Daily Post building, New Street, p. 113). Square turrets hinted at Gilbert Scott's Foreign Office, and in the centre was a huge tower with a concave truncated pyramid top. *The Builder* praised the planning, but compared the elevations to 'a monster railway hotel'.

In 1873 the Estates Committee persuaded Thomason radically to change the exterior, introducing a giant order, a much-praised feature of Lynn's design that was also in sympathy with the Town Hall. The foundation stone was laid by Joseph Chamberlain on 17 June 1874. The Council first met in its new Chamber in 1878, and formal opening followed on 30 October 1879. The courts were not built.

In 1880 the Tangye brothers offered £10,000 to buy works of art, on condition that the Council built a new Art Gallery to replace the one opened within the Central Library in 1867. A deal was struck by which the gallery was built on the empty N part of the Council House site, above new offices for the profitable Gas Department. The foundation stone of *Thomason*'s new design was laid in 1881 and the gallery opened in 1885.

25. Council House, by Yeoville Thomason, 1874–9 and 1881–5; from the north west

The development of council services in the late C19 and early C20, especially the municipalization of the tramways from 1904, required more office space. In 1905 John Feeney, proprietor of the *Birmingham*

Post, left £50,000 to build a new art gallery N of the Council House on a site acquired in 1899. *Ashley & Newman*'s design won a competition in 1907. Following the earlier building, the new galleries are on the first and second floors, with council offices below. The W, S and E ranges were built 1908–12; the N range to Great Charles Street in 1912–17, with delays due to the war. The S side, seriously damaged by bombing in 1941, was reconstructed in 1955–8 by the *City Architect's Department*.

The buildings remain essentially in their original uses, though with many small alterations: most recently, the conversion of two former Gas Department halls into galleries, the Gas Hall and the Waterhall.

Exterior

Thomason's revised façade to Victoria Square speaks a civic language in its giant Corinthian order and central dome, but its opulent Renaissance manner gives it a palatial air.* The main materials are Wrexham and Coxbench stone. Battered rusticated ground floor with a heavy projecting portico on columns and corner piers. Above this, the centrepiece has a deep round-headed niche breaking up into a pedimented attic. The source seems to be French C16: Bullant's Petit Chantilly, but without his syncopated rhythms. Deep cornice of Denby Dale stone, with luscious foliage decoration plundered from Owen Jones's *Grammar of Ornament*, carved by *John Roddis*. The dome, actually a tall double shell, seems small because of the fall of the square. The order is packed very close along the sides, but the fluted columns in the centrepiece are far apart, so the superstructure looks like a heavy body on spindly legs. Big projections burst out near the corners with columns *in antis* and large segmental pediments. The columns continue round a typical Thomason rounded SW corner, marking the Council Chamber and Lord Mayor's Parlour, and answering the order of the Town Hall. **Sculpture**: in the central pediment, Britannia rewarding the Manufacturers of Birmingham; in the segmental pediments of the projections, from W to E, Manufacture, The Union of the Arts and Sciences, Literature and Commerce, all designed by *Thomason* and carved by *R.L. Boulton & Sons*. **Mosaic**: in the niche under the portico, figures representing Science, Art, Liberty, Municipality, Law, Commerce and Industry, by *Salviati*.

Thomason's W façade of 1881–5 is much more successful, with a confident double-storey portico tightly and picturesquely grouped with the NW corner tower, locally nicknamed 'Big Brum'. The first design for the tower had clustered columns at the clock stage, and a dome; in execution it was simplified and given its truncated concave pyramid roof, a delicate version of his proposed tower of 1871. **Sculpture** in the pediment, Birmingham encouraging and advancing the Fine Arts, by *Francis J. Williamson*. A clear and strongly modelled

*The local satirical magazine *The Dart* published a mock plan of the Council's Improvement Scheme with as the largest building the 'Mayor's Palace'.

group well fitted to its high position. On the left, a woman paints and cherubs draw a plan; on the right more cherubs sculpt a head. Birmingham holds a laurel wreath to crown the artists' efforts. Simpler N elevation to Edmund Street with two tiers of windows.

The **Council House Extension** of 1908–17, N, is linked by a chunky bridge across Edmund Street. Its w front, facing Congreve Passage, has a low central dome, now seen in steep foreshortening because of the Central Library attached to its N end (*see* pp. 77–80). Impressively massive Baroque classicism, much more learned than Thomason, but linked visually by its rusticated ground floor and Aberdeen granite basement. The main material is creamy-brown Denby Dale limestone. The *piano nobile* plays variations on the Ionic order: paired pilasters on the w; single columns on the corner pavilions, framed by piers with plain pilasters with typically Edwardian little panels; paired columns free-standing against the blank wall of the galleries on the s. The entrances derive from Wren's St Mary-le-Bow: Doric doorcases, in round-headed niches impressively articulated by alternate rusticated granite voussoirs. The later N front is similar but its central entrance has a rusticated arch below a lintel with the city arms flanked by big seated figures of Art and Industry, probably by *Bloye*. Above, a large staircase window.

Interior

The main elements are laid out clearly and logically. The style is Thomason's normal Italianate, cf. the Colmore Row banking hall (*see* p. 98), with much use of coloured marbles. The **Main Staircase** rises straight inside the entrance to a landing on the ground-floor corridor. On the right the decorative metal grilles of the King's Lift, made by *Waygood* in 1909 for a visit by Edward VII who was unable to climb the stairs. **Committee Rooms** run along the main s front, reached from a long E–W corridor. They are simply but solidly treated with big doorcases and dark wood dadoes. The staircase returns in two flights to the upper corridor and the principal rooms. Above, the inner shell of the dome rises on eight ribs with rosettes decorating the intervening panels, and spectacular squinches with three setbacks. – **Statues** on the half landings: w, Prince Albert in Garter robes by *J.H. Foley*, 1866; E, Queen Victoria by *Thomas Woolner*, 1883, portrayed as a young woman, gently modelled and in a simple gown.

The grandest interiors are the **Banqueting Rooms** (first floor, s front). They have depressed barrel vaults with decorative ribs, a pattern of interlaced hearts. Characteristic *Thomason* articulation by pilasters and round-headed niches. The w room is separated from the central ante-room by paired columns supporting a cornice and an open arcade. It is articulated by paired pilasters, whereas the E room has single panelled pilasters. Wall painting at the E end in the tympanum, Peace, by *Joseph Southall*, in *buon fresco*, 1937–40. Only the top part of his complete design. Central seated figure, in a pedimented aedicule

26. Hall of Memory,
detail of relief, by
William Bloye, 1925

William James Bloye (1890–1975) was the most prolific sculptor of C20 Birmingham, producing work of a consistent and remarkably high standard. He trained at the School of Art and became teacher of modelling there in 1917, while continuing study with Eric Gill, especially in stone-cutting and lettering. Gill's influence is strong in his early work, emphasizing linear patterns in low relief, as in the panels in the Hall of Memory (1925, *see* p. 142), and those on the Legal and General Assurance, Waterloo Street (1932, *see* p. 128). He returned to this manner throughout his career, in e.g. the Mechancial and Electrical Engineering Departments frieze at the University (1954, *see* p. 253).

From the twenties he received many public and large commercial commissions, including many churches, e.g. Christ Church Burney Lane and Queen's College Chapel (*see* p. 252), and pubs, including the splendid pole sign at the Boar's Head, Aldridge Road of 1938. He adopted a fashionable Egyptian manner at the Police Station, Steelhouse Lane (1930–3, *see* p. 116), and New Oxford House, Waterloo Street (1935, *see* p. 126). Much of his later work is more three-dimensional, with a rougher finish, perhaps under the influence of Epstein. His last large work is the Boulton, Watt and Murdoch group in Centenary Square (*see* p. 143).

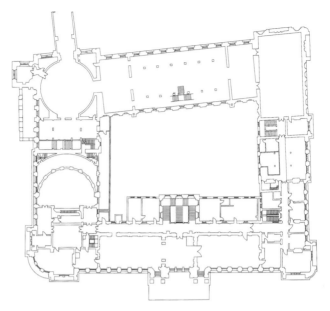

27. Council House, first-floor plan

sculpted by *Bloye*, flanked by a boy and girl in contemporary dress, in twining stylized foliage, as if searching for an elusive ideal.

At the w end of the first floor a square lobby with a glass-domed roof and to its N the semicircular **Council Chamber**. Originally articulated by paired Doric columns and lit by the surviving lunette windows in each bay. Altered in 1911 to accommodate the enlarged Council by *Cossins, Peacock & Bewlay*, who removed the columns, leaving piers with paired pilasters in each third bay, and installed the handsome benches, made by *Marsh, Jones & Cribb* of Leeds. Survivors of 1878–9, *Thomason's* dais, and his screen of Riga oak behind it, richly carved by *Collier & Plucknett* of Warwick. Its coupled pilasters divide carved panels of fruit and flowers with birds and snakes. In the central bay free-standing columns, and a panel with a reminder to politicians, an hourglass inscribed Tempus Fugit. Top cornice with a chunky central circular wreath of Italian walnut, deeply undercut. In the coving above painted panels of Truth and Justice, survivors of a larger C19 scheme.

In the E wing the square former **Rating Hall** with its ceiling supported on four free-standing decorative iron columns.

The **Museum and Art Gallery** [28] is entered through the w portico. It continues the Italianate language of the earlier work but in addition has delicate strapwork ceilings. Its location above the Gas Department led to problems of planning, with very limited space on the ground

28. Museum and Art Gallery, Industrial Gallery, by Yeoville Thomason, 1881–5

floor behind the portico. Thomason's solution has a richly detailed entrance hall and a staircase rising effectively behind a screen of columns, backed by piers. Bronze plaque to George and Sir Richard Tangye, 1908 by *William Robert Colton*. Wall painting on the E wall at the top, Corporation Street in 1914, *Southall*'s most important *buon fresco* panel, painted 1915–16. The title refers to Southall's horror at the outbreak of war; the figures are portraits of friends, with the women in the latest fashions, evoking a lost peaceful world. The upper landing, with coved ceiling and square rooflight, leads to the impressive **Round Room**, with plain walls for hanging pictures and a low conical glass roof above a strapwork band of circles in hexagons. To the E the finest interiors. The **Industrial Gallery** is all in exposed ironwork: seven aisled bays with columns in two tiers, semicircular arcades and cross-arches in the aisles, larger semicircular trusses supporting the roof, all of them exposed I-beams with the rivets prominent. Like a classical version of the Oxford Museum; but the immediate inspiration must be J.H. Chamberlain's Board Schools. Huge pendant gas burners. T-plan staircase of 1893, with a different design of railings. To the E the present **Tea Room** has a cantilevered iron gallery and impressive, slightly Romanesque, details e.g. blind arcading with paired colonnettes.

The **bridge** to the Council House Extension starts with a grand arch of 1912 with Doric columns and a tympanum with inscription in a wreath. The bridge itself and the galleries at the far end were rebuilt plainly in 1955–8. The best remaining early C20 interiors are up the staircase at the N end and through the Pinto Gallery of 1969, W. The **Dome Room** has a ring of eight Ionic columns set in a square; beyond it the **Natural History Gallery** has a shallow barrel vault with roof lights, and a wide E aisle separated by plain pilasters. Then through the upper level of a double-height room with copies of Greek friezes from the Mausoleum of Halikarnassos and the Nereid Monument on the gallery fronts, to the N **staircase**. Its single and double flights rise in a hall with a pronounced Byzantine flavour to its split marble panels and niches with arches checked in at the springing. Stained glass by *Harvey & Ashby*.

Finally two interiors separately reached from Chamberlain Square, between the Council House and the extension. On the old, S side the **Waterhall**. This is below the Industrial Gallery and similarly impressive; a row of six fluted iron Corinthian columns supports I-beams with brick vaults between, the construction again completely exposed. Thomason's wiry strapwork decoration fits very well with the exposed metal. Refurbished with new metal lighting troughs by *Associated Architects*, 2000. On the newer, N side of Chamberlain Square the **Gas Hall**. This was the Gas Payment office of 1910, with barrel-vault and pilasters like the Natural History Gallery. In 1992–3 *Stanton Williams* reconstructed its entrance hall, which had been altered after bombing, in a white planar style, and converted the main hall for an exhibition gallery with new wood flooring and again many plain white surfaces.

School of Art

Margaret Street

The Birmingham Municipal School of Art is *J.H. Chamberlain*'s last work, and his finest. His devotion to Ruskin and his belief in the civic gospel are powerfully expressed in its use of brick Gothic and naturalistic ornament. He was appointed in January 1882 and completed the drawings just before his sudden death in October 1883. His partner *William Martin* executed the designs with *Sapcote & Sons* as contractors. The building owes its existence to a remarkable head teacher, Edward R. Taylor, who was appointed to what was a government school of design in 1877, and persuaded the Council to take it over. He believed that a design was not 'completed until it is executed in the material … intended …', and he changed teaching methods to emphasize craft skills, with 'art laboratories' for e.g. metalwork.

The foundation stone was laid on 31 May 1884 and the school opened in September 1885. It cost £21,254, of which the Tangye brothers gave £10,937 and Louisa Ryland £10,000. The site was given by William Barwick Cregoe Colmore, then replanning his Newhall estate. An extension to the N range, along Cornwall Street, was added by *Martin & Chamberlain* in 1892–3. By the late 1980s the building was in a poor state. The exterior was cleaned in 1990–2 and in 1993–6 a major scheme by *Associated Architects* refurbished the major interiors and cleverly adapted other interior spaces. The building remains in its original use, as the Department of Art of the University of Central England.

The original building covers a nearly rectangular site. It is planned like a compressed H, the three-storey W front to Margaret Street, with its two-storey central porch, placed between slightly projecting four-storey N and S wings to Cornwall Street and Edmund Street, a plan hinting at domestic architecture of the C16–C17. The basic material is orange-red local brick from Adderley Park, a flaming challenge to the stone classicism of the Council House. Grey Derbyshire stone dressings, with a small amount of pink. The W front balances areas of plain brick with rich decoration. An effective blank top storey, with a terracotta blank arcade and discs, hides studios. Tall gabled centrepiece, with the porch contrasting plain brick piers with richly decorated stonework, mostly with leaf patterns in small squares, and buttresses with set-offs like sharp pinnacles. The gable has a tympanum and circles with leaf decoration on a brilliant gold mosaic background.

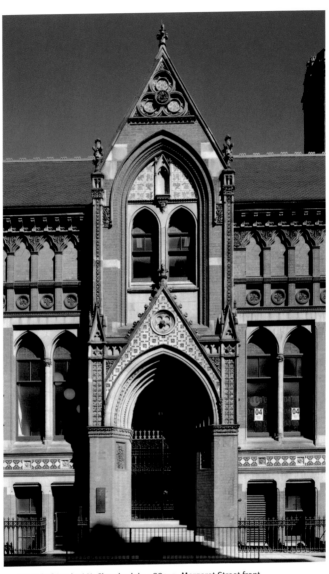

29. School of Art, by J.H. Chamberlain, 1883–5; Margaret Street front

Chamberlain's Darwinian view of beauty evolving through functional purpose is seen in the contrasting designs of the wings. The s one is taller, so that its upper studio can get north light above the N gable. Its large canted mullion-and-transom bay window is supported by a richly decorated bracket, on a chunky three-lobed column above a tall squared base. Flanking it, big buttresses cut back from broad flat fronts in a High Victorian way, enriched by panels of terracotta tracery. The N wing is simpler, with three large plain lancets set in brick walling and just a deep terracotta foliage band at arch level, to set off the glorious circular stone panel in its gable, carved by *Samuel Barfield* of Leicester: huge curving lilies with trumpeting flowers, set against a square trellis.

The s elevation to Edmund Street is an eyecatcher, facing Eden Place and so visible from Colmore Row. Three bays with paired stone windows, successively lintelled, cusped, and plain pointed, rising to exuberant gables enclosing complex little kingpost trusses with blue tiling in the spaces of their curved braces. Between them buttresses which sprout typical little Chamberlain canopies. The vertical force is balanced by the long balcony with its wrought-iron balustrade below the gables. The N side is plainer but impressively functional: five bays of big pointed brick arches with flower and leaf tympana, enclosing first-floor windows with massive shouldered lintels, a motif which repeats below. Above the cornice a long range of wooden-framed studio windows. The 1891–3 extension continues this for another eleven bays, identical except for simpler metal studio glazing, and putti doing arty things in the spandrels. Typical of the firm's engineering approach after Chamberlain's death. The whole exterior is tied together by a continuous plinth band of *Doulton* tilework containing lozenges of lilies and sunflowers on blue backgrounds, and by a repeating motif of a square enclosing a quatrefoil, in turn enclosing a circular disc, usually containing a flower or leaf pattern, seen on e.g. stone panels breaking the tile frieze, and more simply on the original railings made by *Hart & Co.* Crowning the roofs two ventilation towers, chunky chamfered squares with central projections rising to little gablets in the parapets. A charming wooden bridge carrying a duct, best seen from inside, links the s studio roof to the adjacent tower.

The entrance is through the central porch and up a flight of steps. On either side arcading with oak, apple and strawberry designs in the tympana, their very different scales showing that nature is used as pattern. Two pitch-pine screens enclose a lobby which opens into the central corridor. Immediately in front is a two-bay arcade, the central column a deliberately picturesque touch, its capital decorated with sunflowers. Beyond is the **Museum**, not large, but the show interior of the building, and beautifully restored in 1993–6. A tough, rich aisled Gothic hall: three-bay arcades with circular columns of pink granite with grey bases, and complex moulded arches. Their capitals have all kinds of leaves and flowers: oak, lilies, crocus, poppies, anemones. The English bond brick walls stand out sharply, tuck-pointed in white mortar. Steep pine roof trusses with tie-beams and upper collars, linked by kingposts. No clerestory, but roof lights. Pitch-pine dado; mosaic floor by *Craven Dunnill* in curving patterns of brown, gold, grey and white, with spiral borders. Imaginative use of space, e.g. where the upper corridor of the central block opens into the museum, high up, through a triple arcade,

J.H. Chamberlain

John Henry Chamberlain was born in Leicester in 1831, the son of a Baptist minister. He was a devoted follower of Ruskin all his life, and a trustee of Ruskin's St George's Guild until his death. His favourite book was the *Seven Lamps of Architecture*. He moved to Birmingham in 1853. His first house, 12 Ampton Road, Edgbaston (*see* p. 228), was built in 1855 for a relative, John Eld. It shocked a town still used to classical forms and stucco, and he designed little for some years except for Eld's very Gothic shop in Union Street (1862, dem.). His study of nature, inspired by Ruskin, lies behind his mastery of naturalistic ornament, always growing out of the construction of his buildings. It made him an early admirer of Darwin, and he came to see architecture as an art evolving naturally from practical building.

His career developed through his early friendship with Joseph Chamberlain (no relation), and his partnership from 1864 with William Martin, the successor to D.R. Hill, the public works architect of early c19 Birmingham. He was a member of Joseph's inner circle throughout the Liberal transformation of the town in the 1870s. He had many public roles: Professor of Architecture at Queen's College, chairman of the School of Art Committee, secretary of the Midland Institute, secretary of the Archaeological Society, and a magistrate. He was an early conservationist, helping Toulmin Smith to save the Old Crown (*see* p. 183).

Martin and Chamberlain, with Chamberlain designing, became architects to the new School Board in 1871, and surveyors to the new Corporation Street from 1878. Chamberlain designed his Board Schools to be the best-looking buildings in their neighbourhoods, their sources increasingly medieval English instead of Italian: gabled brick blocks with tall airy rooms and big windows grouped round boldly composed but functional ventilation towers, with as much decorative ironwork and terracotta detail as he could afford. The finest include Dixon Road, Small Heath (1879), Oozells Street (*see* p. 149), and Icknield Street (1883). Chamberlain used Gothic consistently, for e.g. Joseph Chamberlain's own house, Highbury, at Moseley (1879–80), and Berrow Court, for William Kenrick, off Westfield Road, Edgbaston (1879). His combination of functional Gothic and naturalistic detail is seen at its best in his masterpiece, the School of Art.

He died suddenly on 22 October 1883, just after lecturing on 'Exotic Art'. His funeral was like a state occasion, with a huge procession from the Town Council, the Institute, School Board, School of Art, Architectural Association and Liberal Party. Joseph Chamberlain and William White, the chairman of the Improvement Committee, led the official mourners.

30. School of Art, Museum

and where the main corridor in front of the Museum opens into the flanking staircases on two levels.* These have pitch-pine dados and continuous handrails. More mosaic floors in corridors and landings.

The main working interiors are the **studios** at the top of the main block and N wing, and on two levels on the S, treated as great halls; the consummation of Chamberlain's Board-School halls. Lines of huge pointed iron trusses, each unit with the disc-in-quatrefoil motif familiar from the exterior, here with a central ivy leaf. The N extension has the trusses boarded in. *Associated Architects* inserted an ingenious mezzanine here, with a cunningly sited glass access lift. The courtyard exteriors, glimpsed through large windows, are plain, with a glass staircase of 1993–6 at the NW end.

*The openings were unfortunately glazed in 1993–6 due to fire regulations.

Victoria Law Courts

Corporation Street
by Ian Dungavell

Until the granting of an Assize in 1884, Birmingham's major civil and criminal cases were heard at Warwick, both inconvenient and an irritant to civic pride. The new building would celebrate the city of Birmingham rather than warn its citizens of the consequences of transgression.

Having inspected the courts in several other assize towns, the Council Committee was in no doubt that it wanted as architect Alfred Waterhouse, the designer of the Manchester Assize Courts (1859–65) – 'the best courts of law in the world', according to *The Times*. But Birmingham architects agitated for an open competition. Waterhouse instead became the assessor, his sketch plans being offered as a guide. Of the top five entries only one came from a local firm, *Bateman & Hunt*, and the winners in 1886 were *Aston Webb & Ingress Bell* of London.

The foundation stone was laid with much ceremony by Queen Victoria on 23 March 1887, her first public appearance in her Golden Jubilee year. The building was thereafter called the Victoria Law Courts. It was opened on 21 July 1891 by the Prince and Princess of Wales, having cost about £113,000.

The winners' pseudonym was 'Terracotta', and the whole building is faced in it, a hard red shade from *J.C. Edwards* of Ruabon. It was guaranteed to catch the attention of the architect, who had made the most extensive use of terracotta to that date. But theirs was more richly decorative, with shafts and mouldings dying back into the wall surfaces. Stylistically eclectic, it draws from both Gothic and Classic (predominantly French Renaissance), combining elements of Flemish, Plateresque and Tudorbethan styles. The profusion of ornament is only possible because it is cast rather than carved.

Webb & Bell also departed boldly from Waterhouse's suggested plan by stepping the front back from the street. As the approach is oblique, this creates a picturesque arrangement of gables and towers instead of a rather flat façade, while keeping the plan regular and basically symmetrical. The principal entrance is at the centre of the long side of the Great Hall, which runs across the front, screening the courts behind from the noise of the street. Two courts open directly off the Great Hall, while a central corridor leads to a smaller square hall in the centre for the civil and criminal courts, and through to the barristers' library at the rear. Parallel secondary corridors at each end of the Great Hall give access to two further courts near the front of the building, and to offices behind.

The steep slate roof of the Great Hall has a large attic window above the central bay of five large segmental-headed first-floor windows. This block is flanked by octagonal tourelles which articulate the former refreshment rooms, projecting on the left, and the offices, receding on the right, both of which are at a lower level. At the corner with Newton Street, far left, the projecting bay with its bow window and the recessed bay five windows wide is a later extension of 1891–4, built by *Webb & Bell* as police offices and now incorporated. Further extensions along Newton Street were designed by *Henry E. Stilgoe*, City Surveyor in a suitable style and submitted to Aston Webb for approval in 1914.

Some of the decoration was supplied by leading figures in the Arts and Crafts movement. On the round-arched entrance porch, inspired by the C16 s transept of the cathedral at Senlis, France, the figure of Queen Victoria enthroned beneath the gable is by *Harry Bates*; the other figures representing the attributes of justice were designed by *Walter Crane* and modelled by *W.S. Frith*, who also modelled the figure of Justice crowning the clock gable. Much ornament elsewhere – putti supporting the brackets of the cornice, dolphins, and classical mouldings, all by *William Aumonier* – but little specifically to do with the function of the building apart from the scales on the piers flanking the entrance.

Interior

Inside is one of the most striking interiors of any C19 court building in England. Instead of red terracotta, the **Great Hall** and public corridors are faced in a sandy-yellow shade by *Gibbs & Canning* of Tamworth, and judicial gravitas takes second place to the golden glow of civic pride. The decoration is lavish and intricate. The great hammerbeam roof of dark stained deal and pitch pine is no doubt intended to recall Westminster Hall, the traditional hub of British justice. The first-floor corridors across each end, with their curved central balconies on profusely ornamented corbels, look like minstrels' galleries, and the pairs of exceedingly pretty putti which support the empty niches between the windows give a playful touch. Only the inscriptions from Chaucer ('Truth is the highest thing a man may keep') and the Magna Carta ('To none shall Justice be denied') remind the visitor of the seriousness of the business at hand. The five great electroliers are by *Starkie Gardiner*.

The stained-glass windows, designed by *H.W. Lonsdale* and executed by *Heaton, Butler & Bayne*, are Birmingham's Golden Jubilee memorial. Along the street front the theme of 'just balance' refers to Birmingham's civic accomplishments in scenes that show the contribution of the Queen or Prince Consort. The windows at the short ends have figures representing Birmingham manufacturing trades at one end and Warwickshire worthies at the other.

31. Victoria Law Courts, by Aston Webb & Ingress Bell, 1887–91. Detail of Corporation Street front

The **Courts** themselves are more sombre. The most impressive is Court 5, the criminal court, panelled in dark oak linenfold with an elaborate carved oak canopy over the bench by *H. Martyn* of Cheltenham. The first-floor balcony on the right leads to the Grand Jury Room. Elaborate plasterwork throughout by *George Jackson & Sons*.

Central Library

Paradise Circus

The finest example of the Brutalist aesthetic in Birmingham, and a civic project of European importance, the largest of its time in the city. Typical of Birmingham, but unusual nationally, in being entrusted to local architects, the *John Madin Design Group*; also typical in finally being approved so the Inner Ring Road could be built. It was the first library in Western Europe to be designed as a complete cultural centre including exhibition areas, lecture hall, children's and music departments under one roof. The scheme covered all of Paradise Circus, and was to have included a drama centre and athletic institute, and tough landscaping, with extensive water features. What was built is the Reference and Lending Library complex, a linking wing to the Council House Extension and, detached to the s, the Conservatoire. They combine the grand romantic gestures of the Brutalist period with subtle use of internal space, and remarkable tact in relating to their c19 neighbours [15, 32].

History

Birmingham adopted the Free Libraries Act in 1860. A Central Library was built in 1864–5 to designs by *Martin & Chamberlain*, w of the Town Hall. Its classical façade continued that of *E.M. Barry*'s Midland Institute of 1855–7. Burnt out in 1879, it was rebuilt splendidly by *J.H. Chamberlain* in Lombardic Renaissance style, with a tall clerestoried Reading Room, but was demolished, after a long campaign to preserve it, in 1974.

The City Council resolved in 1938 that a new library was 'an urgent necessity', but nothing was done until the previous site was needed for the Inner Ring Road. In 1959 the City Librarian selected the new site, and in 1960 a general specification was agreed. A box-like 1963 design by the *City Architect* was rejected, and in 1964 the *John Madin Design Group* was appointed. Drawings are dated 1964–6. Construction started in 1969 and the main shell was completed in 1971. Fitting out took until 1973. Structural design was by *Ove Arup & Partners* and the main contractor *Sir Robert McAlpine & Sons*. Formal opening by Harold Wilson was on 12 January 1974, when it was the largest public library in Europe.

The Library became a focus of changing taste in 1989, when the Prince of Wales likened it to 'a place where books are incinerated, not

32. Central Library, by John Madin Design Group, 1969–74. Photograph 1974

kept'. In 2001 the City Council announced plans to demolish it and build a replacement in Eastside. Drawings by the *Richard Rogers Partnership* were unveiled in 2002. Huge increases in book and archive holdings have made it too small to fulfil contemporary requirements: ironically, the same reason used to demolish its C19 predecessor. It will be tragic if history repeats itself and the building is destroyed.

Exterior

From the main approach, across Chamberlain Square from the E, the basic concept is immediately visible. The 'introvert' Reference Library, designed for lengthy stays and academic study, is an inverted ziggurat on tall piers. The 'extrovert' Lending Library, designed for short visits to renew books, is a curving three-storey wing E and in front. This contrasts with the ziggurat and links it visually to the Council House. Before the alterations of 1988–9 (*see* below) it was much more clearly separate. It ends in a well-calculated sharp little cut-off stair-tower. The original source is clearly Le Corbusier, particularly the monastery of La Tourette, appropriate for a place of research and scholarship, but more immediately through Denys Lasdun's Royal College of Physicians, London, Leslie Martin & Colin St J. Wilson's Law Library at Oxford, and their Harvey Court, Cambridge.* Bill Taylor, the City Librarian, knew Basil Spence's library at Swiss Cottage, London (1963–4) and wanted departments linked so that users would be aware of the whole library,

*Boston City Hall, often suggested as a source, was not known to the design team at concept stage.

not just the part they were using. The structure is complex, built over the Ring Road and an uncompleted bus station. The bus bays imposed a 36-ft (11-metre) pier spacing on the main block, and led to the standardization of a 1 ft 6 in. (45.7-cm.) module for the design.

The massive central ziggurat, contrasted with a lighter curving wing, perhaps hints at James Wyatt's Dodington Park of 1796–1800. Typical of Madin the abrupt junction between the parts, now masked. Here a quiet link was provided by the administration block which continues behind the Lending Library, weaving between the piers of the Reference Library. The scale is carefully calculated not to overwhelm the Town Hall and Council House, and the use of the Golden Section in e.g. the piers and decks of the ziggurat gives an underlying harmony and restfulness to the design. Concrete is strongly expressed with its texture roughened by abrasive blasting. The outer faces of the ziggurat and the front of the curved block are clad in pre-cast panels of Hopton Wood limestone, Derbyshire Spar and white cement.

After the tact of the exterior, the concourse, inside the ziggurat, is overwhelming. It is quite small. The pier spacing limits light to the library floors. The terraces with their rough aggregate finish, and the cruciform shape of the inner piers, create an impression of exceptional force. A weightlifter has taken Harvey Court and pushed it thirty feet into the air. Its power was too much for Brummies: in 1989–91 it was enclosed with a glass roof and boxy screens by the *City Architect's Department*, and filled with a clutter of cheap shops and a central clock by *Tibbatts Design*. Worst on the E by Chamberlain Square, where they obscure the structural glass wall to the entrance hall. A small example of Madins' water features remains on the N. On the w side the ziggurat stands impressively alone except for the small but telling elliptical Library Theatre block on its N, designed in 1969–70 but only built in 1983. To the N of the library, a wing running to a romantic castle-like service core, and then into the NW corner of the Council House Extension. Relief **sculpture** by *David Patten*, 1990, Cader Idris, N side of the lending library. At the far s, the Birmingham Conservatoire faces Paradise Street. Blue brick and concrete, its blank front the least effective aspect of the building.

Interior

Entrance from Chamberlain Square and lobby altered by the city's *Urban Design* team, 2001. The **entrance hall** is a long tall space deliberately drawing you in. The **Lending Library** on the N opens into it by two stepped galleries, reflecting the concourse and integrating exterior and interior. Effective sloping access bridges near the E end. The s side is the glass wall.

The way into the **Reference Library** seems awkward – escalators, a long corridor, another escalator, a landing, a third escalator – but was designed for a coat and bag store along the corridor, and a control desk

Shakespeare Memorial Room

The reconstructed **Shakespeare Memorial Room** comes from *Martin & Chamberlain*'s library, opened in 1882. Their richest interior, a small room like a casket in a refined Elizabethan Revival, to evoke Shakespeare's time. Entrance composition like a triumphal arch. A very rich piece culminating in a built-up centrepiece topped with a shell. Small square panels of carved leaves, and a frieze of appropriate laurel. Tall oak bookcases run all round, their arched tops decorated with patterned glazing. Upper and lower parts separated by a brass rail, for attaching service ladders. They stand on a low panelled dado which projects in the middle of each side as a service counter. Rich tympana at each end between bookcases and vault, with arcading, central niches, and beautiful marquetry of flowers, leaves, and occasional birds, those on the N side rather Byzantine, drinking out of a birdbath. The ceiling, with alternating plasterwork and glazing, was reconstructed from photographs (contractors *Trumper Bros*).

on the landing. Above the first escalators, the Royal Warwickshire Regiment war memorial of 1899, a bronze gazelle on a grey marble pedestal. On a pier, circular *Coade* portrait medallions of Shakespeare and Garrick from *Samuel Wyatt*'s façade of the Theatre Royal, New Street (*see* p. 7). At the third floor, a glass wall looks back to the entrance hall. The four main reference floors are low and deep, the concrete floor slabs left exposed as coffered ceilings. In 1974 the *Architects' Journal* said that 'one glides through the succession of volumes smoothly, sleekly'. Space flows magically through an inter-related series of double-height wells, fulfilling Taylor's scheme of linking departments. On the E side of the fifth floor the flow is increased by setting back the floor slab from the concourse wall, creating a bridge-like structure. Stabilizing points on each floor are the corner core structures, marked by ribbed concrete. Delightful reused *Martin & Chamberlain* iron spiral staircase to the seventh floor.

Later Additions, from 1983

In 1983 the City Council infilled between the Library and Conservatoire with a lecture hall and book storage. A design-and-build job with the *John Madin Design Group* as consultants, in a timid version of the 1969–74 work. In it, the reconstructed Shakespeare Memorial Room (*see* topic box, above).

Other parts of this commercial development: Two cheap-looking blocks of 1985–7 by *Leonard J. Multon & Partners*, W, with wedge-shaped ends. N of them an office tower with an ugly folded roof, also *Multon*, 1988–9.

City Centre

(Area bounded by the Inner Ring Road w, n and e , and New Street station s)

N

LIVERY STREET

BIRMINGHAM & FAZELEY CANAL

LIVERY STREET

St C
Cath

NEWHALL STREET

CHURCH STREET

GREAT CHARLES STREET

NEWHALL STREET

CORNWALL STREET

EDMUND STREET

STREET

COLMORE ROW

Sno
Sta

St Philip
Cathedr

School
of Art

Council
House
Extension

CHAMBERLAIN

Council
House

VICTORIA SQ

WATERLOO

BENNETT'S HILL

TEMPLE ROW WEST

TEMPLE

Central
Library

PARADISE CIRCUS

Town
Hall

NEW STREET

TEMPLE STREET

NEEDLESS ALLEY

Birmingham
Conservatoire

PARADISE ST

HILL STREET

PINFOLD STREET

ETHEL ST

LWR TEMPLE ST

CANNO

NE

STEPHENSON STREET

New Stree
Station

SUFFOLK STREET QUEENSWAY

0   1/4 mile

0   250   500 metres

33. City Centre

WHITTALL STREET

Birmingham
Children's Hospital

STEELHOUSE LANE

Law Courts

NEWTON

PRIORY

County
Court

CORPORATION STREET

Queen Elizabeth II
Law Courts

UNIVERSITY
OF ASTON

OLD
SQUARE

QUEENSWAY

L STREET

RATION STREET

BULL STREET

DALE END

ALBERT STREET

MOOR STREET QUEENSWAY

UNION STREET

St Michael
(R.C.)

CARRS LANE

Carrs Lane
United Reformed
Church

HIGH STREET

Rotunda

Moor Street
Station

Bull Ring
Shopping Centre

Selfridges

St Martin
in the Bull Ring

EDGBASTON STREET

The Commercial Centre

A network of streets, alleys and precincts, sloping up NW from the Bull Ring to the ridge of Colmore Row. Bennetts Hill, e.g., is quite steep. Late Georgian survivors in the Waterloo Street area; otherwise the character is late C19 onwards, with much late C20 rebuilding in High Street, lower New Street and the middle part of Corporation Street.

Streets are listed alphabetically.

Albert Street

Runs E off Dale End. On the s Nos. 20–26 of 1898 by *J.A. Chatwin*, the entrance with a big broken pediment biting a two-light window. Nos. 28–34 of 1888 by *Arthur Harrison* for William Marston, a carriage lace manufacturer who turned to car trim. A good Queen Anne design in pinky-red brick with a rusticated stone ground floor. This and the segmental windows look almost Neo-Georgian of 1930. Only the dormers and the ground-floor window transoms give the date away. Beyond and behind, facing **Moor Street Queensway**, **St Michael's (R.C.) church** is the wreck of the Unitarians' New Meeting House of 1802, the replacement for Priestley's chapel burnt down in 1791. Temple front with segmental ground-floor arches, formerly an open arcade. Paired Ionic pilasters and pediment. Two tiers of windows. In 1975 *Cyril Horsley* of *Horsley Currall & Associates* roughcast the exterior, infilled the arcade, built the porch with hanging arches, fitted new windows and gutted the interior, destroying box pews and galleries. Its only feature now a canopy over the altar with hanging arches like the porch. Small presbytery of 1933–4 by *Victor S. Peel*.

Bennetts Hill

Part of the early C19 Inge estate development (*see* Waterloo Street, p. 125). Starting from New Street, on the w side No. 13, a charming stucco survivor of 1823, perhaps by *Charles Edge*. Windows in cut back panels, which form fluted pilasters at the sides. Then two six-storey offices. Nos. 11–12, the **Scottish Widows Building**, of 1930–1 by *E.C. Bewlay* of *Peacock & Bewlay*. A heavy block, but with a wiry appearance partly due to the architraves projecting forward of the pilasters. Neo-Egyptian capitals and sculpted heads. The **Sun Building** is by *S.N. Cooke*, 1927–8, stripped classic, almost a copy of No. 126 Colmore Row (q.v.). On the E side, No. 21, commercial moderne of 1933–4 for Horton's Estate by *W.S. Clements*: slightly recessed centre with shooting fins, flanked by big angled steel windows with heavy sills and lintels. Nos. 23–24 is very late Neo-Georgian of 1961 by *E. Bower Norris* of Stafford, best known for Catholic churches. No. 25 is by *Riley & Smith*, 1926–7, for the Commercial Union Assurance. Handsome but slightly coarse, with giant fluted Ionic pilasters and a bowed central bay.

Beyond Waterloo Street on the w side, early C19 fronts. First No. 6 of five bays, then Nos. 7–10, two-bay shops stepping uphill. All with windows in recessed panels, typical of *Charles Edge*. Façaded in 1976 as part of Waterloo Court (*see* Waterloo Street, pp. 125–6), with an oppressive double mansard on No. 6.

The e side was developed later, after the demolition of Bennetts Hill House (*see* p. 125). Two elegant three-storey Italianate office buildings of *c.* 1860. No. 37 has first-floor windows with decorative spandrels, below alternating pediments. They suggest the work of *Edward Holmes*, cf. the former Masonic Hall, New Street. No. 38 is plainer with a rich cornice. Late C19 rusticated ground floor.

Bull Ring

The historic town centre, demolished and rebuilt in the 1960s and again in 2000–3. Peter de Bermingham, the Lord of the Manor, obtained a market charter in 1166, though the name Bull Ring dates only from the C18. The original layout fell sharply s from the junction of High Street and New Street, widening out in front of St Martin's church and forking into Well Street, later called Digbeth, to its e, and Spiceal Street and Jamaica Row to its w. There is evidence that the market continued se of the church, where the island site between Digbeth and Moat Lane probably represents late or sub-medieval encroachments. The medieval Manor House survived until 1822, sw of Moat Lane.

In the early C19 the market place was dignified by the statue of Nelson, and by *Charles Edge*'s massive Doric Market Hall of 1831–5 on the w side. The following century saw piecemeal rebuilding of poor quality. Bombing in 1940 destroyed some buildings and gutted the Market Hall. The City Council planned complete rebuilding, but its scheme, formulated after a big round-table conference in 1958, had to accommodate the Ministry of Transport's preference for separation of roads from pedestrian routes. The result, of 1961–7 by Laing Investment Co. and their architects *Sydney Greenwood* and *T.J. Hirst*, was the Bull Ring Centre, a large block of indoor shopping squares and markets. The elevated roads of the new St Martin's Circus ran NE–SW, with pedestrian subways beneath, unlike the slightly earlier boulevard layout of Smallbrook Queensway (*see* p. 201). The Rotunda was the visual focus of the whole.

The result became vilified as a classic case of inhuman post-war planning, subjugating people to the needs of traffic. Redevelopment schemes started in 1987. *Chapman Taylor*'s grand classicizing project of

1995 was perhaps the finest. The City Council insisted on the re-creation of an open pedestrian route from High Street and an open space in front of St Martin's. Suggestions of a thirty-storey tower were killed by the listing of the Rotunda in 2000.

What we see now is a scheme approved in 1997 and built by the Birmingham Alliance in 2000–3. Starting from the junction of New Street and High Street, the sole survivor of the 1960s rebuilding, the **Rotunda**, by *James Roberts*, 1964–5. A twenty-four-storey reinforced concrete circular tower, a simple and dramatic shape well suited to its commanding site, on a podium which is satisfyingly concave on the w. The mosaic cladding panels are not curved and have angles at the joins. The result looks cheap, but re-cladding in glass, approved in 2004, will destroy its historic integrity. *Ciment fondu* relief by *John Poole*, richly textured abstract patterning, now in a ground floor shop.

Beyond, the new pedestrian street runs s to St Martin's. It rises slightly to cross an underground bus route, then falls steeply. On either side covered malls run out to department stores anchoring the e and w ends, then return further s to the central street. The fall of the site means that the s legs of the malls are on three levels with balconies and bridges. It also produces a dramatic stroke at the s end of the walkway, a curving balcony high above the open space in front of the church.

Here is the bronze **statue** of Nelson [34] by *Sir Richard Westmacott*, 1807–9, the earliest memorial to him, paid for by many small sub-scribers.* The result is a democratic monument, without heroics. Westmacott aimed at simplicity, in contrast to his idealized Nelson at Liverpool of 1808–13. The admiral wears modern dress. He stands so easily that the anchor he leans on, and the model of HMS *Victory*, do not appear incongruous. There is no attempt to disguise his missing arm. 12-ft- (3.7-metre-) high drum pedestal, in contrast to the column and pillar of London and (formerly) Dublin. But the original concep-tion, lost in the rebuilding of 1961, was like a modern installation sculpture, with a pedestal relief of Birmingham mourning her dead hero, and four surrounding lamps formed from naval cannons supporting piled muskets and ships' lanterns. The surviving railings are shaped as pikes linked by twisted rope.

In 1966 Alexandra Wedgwood said of the Bull Ring Centre, 'The technical problems have been solved efficiently, even excitingly, but much of the architecture is disappointing.' Plus ça change . . . The replacement is retail architecture at an uncomfortable moment of tran-sition. All except Selfridges (*see* below) is by *Benoy*, without the many-handed re-creation of urban fabric we find at Brindleyplace. The treatment varies uncertainly from crude Postmodern classical in recon-stituted stone, to panels with abstract reliefs which look like Victor

*Nelson, with Sir William and Lady Hamilton, visited Birmingham in 1802, when he was 'repeatedly greeted with the applauding shouts of the surrounding multitude'.

34. Horatio, Viscount Nelson, statue by Sir Richard Westmacott, 1807–9

Pasmore work of *c.* 1955. The mall entrances are marked convention-
ally by full-height glazing, and Debenhams store at the w has a trite
circular tower. It is all very depressing.

Artworks. On the w side of the walkway near the top, a slightly over-
life-size bronze bull by *Laurence Broderick*, 2002. – On the w entrance
of the w mall, by Debenhams, a large silkscreen print like a blue flower,
by *Martin Donlan*, 2002–3.

Attached at the e end of the new development, **Selfridges** [2] department store of 2001–3 by *Future Systems*, an adventurous choice for a
major retail firm. The brief specified the separation of the interior from
the outside world. The result is an organic, waveform shape, as instantly
recognizable an icon as the Rotunda was for the 1960s, and a joy to car-
toonists. It tries so hard to be populist that one may as well begin with
its nicknames, the Blob, the Digbeth Dalek: cruel suggestions that nos-
talgia for the science fiction thrills of 1960s adolescence lurks behind the
silver anodized aluminium discs bolted to the skin. The architects suggest the influence of Paco Rabanne. A plasticine model by *Jan Kaplicky*

of Future Systems started the design. The outside wall tapers in from the ground like a fortification, then sweeps out and up and rounds back at the top. The shape goes round w, s and e. Aerial views suggest an enormous sofa. Glass entrances like mouths: four on the se corner hint at a monstrous face. A vertiginous glazed steel-box footbridge shoots out like a huge tongue over Park Street to the car park. The anti-urban rejection of traditional scale, massing and relationships is a hallmark of its designers. The sources of their 'plastic freedom' lie more in design, e.g. the Ya table of Karim Rashid, than in architecture, though there is an obvious influence from Archigram (a 1960s group of course) and their rejection of traditional form, devotion to the space age, and welcome to a hedonistic consumer culture. The free curves of Mendelssohn's Einstein Tower also lie somewhere in its ancestry. But the organic concept is only skin-deep – a skin of blown concrete on steel mesh, covered in fibre insulation and a coat of blue render. Behind is a conventional and cheap steel post-and-beam construction. It is an appalling neighbour, because of its overwhelming bulk, looming over St Martin's from the s, with the vehicle entrance close to the church's e end.

The interior is arranged around two light-wells, the smaller w one oval, the larger e one curved like a surgical dish, and raked upwards. Escalators and balconies are faced in shiny plastic resembling vitreous enamel. Detail is poor, e.g. where escalators join balconies. The floors are fitted out by separate architects: going up from the ground *Future Systems*; *Eldridge Smerin*, with green cylindrical lamps and dividers like children's bricks; *Stanton Williams*, easily recognizable with black free-standing open frames for hangers; and *Cibic & Partners* with *Lees Associates*, very pale, with glass fittings and big roof slats. But the low ceiling heights and enclosing walls are claustrophobic, and ovals of white enamel have unfortunate associations.

In the amphitheatre, café by *Marks Barfield*, 2004; elegant overlapping shells of beautifully patinated copper. The open market, which survived n of St Martin's from the c12 until 1999, has been banished s of it. The new **covered market** by the city's *Urban Design* team, 2000, has a barrel roof. To the se, **Moor Street Station**, by the Great Western Railway's Superintendent Engineer *W.Y. Armstrong*, 1911. A twin-gabled brick block, a standard G.W.R. design, with open canopies to the platforms beyond. Restored by *Simons Design*, 2002–3, with a new n porch.

Bull Street

The section se of Corporation Street is now the Martineau Place and Corporation Square shopping precincts. nw of Corporation Street, beyond Temple Row, **Pearl Assurance House** of 1958–60 by *S.N. Cooke & Partners*. On the ne side, set back, the **Friends' Meeting House** by *Hubert Lidbetter*, 1931–3, cubic Neo-Georgian. The first meeting here began in 1703. Beyond, No. 41 by *Gerald de Courcy Fraser*, 1936–7, and Nos. 42–43 by *S.N. Cooke*, 1934.

Cannon Street

Cut in 1733 by the Guest family who owned a cherry orchard on the site. It runs NE from New Street, parallel to Corporation Street, to which it now looks like a rear access. The houses were all replaced in the late C19. Still Late Victorian in appearance, except for the upper NW side. Ornate globe **lamps** on brackets, 1980s copies from a surviving C19 example in Needless Alley.

Starting from New Street, on the NW side No. 7, 1906 by *Frederick W. Lloyd*. Big canted terracotta bays and a doorway with huge head masks and a pediment perched on a lintel. The **Windsor** pub was rebuilt in 1990 by *PCPT Architects*, the stucco Jacobean façade a near-replica of that of 1888 by *William Wykes*. The **City Plaza** shopping development is of 1987–9 by the *Halpern Partnership*. Quite a contextual brick front, aggressively changed in 2002 by *Rolfe Judd Planning*'s green arches, and their oriel which dominates unpleasantly. **New Cannon Passage** to its NE has a dramatic view of the Cathedral tower. Beyond, the former Bank of England development (*see* St Philip's Place and Temple Row).

Returning down the E side, Nos. 13–14 on the corner of Cherry Street, by *J.L. Ball*, 1881–2, for Thomas Smith. Queen Anne style early for Birmingham. A massive, gabled brick block, but with delicate detail, e.g. the band of steep pitched triangles between first and second floors. Casement windows and shallow bays, all painted white. Two-storey corner oriel. Steeply pitched dormers. Bare areas of brick hint at Ball's later, Lethaby-influenced work. The design has a Dutch flavour, suggesting a city Protestant, commercial, but artistic. Ball was a lifelong Methodist.

Then the very bald rear of *A.B. Phipson*'s Midland Educational shop of 1883–4 in Corporation Street (q.v.). Nos. 10–11, 1887 by *J.P. Sharp & Co.*, with stone lintels and lots of terracotta rosettes. Tactful top floor of No. 10 added 1987. Beyond Fore Street the rear of *Martin & Chamberlain*'s building of 1880–1 for Marris and Norton (*see* Corporation Street, p. 101). Then parts of the 1996–7 *Seymour Harris Partnership* scheme for the former Post & Mail site: a replica of *W.H. Ward*'s 1881 rear façade of the Central Arcade, nicely done, and some mildly Postmodern infill. Plaques of Shakespeare and Walter Scott from the former W.H. Smith shop in Corporation Street.

Carrs Lane

On the N a wonderful survival, **Powell's Gun Shop** [35] of 1860–1, a late work of *Charles Edge* in Italian Gothic. Four storeys and dormers, rendered below, red brick with blue brick patterns above, and stone dressings. The ground floor, originally two shops with a central rear access, has four-centred arches. Above, the window arrangement narrows on each succeeding floor, creating upward movement. Many sculpted heads. The first-floor projections are recent. At the rear a narrow five-storey contemporary workshop wing.

Beyond, across a small grassed space, **Carrs Lane United Reformed Church**. Founded in 1748 and rebuilt in 1802 and again in 1820 by *Thomas Stedman Whitwell* in Greek Revival style, to seat 1,800. Refronted in 'Renaissance style' by *Yeoville Thomason*, 1876. Rebuilt 1968–71 by *Denys Hinton & Partners*. A tough piece, typical of its date with its echoes of Aalto and Butterfield. A mixture of red and plum Staffordshire brick, laid in Sussex bond. Four blocks linked by a central glass foyer peeping between. At the s end the octagonal chapel, to E and w hexagonal meeting-room blocks, at the N flats for overseas students. The chapel has blank brick gables split by V-shaped recesses with narrow strip windows. The meeting rooms a deliberate contrast, with horizontal windows. Tall dark steel cross at the Moor Street entrance. On the N side of the grass space, surviving *Thomason* **gatepier** and walling.

In the foyer, seated **statue** of R.W. Dale by *E. Onslow Ford*, 1897, and **mural** by *Edward Bawden*, 1971: three relief panels of the former chapels [36] and a list of ministers. Simplified architecture in bright monochrome, surrounded by circular patterns of nail heads, 20,000 in all. The chapel has rendered walls and quite a low ceiling, with light entering side alcoves Ronchamp-fashion. Plain tablet to three C18 and C19 ministers. R.W. Dale d. 1895, simple brass tablet. John Angell James d. 1859, a stone Ionic aedicule.

Chamberlain Square

NW of Victoria Square, between the Town Hall and the Central Library. Remodelled to *Madin's* designs as part of the Library scheme (*see* p. 77), but not completed until 1978. In the centre, the **Chamberlain Memorial Fountain** of 1880 by *J.H. Chamberlain*, commemorating Joseph Chamberlain's mayoralty. A High Victorian combination of strong primitive masses, influenced by medieval reliquaries, the planes cutting backwards as we look up. The belfry-like main storey with steep gables is set straight on a tall base with massive clasping buttresses. Set in its arches, mosaics of aquatic plants, and a portrait medallion of Chamberlain by *Thomas Woolner*. Above, a tiny pierced octagon, and an insistent spire with lucarnes and bristling crockets. The carving is by *Barfield* of Leicester. The curving pools are of 1978.

Behind the fountain, curving steps, needed to bridge the Ring Road, lead up to the Library. On top, two **statues**. James Watt by *Alexander Munro*, 1868, hand resting on a steam-engine cylinder. Joseph Priestley by *Francis Williamson*, 1874, re-cast in bronze in 1951. He is shown absorbed in the experiment which led to his discovery of oxygen. Below, an installation sculpture of Thomas Attwood by *Sioban Coppinger & Fiona Peever*, 1993, reclining on the steps with his pamphlets and his box nearby.

Colmore Circus

A roundabout on the inner Ring Road at the E end of Colmore Row, replanned in 2002 to re-create the street line through to Steelhouse Lane. Starting from Colmore Row, on the N the **Wesleyan and General Assurance** by *Peter Hing & Jones*, 1988–91. A poor attempt at

Postmodern, and very big. Central core with a pyramid roof, and four radiating wings, like a workhouse. Artificial pink granite facings, angled between floors, like the legs of a huge insect. On the s a bulky piece by *Fairhursts Design*, 2002. Oddly like an inflated house, with enormous two-storey high 'windows'. Across the road here, on the s the Bell Nicholson building (*see* Corporation Street, p. 103).

On the N, the **Post and Mail Building**, offices and printing works by *John H.D. Madin & Partners*, designed 1961, built 1963–6. The finest commercial building of its time in the city. A podium and slab block, inspired by Skidmore, Owings & Merrill's Lever House, New York, of 1951–2. Offices and works form an integrated production facility. Three-storey podium faced beautifully in Argentine black granite, with inset fillets of Sicilian marble. In the centre it is recessed, forming a courtyard, with the cornice carried dramatically across on piers as an open arcade. Sixteen-storey slab above, carefully detached, with light aluminium mullions. The printing works is treated quite differently, with concrete cladding, and the junction is deliberately abrupt – a Birmingham habit going back to the radical Arts and Crafts. Marble-clad entrance hall, and a double-height advertisement hall, N end, with a gallery distinguished by bronze anodized railings and staircase. Dem. 2005. Big bland replacement by *Aedas Architects*. sw of the printing works, across Weaman Street, **Lloyd House** [14], by *Kelly & Surman*, 1960–4.

Colmore Row

This was rural New Hall Lane, linking the Lichfield and Dudley roads out of Birmingham. St Philip's church (*see* p. 40) was built on the s side from 1709 but general development only began on the N side after the Colmore Act of 1746 (*see* Newhall Estate, p. 129). The s side w of St Philip's was developed by the Inge estate from 1823 (*see* p. 125). The N side was redeveloped from 1869 after leases fell in and the section w of Newhall Street again in the later C20. Starting at Victoria Square, w, there is a sharp contrast between these and the s side. Here C19 and early C20 buildings survive, ironically, because total demolition was planned later in the C20 for the Inner Ring Road.

On the s, No. 130 by *Goddard & Co.* of Leicester, 1903, for the Alliance Assurance. Two ample storeys in Wrenaissance style. Good domed corner turret, and a canted bay to Waterloo Street. Juicy garlands. No. 126 of 1926 by *S.N. Cooke* for the North British and Mercantile Insurance starts a line of four- and five-storey fronts. Cleanly articulated, with giant Ionic pilasters. On the N side No. 125, offices by the *Sidell Gibson Partnership*, 1999–2001. Tactful but less adventurous than their No. 5 Brindleyplace. The frame is heavily expressed in reconstituted stone, enclosing grey anodized metal windows, and a corner turret reflects a traditional Birmingham form.

Nos. 122–124 are the former **Eagle Insurance offices** [38], by *W.R. Lethaby & J.L. Ball*, 1900. One of the most important monuments of the Arts and Crafts Free Style in the country. The design is essentially Lethaby's; Ball was the executant. Pevsner saw it as an early example of functionalism. Recent research has emphasized Lethaby's interest in symbolism and primitive forms, described in his *Architecture, Mysticism and Myth* (1892), most obvious here in the eagle, symbolizing the sun god. The structure of load-bearing walls, concrete floors, and steel joists is expressed directly and simply in the façade. Ground-floor banking hall lit by a large mullion-and-transom window carried down to the ground. The doorways have segmental hoods and three-part mouldings deriving from Buddhist temples. Glowing bronze doors with moulded discs representing the sun. Above, three floors of offices with a grid of chamfered pilasters between chunky cornices again with three-part mouldings. Over the top floor a dramatic motif of alternating round- and triangular-headed arches. Godfrey Rubens suggests a re-working of the basic round and pointed architectural shapes Ruskin identified in *The Nature of Gothic*; Alexandra Wedgwood noticed the primitive, Anglo-Saxon appearance of the triangular heads. Finally a parapet of two layers with a chequer design of alternating wide and narrow brick and stone panels, with more sun discs and an eagle relief in the centre.

The interior is confused by alterations of 1982 by *Nicol Thomas Viner Barnwell*. Ground-floor banking hall, not large, but tall and full of light from the big window. Sharply rectilinear, mirroring the façade grid.

38. Former Eagle Insurance offices, Colmore Row, by W.R. Lethaby & J.L. Ball, 1900

Curves are treated as something precious: the circle in the centre of the beamed ceiling, and the elliptical relieving arches to the doorways. The walls have a very deep frieze with framed panels of green marble, cut and laid outward from single stones to give a symmetrical effect, like the Byzantine pavements which for Lethaby symbolized the sea. The octagonal Director's Room behind has been knocked through into the banking hall, and its skylight roof filled in. It has the best surviving fireplace, again stressing right angles; slabs and panels of stone without decoration, following the nature of the material. A relief panel of an eagle above it has gone. Simpler fireplace at the rear of the banking hall. The left-hand corridor has a typical Lethaby plain groin-vault ceiling, like the (demolished) hall of The Hurst, Four Oaks, Sutton Coldfield. The staircase has a nasty tiled floor of 1982 but retains the original balustrade with knot patterns, squares with the lines projecting as loops, and a cusp pattern symbolizing the heavens.

Nos. 118–120 is entertaining but mongrel stucco Italianate of c. 1875. Nos. 114–116 [39] is a full-blown Baroque wedding cake of 1912 by *Paul Waterhouse*, for the Atlas Assurance. A big portico is hoist aloft above much rustication, circular windows, garlands and all the panoply of commerce. An extreme contrast to Lethaby: pure scene-painting, with regular office floors behind, but very effective. The façadism is expressed by Mannerist detail: the large lunette window on the ground floor directly below the portico, and the two small, heavily blocked windows immediately under the pilasters.

No. 112 of c. 1823 has a crisp stucco front with delicate detail: pediments with anthemion decoration, garlands, and oval discs. Stepped-up lugged architraves. No. 110 is a picturesque and original piece of 1903–4 by *Henman & Cooper* for the Scottish Union and National Insurance Co. Aberdeen granite, appropriately, and limestone, with inset bands of red brick. Two-storey centre with big semicircular oriel and fine original railing, clamped between three-storey towers with tapering tops, ogee caps and tall finials. Nos. 104–106 have a three-bay Georgian front of c. 1827, the doorway with Tuscan pilasters, and paired pilasters to the first floor. Top altered. No. 102 is of c. 1829 when the plot was leased to Thomas Edge. His son *Charles Edge* was probably the architect. Now façaded as part of the Waterloo Court development (*see* Waterloo Street, p. 126).

Opposite, the **National Westminster Bank** [40] development by the *John Madin Design Group*, 1973–4. The most important Brutalist commercial building in the city, disastrous in context but with its own tremendous integrity. Low banking hall to the corner of Newhall Street, tower behind stepping up from sixteen to twenty-one storeys with horns on top, and originally a five-storey block to Colmore Row. The first designs of 1964 show influence from Louis Kahn's Richards Medical Center. The layout as built draws on the Smithsons' Economist development in St James's, London. Rough concrete aggregate and plum-

coloured Staffordshire bricks: industrial, romantic materials. Canted corners to the banking hall, the original metal doors with an abstract pattern of triangles. The Colmore Row block re-clad and heightened to eight storeys in 1996–7 by the *Seymour Harris Partnership*, in an attempt, sponsored by city planners, to recreate the lost streetscape of Colmore Row. Well intentioned, but it makes nonsense of Madin's design.

Beyond Bennetts Hill, on the s, **Wellington House** by *Essex & Goodman*, 1928, uninspired but contextual Portland stone with a big mansard. Nos. 78–84 was the **Phoenix Assurance Co.** [11], 1915–17 by *Ewen Harper & Brother & Co*. A very impressive example of Monumental Classic, in Albert Richardson's phrase, influenced by Selfridges in London. Seven bays of giant fluted Doric half-columns and tower-like end bays with slightly stepped-back tops. Concave corners with inset porches, and intelligent use of channelled rustication.

On the n side beyond Newhall Street a fine mid-Victorian commercial row, nearly all in Florentine Renaissance, and with a common cornice height, a requirement of the Colmore Estate. No. 85 is the former **Union Club** [7] by *Yeoville Thomason*, 1869. He altered it and rebuilt the façades in 1885, to match the new street line. Perhaps his finest building. Two ample storeys faced in Derbyshire limestone. Rusticated ground floor. Typical Thomason rounded corner and rich detailing, with big bearded-head keystones and juicy foliage frieze. Slightly inset corner, balancing the slightly projecting right-hand end to Colmore Row with

its big canted bay. Porch with coupled columns; tactful flanking shopfronts by *S.T. Walker & Partners c.* 1968. Two mansard storeys added in 1988 by *I S H Partnership*, consultant *Douglas Hickman* of the *John Madin Design Group*. Carefully detailed with a railing dividing the storeys. Thomason's cornice with its line of urns still registers on the skyline.

Nos. 79–83, **Royal Bank of Scotland**, is by *J.A. Chatwin*, 1871–3, for William Spurrier. He sold silver and plated goods, hence the sculpted heads of Renaissance goldsmiths, Ghiberti and Cellini, in roundels on the top floor, which also reflect the Chamberlainite programme of creating in Birmingham an Italian city state. A rich, original and functional three-storey front. Five bays: the three wide central ones project slightly and have an ornate bracket cornice. The ground-floor showroom has a rich central porch with coupled fluted Corinthian columns, arched side windows with vermiculated rustication, and former side entrances with segmental pediments on odd consoles like headless birds. First-floor offices with rich aedicules and pediments with foliage and vases, second-floor workrooms lit by a row of round-headed windows.

The rest of the row are of four storeys, but little more than façades survive. Nos. 75–77 of 1872–3 by *Yeoville Thomason* for Sanders & Co., metal brokers. An overall rich treatment with arched windows throughout and ornate three-storey central feature. Nos. 69–71 of

1873–4 is more sober, with rows of half-columns, Corinthian over Doric. Cast-iron columns to the ground floor, probably part of the original shopfront for Rogers & Priestley, piano makers. Then three more by *Thomason*, all for the Birmingham Town and District Banking Co. Two five-bay blocks flank a six-bay centre. All originally faced in Bath stone. The centre is the earliest, designed in 1867 and built in 1870. Its rich cornice survives, and the composition with porches in the end bays is original. The rest dates from alterations of 1937 by *Peacock & Bewlay*, who put Corinthian pilasters on the central four bays, creating the awkward effect of a pilaster in the middle. They altered the ground floors of the side buildings to match, but the rest of Thomason's elevations here remain. Left-hand block designed 1872 and built 1875, right-hand block of 1873–4, both with plain rustication and simple architraves. The left-hand one has a little more decoration.

No. 59 runs round into Church Street and down as far as Barwick Street. A very different flavour, the best piece of Second Empire French in the city. 1878 by *J.J. Bateman* for the Midland Land and Investment Corporation. Rich yet with classical discipline. First and second floors articulated by free-standing pink and dark grey granite columns, Corinthian over Doric. The corner has a first-floor oriel and a Venetian window above.

In 1991–2 Barclays Bank rebuilt the Thomason and Bateman buildings behind the façades to designs by the *Seymour Harris Partnership*. The dormers and roofline are theirs, a more tactful scheme than that of 1986 by *Peter Hing & Jones*, consultant architect *Anthony Blee* of the *Sir Basil Spence Partnership*, which established the principle by a successful planning appeal. Seymour Harris's rear façade in Barwick Street is impressive Postmodern, with semicircular and canted oriels in red Butterley brick and Portland stone. Their foyer is ingenious in a small space: a shallow double-height lobby leads into an entrance hall with a classical cornice. This prepares for the retained *Thomason* banking hall of 1869, refurbished by *Seifert Ltd*. The very first piece of C19 redevelopment on the street, built before the front block. A grand classical interior like Chatwin's bank of 1864 in Temple Row West (q.v.). Nine bays by five, all articulated by round-headed arches and Corinthian pilasters. Former entrances (right) have huge head keystones. Rich coved ceiling with central dome and panels of leaf decoration. The two main supporting ribs have plaster roses and foliage. Thomason's roof structure survives above: six large queen-post trusses.

Beyond Church Street the **Grand Hotel** [41], built in 1876–8 for Hortons' Estate and designed by *Thomson Plevins*. *J.A. Chatwin* was possibly also involved. Classical front, rendered *c.* 1974, its French pavilion roofs a picturesque sight from the Cathedral churchyard. Entrance porch with paired granite Corinthian columns on elegant tall elongated bases, probably of 1890 when *Martin & Chamberlain* extended the building at the rear in Barwick Street. Another extension by them here,

41. Grand Hotel, Colmore Row, Withdrawing Room, by Martin & Chamberlain, 1893–5. Photograph 1983

of 1893–5, eight storeys in red brick and terracotta with canted bays running right up. This includes the best interiors, the **Grosvenor Room** and adjoining withdrawing room, with rich French C18 plasterwork. (Important **stock rooms**.) Extra bedrooms by *Henman & Cooper*, 1900. On the corner of Livery Street, a four-storey block in creamy-brown stone, of 1986–7 by *The Weedon Partnership*, still for Hortons' Estate. Large round-headed dormers which stare alarmingly.

Beyond the churchyard on the s side, the former Prudential Assurance (*see* St Philip's Place, p. 115). Then the Colmore Row entrance to the Great Western Arcade, a replacement of 1988 by *Douglas Hickman* of the *John Madin Design Group*. A late work, showing his elegant and austere style moving towards Postmodernism. Frame and cornices polished blue pearl granite, and square bays of grey tinted glazing in stove-painted aluminium frames. Central tall round-headed niche with top pediment and round window inspired by S. Miniato al Monte, Florence. (For the arcade itself *see* Temple Row, p. 118). Finally on the corner of Bull Street, **Colmore Gate**, shops and offices of 1990–2 by the *Seymour Harris Partnership*, with a fourteen-storey tower. Silver reflective glass and more blue pearl granite. The mullions defining the centre of each side end at the top in half-rounds, like Cass-Gilbert-period New York. Very dominating from Colmore Row and the Cathedral churchyard. Built for the Church Commissioners.

Beyond Livery Street on the N side, the **Snow Hill Station** site. The first station was built by the Great Western Railway in 1852. *J.A. Chatwin's* **Great Western Hotel** of 1875 on the Colmore Row frontage, the finest C19 hotel in the city, was demolished in 1971. The station itself, rebuilt in 1911–12 to designs by the G.W.R.'s engineer *Walter Y. Armstrong*, lost its main line services in 1967, and came down in 1976–7. An archway survives in Livery Street. Its replacement is Nos. 1–9 Colmore Row, six- and ten-storey mauve brick and glass blocks of 1983–6. Contemporary multi-storey car park over the platforms with blue brick facings. All by the *Seymour Harris Partnership*.

Corporation Street
With Old Square and Priory Queensway

The largest of the municipal improvements of the 1870s (*see* Introduction, p. 13). Work began at New Street, S, in 1878 and reached Steelhouse Lane by 1882. The surveyors were *Martin & Chamberlain*. It is 66 feet (20.1 metres) wide, influenced by Haussmann's boulevards in Paris. The first building plan was approved in March 1879. In 1902 the *Birmingham Daily Post* reported that Corporation Street had 'quite eclipsed New Street as the premier street of the city'.

The original buildings are very different from earlier C19 developments such as the N side of Colmore Row. The skyline has gables and turrets instead of regular cornices. There is a mixture of styles: French Renaissance, Gothic, Flemish and Jacobean. W.H. Bidlake, speaking in 1908, was rude about this and said, 'Corporation Street consists of what a seedsman would call "selected varieties of sorts"'. There are hints of the contemporary New York of architects like *George B. Post*, e.g. his Western Union building of 1875.

1. From New Street, north to Old Square

The original NW side, mostly four storeys, survives as far as Cherry Street, and fortunately the corner building on the SE side. This is **Prince's Corner**, by *Dempster & Heaton, 1890,* very worn Italianate. The curve of the street means that the view from New Street is largely intact. On the NW good commercial façades. **Queen's Corner** is of 1879–80 by *W.H. Ward*. It continues the elevation of *Yeoville Thomason's* Daily Post buildings in New Street (q.v.), but with slightly more licence in the rich triplet corner windows and the sandstone pilasters with sunk panels. **Victoria Buildings** is also by *W.H. Ward*, of 1879–80, handsome French Renaissance. Decorated pilasters link the design to Queen's Corner, and a repeated motif of two smaller windows above one large one runs through. Two-storey rounded bays, and a great variety of pediments. The central doorway has a Michelangelo motif: broken concave pediment with a central panel topped by a broken segmental pediment.

Nos. 9–13 by *Yeoville Thomason*, of 1879, was built for John Feeney of the *Birmingham Daily Post*. Linked behind to his New Street offices (q.v.), but quite different in style, picturesque French-cum-Flemish. Two-storey canted bays, a plain storey with paired round-headed windows, then elongated shaped gables with small almost semicircular broken pediments (restored 1996–7).

Then the former **Central Arcade** by *W.H. Ward*, 1881, again French Renaissance, but very tightly composed. The right-hand entrance bay has a lunette enclosed in a giant arch, an oriel above, and a complex Chambord gable with Corinthian columns, a concave pediment, and a little semicircular top.

Finally in this row Nos. 19–21 by *Martin & Chamberlain* of 1880–1 for Marris and Norton, a furniture shop; their only surviving building on the street they planned. Flemish style in red terracotta, with some brick on the upper storeys. Five bays to Corporation Street with a big central gable, the symmetry carefully broken by the off-centre entrance and first-floor windows. The two floors of display windows reflect the original retail use. Octagonal corner turret with a short spirelet, the only complete survivor of many in the street. Iron frame structure concealed inside.

In 1996–7 all the buildings between New Street to Fore Street were façaded, except for the iron frame at Nos. 19–21, by the *Seymour Harris Partnership* (*see* p. 113). The rear elevation of the Central Arcade was rebuilt in replica in Cannon Street (q.v.).

Beyond Fore Street Nos. 25–39 were built in two parts, the left 1884–5 and the right 1887–8, both by *Dempster & Heaton*. The division is marked by an alteration in the second floor windows. A.E. Dempster owned the left-hand part. Builder's Gothic turning Queen Anne, in attractive orange brick. The octagonal corner turret has windows under triangular hoodmoulds, but has lost its spire. Nos. 41–43 were the **Midland Educational Co.**, of 1883–4 by *A.B. Phipson*. Five storeys, severe French Renaissance, relieved by pilasters with decorated panels. A big gable, built up in tiers of arcading; typical of Phipson, who always liked something impressive on the mantelpiece (cf. No. 10 Church Street).

Finally Nos. 45–49 of 1887 by *J.P. Sharp & Co.* for William Gammon Grenville, an outfitter. A commercial version of Ruskinian Gothic, with a lively rhythm of windows and a rounded corner to Cherry Street. Two-storey decorative aedicules with big lintels.

On the SE side after Prince's Corner, **Beattie's** store, formerly C&A, of 1949, extended 1958 and 1969 by *North & Partners*, linked with their work on New Street (q.v.). Glass top storey of 2000. **Victoria House** is of 1996 by *Robert Seager Design*, modified by *Peter Hing & Jones*: revived late C19 in terracotta and brick, not well done. On the NW here **House of Fraser** (formerly Rackhams), by *T.P. Bennett & Son*, 1957–61, eight storeys rising higher to Bull Street and including a new **North Western**

42. Corporation Square shopping precinct, by Frederick Gibberd, 1963–6

Arcade, replacing *William Jenkins*'s classical structure of 1884. Restless glazing patterns.

On the SE, Martineau Street, cut in 1887 as part of the Improvement Scheme, was replaced by the **Commercial Union** development of 1959–65 by *J. Seymour Harris & Partners*. Bold Pirelli-style fourteen-storey tower with tapered ends and top arcade, set well back. Shops around it replaced in 1999–2001 by *Leslie Jones Architects* as the first part of the **Martineau Galleries** scheme. Blue mullions topped with gold saucers, an entrance on Corporation Street with hugely inflated silver metal keystones, a pointed prow canopy in Union Street, and at the corner of Bull Street a miniature Odeon in blocky moderne. A gimmicky mishmash.

The Martineau Galleries scheme threatens the **Corporation Square** shopping precinct [42] beyond, by *(Sir) Frederick Gibberd*, 1963–6, job architect *Gerald Goalen*. Gibberd's only building in the city where he trained, and Birmingham's best 1960s shopping development. A cool Portland stone podium with carefully placed slit windows, over a recessed ground floor. Plant rooms treated as rectangular sculptural masses, with vertical slits linking visually to the podium: an early hint of late Corbusier in the city. The plan is defined by walkways from Bull Street (Dalton Way) to a central square and through to the Priory. Along Corporation Street, the 'Oasis' indoor fashion market. Mangled in 1990 by *Bob Bowyer Associates*, with heavy glazed canopies and in the square, a lumpy Toytown clock tower (with electric chimes) replacing Gibberd's minimalist advertising tower.

Opposite on the NW side, the former Lewis's store of 1924–5 by the firm's architect *Gerald de Courcy Fraser* of Liverpool. Another block behind, of 1931–2, linked by bridges across the narrow Minories. The result is a huge but chaste and carefully proportioned classical block, the sw and NE sides, to Bull Street and Old Square, articulated by fluted Doric columns (restored 1993). Impressive spatial effect in the Minories, which was originally open. Between the entrance bridges with paired columns and lintels is a deep narrow canyon. Built over in 1971, reopened and glazed in by *Peter Hing & Jones* in the 1993 conversion to offices and courts. Tactful extra storey all round.

2. Old Square and further north

Old Square, beyond, was developed from 1697 by John Pemberton, ironmaster. Corporation Street cut through it, and Upper and Lower Priory, running NW–SE, were reconstructed in the 1960s as **Priory Queensway**, part of the Inner Ring Road. Some original houses, typical of the period, with hipped roofs and giant corner pilasters, lasted until the early C20. Central paved space of 1998, when subways were filled in. Eight Festival column lamp-standards, moved here from Colmore Row, and two **sculptures:** Tony Hancock, the comedian, an impressive, looming presence, by *Bruce Williams*, 1996. A 10-ft- (3-metre-) high sheet of bronze with the famous image of Hancock, in Homburg hat, with cup of tea, made in glass rods set into the metal, symbolizing the dots of an analogue television screen, on a polished black stone plinth. On the N, *Kenneth Budd*'s relief panel of scenes from the history of Old Square, in cast brass and iron and moulded fibreglass. Made 1967, repositioned and restored by the artist 1998.

On the N, the **Bell Nicholson and Lunt** building of 1961–4 by *Essex, Goodman & Suggitt* with *J. Alfred Harper & Son*. Very big – it runs right along Priory and round into Steelhouse Lane – and plain, but its sweeping curves and continuous canopy (an obvious crib from the Peter Jones store in Chelsea) give it elegance.

On the E, **Maple House**, a re-casting of 1996–7 by *Level Seven Architects* of a 1966 block by *Cotton, Ballard & Blow*. The health club beyond was **Thomas Woolf's** furniture store, of 1972 by *Paul Bonham Associates*. Elegant Travertine façade, its slit windows taking their cue from the Gibberd opposite (*see* above). Dramatic interior with a two-level showroom on ground floor and basement. The **McLaren Building** tower beyond is also of 1972 by *Bonham*.

Beyond Old Square the finest remaining stretch of the street. On the SE side **Gazette Buildings** [8], originally Lincoln's Inn, lawyers' chambers of 1885–6 by *W.H. Ward*. Ground floor altered 1928 by *W.H. Martin*; mutilated top. What remains is Ward's finest surviving commercial design, an expansion of City Chambers, New Street (q.v.). The giant arches with their Venetian arrangement recall the splendours of his demolished Colonnade Building. The rich all-over treatment derives from Italian Mannerism; the first-floor niches placed illogically above

43. Nos. 153–161 Corporation Street, by Crouch & Butler, 1896–9. Detail, showing Allegory of Birmingham and Industry, by Benjamin Creswick

the ground-floor piers from Raphael's Palazzo dell'Aquila. The **Crown Inn** is of 1888 by *Charles J. Hodson*. Very French with tall canted bays.

On the NW, Nos. 153–161 of 1896–9 by *Crouch & Butler*. An exuberant and joyous design in red brick and buff terracotta. Giant arches on the ground and first floors, cut by swinging balconies above the shopfronts. For A.R. Dean, house furnisher, and Pitman's vegetarian restaurant, so we have *Benjamin Creswick*'s frieze of carpenters at work and diners at table above the shops, his city coats of arms above the arches, and the string course with its amusing cable moulding pulled by putti at either end.* Picturesque and effective skyline: a small oriel at the left with a tiny octagonal domed top, then a huge Flemish gable, and finally a smaller gable, right, flanked by small turrets. On the large gable an allegory of Birmingham and Industry, also by *Creswick* [43]. The **County Court** is of 1882 by *James Williams*, the first building on this part of the street. A conservative but beautiful Italianate palazzo, like a Charles Barry club of 1835, strayed from Pall Mall. Ground floor with channelled rustication and Doric porch. *Piano nobile* with pedimented windows.

To the SE in **James Watt Street** the **Queen Elizabeth II Law Courts** of 1981–7 by the *Property Services Agency Midland Region Design Unit Architects*. Three storeys, long low-pitched intimidating roofs, glazed entrance. **Sculpture** by *Vincent W. Woropay*, 1988: the 'Wattilisk', five surmounted heads based on Chantrey's head of James Watt in the city art gallery, becoming smaller and more defined as they go up. Black Indian granite.

On the NW, the **Victoria Law Courts** of 1887–91 by *(Sir) Aston Webb & Ingress Bell* (see Major Buildings, p. 74). On the SE, the Court Restaurant, now Yates' Wine Lodge. 1882 by *George Henry Rayner*, altered in 1925 by *Arthur Edwards*. Then the former **Salvation Army Citadel** of 1891–2 by *W.H. Ward*. Cleanly articulated, with a pair of domed turrets. Rebuilt as offices behind. No. 190 was built as shop and works for Coopers, bookbinders, in 1890 by *W. Hawley Lloyd*. Red brick and terracotta. The ogee mouldings to the second-floor windows give a Gothic feel. Entrance with a little flying arch. The first design had a simple cornice; the tall gable is pencilled on the drawing as an amendment, a quick change approved by the Council Surveyor, and evidence of the picturesque approach to design in the street.

Beyond the Courts on the NW, **Coleridge Chambers** of 1898 by *John W. Allen* of West Bromwich, for the Birmingham Mutual Sick Benefit and Old Age Society. A modest but effective foil, the structure well expressed in red brick and cream terracotta. Flemish gables, piers topped by heraldic beasts and a little onion dome. **Ruskin Buildings** is

*The joke is a clever one. Creswick was a Sheffield knife grinder discovered as a sculptor by Ruskin. At the start of *The Seven Lamps of Architecture* Ruskin makes a distinction between architecture and building, using as his example the addition of a cable moulding. Here it is pulled by classical putti, symbols of a style Ruskin despised.

a much grander thirteen-bay block of 1900 by *Ewen & J. Alfred Harper* for themselves as developers. Carefully articulated, with a very big Flemish gable, projecting ends, two-storey canted bays, and the top floor recessed behind stubby attached columns. Many original iron shopfronts, divided by terracotta columns with reversed volutes supporting shields.

Opposite on the SE side, the former **Methodist Central Hall** [10, 44] of 1900–3 by *Ewen & J. Alfred Harper*. The town's first Wesleyan chapel opened in Cherry Street, 1782 (rebuilt 1822). In 1887 it was replaced by a Central Hall by *Osborn & Reading*, seating 1,100, in Corporation Street near Old Square. By 1899 this was already inadequate. The Harpers' successor has a main hall to seat 2,000 and over thirty other rooms including three school halls. It cost £96,165. As Alexandra Wedgwood said in 1966, it is 'clearly the local men's answer to the Victoria Law Courts opposite, to which it does indeed form the perfect complement'. Faced entirely in terracotta like the Courts, it is otherwise a sharp and deliberate contrast. The courts are angled to the street, the Hall follows its curve. The courts are picturesquely informal, the Hall's three very tall storeys are powerfully defined by vertical piers, cornices and a parapet. The central tower marks a step down, following the fall of the street. It

44. Former Methodist Central Hall, Corporation Street, by Ewen & J. Alfred Harper, 1900–3

rises sheer to a complex and strongly modelled square belfry, partly enclosing an octagon, and a convex spirelet. The grid of the façade unifies but does not disguise the change in elevations between the parts: five bays of school rooms and offices to the left have canted bays, with an arcade including paired windows above; seven bays with the main hall to the right are lit by big three-light Perpendicular windows above gently curving bays. The detail is remarkably eclectic, with e.g. corner turrets resembling Indian chattris.

The ground floor is articulated by pilasters and has several original shopfronts with elegant thin mullions. Baroque entrance porch with swinging voussoirs and paired stubby blocked Ionic pilasters. Much sculpture, modelled by *Gibbs & Canning*. On either side of the pediment, allegories of Methodist Teaching. Large draped figures instruct naked cherubs with discreetly placed books. Inside the porch on each side, panels of scenes from the life of Wesley. The charming triangular lamp over the right-hand door is by *Ewen Harper & Brother & Co.*, 1928.

Inside, the main staircase rises on the left of the entrance hall to a seven-bay aisled and clerestoried hall with SE apse, which rises to the roof. Iron arcades. The gallery has a good iron balustrade of Art Nouveau flourishes. Narrow corridors between hall and outside walls, largely glazed. **Organ** by *E.F. Walcker* of Ludwigsburg, 1898.

On the NW side, turning the acute corner into Steelhouse Lane, the **King Edward Building** of 1900–1 by *E. & J.A.Harper* for John Hawkins & Sons, cotton spinners. Nine bays running round. The rich terracotta style of Ruskin Buildings already going plainer. Doric columns on the ground floor and plain giant pilasters above. Classical clock pediment.

Dale End

The N continuation of High Street. The last Georgian survivor, on the E, went in 1987. The W side is Corporation Square (*see* Corporation Street, p. 102). On the E a Postmodern block by the *Seymour Harris Partnership*, 1989–90. Beyond Albert Street offices and car park of 1973–6 by *Ardin & Brookes & Partners*.

High Street

High Street, running N from the Bull Ring, is probably the oldest street in the city. C16 timber-framed buildings of typical West Midlands form survived until the late C19. Victorian rebuilding, including the spectacular Louvre department store of 1896 by *Essex, Nicol & Goodman*, was replaced after the war to depressingly poor standards.

The whole W side is two dull Portland stone commercial blocks. The **Big Top** of 1956–61 by *Cotton, Ballard & Blow*, with a thirteen-storey tower behind. Clever planning, with underground servicing from the Inner Ring Road. To its N the former **Littlewoods** store of 1959–64 by *Littlewoods M.O.S. Ltd Architects' Department*. Alterations 1997–8 by the *Seymour Harris Partnership*. At the entrance to Union Street, **clock** of

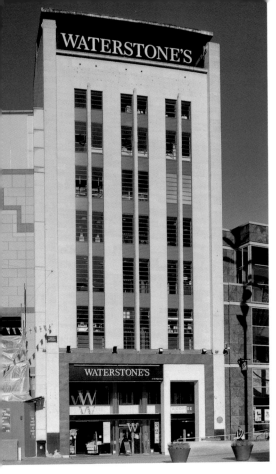

c. 1900 by *J. & A. Law* of Glasgow, brought in 1979 from the King's Head, Bearwood. Banded Corinthian column pedestal, domed top.

The E side starts with **Waterstone's** bookshop [45], built for Times Furnishing in 1936–8 by *Burnett & Eprile*. An eight-storey moderne tower, its height emphasized by tall strips of windows linked by lead panels, their central fins with a kind of cubic billet moulding. Side pilasters with curved tops, and roof canopy floating free. Then the **Pavilions** shopping development of 1986–8 by *Chapman Taylor Partners*. It started the commercial revival after the 1970s recession, and its pink granite and glass façade with Art Deco detail brought Postmodernism to the city centre. Its planning is ingenious. The atrium, with the city's first glass lifts, rises and twists round to the N to link inside with Marks & Spencer (*see* below). Altered entrance and huge disfiguring metal panel, 2002. **Marks & Spencer** is by *James M. Munro & Son*, 1956–7. A big old-fashioned classical job with moderne details – but a welcome relief here. Beyond Carrs Lane, Nos. 50–53 by *Kenneth W. Norton*, 1974, and Nos. 54–58 by the *Seymour Harris Partnership*, 1980.

Lower Temple Street

On the w the Neo-Georgian **Shakespeare** pub by *Arthur Edwards*, 1911. The successor to the Pit Bar of the Theatre Royal, hence the name. Before the block was reconstructed in 1910–11, the theatre ran through to Lower Temple Street here. Then a cream terracotta shop of 1914 by *Essex & Goodman*, with inset canted bays and two floors of display windows. The first floor was originally a car showroom, with a 'motor lift' at the rear.

New Street

First mentioned in 1397 and probably cut in the C14 as a better graded and more direct route E from the junction of the Halesowen and Dudley roads, now Victoria Square, to the top of the Bull Ring, replacing what are now Pinfold Street and Dudley Street. The lower, E, end built up in the C15, included the Gild Hall of the Guild of the Holy Cross, later used for King Edward's School. The rest was a scatter of cottages and barns until the C17. Consistent urban character appeared in the early C18, with houses in a provincial Baroque style. Warwick House, rich classical of 1839 by *William Thomas*, was the first department store in the town. In the mid C19 New Street was Birmingham's most fashionable shopping street, supplanted only by Corporation Street at the end of the century. It now links the new Bull Ring to the whole Victoria Square, Convention Centre and Brindleyplace area.

The E end has suffered badly from poor mid- and late C20 redevelopment, but a precious stretch of good Victorian and Edwardian commercial survives between Bennetts Hill and Corporation Street. Starting from Victoria Square, on the s Nos. 79–83, 1870, on the corner of Pinfold Street. Brick with stone dressings in enjoyable but ignorant Venetian Gothic, see the second-floor clutter of pilasters. Suspiciously classical cornice and keystones. Top storey on the corner originally an iron and glass photographer's studio, rebuilt in brick by *Nicol & Nicol*, 1912, as a showroom for Dale Forty's pianos. Nos. 84–86, **City Chambers**, for the stationer E.C. Osborne, *c.* 1871, must be by *W.H. Ward* as its handsome front is a simpler version of his Gazette Buildings, Corporation Street (q.v.). Giant arches, pairs of round-headed windows, plain triplets above. Nos. 88–91, **Town Hall Chambers**, is of *c.* 1868 for Isaac Horton, probably by *Thomson Plevins*. Brick with stone dressings, mongrel classical, but with real character in the giant pilasters banded with rows of nailhead and cogging.

On the corner of Ethel Street the former **Masonic Hall** of 1865–9 by *Edward Holmes*. He won a competition judged by 'Mr. Cockerell, the architect' (presumably F.P. Cockerell) jointly with *Henry Naden*, and after an attempt to amalgamate their designs, Holmes got the job, to protests from other competitors. Classical, rendered. Ornate first floor windows with decorative panels and spandrels. The corner oriel lit club rooms with a view down New Street. Converted to a cinema by *Bertie*

46. New Street Station, North Western side, 1849–54. Photograph *c.* 1895

New Street station was built in 1849–54 as a 'Grand Central' station for through services, to replace the termini of the London & Birmingham, Grand Junction, and Midland railways on the edge of the town – Curzon Street, Vauxhall, and Lawley Street. The site was densely built up with shops, chapels (including the Old Meeting of 1689 and 1795) and some of the town's worst slums. The station was owned by the London & North Western Railway – the amalgamation of the London & Birmingham and the Grand Junction – but Midland trains used it from the start. The station buildings facing Stephenson Street, designed by *John Livock*, were a handsome restrained block in the Italianate style of Charles Barry, incorporating the Queens Hotel. A public footbridge across the platforms replaced the lost streets of Peck Lane and lower Pinfold Street.

In 1881–5 the station was extended southwards and Station Street, aligned on the w entrance of the Market Hall, built along its s side. In its final form, the N, North Western, side was separated from the s, Midland, side by a road, the Queen's Drive. The North Western side had a single-span iron trussed-arch roof with a maximum width of 212 ft (65 metres), the largest in the UK when built. It was designed by *E.A. Cowper* of *Fox, Henderson & Co.*, the firm which built Paxton's Crystal Palace. After the Charing Cross station roof collapse of 1905, Cowper's roof was strengthened with additional tie bars in 1907. It was destroyed by bombing in 1940. The remainder of the station was demolished in 1964–6.

Crewe of London in 1910; heavily reconstructed within by *William Glen* in 1929–30 for ABC cinemas. The steep pitched attic is his.

On the N side, **Waterloo House** of 1926–7 by *Essex & Goodman*, a weak faience design with old-fashioned classical details. The side elevation steps up Christ Church Passage and round into Waterloo Street. Ugly 1970s granite facing to the lower floors. Then the former **Royal Birmingham Society of Artists** building by *Crouch & Butler*, 1912, on the site of *Rickman & Hutchinson*'s 1829 gallery. A good faience design, influenced by contemporary London fashion: canted inset bay windows, and slightly projecting end bays rising into built-up dormers. The former gallery is a top-lit room in a two-storey rear block. Next, a ten-bay former Lyons Corner House by *F.C. Baker* of their architects' department, 1926–7. On the corner of Bennetts Hill, one of Birmingham's earliest post-war office buildings, **Grosvenor House** by *Cotton, Ballard & Blow*, 1951–3. The first designs of 1949 were plain. Manzoni asked for 'some improvement in the architectural treatment' and the result has rows of sawtooth projections, little pointed iron balustrades on the corner, and a brise-soleil. Flashy but undeniably effective.

Opposite is New Street's architectural disaster, the **Woolworth Building**, designed by *Cotton, Ballard & Blow* and built in two parts, the E 1958–61 for Woolworth's, the W 1962–4 for Jack Cotton & Partners.* A shapeless mass of Portland stone, mosaic cladding and green slate, stepping up to ten storeys. A 1990 refurbishment of the E half by *Temple Cox Nicholls* included the clunky and exceptionally prominent glass lift tower, now the principal accent in the street from Victoria Square.

Beyond this the best surviving part. The N side starts with the former **London & Lancashire Insurance Co.** of 1906–8 by *Riley & Smith*. Edwardian Baroque, rare in Birmingham, and significantly by commercial architect-surveyors. But its big pediment and low dome are excellent street scenery. Good sculpture: cherubs and garlands, and the company's arms with fearsome gryphons. The *Birmingham Guild* did work here. Partly original shopfronts.

On the S opposite, the **Piccadilly Arcade** [47] has a handsome Baroque façade in white and green faience. Built as a cinema in 1910 by *Nicol & Nicol*. Giant arch entrance, open arcade above, Wren-style turrets. It runs through to Stephenson Street. Bronze fascia and shopfronts of 1926 by *J.R. Shaw*, who made it a shopping arcade. Inside, the slope reflects the original rake of the seating. More original fronts with thin metal mullions and decorative top lights. Refurbished in 1989 by

*It replaced both the **Theatre Royal** [3] by *Runtz & Ford*, 1904, replacing one originally by *Thomas Saul*, 1773–4, with a façade by *Samuel Wyatt* of 1780 retained in rebuildings by *George Saunders*, 1793–4, and *Samuel Beazley*, 1820; and *W.H. Ward*'s masterpiece, the **Colonnade Building** of 1881. The portrait plaques from Wyatt's façade are now in the Central Library, *see* p. 77.

47. Piccadilly Arcade, New Street, by Nicol & Nicol, 1910, ground floor 1926

Douglas Hickman of the *John Madin Design Group* with *trompe l'œil* ceiling paintings by *Paul Maxfield*. No. 111, **The White House**, started as a similar building to the Burlington Hotel block beyond Lower Temple Street, of 1874–5 by *Plevins*. Reconstructed 1911–12 by *Nicol & Nicol* for Hortons' Estate with a new steel frame and elevations of fine concrete render scored to imitate faience. Open top arcade mirroring Piccadilly, the uneven spacing betraying the reconstruction.

On the NW corner of Temple Street, a modest three-storey block of 1842. Typical cornice for the date, with paired brackets. Probably by *Charles Edge*, see the windows in panels cut back from the wall plane. Baroque side doorway of 1910 with gilt lettering. Beyond, shops and flats by *GMW*, 2003–4, blocky and over-scaled, repeat all the mistakes of Woolworths, in glass panels.*

On the s here the **Burlington Hotel**, formerly the Midland. Built as a hotel and offices between 1867 and 1875 for Isaac Horton and designed by *Thomson Plevins*. Two blocks flanking the former Burlington Passage, made the hotel entrance *c.* 1994, with obtrusive vertical signs. Italianate in white brick, now painted. The scale reflects its important location by the original entrance to New Street Station. Impressive street architecture; the detail carefully increasing upwards.

On the N between Needless Alley and Cannon Street an exuberant free Jacobean office and shops block of 1898 by *Essex, Nicol & Goodman*, in pale orange terracotta with red bands. Giant three-centred arches with soffit scrolls enclose the shopfronts. Canted bay windows above. Picturesque roof-line with domed corner turrets, and a wide Flemish gable with a little serpentine balcony. The Cannon Street elevation has a three-storey tower entrance to the upper offices. Big arch with a wild soffit of almost detached, S-shaped cusping.

Beyond Cannon Street the former **Daily Post** offices and printing works, by *Yeoville Thomason* for its proprietor John Feeney. Four storeys. The start is the six-bay middle section of 1864–5. Rich Italianate. Windows set in double arches with decorative soffits and spandrels. Strong horizontal emphasis from cornices and the impost bands carried across the building. Top floor with panelled pilasters. Extended W, turning into Cannon Street, in 1871, and E with an identical design of probably the same date. Richer architecturally, with paired columns and pilasters, but less decoration, e.g. plain spandrels. Taller top floor to gain attic space, with segment-headed windows and a frieze of panels and discs inserted below the cornice. In 1879, when Corporation Street was cut, a very different kind of building was added facing it (q.v.). 1882 extension up Cannon Street, with a plainer round-arched three-storey elevation. In 1887 large additions were made behind the façades by *Thomason & Whitwell*. In 1959–62 the developer Jack Cotton proposed a huge development stretching from here to the Cathedral churchyard, with *Walter Gropius* as consultant but nothing was built. The *Post* moved to Colmore Circus in 1966 (q.v.) and the printing works was demolished. In 1996–7 the whole block bounded by New Street, Cannon Street, Corporation Street and Fore Street was redeveloped behind retained façades by the *Seymour Harris Partnership*. Evidence of this the extra floor behind a mansard roof, and Postmodern infill in Cannon Street.

In front now, a free-standing **Welcome Centre** by the City Council's *Urban Design* team, 2003. Heavy freeform steel structure and glass walls, slanting roof and sides, E prow. It clashes horribly with both the

*They replaced **Temple House**, by *W.H. Ward*, 1890–1, altered but retaining a charming corner oriel; in Temple Street five shops of *c.* 1825 with living space above, stepping up one by one; also delightful small-scale early C19 buildings in Needless Alley.

Post buildings and the rich classical former **Midland Bank** [48] of 1867–9 by *Edward Holmes*, opposite on the sw corner to Stephenson Place. Two tall storeys. Ground floor with wide rusticated pilasters and big round arched openings with decorative transoms; first-floor windows in aedicules separated by Corinthian half-columns, paired on the New Street front, and becoming pilasters at the corners. Some Greek detail e.g. the acroteria breaking the top balustrade. Chimneys form the corner turrets. Grand entrance porch on New Street with paired Greek Ionic columns of Cornish granite. Original railings by *Hart & Son*. Inside, the former banking hall has giant Corinthian pilasters and a heavily coffered ceiling. The central domed lantern was raised up a full storey in alterations of 1992–3 for Waterstone's by the *Malcolm Payne Design Group*. At the rear a five-storey office extension of 1875.

Beyond Corporation Street, New Street has less interest and too much Portland stone. On the N the former **Marshall and Snelgrove**

48. Former Midland Bank, New Street, by Edward Holmes, 1867–9

store, on the site of Warwick House. By *North, Robin & Wilsdon* of London, started in 1938 but not completed until 1956 due to the war. Former entrance with the upper floors recessed in a segment of a circle, contrasted with projecting segmental balconies with curly ironwork. Hotel conversion by 1970 by *Ted Levy, Benjamin & Partners*, with a high mansard. (For the Big Top development beyond, *see* High Street, p. 107).

On the s side the bland classical **King Edward House** of 1936–7 by *Essex & Goodman* replaced *Charles Barry*'s King Edward's School of 1833–7 (*see* Edgbaston, p. 246). The **Odeon** cinema, by *Frank Verity & Samuel Beverley* for Paramount Pictures, 1936–7, retains a tall roof feature, a concave stripped-classical aedicule. Central fin altered.

Paradise Street

It runs w from Victoria Square. On the n first the Town Hall, then the Conservatoire (*see* Central Library, p. 77). On the s, first a plain block by *Watkins Gray Woodgate International*, 1983–5. The corner attempts an oriel, nicknamed 'the Chieftain tank' by a former chair of the City Planning Committee. Then the retained 1904 façade of **Queen's College Chambers**, by *Mansell & Mansell*, French Renaissance in cream terracotta, sharply gabled but restrained in detail. The offices behind, by *Watkins Gray Woodgate International*, 1975–6, replace the original college buildings of 1843 (for the present college, *see* the University, p. 252). No. 36 is a rare piece, for Birmingham, of full-blown Postmodern, a single gable front of 1991 by *David Delaney-Hall* of *Sinclair Architects*, refacing a plain block of 1959. No. 35 is latest classical by *H.W. Way Lovegrove*, 1955. No. 34, **Daimler House**, is a swagger Baroque piece by *A. Gilbey Latham*, 1911, originally a showroom and repair shop for the Daimler motor company. Finally a block on the corner of Suffolk Street by *J. Seymour Harris & Partners*, 1959–61, one of their best and simplest works, its Portland stone façades defined by close-set fins. Sadly re-clad in aluminium, 2002.

St Philip's Place

The E side of the Cathedral churchyard, originally with the Blue Coat School of 1722, rebuilt in 1792–4, at the N end, and the rectory at the s, with its garden between. At the N end now the former **Prudential Assurance** building of 1935–7. By the *Prudential Assurance Architects' Department*, but *P.B. Chatwin*'s papers suggest he was involved. Beaux Arts classicism in Portland stone. The Doric order imitates that of the Cathedral. Extra storey and irritating canopy by *Temple Cox Nicholls*, 2002. The former **Provost's House** has a Cotswold stone front. Ground floor with three-centred arches, and first floor with canted bay, from the replacement Rectory of 1885 by *Osborn & Reading*. The rest of 1950 by *Caröe & Partners*. Reconstructed behind as offices by *Temple Cox Nicholls*, 1981–2. At the s end an office building by *Level Seven Architects*, 2001–2, in cream stone with silver-grey anodized bay windows.

Steelhouse Lane

The E continuation of Colmore Row, now Colmore Circus, to Lancaster Circus. On the N side **Fountain Court**, barristers' chambers by *Holland W. Hobbiss & Partners*, 1963–4. A conservative brick classical block, with a majestic Bath stone cornice. In the courtyard a **bronze**, Fountain (Nude Girl), by *Bloye*, 1964.

Beyond, a nurses' home by *Martin & Martin & W.H. Ward*, 1947, a late example of their cubic Neo-Georgian. It heralds the **Birmingham Children's Hospital**, the former General Hospital of 1894–7 by *William Henman*. The original E-shaped plan altered but still recognizable. In the Romanesque style of the Natural History Museum in London. Rich red brick and terracotta. The wings end in pairs of spires with (infilled) triplet arcades between. In the rear corners huge octagonal ventilation towers with spires cut off for tapering open caps. Rebuilt central entrance, now with a glass and silver anodized metal porch, part of 1995–8 alterations by *Powell Moya Partnership* for the Children's Hospital, which also included operating theatres at the rear.

The s side has the **Queen's Head** pub of *c.* 1960, then the **Juvenile Court** of 1930 by *Peacock & Bewlay*, brick with stone dressings, the corner nicely turned by Ionic pilasters. In **Newton Street** their good **Coroner's Court** of 1936–7. Early C18 style with rusticated ground floor, swept-up parapet, and curly broken pediment over the entrance. Further E down Steelhouse Lane the rear of the Law Courts (*see* p. 74) including a small **police station** of 1897, and its ponderous 1930–2 successor by the *City Engineer & Surveyor*. Sculpted heads by *Bloye*.

Stephenson Place and Stephenson Street

Stephenson Place runs s from New Street opposite Corporation Street, turning w into Stephenson Street. On the E the uninspired ten-storey replacement for *Holmes*'s Gothic **Exchange Building** of 1865, by *Cotton, Ballard & Blow*, 1965–7. In front, a ramp leads to the same architects' **Pallasades shopping centre** of 1968–70, with a nine-storey office block, on a 7.5-acre (3-hectare) concrete raft over **New Street Station**. Piers refaced *c.* 2000. The station itself (*see* topic box, p. 110) was rebuilt 1964–7 by *British Railways, London Midland Region*, planner in charge *Kenneth J. Davies*. The shops and office block are bland, the station underneath dark and claustrophobic. (For the signal box, *see* p. 207.)

On the N side, *Henman & Cooper*'s 1900 additions to the **Burlington Hotel** (*see* also New Street, p. 113). Brick with stone dressings, Jacobean. The central gable shows Cooper's Waterhouse ancestry. Further w, in the triangle with Navigation Street and Pinfold Street, **Guildhall Buildings** by *Frederick W. Lloyd*, 1899. Brick and terracotta, well proportioned, and with delightful mosaic floors in the entrances.

49. Great Western Arcade, Temple Row, by W.H. Ward, 1874–6. Arch infill by Douglas Hickman of JMDG, 1984–5

Temple Row

The s side of the Cathedral churchyard, developed by William Inge in the early C18, it continues E to Bull Street. The original houses were in a provincial Baroque style. The last survivors were demolished in the late 1950s.

Starting at the E end at Bull Street, on the s the rear of House of Fraser (*see* Corporation Street, p. 101). On the N, the **Great Western Arcade** [49] of 1874–6 by *W.H. Ward*. The best survivor of the city's many C19 arcades, built on iron supporting arches which span the railway line into Snow Hill. The builder was Henry Lovett of Wolverhampton. Rich Renaissance façade to Temple Row: paired columns with much banding and decoration, and heavy cornices. Giant arch to the arcade with figures of Art and Industry in the spandrels. Top floor lost in the Second World War. Inside, shops divided by plain pilasters lead to a central space with side apses. Upper storey with rows of round-arched windows recessed behind a balcony with original ironwork. Simple steel post-war roof. Refurbished in 1984–5 by *Douglas Hickman* of the *John Madin Design Group* with decorative transverse plaster arches which deliberately don't touch the roof ribs. Brass electroliers to the original 1874 design by *Best & Lloyd*, and a chiming clock at the N end. (For the Colmore Row front, *see* Colmore Row, p. 99.)

Continuing w, on the s the **TSB**, by *James A. Roberts Associates*, 1980, a heavy design in Travertine and dark pink-grey granite. Then the former **Bank of England** (now Bank of Scotland) of 1969–72 by *Fitzroy Robinson & Partners* of London, extending back to Cannon Street. Heavy podium block set back up steps. Dark granite facings below, copper clad cantilevered beams and bronzed window surrounds, and long pierced rectangles of Portland Roach, like huge architraves, above. Blocky recessed attic. Twenty-storey office tower behind, the successor to *Walter Gropius*'s proposal of 1962. A dominating, authoritarian design, very damaging in context. Just into Needless Alley, a blunt fat glass turret of City Plaza (*see* Cannon Street, p. 89). **Union Chambers** by *Ewen Harper, Bro. & Co.*, 1936, is a plain nine-storey block of Portland stone with concave corner. Then a tactful piece in cream and brown reconstituted stone by *Robert Turley & Associates*, 2001, defined by square turrets of differing heights. Across Temple Street, a big range, of 1963 by *Tripe & Wakeham*.

Temple Row West

The w side of the Cathedral churchyard, developed from *c.* 1820 by the Inge estate (*see* Waterloo Street, p. 125). At the s end the **Birmingham Midshires** [9], 1900–2 by *Mansell & Mansell*. A fine office block in brick and cream terracotta, the steel structure firmly expressed in the brick and terracotta grid of the façade. Built for the Ocean Assurance Corporation, with their initials, and bands of roses and thistles, and waves and fishes, on the corner oriel. Finely moulded entrance. Shallow canted end bay. Delightful fantasy at the top: ogee windows, parapet with heart-shaped piercings, two-stage corner turret, end gables with brick and terracotta diapering. Ground-floor windows lowered 1983. Along Waterloo Street an extension of 1983–4 by *Peter Hing & Jones*. Brutalist but contextual, with narrow triplet fins of tinted glass. Corbelled-out brick piers above. Beyond, Nos. 5–7, 1876–7 for James Knowles Roderick, probably by *George Ingall*. Stucco, debased classical, with end pilasters topped by consoles. Terrible 1970s ground floor.

The **Old Joint Stock** [50] pub was built as the Birmingham Joint Stock Bank in 1862–4 by *J.A. Chatwin*. His first bank building, which made his reputation. A subtle, scholarly and beautiful Renaissance palazzo, its façade a study in interpenetrating orders. Doric lower order on panelled bases. Its cornice has a feeling of weight produced by compressing the frieze. The band above can be read as the attic of the lower order – lunette windows with head keystones – or the base of the upper order – rustication and panelled column bases. Corinthian upper order, with round-headed windows in aedicules. These have Corinthian pilasters and their cornices, repeated between the columns, read almost as part of the upper entablature, increasing its depth and relating it to

50. Old Joint Stock (formerly Birmingham Joint Stock Bank), Temple Row West, by J.A. Chatwin, 1864

the overall height. The balustrade has unfortunately lost its urns. Inside, a banking hall with deep coved ceiling supported on decorated ribs. It is taller than the lower external order, and the lunettes outside light the cove: a Mannerist relation of interior and exterior (cf. Peruzzi's Palazzo Massimi in Rome). Converted to a pub 1997 by *Langford & Williams*. Spoilt by prominent floodlights and heavy texturing inside.

No. 3 has a stucco front of five low storeys and attic. Its complex history starts with U-shaped farm buildings here by the early C18, the wings facing E. The plot was leased to the artist Samuel Lines in 1820, a good date for the two-storey Regency pavilion shown here on mid-C19 drawings, and probably a rebuilding of the left hand wing of the U. The pavilion represents the ground and first floors of the present building. The ground floor has a mid-C19 shopfront with attached Corinthian columns. In 1877 two storeys were added, the first floor refronted, and the narrow entrance bay built over a former passage. Almost certainly by *George Ingall*, who occupied the ground-floor office. Round-headed windows in straight-headed aedicules. Reconstructed with extra storey and attic by *Edwin Hill & Partners*, 1972.

Temple Street

Cut in the early C18 to link New Street to St Philip's churchyard, as part of the development by William Inge and Elizabeth Phillips. The plots on the W side were leased again by the Inge family 1842–53. Now a mixture of C19 and C20 office buildings, its intimacy damaged by recent demolitions at the New Street end (q.v.).

On the W, Nos. 19–20 were plain classical of *c.* 1846, rebuilt by *Newton & Cheatle* in 1900 for Ludlow and Briscoe, surveyors, in red brick with delicate Jacobean windows. The outer bays have Free Style wavy parapets and little domes with tapering finials. No. 17 was the Norwich Union's **Fire Engine House** [51], of 1846 by *Edge & Avery*. Four bays, recessed centre, still stucco Cheltenham Regency. Small sashes and heavily rusticated quoins. In 1883 *W. Luke Dennis* altered the ground floor for the Bodega wine bar, but the present sumptuous tiled front with Corinthian pilasters and mosaic frieze with decorative garlands is probably by *Maw* of 1902, when it became the Trocadero. Inside, part of a contemporary Smoke Room at the rear: panelling and a fireplace with stressed verticals, rather Art Nouveau.

Nos. 14–16 is a grand four-storey Italianate palazzo of 1854 by *Samuel Hemming* for the Unity Insurance, their crest in the Baroque two-storey centrepiece. On the cornice, pedestal of a lost sculpture of Prudence and Justice. The ground floor partly survives, with chopped-off keystone heads. Beautiful, deeply modelled, world-weary lion's head over the former fire-engine-house entrance.

Nos. 11–13 are moderne of 1931 by *S.N. Cooke* for Smart Bros, house furnishers. Three bays of offices expressed as a bronze fascia decorated with rosettes, set in a Portland stone surround. Giant pilasters

51. No. 17 Temple Street (Trocadero), front probably by Maw, *c.* 1902

play hide and seek at the corners. Coved cornice with a touch of Art Deco zigzag. Nos. 9–11 are an intrusive eight-storey tower of 1962 by *Essex Goodman & Suggitt*, refurbished in 1976.

No. 8, the **Birmingham Law Society** [52], hides a complex history behind *C.E. Bateman*'s deceptively plain, Neo-Georgian, Portland stone façade. Cornice with plaques bearing the society's initials and the date, 1933. In the left-hand bay, door with bronze relief of the society's seal as a wavy sunrise over the sea. The building started in 1858 as a Temperance Hall, designed by *Yeoville Thomason*. His brick side elevation to Temple Passage is still recognizable. Two storeys of windows set in shallow giant arches, the style of his master Charles Edge. The rear of the hall is a semi-ellipse, now disguised by additions, part of *E. & J.A. Harper*'s alterations of 1900–1, which also included a terracotta façade with twin towers. Bateman replaced this, and filled the hall with three floors of offices and a library for the society. His is the dignified oak staircase with square newels and hanging arches leading to a double-height library with square giant Doric columns made of single pieces of oak. Original bookcases and pedimented doorcases with eared architraves and pulvinated friezes. Gold sunburst clock. Above the ceiling with its large skylight is the 1858 roof of massive queen-post trusses.

52. Birmingham Law Society, Temple Street, by C.E. Bateman, 1933. Library

Beyond the upper entrance to Temple Passage, No. 4 started as a classical office building of 1862 for Copestake, Moore and Crampton, lace merchants. The side elevation in white brick with red detail is still there, but the front was crassly refaced in black granite in 1964 by *Thurlow Lucas & James* for the Gateway Building Society.

Returning down the E side, Nos. 41–42, a delightful survivor of *c.* 1824. Pedimented first-floor windows and Greek key frieze above. Tuscan pilasters on the ground floor. Then big streamlined **Somerset House** of 1936 by *Essex & Goodman*, with bands of wide windows between tower-like end bays. Over the entrance, relief of a sailing ship. **Imperial House** is a bulky seven-storey intruder of 1996–7 by *Temple Cox Nicholls*. Red brick and reconstituted stone. The four lower storeys, crushed by the additions, are the retained façade of the **New Imperial Hotel** of 1905–7 by *Wood & Kendrick*. Mildly Baroque, with blocked segmental arches, stubby stone columns, and a centrepiece with a big broken pediment. Finally **Essex House** of 1924–5 by *Essex & Goodman*, who were also the developers. Their usual watered-down classical faience.

Union Street

On the sw side, the surviving part of the **Midland & City Arcades** [53], of 1900–1 by *Newton & Cheatle*. Pink terracotta and brick, with cream terracotta dressings. The entrance has a giant arch and a big shaped gable. Flanking it, canted bays rising into domed turrets with bold curving buttresses. Jacobean details but a Baroque feeling of movement. Enjoyable sculpture by *W.J. Neatby*. Above the entrance two sculpted heads, then a frieze of angry sea monsters emerging from strapwork and separated by tridents. On the towers, atlantes playing wind instruments. Green terracotta interior. Shopfronts divided by pilasters with niches and domed tops, balcony with more sea monsters. Semicircular iron roof with swirling metal supports to the top rib.

Victoria Square

Now the premier civic space of the city. It began as a road junction, at the far w end of New Street from the historic centre, where the Dudley road went N along the line of the present Congreve Passage, Parade and Sand Pits, and a lane w along what are now Paradise Street and Broad Street. Development reached here in the late C18, and ran along Paradise Street to the canal wharf.

Civic identity began with Christ Church, built in the angle of New Street and Colmore Road in 1805, and the Town Hall [13, 24] on the w side in 1832–4. The Council House [25, 27] followed on the N in 1874–9, the General Post Office on the s in 1891. They defined a much smaller space, essentially the w half of today's square. In 1899 Christ Church was replaced with picturesque, French Renaissance style offices by *Essex, Nicol & Goodman*, 1901 ('Galloway's Corner'). Demolished in 1970 for an unbuilt part of the Inner Ring Road. On the E side, the bend of Waterloo Street and the steps of **Christ Church Passage** still define its boundary. In 1973 permission was granted to replace the Post Office with an office tower, sparking a campaign led by the Birmingham Group of the Victorian Society. Their success in 1978 marked the end of the post-war comprehensive development philosophy in the city.

The square gained its name when *Thomas Brock*'s **statue** of Queen Victoria was unveiled in 1901. A copy – at the insistence of the patron, W.H. Barber, a Birmingham solicitor – of Brock's statue at the Shire Hall, Worcester. Originally white marble, re-cast in bronze in 1951 by

53. Midland & City Arcades, Union Street, by Newton & Cheatle, 1900–1

William Bloye. To its E, **landscaping** of 1991–3 by the city's Landscape Practice team, sculptor *Dhruva Mistry*, adviser *Rory Coonan*. Dramatic in conception, exotic in detail, and triumphantly successful as urban planning, creating a N–S axis of steps either side of upper and lower pools with water flowing down between them, it aligns the expanded square on the Council House portico. Sandstone walls. In the top pool, a large reclining female nude, The River. In the floor of this pool, six bas-reliefs of salmon. In the lower, two smaller figures representing youth face a fountain of three vertical bowls. To either side here, the two sphinx-like **Guardians** (Mistry suggests a C1 Indian source). To each side at the top, an **Object/Variation**, a tapering pillar suggesting lighthouses or pyramids. The sculptor wanted a scheme of many associations: hints are given by the quotation from T.S. Eliot's 'Burnt Norton' carved round the rim of the top pool by *Bettina Furnée*.

For the Town Hall, *see* p. 57, for the Council House, *see* p. 61; for the E side, *see* Colmore Row, p. 93, and New Street, p. 109.

On the S side the former **General Post Office**, now **Victoria Square House**, by *Sir Henry Tanner* of the Office of Works, 1889–91. *The Builder* called it 'coarse and commonplace . . . Pots and tea urns of abnormal dimensions are perched about on ledges and on cornices; the whole of it is fussy, pretentious and totally lacking in dignity.' Its simple French Renaissance style now seems reticent, and the 'pots and urns', actually pediment and cupolas and a dome on the left, make their mark against C20 neighbours. **Sculpture** in front, Iron : Man [17], by *Antony Gormley*, 1993, instantly recognizable: a 12-ft- (3.7-metre-) high human torso, enclosed by beams, in rusted iron, leaning slightly backwards and to its left, intended to refer to the industrial tradition of the area, and 'standing absolutely motionless at a slight angle to the universe'.*

Waterloo Street

The principal street of the Inge estate, the area between St Philip's on the E, Colmore Row on the N, Victoria Square on the W, and New Street on the S. It remained fields and orchards, the grounds of Bennetts Hill House, until the early C19. Development started in 1818 on New Street, and plots on Waterloo Street and Bennetts Hill were leased between 1823 and 1838, mainly working W. The first buildings included houses, banks and shops. *Charles Edge* was active here, but nothing surviving is definitely his, though his Norwich Union fire engine house survives in Temple Street (q.v.).

By the late C19 commercial uses had taken over, and many houses were rebuilt in the 1930s when the original leases ran out. Several early C19 buildings remain, uniquely in the city centre. Most were façaded in the 1970s for the Waterloo Court development (*see* below), an early development of this kind in the city. Several banks and offices have recently been converted into wine bars.

Waterloo Street leaves Colmore Row at the NE corner of Victoria Square and turns E, the bend still marking the vanished Christ Church (*see* Victoria Square, p. 123). The N side has an unbroken early C19 three-storey stucco row, mostly with rusticated ground floors. The first are all of *c.* 1835. Nos. 27–30 is a thirteen-bay range curving round the bend. Almost certainly by *John Fallows* as it has his trademark Graeco-Egyptian tapering architraves. Dentil cornice. Nos. 31–32 look like *Edge*: four bays with the centre slightly projecting, and channelled rustication. Nos. 33–34, **Wellington House**, is like Nos. 27–30 but without the cornice. Attic added in 1976 (*see* below).

No. 35, **Apsley House**, is *c.* 1831. Six bays. A Palladian 1–3–1 villa composition, with the extra bay recessed at the right. Central first-floor window with pediment on consoles; porch with free-standing Ionic columns. Pilasters with incised decoration, and a blocking course hinting at a pediment. No. 36 is *c.* 1828, in a version of Soane's Bank of England manner, perhaps also by *Fallows*. Four bays, the ground floor

*E.M. Forster's description of C.P. Cavafy. The maker was *Firth Rixon Castings* of Wednesbury.

54. No. 36 Waterloo Street, *c.* 1828

recessed behind an open fluted Corinthian arcade. Heavy attic with paired pilasters. In 1976 all these and the upper w side of Bennetts Hill were façaded as **Waterloo Court** by *James Roberts Associates*. The attics on e.g. Nos. 33–34 are theirs. A hole punched through the ground floor of No. 36 [54] leads to an internal courtyard. Brick and render elevations and imitation sashes.

The s side was rebuilt between the wars. For **Waterloo House** *see* New Street (p. 111). **New Oxford House** is poor stripped-classical of 1934–5 by *S.N. Cooke*. Swan-neck pediment with a putto by *William Bloye*, who also did the stylized Neo-Egyptian heads facing each other with expressive closed eyes and fan-like hair, emerging from the stonework of the porch. **Neville House** of 1934 by *W. Norman Twist* is a good seven-storey moderne block, with long bands of windows cutting fluted pilasters, a big frame with channelled rustication, and an Art Deco cornice. Then two plain surviving bays, half of a passage-entry pair of *c.* 1834.

The crossroads with Bennetts Hill has fine Victorian and Edwardian buildings on each corner, a unique survival. On the sw, the former **National Provincial Bank** of 1869–70 by *John Gibson*, replacing a building of 1833 by *C.R. Cockerell*. In the opulent Renaissance style Gibson used for many of their buildings (e.g. Bishopsgate Street, London). Warm pink-grey Wrexham sandstone. Two tall storeys, giant Corinthian pilasters. Big round-headed windows to the banking hall, simple paired lights above. Rich cornice, frieze with a long date inscription, and foliage band between the windows with the bank's initials. Main entrance in the rounded corner, where the giant pilasters become fluted half-columns. On the cornice a monumental Birmingham coat of arms crowned by a helmet and veil, and seated figures of Art and Industry, by *S.F. Lynn*. The porch has a rich coffered half-dome and fine relief panels of Birmingham industries by *Lynn*: metalworking, glass-blowing, electroplating, gunmaking. Composed like classical friezes but modelled realistically, and almost in the round.

Gibson's building had only six bays to Waterloo Street and three to Bennetts Hill. In 1890 *Charles Risdon Gribble*, the bank's architect, added two bays on Waterloo Street, right. In 1927 *C.E. Bateman* added two in Bennetts Hill, left, with a staircase lit by slit windows between paired pilasters. Walking in is a shock, as *Bateman* re-cast the whole banking hall (now a wine bar) in a grand but cool and sophisticated Neo-Grec. Huge Doric columns with correctly profiled Greek capitals but leaf decoration hinting at Art Deco. Theatrical cornice with mutules set with exaggerated correctness downwards and outwards.

On the se corner the former **Birmingham Banking Co**. [55] of 1830–1 by *Rickman & Hutchinson*. The best survivor of their work in Birmingham. The original building is a classical box, five bays by seven, articulated by plain pilasters. Grand attached Corinthian porticoes of three bays with a pediment to Waterloo Street, and five bays without a pediment to Bennetts Hill. Its isolated formal quality is unusual in a commercial building. The corners of the box were originally exposed, as can still be seen at the left-hand end of the Waterloo Street front. A single tall window in each bay lights the banking hall. In 1877, following the rebuilding of the National Provincial, *Yeoville Thomason* added the rounded corner between Rickman's porticoes. Its blank façade continues Rickman's cornice but adds a blank attic, linking the porticoes. Typical doorway with Aberdeen granite pilasters and luscious foliage frieze. Also *Thomason*'s the Vanbrughian paired arched chimneys over the pediment. He remodelled the interior with paired Corinthian columns running down the banking hall. Plain block behind in Bennetts Hill by *Harris & Martin*, 1881–4.

The nw corner is a heavy three-storey French Renaissance block, built *c.* 1872 for the Inland Revenue. Thumping dentil cornice. The ne corner is the former **Parr's Bank** of 1904 by *Cossins, Peacock & Bewlay*. Originally three storeys, the upper ones unfortunate later additions.

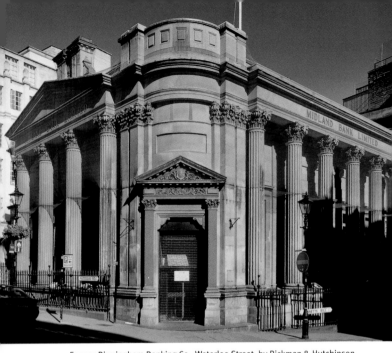

55. Former Birmingham Banking Co., Waterloo Street, by Rickman & Hutchinson, 1830–1, altered by Yeoville Thomason, 1877

Grey sandstone, perhaps Quarella. An elegant design with a French C18 air to its rusticated pilasters and end bays. Restrained high quality decoration of garlands, and a fine cornice. Ground floor with segment-headed windows and cartouches, a 1990s reinstatement. Walking E, **Cavendish House** of 1937–9 by *W.T. Orton* with *T. Cecil Howitt* as consultant. A thirteen-bay moderne block, the seven-bay centre projecting slightly in a frame, with reeded pilasters. *Howitt*'s involvement explains its impressive urban scale. On the s side the former **Legal and General Assurance** of 1931–2 by *S.N. Cooke*. A distinguished piece of cubic, stripped classicism moving towards Modernism, quite unlike his other contemporary work, and probably by his assistant *E. Holman*. A square block, five bays by five, five storeys. Portland stone with bands of green instead of a cornice. Recessed lantern-like attic. Windows set behind piers with very slightly concave faces, which rise to more deeply concave-sided pinnacles. Their strong vertical emphasis is only just controlled by the almost sheer square corner piers. Near their tops, relief panels by *William Bloye*: simplified, hieratic figures of Wisdom, Fortitude, Charity, and Faith, sharply cut in low relief, their tight rectangular frames emphasizing the geometric quality of the building. Plain ground floor; central entrance with deeply moulded lintel to Waterloo Street with a central panel of Temple Bar, the Legal and General emblem, also by *Bloye*. Entrance to the upper storeys in a six-storey sw tower. Original cylindrical lanterns.

The Newhall Estate

The Newhall Estate lies NW of the medieval and C17 town, bounded by the present Livery Street, Colmore Row, Paradise Street, Summer Row and The Parade. It includes part of the present Jewellery Quarter (q.v.) as far as St Paul's Square and Caroline Street. In the later Middle Ages it was owned by St Thomas' Priory and in the C16 acquired by the Colmore family. Their house, New Hall, stood roughly where Newhall Street now crosses Great Charles Street. Westley's map of 1731 shows a curious building, probably C17, with a large central pediment and small projecting wings. In the early C18, the development of St Philip's and the streets surrounding it brought the urban area to the edge of the estate.

In 1746 Ann Colmore obtained an Act of Parliament making leases of up to 120 years binding on her heirs, which allowed development. The NW side of Colmore Row was built up during the 1750s. Hanson's map (1778) shows the estate built up beyond Great Charles Street to Lionel Street, with streets laid out around St Paul's Square, where the church was under construction. The grid of streets named after Colmore family members is still recognizable. The Digbeth Branch Canal was cut through NW of Lionel Street in 1786–8, giving direct access to industrial premises. New Hall was demolished in 1787, and Kempson's map (1810) shows the whole estate built up.

Leases fell in from the mid C19, with large groups in 1867 and 1892. William Barwick Cregoe Colmore and his surveyor *Thomson Plevins* replanned the area between Colmore Row and Great Charles Street, cutting new streets and realigning others. Rebuilding started with the Birmingham Town and District Bank in Colmore Row in 1869–70 and was almost complete by 1900. Early rebuildings were for commercial premises, with many merchants' warehouses like the surviving row at the NE end of Edmund Street. The establishment of the Eye Hospital in Church Street, 1883, and the Ear and Throat Hospital in Edmund Street, 1890, led to the building of many doctors' houses and consulting rooms. The best architects in the city designed these and other professional offices in the late C19 and early C20, producing a very fine and consistent townscape. After the First World War, redevelopment continued NW to the canal. C18 and early C19 buildings now survive only around St Paul's Square.

Great Charles Street became part of the Inner Ring Road in the 1960s, cutting the estate in two. This walk covers the part inside the Ring Road. Its Victorian and Edwardian character remained almost unbroken until the 1960s. In 1966 Alexandra Wedgwood hoped that it would not be redeveloped piecemeal, but exactly this has happened, particularly since designation in 1984 as the city's Primary Office Area. At the start of the C21 it is still threatened by unsympathetic development, with façadism rampant in e.g. Edmund Street. For the estate outside the Ring Road, *see* the Jewellery Quarter, p. 158.

We start in Chamberlain Square and walk under the arch of the Council House Extension into **Edmund Street**. On the NW side beyond Margaret Street the School of Art (for this and the Council House, *see* Major Buildings). Beyond it C19 façades, the former **Medical Institute** of 1879 by *Osborn & Reading* is Victorian classical turning Queen Anne. Old-fashioned stone porch with paired Corinthian columns and tall windows with Venetian tracery, but elongated consoles, relief panels of flowers and a pretty little pediment. Good original railings. The former **School Board Office** of 1881–2 by *Martin & Chamberlain* is brick Ruskinian Gothic like the firm's schools, here with stone dressings. Sashes under Gothic lintels or cusped relieving arches. Vigorous central entrance with the porch parapet returned as buttresses on either side of the canted bay window above. Beautiful low-relief flower decoration, e.g. the band above the second-floor windows.

Then the former **Parish Offices** and **Board of Guardians** of 1882–5 by *W.H. Ward*. Very large, cleanly articulated French Renaissance, eleven bays (seventeen to Newhall Street), in cream stone with banded Cornish granite columns to the centrepiece and ends, rusticated ground floor, and panelled pilasters flanking windows and doorways. Central dome lost in the Second World War. In 1984–6 the School Board office, Medical Institute, and Parish Offices were all façaded by *PCPT*, with mansard roofs and dormers.

On the SE side, first the rear of No. 125 Colmore Row (*see* p. 93) then Nos. 12–22 Newhall Street, 1962–3 by *Fitzroy Robinson & Partners*, eleven storeys, Portland stone with pale grey infill panels.

Across Newhall Street, on the E corner, Nos. 17–19 [56] of 1896 by *Frederick Martin* of *Martin & Chamberlain*, built as the National Telephone Co.'s offices and exchange. The finest commercial building of Birmingham's brick and terracotta period. Ten years after the School of Art, Chamberlain's successors are more eclectic, less Ruskinian, but still enormously original. Massively articulated by three-storey brick piers with bands of pierced terracotta high up, linked by decorative arches. These have fierce beast-head keystones, and lots of foliage with heads peering out. The piers rise to turrets, but on two bays of the Edmund Street front they run dramatically up through big Dutch gables to form tall chimneys. There is a Baroque sense of movement and of volume in the three-quarter-round corner oriel and two-storey

56. Nos. 17–19 Newhall Street, by Frederick Martin of Martin & Chamberlain, 1896

canted bays. They dance in and out between the piers and leave dark spaces above, with deeply recessed lunette windows. More fantastic animals, like gryphons but with fish tails, reclining against the balustrade ends. The gables above the entrance and corner bays have roundels with tracery, like the School of Art's. The Newhall Street entrance has fine wrought-iron gates with writhing bunches of poppies. The porch has cream tiles with restrained pie-like patterns and the company's emblem. Simple interior. The corridors are spanned by three-centred arches all tiled like the porch. The staircase has paired cast-iron balusters with tiny square tapering Ionic pillars. The top floor was the equipment room, articulated by full-height pointed trusses like at the firm's school halls. Alterations of 1994 by *Mark Humphries Architects* included the stairwell lift and an extra floor in the equipment room.

Opposite, on the N corner, No. 29 Newhall Street and Nos. 106–110 Edmund Street [57], by *Frank Barlow Osborn*, 1895, for W.M. Smythe. Solicitors' offices with sets of doctors' consulting rooms on either side. A fine subtle Shaw-influenced design in red brick and dark grey stone, perhaps Cefn. It can be read in two ways. There is a main block to Newhall Street with its central bay marked by broad pilasters ending in volutes, and a high roof with finely moulded chimneys, with a side wing to Edmund Street. But the canted bays rising to Queen-Anne-style

57. No. 29 Newhall Street and Nos. 106–110 Edmund Street, by F.B. Osborn, 1895

gables, and the continuous balconies with iron railings, impose a grid which clearly expresses the offices behind. Osborn's typical elongated consoles to the doorway. Blunt, unmoulded windows, especially in the corner oriel with its charming ogee cap.

A glance SE up Newhall Street towards Colmore Row. On the NE, Nos. 1–3 of 1967–9 by *Fitzroy Robinson & Partners*, brick faced with narrowly divided bays, and Nos. 7–15 of 1962 by *Essex, Goodman & Suggitt*. Portland stone with fins, recently re-clad in grey.

Continuing down Edmund Street, on the SE the former **Ear and Throat Hospital** of 1890–1 by *Jethro A. Cossins & Peacock*. Severe but elegant Queen Anne. The façade directly expressed the plan, with Dutch-gabled three-storey brick blocks for wards and theatres flanking the central entrance with a double-height canted bay, enclosed at the top by an elliptical brick arch. The window lit the staircase. Extended along Barwick Street by the same, 1902–3. Reduced to façades and one side gable for a bulky office scheme by *Glazzard Associates*, 2002–3.

On the NW opposite, No. 120, plain eight-storey Portland stone by *Watson, Johnson & Stokes*, 1956–7. New windows, porch and forecourt wall of 1994–5 by *GMW* (*Gollins Melvin Ward*). Intrusive glass canopy of 2001. Then No. 134 of 1897 by *Newton & Cheatle* for G.J. Eveson, whose initials appear above the ground floor. Brick and terracotta, with double-height sunk canted bays. Very different from their Free Style work opposite, but a typical slightly projecting square centre and semi-octagonal dormer. Lots of jolly moulded ornament on swinging balcony-like bands between floors. Nos. 136–138 are Venetian Gothic of *c.* 1875 and must be by *J.H. Chamberlain*. Arcaded ground floor with a gabled doorway breaking the cornice, double-height brick arches enclosing the office floors, and an unusual attic, probably built as a workshop, with twelve tightly packed lancets with round lights above, and a rich cornice. A new block behind Nos. 134–138 by *Associated Architects*, 2004, aggressively cantilevered, has made them into little more than a grand porch. Nos. 140–146 is by *Jonathan Wingfield* of *WSM Architects*, 2000. Minimalist blue-tinted glass façade, but dominating top canopy. No. 148 on the corner of Church Street by *Trehearne & Norman, Preston & Partners* of London, 1959–60.

Beyond Barwick Street on the SE, the former **White Swan** pub, plain classical with brick pilasters, mostly of 1890 by *J.S. Davis*, façaded in the early 1990s. Then a very fine late C19 row, showing Norman Shaw influence, and the approaching Free Style. Nos. 121–123, of 1898–9 by *Newton & Cheatle* for G.H. Willetts, have a simple brick sash-window front given character by the giant relieving arch. Swept-up parapet and dormer window with shouldered gable. Original ground floor with stone pilasters and typical Newton & Cheatle doorways with round arches breaking across little pilasters. Nos. 125–131, also *Newton & Cheatle*'s, 1898–1900, were their own offices. One of their finest and freest designs. The ground floor is a four-bay open stone arcade. Powerful short columns, rather Jacobean round arches with big keystones. Four Shaw-like two-storey wooden canted bays, linked in pairs by perky top arches and a deep cornice. Their upward movement is stopped by a pair of seven-bay mullion-and-transom windows and the plain severe gables which break at the top and rise to little swan-neck pediments. All through, horizontals and verticals are held in perfect balance. Bays almost entirely renewed 2000–2 (*see* below).

No. 133, **Chamberlain House** is of 1895–6 by *Mansell & Mansell* for Thomas Savage, surgeon. Delightfully Shavian. The brick front has stone bands linking the cross-windows. Cornice with Savage's initials and the date, swept-up parapet, and tall hipped roof with finials. The doorcase is a combination of two demolished Shaw designs in the City of London, New Zealand Chambers and Barings Bank. A large segmental pediment supported on long consoles and short pilasters, the pediment broken by a tiny window, itself pedimented and with a big keystone. No. 135 on the corner of Church Street is a well-proportioned but basic Gothic block of 1877–8 by *J.A. Chatwin* for the merchants Scholefield Goodman. Their chairman, John Goodman, kept a notebook recording construction costs down to the last halfpenny, and it shows. Beyond, going up **Church Street** towards Colmore Row, No. 10, 1885 by *A.B. Phipson & Son*, Queen Anne style. Terracotta relief panels, and a big built-up gable, typical of Phipson, with a shell niche and pediment. On the corner of Barwick Street, a former hotel of 1876–7 by *Yeoville Thomason*. A distinctive elevation: broad brick pilasters separating paired windows with delicately shouldered lintels. The whole block from No. 121 Edmund Street to here was savagely restored, with much demolition behind, by *Glazzard Associates*, 2000–2.

Opposite on the NE side the former **Eye Hospital** of 1883–4 by *Payne & Talbot*. Queen Anne style in red brick, progressive for Birmingham at this date. Tall windows, originally sashes, with moulded brick surrounds and glazing bars in the upper lights only. Dormers with fluted pilasters and a variety of pediments. Corner oriels with impressive leaf corbels. Let down by the old-fashioned mansard roofs, and the heavy entrance with banded columns. Refurbished as a hotel and bar in 2000–1 by *Michael Phillips Associates*, with a wavy glass canopy.

Back and NE down Edmund Street again. On the NW, No. 158 of 1891 by *J.W. Allen* of West Bromwich for Keay & Co. A handsome classical job, disciplined by giant Ionic pilasters but with ornate stepped-up swan-neck pediments and corner doorway. Chimneys with pedimented tops, rebuilt to the original design 1986. Then infill blocks of seven and four bays of 1986, the sign of a big refurbishment and reconstruction scheme by *Bonham Seager Associates*, consultant *Douglas Hickman* of the *John Madin Design Group*. It retained the façade of Nos. 168–170, simple brick classical of 1873 with moulded brick window reveals and sunk panels. Perhaps by *Thomson Plevins* who surveyed the plot for the lease. Beyond, No. 172, 1874–5 for H.A. Fry, a merchant, also perhaps by *Plevins*, slightly richer, with paired brackets to the cornice. No. 174, with windows linked vertically, was built with the corner building to Livery Street. This is the **Old Contemptibles** pub [58], originally the **Albion**, of 1880–1 by *William Hale* for Henry Herridge. A rare survival for Birmingham of a Victorian commercial hotel. 'Mixed Italian', with e.g. first-floor pediments poking up into Gothic windows. Chimneys on the eaves give a fine silhouette. Surviving ground floor with segmental windows and pedimented doorway. The corner has Corinthian pilasters and big, mostly original, windows with delicate colonnettes. Plain high public bar, strongly articulated by a continuous cornice, with shouldered relieving arches as the bar back. Original bar front. Lounge bar: the rear part a former billiard room, with skylight. Large fireplaces in pink veined marble. Service passages with chunky, almost Romanesque, supporting arches. Opposite, large new offices by *Associated Architects*, 2003–4.

Back and NW down Church Street. On the NE, Nos. 37–39, of 1901–2 by *Newton & Cheatle* for H.B. Perry, export hardware merchants. Simple free Neo-Georgian in brick with stone bands and ground floor. Four bays, slightly projecting ends. Typical Newton & Cheatle doorways with semicircular hoodmoulds breaking across a three-light window. Dormers arranged 2–1–2–1–2, in counterpoint. Nos. 41–43 [60] also *Newton & Cheatle*, of 1900–1. A beautiful and original Free Style composition, like a fantastic castle in low relief. Wide shallow bays, with large windows separated by lead panels, rise to concave, set against seg-

58. Old Contemptibles pub, Edmund Street, by William Hale, 1880–1

mental brick gables. A perfect balance of delicacy and mass. Brick entrance bay with a stone canted turret-like top. Semicircular doorhead on piers and stubby columns, linked by a subtly moulded stone panel to the shallow bay above. No. 45, **Peat House**, by *James A. Roberts*, 1973–4 is being replaced by a new office tower by *SMC Corstorphine & Wright* (2007).*

Across Cornwall Street the jolly **Old Royal** public house, originally the **Red Lion**, 1899–1900 by *Arthur Hamblin*, in pinky-red brick and cream terracotta. Concave gables rise to little pediments. Lots of Jacobean decoration. Corner turret with a conical top and lion weathervane. Big canted bays on the first floor mark the assembly room. Glancing NE down **Cornwall Street**, No. 2, **Cornwall Court**, 1989–92 by the *Seymour Harris Partnership*. Orange brick with insistent blue bands. Bulky, with a big top hamper, but redeemed by lively Neo-vernacular gables and semicircular projections responding to its neighbours.

Continuing down Church Street, on the SW, stretching through to Great Charles Street, **Embassy House**, 1982–3 by the *Hitchman Stone Partnership*. Glass walling with big chamfers, retaining the brick façades, with stone oriel and a nice doorway on Cornwall Street, of a building of 1899 by *Owen & Ward*.

*It replaced *Newton & Cheatle*'s superb Buckler & Webb printing works of 1898.

59. Guild House, Great Charles Street, by Arthur S. Dixon, 1897–8

Opposite Embassy House on the NE side, Nos. 57 and 59 are of 1909 by *G.A. Cox* for F. Keay & Co., paper merchants. Massive Free Style with heavy cornices and a grid of big mullion-and-transom windows separated by massive brick piers. Tower-like end bays. Off-centre doorway with its own cornice and big keystone. No. 63 is Postmodern imitation by the *Seymour Harris Partnership*, 1990. Finally, No. 65, the former Diocesan Lodge of the **Girls' Friendly Society**, i.e. a women's hostel, 1908 by *Osborn, Pemberton & White*. Warm orange-red brick with giant Ionic pilasters, appropriately feminine and domestic. Many small sashes, and oval windows under the swept-up parapet. Large stone panel with the date split in the corners.

Now SW up **Great Charles Street**, with the Queensway tunnels of 1967–71. **Britannia House**, nine storeys, by *Hurley Robinson & Son*, 1955–7.

Guild House [59], on the corner of New Market Street, is the former **Guild of Handicrafts** building of 1897–8 by *Arthur S. Dixon*. The pioneer building of Arts and Crafts radicalism in Birmingham and a perfect example of the quiet understatement which Dixon and others cultivated around 1900. Artfully simple, its complex composition has subtle references. Facing New Market Street, two three-storey gabled blocks separated by a two-storey range with a deep swept roof and big dormers. The gabled blocks differ slightly, the left one with windows linked vertically by shallow recessions. The contrast between gables and big roof, also used by Bidlake at e.g. St Winnow, Four Oaks, Sutton

Coldfield, comes from c16–c17 Midlands vernacular. The Great Charles Street front is a compressed version of the same composition, stepped uphill. So the corner block is a small cross-gabled tower, surely inspired by the High Building at Daneway House, Glos., which Ernest Barnsley, whom Dixon knew, repaired in 1896. Rough textured brick, probably local seconds, with wide mortar joints. Casement windows. Typical Dixon round-headed relieving arches. The roots of his style lie in Gothic Revival picturesque functionalism, but he never pointed an arch unless absolutely necessary. Inside, the attic is supported by a complex timber structure, a tie- and collar-beam roof supported on posts rising from the first floor. Originally there was a rear workshop wing with a fully glazed upper floor. Alterations in 1988–90 by the *ISH Partnership* replaced the windows and destroyed the original interior. Poor repairs to the brickwork. *ISH* also designed the five-storey block beyond, higher up Great Charles Street. Beyond this, No. 40 of 1954 by *Essex, Goodman & Suggitt*. Nine storeys, Portland stone, fins. Still with very basic classical columns on the ground floor. Original bronze doors.

At the Newhall Street crossroads, Great Charles Street regains urban character, as a wide boulevard. From here to Paradise Circus the street still looks like a mid-c20 town planner's drawing, with mostly anodyne Portland stone blocks moving from Beaux Arts to plain modern.

On the N corner of the crossroads, **Lancaster House** of 1932–3 by *Essex & Goodman*, minimal classical with careful rustication. Across Newhall Street No. 141, **Galbraith House**, of 1960 by *Surman, Kelly & Surman*. **Lombard House** is by *S.N. Cooke*, 1933. Nos. 148–149, **CML House**, is a nine-storey stepped-up tower of 1939 for Colonial Mutual Life Assurance by *Hennessy, Hennessy & Co.*, of Sydney, in association with *Stanley Hall & Easton & Robertson* of London. The best building is Nos. 150–152, the **Birmingham Chest Clinic**, by *John P. Osborne & Son*, 1930–2, part of the national effort to eradicate tuberculosis. Elegant and subtle Neo-Georgian. Nine bays. The central seven project slightly and have a cornice. Careful use of smooth rustication and raised panels. Entrance with two Doric columns in antis and **relief** of Aesculapius by *Bloye*. Nos. 154–155 is by *Surman, Kelly & Surman*, 1958–60. **Civic House** is a replacement of 1981 by *Scott, Brownrigg & Turner* of London.

On the SE side, on the corner of Newhall Street, York House of 1930 by *Crouch, Butler & Savage*. Red brick, the windows with Portland stone dressings recessed in vertical strips. No. 36 of 1973 by *S. Elden Minns & Partners* of Sheffield has Inca-like abstract reliefs.[*] Beyond it on the Margaret Street corner the **Stock Exchange** of 1928 by *S.N. Cooke*. A seven-bay Portland stone block, the tall ground floor with smooth rustication. Pulled together by a well-proportioned cornice.

Back down Great Charles Street and SE down **Newhall Street**. On the NE side, No. 61 by *Newton & Cheatle*, 1904. Dixon-style round-headed

[*]It replaced *W.H. Bidlake*'s offices for Keep Brothers of 1902, his only commercial building.

brick relieving arches with herringbone work. Carefully casual side elevation to Great Charles Street, with a hint of Mackintosh in the small, perfectly placed bay window. No. 55, **Avebury House**, is of 1905–6 by *Marcus O. Type*. Classical, with quirky detailing, e.g. the keystone of the relieving arch pushing up into the pediment, a touch of the London Neo-Mannerism of e.g. J.J. Joass. The ground floor uses the paired Doric columns of Peruzzi's Palazzo Massimi in Rome.

On the SW side, Nos. 56–60 by *Newton & Cheatle*, 1900–1. Two buildings designed as one, the left part for Rheece W. Palk, their client in Church Street, the rest for the Birmingham Office Co. Flemish and Jacobean Renaissance, fused with elements of Arts and Crafts Free Style. Pink brick – which must have looked shocking when new – and terracotta details. Seven bays, divided at the top 3–1–3, with big shaped gables separated by a central bay, like an expanded version of Cossins's Ear and Throat Hospital (*see* p. 132). Two-storey terracotta porches with tent roofs, their height important in the overall composition. Sinuous cartouches, with little columns and plaques above the doorways, hint at Harrison Townsend; the chequering in the gables suggests Lethaby. In the central bay on the top floor, and the ends, plaques of St George and the Dragon modelled by *W.J. Neatby*.

No. 54 is of 1897 by *Henman & Cooper* for F.W. Richards, dentist. A quietly three-dimensional design in restrained Jacobean. Brick with dark stone dressings. Porch with banded columns and Cape-style pediment. Ground and first floors with canted bays recessed behind brick pilasters, almost the architects' signature. The top-floor windows sit behind full Doric columns. Then the corners of Cornwall Street, guarded by a pair of balancing but not identical brick and terracotta corner turrets with domed tops, a delightful piece of townscape. Both are by *Essex, Nicol & Goodman*, in a Flemish-cum-Jacobean Renaissance style. The smaller circular turret on the W corner belongs to Nos. 50–52, doctors' consulting rooms of 1896–7. Picturesque functionalism, the wide bays with large windows lighting the consulting rooms. Shaped gables link the design to the larger Nos. 43–51 of 1898–1900, opposite on the N corner. A very big development for the Birmingham Hospital Saturday Fund (a low-cost medical insurance society). Shaped gables and two-storey canted bays. Big entrance portal with a shaped parapet and canted corners, and stylized flower sculpture. The octagonal corner turret picks up the shaped parapet. The round arch of its ground-floor door repeats in turn down Cornwall Street, where the far end was largely rebuilt after the Second World War.

On the E corner Nos. 33–41 of 1986–7 by the *Percy Thomas Partnership*, was contextual Postmodern with many local references. Brick with stone bands. Refronted and heightened by *Aedas Architects*, 2006: vacuous. Free-standing steel entrance arch. On the W corner, the Parish Offices (*see* p. 130).

Now sw up Cornwall Street. On the SE side the studio block of the School of Art (*see* Major Buildings, p. 73). On the NW, a fine row of doctors' houses and consulting rooms. Unique in the city as high-quality houses in a tight urban street, the equivalent of e.g. parts of Chelsea. Because Edgbaston is so near, this kind of house was only built in Birmingham for this special purpose. No. 87 is by *Henman & Cooper* for Dr Parrott, 1899. Three storeys and a big gable. Subtly asymmetrical windows with the firm's characteristic canted bays set deeply into the wall surface, behind piers and Tuscan columns (cf. No. 54 Newhall Street, above). Nos. 89–91 by *C.E. Bateman*, 1905, for J. Mountford, 'surgeon-dentist'. Arts and Crafts Neo-Georgian, showing the revived interest in local early C18 buildings, driven partly by demolition of the real thing in e.g. Old Square. Four storeys, with three-storey canted bays ending in a cornice with a gadrooned frieze. Tall attic showing Lethaby influence in the segmental pediments and diapering. The doorcases, up steps, have pilasters and scrolly broken pediments. A tablet above the door to No. 89, a little window with a shell hood above that to No. 91.

No. 93 is by *Newton & Cheatle*, 1902, for Sir James Sawyer, with sash windows linked by blocked surrounds extended as stone bands.

60. Buckler & Webb works, 1898 (left, dem.), and Nos. 41–43 Church Street, 1900–1, both by Newton & Cheatle. Photograph 1901

Doorway with a flat canopy hanging from iron brackets. Dramatic parapet with big segmental curve and swept-up ends. Finally No. 95, also *Newton & Cheatle*, 1901 for Dr Priestley Smith. Stone ground floor with heavy porch; giant pilasters in brick above; heavy dentil cornice and sharply swept-up parapet. Both Nos. 93 and 95 have good iron railings.

At the end of Cornwall Street, the Council House Extension (*see* Major Buildings, p. 64) faces us on Margaret Street. On the N corner, the **Birmingham and Midland Institute**, built 1898–9 as the Birmingham Library (a private members' library) and designed by *F. Barry Peacock* of *Cossins, Peacock & Bewlay*. Loose but friendly Jacobean, brick with big stone windows, many divided by banded columns or pilasters. Its composition with two end gables is a rather deliberate simplification of its neighbour, the School of Art. Slightly fussy entrance with banded columns, rusticated arch, and side panels with semicircular pediments, the left one containing a contemporary clock. Interior altered, but retaining a handsome entrance hall and staircase. The Institute moved here when its building in Paradise Street was demolished. To accommodate it, in 1972–3 *Associated Architects* extended the Library building into No. 95 Cornwall Street, and expanded it internally, adding a basement auditorium. A narrow glazed link faces Margaret Street. Canopy of 1980. Finally SE along Cornwall Street past the School of Art, and back up Edmund Street to Chamberlain Square.

Inner Areas

Walk 1.

Broad Street and Brindleyplace

Broad Street was a medieval lane linking Newhall Lane (now Colmore Row) with the Hagley Road. Development started when the Birmingham Canal was cut in 1768–72, with its terminal basin s of the street at its E end. Iron and brass manufacturing grew up around it. On the N side the Brasshouse and the Crown Inn were both built in 1781, and housing followed. In the early C19 a separate development, Islington, began at the w end, and by the 1840s the area was almost completely built up. The street was a fashionable shopping area until the mid C20. By the 1960s decay had set in, except for the Civic Centre area at the E end. Regeneration started in 1988–91 with the creation of Centenary Square, and the Convention Centre and Hyatt Hotel complex at the E end, followed from 1993 by the Brindleyplace redevelopment on the N side.

We walk from Victoria Square through the tremendous Central Library concourse (*see* p. 79) and along **Centenary Way** of 1989, the first level bridge across the Inner Ring Road. From it, a spectacular view s to the ATV development of 1969–73 [16], on the site of the canal basin. A twenty-eight-storey Alpha Tower, hotel and offices by *H. George Marsh* of *Richard Seifert & Partners*. A good example of Marsh's dramatic and angular style (cf. Centre Point, London). The tower cranks in the middle and has Pirelli-style tapered ends. They house the staircases. The window surrounds have tapered sides, and the angles are reflected in the ground-floor arches. To its w, offices with a similar arcade and a skyline of jazzy projecting triangles, a Marsh signature. Lovely surreal collection of service vents and accesses in the surrounding piazza. To the right, the retained façade of the **Masonic Hall** of 1926–7 by *Rupert Savage* of *Crouch, Butler & Savage*. Good stripped classical, with Egyptian-style low relief frieze of building workers by *Gilbert Bayes*. Entrance mutilated 1961 by removal of the Ionic columns *in antis*.

At the end of the bridge, the suitably solemn **Hall of Memory** of 1922–5 by *S.N. Cooke & W.N. Twist*, who won a competition assessed by Sir Reginald Blomfield. A classical domed octagon, or chamfered square. Portland stone, new to Birmingham then, with a base of Cornish granite. The short diagonal faces are set slightly back, framing bronze seated figures on pedestals representing the services by *Albert Toft*. Pedimented projections on the main sides. Heavy Doric

entablature and attic, and a low dome. SE entrance, originally facing the corner of Broad Street and Easy Row. Interior also Doric, in Beer stone, with curiously spreading pilasters. The focus is the central **Shrine**, a Siena marble tomb with boldly moulded base and top, crowned by a bronze casket made by the *Birmingham Guild* containing the Roll of Honour. Marble paving and seats in the angles, bronze flambeaux. Ribbed and coffered dome set below the outer one. Stained glass by *Richard Stubington*, and three sculpted panels, high up, by *William Bloye* [26], showing soldiers joining up, in the firing line, and returning wounded. Fine Primitivist work in low relief, showing the influence of Eric Gill. The returning figures particularly haunting, walking on angular ground against a background of receding graves, marked by crosses.

The Hall of Memory stands at the E end of **Centenary Square**, a long rectangle oriented E–w with Broad Street forming its s side. The current layout of 1989–91 by the *City Architect* is the last of many schemes for a Civic Centre (*see* topic box, p. 144). Lamps, and railings on the s side screening Broad Street, by *Tess Jaray*. **Sculpture** of 1991 (N side), bronze and wire fountain by *Tom Lomax*, The Spirit of Enterprise. Elegant surrealism, with three heads representing Industry, Enterprise and Commerce emerging from shallow angled bowls. *Bloye*'s 1956 bronze conversation piece of Boulton, Watt and Murdoch, intended for the Civic Centre scheme, is to be reinstated further w. They are grouped discussing drawings, the butt of many jokes, but a skilful solution to relating three standing figures.*

Raymond Mason's Forward, a large painted group in fibreglass and resin, was destroyed by fire in 2003.

The Civic Centre Schemes

62. Model of the Civic Centre Scheme, by William Haywood, 1940–1

Centenary Square and the Convention Centre are the products of a long history of proposals for a Civic Centre and Exhibition Hall on the site. William Haywood's influential polemic of 1918, *The Development of Birmingham*, proposed a civic complex, including a cathedral and exhibition hall, w of Victoria Square. Its centrepiece was a thirty-six-storey 'Municipal Tower', showing strong American Beaux Arts influence. In 1926–7 a competition assessed by H.V. Lanchester was won by *Maximilian Romanoff* of Paris, but his scheme was judged too expensive, and a basic plan was made by *S.N. Cooke*, *A.J. Swann*, and the City Engineer *Hubert Humphries*. This established the idea of an E–W space aligned along Broad Street, with a three-sided court of council offices to its N. In 1940–1 *Haywood* produced another spectacular Beaux Arts design, centred on a 140-ft (42.7-metre) high column topped by a 10-ft (3-metre) male nude statue representing the Spirit of Birmingham. Baskerville House formed the E wing of its U-shaped court. The Council adopted the proposal in 1944, and *William Bloye* produced a maquette for the statue in 1948, but the next year it was abandoned as too expensive.

In 1958 *A.G. Sheppard Fidler* produced a less formal layout, with water features and a line of residential towers linked by a municipal office podium on the N side. The Crescent Wharf blocks N of Cambridge Street, by the City Architect *Alan Maudsley*, 1968, are a much-modified version of its proposed towers. The Repertory Theatre is the w wing of this scheme, and has no front entrance because it was to have faced a pool.

On the N side, **Baskerville House** of 1939–40 by *T. Cecil Howitt* of Nottingham, who won a 1935 competition, again assessed by Blomfield. Portland stone, to match the Hall of Memory, and Cornish granite. Academic classicism, but with real urban scale and dignity. The *piano nobile* with pedimented windows marks the most important offices. It represents the front half of the E wing of the proposed Civic Centre, hence the big pavilion with columns *in antis* stranded at the NW corner. Stepped-up centrepiece with a big niche behind a free-standing Ionic order. In this context, probably a reference to Lutyens's Thiepval memorial arch.* Cool, double-height galleried entrance hall with a fine hanging light fitting, to be retained in a scheme of 2004 etc. by *Rolfe Judd* which will add two glazed storeys.

On the s side of Broad Street the massive former **Municipal Bank** [63] by *T. Cecil Howitt*, 1931–3. It has his grand sense of urban scale. Four giant fluted Ionic columns *in antis*, complex deep entablature, attic supported by big consoles laid flat. Modest **Register Office**, 1951 by *Alex Steele*, altered 1961 by *Harry Gibberd*.

Opposite on the N, the **Repertory Theatre** of 1969–71 by *Graham Winteringham* of *S. T. Walker & Partners*, with an E extension of 1990 by the same firm (*Graham Winteringham* and *Paul Burley*). Controversial when built: called by Colin Amery 'a mess, a melée of misunderstood stylistic gimmicks'. A picturesque and complex grouping of masses unified by functional relationships, and showing the roots of the Birmingham tradition. A good Modernist analogy might be a ship (reflecting its architect's naval career). The flattened curve of the façade resembles the captain's bridge. Its knapped concrete fins are linked by arches, and it follows the shape of the auditorium. No front entrance because the 1958 Civic Centre scheme envisaged a water feature here. At the sides, now only visible on the w, sharply angled volumes cut in to the stage and fly tower at the rear. This is a chunky piece with rounded corners, echoed in brick staircases on the N but contrasted with angular boxes for the dressing rooms. The **Extension** is almost the only city building of its date to show awareness of High Tech: a minia-ture Norman Foster-style glass front, its flattened curve reflecting the main façade. Interior remodelling by *Pawson Williams*, 1999, left the foyer's cantilevered staircases and rough concrete ceiling, but removed impressive Brutalist exposed heating ducts. New counter canopy and planar surfaces, e.g. the bar surround. The unusual single-rake audito-rium with wide proscenium was refitted except for the angled ceiling reflectors.

On the w side is the **International Convention Centre** and **Hyatt Regency Hotel**, 1987–91 by the *Convention Centre Partnership*, made up of *Percy Thomas Partnership* and *Renton Howard Wood Levin*, with acoustic consultants *Artec*. A linked complex of hotel, concert hall and

*Howitt won the M.C. in the Great War.

63. Former Municipal Bank, Broad Street, by T. Cecil Howitt, 1931–3

64. Café, Brindleyplace, by Piers Gough of CZWG, 1995

conference facilities, the first such in the U.K. Architecturally a huge disappointment. The 2,200-seat concert hall, **Symphony Hall**, faces the square. A heavy mass of grey granite banded with red, and blue tinted glass. Its top drum with corner wings defines a symmetrical block, but the entrance is pushed N, under a blue metal canopy, with more halls and a theatre beyond. To the S across Broad Street, linked by a bridge, the hotel. A twenty-five-storey mirror glass slab, pure commercial American.

Inside the Centre, a mall-like through route runs E–W, another American concept. Awkward forty-five-degree angles run through the design inside and out. The interior of the concert hall is tall and narrow, with three tiers of balconies and big adjustable sound holes, acoustically superb but visually uncomfortable.

Sculptures. In the entrance canopy, Birdlife, neon tubes, by *Ron Hasleden*, 1991. – N side of mall, Construction, delightful chromed bronze by *Vincent Woropay*, 1990. – S side, high up, Convention, limewood relief by *Richard Perry*, 1992, overlapping tree forms.

Beyond the mall a canalside space, with a bronze **sculpture** of 1990 by *Roderick Tye*, Battle of the Gods and the Giants, a cloud shape split vertically. To the N above a retaining wall, the **Brewmaster's House** of 1816, repaired 1983–4 by *Remo Granelli* for the Birmingham Conservation Trust. Built as the owner's house and office of a small brewery. Almost symmetrical three-bay façade with hipped roof. Typical Birmingham lintels on consoles. Doric porch with open pediment. At the rear a former **cart shed** with cast-iron columns and slate roof in beautiful diminishing courses. Glazed in and extended by the *City Architect*, 1989.

To the N, the modest brick **ICC Energy Centre** by the *Convention Centre Partnership*, 1986, and a pub by *John Dixon & Associates*, 1995. Further N in **Cambridge Street**, **Kingston Buildings**, built *c.* 1803 as Price's nail warehouse, on a courtyard plan. Symmetrical two-storey front, arched central entrance with pediment. Sash windows, in simple triplets at the rear facing the canal where former loading bays can be seen. Heavily restored by *David Robotham*, 1995. Behind all these, the **National Indoor Arena** of 1989–91 by *HOK* and *Percy Thomas Partnership*. A huge uninspired lump with brick projections for staircases. It seats 8,000 to 13,000.

Now back past the Brewmaster's House and W across the canal into the **Water's Edge** restaurants and shops, by *Benoy*, 1993–5. Postmodern industrial vernacular, the most obvious joke the steel-pipe column on top of a huge sloping buttress. It succeeds by strong detailing, e.g. English bond brickwork with red stretcher rows alternating with blue headers. Part of the *Terry Farrell Partnership* plan of 1991 for this area, retained in the 1993 version by *John Chatwin*. A passage runs NW to the main square of **Brindleyplace**, laid out in 1995. The master-plan's combination of informal relationships within strong townscape disciplines is evident in the buildings and the apparently casual layout with trees, pools and carefully aligned pathways, by *Townshend Landscape Architects*. At the centre, set on radiating paving which continues as its floor, a **café** [64] by *Piers Gough* of *CZWG*. Small, angular, sculptural: a pointed oval of grey-painted steel and glass, its roof slopes extended across each other and up, like the wings of a bird about to fly. **Sculpture** in the NW corner by *Miles Davies*, 1995, blackened arches.

The buildings share a common scale, the use of brick, and a tripartite division into base, main storeys and attic. On the E, No. 3 [65] by *Porphyrios Associates*, 1997–8, the most classical design, its seven storeys ingeniously fitted in. Doric colonnade with intersecting arches hinting at both Gothic and Romanesque. Huge attic, like a temple set sideways. Clock tower with cornice on big consoles. The strong influence of early C19 Germany, Schinkel and Klenze, filtered through Leon and Rob Krier, is characteristic of the late C20 classical revival. Inside, a Doric screen leads to an atrium with Mannerist stretched Corinthian pilasters, and first-floor windows breaking into the base mouldings above.

On the S, two plainer buildings by *Allies & Morrison*, also with open colonnades. No. 2 of 1996–7, buff brick. No. 6 of 1998–9, red brick carefully detailed, with two-storey attic recessed behind brick piers. Beyond

65. No. 3 Brindleyplace, by Porphyrios Associates, 1997–8

them No. 7 by *Porphyrios Associates*, 2003–4, in red sand-faced brick. Open colonnade and grey-clad attic with deep canopy. On the w, No. 5 by *Sidell Gibson*, 1996. A highly asymmetrical picturesque composition, in buff brick with stone bands, pulled together by the classical tripartite division. Deep glass atrium on the s, flanked by a massive turret to the square and a bullnose end beyond. The strong base adds bands of blue brick and has its own tripartite division.

On the N, No. 4 by *Stanton Williams*, 1997–9. Moving beyond its Postmodern neighbours into the resurgent planar Modernism of the late 1990s. A louvred screen of metal and glass, a recessed entrance, and a left block and cornice of pink Belgian brick, flush-pointed to emphasize mass. Crisp but coldly threatening, and unpleasantly bulky at the rear. To the NE, between and behind Nos. 3 and 4, the **Sealife Centre**, an aquarium by *Foster & Partners*, 1996, its three-dimensional ray shape spoilt by poor grey-blue cladding.

The walk continues s between Nos. 2 and 6 into **Oozells Square**. On the E, the **Ikon Gallery** [6, 66]. This was Oozells Street School, by *Martin & Chamberlain*. 1877 in Ruskinian Gothic with E wing added 1898. The confined site dictated a compact three-storey block. Renewed sash windows, stone and tile tympana in pointed openings, typical naturalistic sculpture. Converted by *Levitt Bernstein*, 1997. They reinstated the tower, removed in the 1960s, to the original design, and added glass N and s extensions for lifts and stairs: tough additions to a tough building. Inside, new and old spaces flow intriguingly. New floors inserted in the main classrooms and hall, but C19 roofs visible on the second floor. Big wooden arch braces and iron ties, but the 1898 wing has iron arches. New entrance in the NW turret, cut in awkwardly.

The landscaping in the square, with a diagonal rill aligned on the gallery tower, is by *Townshend Landscape Architects*. Granite sculptures by *Paul de Monchaux*, 1998. At the w end, No. 8 by *Sidell Gibson*, 2002–3. Tall, with a gimmicky prow. Disappointing.

Back to the main square and sw between Nos. 4 and 5. On the N, car park and health centre by *Benoy*, 1998; canted glass-block stair-tower and delicate steel panels covering the concrete structure. Beyond it to the w, the **Crescent Theatre** by *John Chatwin*, 1998. Brick with a blue-painted front, cut down from the original design. On the s, the **City Inn** hotel by *Hulme Upright Weedon*, 2000.

Opposite the theatre, **Grosvenor Street West** runs sw. On its NW side, the **Union Mill** [5] of 1813, perhaps by *William Hollins*. When built, it was the largest flour mill in the town. Simple two-storey front range with a pedimented gable over the central carriage arch. Now back to the theatre and NW along **Sheepcote Street**. On the NE, **Symphony Court**, the Brindleyplace private housing scheme, of 1995 by *Lyons & Sleeman & Hoare*. Friendly canalside scale, but fake shaped gables. On the sw, retained C19 façades to a large private flats scheme, with white-clad end pavilions, by *Associated Architects*, 2000–2. Then a good Queen Anne

66. Ikon Gallery, Brindleyplace, by Martin & Chamberlain, 1877, converted by Levitt Bernstein, 1997. Detail of staircase

office building by *Osborn & Reading*, 1890, with massive flats behind by *Turner Woolford Sharp*, 2000–2, turning the canal here into a dark canyon. On the corner of St Vincent Street, the former **Corporation Depot** of 1873 by *W.H. Ward*. Picturesque paired Gothic lodges. Inside, a more than semicircular range with a cartway running under its centre to the canal. Evocative cobbled pavements.

Back to the Crescent Theatre and s down Sheepcote Street. On the w, the classical former **South Staffordshire Waterworks Co**. offices,

1931–2 by *Crouch, Butler & Savage*. Brick and Portland stone. Heavy Doric porch and small top pediment with long consoles embracing a round window. Opposite, the low moderne **Liberal Jewish Synagogue** by *Josephs* of London, 1938, dem. 2006. On the NE corner to Broad Street the former **Birmingham and District Bank** of 1898 by *C.E. Bateman*. A beautiful Shavian classical piece with Arts and Crafts touches, see the stone bands marking the quoins, and a slight French air e.g. the little iron balconies. Sumptuous angled corner porch with Ionic columns.

On the NW corner the **Old Orleans** bar, originally the Islington Glassworks of 1815. Three-bay, three-storey centrepiece built as the owner's house. Stone strings between the floors, Doric porch. The windows with heavy architraves and lintels are probably of 1863 by *J.J. Bateman*, who added the wings then, when it became the Lying-In Hospital. Railings with Gothic piers by *Martin & Chamberlain*, 1869.

Now SW along **Broad Street**. On the S side, the **Transport and General Workers' Union** is by *Culpin & Bowers* of London, 1927–9. Friendly, slightly overcrowded cream faience front with Ionic pilasters and a perky oriel. **Cumberland House** is of 1963–4 by *Lewis Solomon, Kaye & Partners*, the podium dressed up by *Halpern Partnership*, 1998. Further W, a large cinema and leisure complex, two brick blocks with deep recessed attics and big canopies, by *Abbey Holford Rowe*, 2000–2. W from here lie Five Ways and Edgbaston (p. 215).

From here we can return NE down Broad Street past Sheepcote Street. Alternatively we can take an optional excursion SE down **Bishopsgate Street**. On the NE side the **City Tavern**, a terracotta pub of 1901 by *James & Lister Lea*. On the SW, municipal housing of 1968–72 by the *City Architect*. Low-rise courtyard blocks with deck access, unusual in Birmingham, over ground-floor garages. Restless, cubic elevations in pink brick, perhaps influenced by Eric Lyons. Metal roofs 2002–3. Further down on the NE No. 5, a surprising survivor, Arts and Crafts offices and warehouse by *Harvey & Wicks*, 1913–14, with linked first- and second-floor windows under typical relieving arches. At the far end, **Bath Row** runs E. On the N side, student flats by *Barton Fellows*, 1994–5, and two retained blocks of the former **Queen's Hospital**. Handsome, delicate Italian Romanesque façade of 1871–3 by *Martin & Chamberlain*. Raised centrepiece with a big arch. Doorway of 1995. Then the original 1840–1 building by *Bateman & Drury*: heavy square classical. Porch on unmoulded piers, its only decoration a coat of arms. Further E the former **St Thomas' church** [67] of 1826–9 by *Rickman & Hutchinson*. Only the W end survived a 1941 bomb, the worn Bath stone now very poignant. An elegant and original Greek Revival composition. Four-stage tower with ground floor open to N, S, and W, linked to the W wall by tightly packed Ionic quadrant colonnades. Above, a plain stage, then a square with pedimented aedicules, and an octagon. Originally topped by a ball and cross, now missing. **Churchyard** laid

out as a Peace Garden in 1992, incorporating a Doric loggia by *S.N. Cooke* and *W.N. Twist*, once part of the Hall of Memory scheme, brought from Broad Street. Opposite on the s side, **Colston Health Centre** of 1989 by *Associated Architects*. Two yellow brick wings at right angles, foyer in a glass-roofed quarter-circle between, like a squashed version of Stirling & Gowan's Cambridge History Faculty. We can return to Broad Street by retracing our steps up Bishopsgate Street, or by walking N from St Thomas up Granville Street.

Back on Broad Street, going NE from Sheepcote Street, on the s side Nos. 214–215 by *W.T. Orton*, 1931, linked to a six-storey block by *Brian A. Rush*, 1975. **Lee Longlands** furniture shop is by *Hurley Robinson*, 1931, in his distinctive squared-up Art Deco. Three-bay E extension 1939. The **Travelodge**, 1961–3 by *John Madin*, was badly re-clad *c.* 1990. **Granville Street** runs s here, with on the opposite corner the former **Granville** pub, prominently dated 1923. By *Arthur Edwards*, still Jacobean, but toned down, in white faience. Original lamp brackets. In Granville Street on the w side, **Granville Square**, red brick housing of 1978–80 by *Peter Hing & Jones*. Low-rise blocks surrounding a tower breaking into horns at the top.

Back on Broad Street on the N, the **Novotel** by the *Percy Thomas Partnership*, 1988–9. No. 10 Brindleyplace, orange brick, by *Sidell Gibson*, 2003, then No. 9, by *Associated Architects*, 2000–1, rather reticent, the base signified by two-storey stone framing. It wraps tactfully round the former **Presbyterian church** of 1848–9 by *J.R. Botham*. Blue Staffordshire brick, locally fashionable then for churches.* A rectangular box with two tiers of windows, still in the Georgian tradition. Four-stage tower showing the influence of Rickman's St Thomas (*see* above), see the Doric quadrants on the belfry stage. Pagoda top. Big, handsome doorcase. Interior altered.

Then No. 1 Brindleyplace [68], a fine gateway building to Broad Street, by *Anthony Peake Associates*, 1994–5. It cleverly addresses the curve of the street, and reduces scale by the church, by telescoping a three-storey front block into a separate five-storey one behind, aligned with its neighbours to the E. Brick skin with deliberately unstructural detailing e.g. broken lengths of cornice. Slightly Chinese turrets echo the church's suggestion of a pagoda.

On the s side opposite, the Art Deco **Figure of Eight** bar by *Bernard G. Warr*, 1932, started as a car showroom. On the corner of Berkley Street, sixteen-storey Seifertian tower of 1974–5 by *Ian Fraser, John Roberts & Partners*, now the **Jury's Inn**. Brutal as townscape. Heavy

---

*Cf. the first St Luke, Bristol Street, 1842 by *Harvey Eginton*, (dem. 1899); St John, Walmley, Sutton Coldfield, 1843–4 by *H.J. Whitling*, completed by *D.R. Hill*; St John, Brockmoor, by *Thomas Smith*, 1844–5.

---

67. St Thomas, Bath Row, by Rickman & Hutchinson, 1826–9. West end and tower

68. No. 1 Brindleyplace, by Anthony Peake Associates, 1994–5

chamfered concrete lintels define the podium. Tower fins tapering at the top. **Berkley Street** runs s here. At the far end on the w, the **CBSO Centre**, offices and rehearsal rooms. Retained façade of Rowe's lead works, 1921–2 by *H. Peter Hing*, to a development by *Associated Architects*, 1997. Their s front is a grid structure of dark grey steel I-beams with characteristically varied infill including wooden trellising. Round-ended staircase faced in glass blocks, inside the open steelwork. Barrel roofed hall behind. Back on Broad Street going E, **Quayside Tower**, a sixteen-storey slab between Berkley and Gas streets, of 1965 by *John Madin*. Podium enlivened by textured abstract reliefs. Re-clad 2003 by *Richard Johnson & Associates*.

At the junction of Broad Street and Gas Street some good survivors. On the N the **Brasshouse** of 1781. The finest surviving secular building of the C18 town, the front range of a brassworks, built to serve local brassfounders, and to cut imports. The façade is an early attempt to articulate a long, low office and factory range, a problem for C20 archi-

69. Retort House, Gas Street, 1822. Detail of roof

tects. Seven bays, the ends slightly recessed. Two storeys with a parapet over the central bays breaking into balustrades over the main windows, and supported by consoles at the ends. Attractive but slightly overdone fenestration: tripartite compositions in the second and sixth bays, divided by slender colonnettes; central Venetian window. Sills tied together by string courses. Romanesque central doorway by *Martin & Chamberlain*, 1866. Restaurant conversion 1987–8, with rear extensions, by *Temple Cox Nicholls*.

To the E over the canal, the former **Crown Inn** was William Butler's brewery tap.* Small irregularly spaced sashes on first and second floors survive from the building of 1781. Reconstructed in 1883 by *William Jenkins*, and again in 1930 by *E.F. Reynolds*, who did the ground floor with its rusticated piers, the Brasshouse-style parapet and the domed clock tower. Cheap classical w façade by *Alan Goodwin & Associates*, 1991.

Opposite on the s, a block of 1887 by *Martin & Chamberlain*. Informal composition with one big gable decorated with brick mullions, balanced by two smaller ones. These have paired lancets and big stone heads with cusped roundels. Next E, a slightly earlier Italian Gothic block. Paired and triplet lancets and second-floor tilework frieze. Then a block of 2000 by *Level Seven Architects*. Undeniably elegant, but almost a caricature of fashionable Millennium details, mostly Constructivist or early Le Corbusier: pilotis, countless floating panels, terracotta tiles, and a choice of wavy and wired canopies.

Back and s into **Gas Street**, which dates from the early C19. On the E, a rendered range followed by two cottages of *c.* 1810 with typical lintelled windows and doorcases. On the w, **Carlton Television** retains a house and factory of 1821 with segment-headed iron-framed windows and a massive doorcase. Behind, offices of 1995 by *Peter Hing & Jones*. A Postmodern attempt at canalside vernacular, with chunky tapering columns.

---

*His C19 tower brewery survived at the rear until 1987.

70. Gas Street Basin, west side, mostly 1820s and 1830s

Next a plain brick range of 1857 with a segmental roof, built as a store for the building beyond. This is the Birmingham Gas Light & Coke Co.'s **Retort House** [69] of 1822, designed by its engineer *Alexander Smith*. Simple street front with windows in three-centred relieving arches. It was built with a fireproof 'iron roof and slates', and the roof survives inside: cast-iron trusses, wrought-iron tie rods. On the s side, originally open, the roof is supported on cast-iron columns. Extended w 1828 with a similar roof; contemporary **Coal store** to the N with louvred roof. All restored drastically in 1998–9 by *Richard Johnson & Associates* who also designed the blocks of flats beyond, red brick with grey-clad roofs.

No. 46 on the E is the former **Worcester and Birmingham Canal Co. office** of 1864 by *James Lea*. A severe and dignified L-shaped block with heavy porch in the angle. Rendered ground floor with big cornice, blue brick above.

Back N a few yards, to where a gate in the wall leads into the hidden **Gas Street Basin** [70], still a great surprise to enter. A small basin on the Birmingham Canal of 1772, it became important as the junction of the Worcester and Birmingham Canal from 1795. Its sense of enclosure, highlighted in Gordon Cullen's *Townscape* (1961), was seriously compromised in the late C20; best now viewed from the traditional-style footbridge of 1988, to the right as we enter. The Birmingham Canal enters from under Broad Street and its old E exit to the terminal basin is still visible. The **Worcester Bar** runs w–E across the basin, originally separating the canals. **Stop lock** of 1815, now crossed by the bridge.

Surrounding buildings are taken clockwise from the Gas Street entrance. The w side is best. Here, going N, the Gas Street cottages have an extra lower storey facing the canal, and the rendered range is revealed as a three-storey corn warehouse of *c.* 1830 with a battered base. To the N and NE, backs of buildings in Broad Street, one incorporating walls of an 1820s grain store. Altered and extended in the mid 1860s for a foundry, hence the chimney. Then the terribly dominating rear of the Hyatt Hotel (*see* p. 145). s of the E arm, late C20 replacements for C19 warehouses. Modest scale and brick facings, but not of high quality. The best is the **James Brindley** pub of 1985 by *Alan G. Goodwin*, with a typical 1980s semicircular glass roof, and a decent attempt at an imitation hoist extension, on Doric columns. Then a long range of 1985–6 and 1989 by *Carter Green Associates*. At the s end a horrible five-storey hotel with cantilevered top and pseudo-classical detail. 1988 by *Tibbatts & Co. Design Group*. Opposite, a long C20 factory runs s. Beyond, former Worcester Canal stables of 1876, now a restaurant, then a cast-iron **aqueduct** of 1870 over Holliday Street, with segmental brick vaults supported on decorative iron columns. Then, returning N, a nice group. A Worcester Canal lock cottage of 1876, the rear of the Worcester Canal offices, and finally a Birmingham Canal lock-keeper's cottage of 1815. Across the bridge and along the bar, past the pub, is the exit to Bridge Street, and so N back to Centenary Square.

Walk 2.

The Jewellery Quarter

The area NW of the centre, divided from it since the 1960s by the Inner Ring Road, and bounded by the Dudley road (The Parade and Sand Pits), SW, the Middle Ring Road, NW, and the Wolverhampton road (Great Hampton Street and Constitution Hill), NE. Development started nearest the centre, as part of the Newhall Estate (*see* p. 129). The grid of streets focused on St Paul's Square was laid out, and the church built, in 1776–9. Hanson's map of 1778 shows church and layout but no houses; the sole surviving lease for the square is dated 1791. The W part was developed in the early C19 with substantial villas in private grounds, but industry arrived quickly. The N end, around Vyse Street, was built up *c.* 1845–70 with houses and workshops, the latter taking over in the later C19.

Early industry was encouraged by canals: the Digbeth branch of the Birmingham Canal of 1786–9 along the SE edge, and the Whitmore Arm, cut in stages through the W part 1800–*c.* 1824. There was a great variety of manufacturing, especially of the small metal 'toys', trinkets and boxes, for which Birmingham was famous. Electroplating, invented by Elkingtons of Newhall Street, was particularly concentrated around Great Hampton Street. From the mid C19 the precious metal trades became concentrated in the area, helped by the large number of interdependent trades needing close proximity. This encouraged related businesses such as diamond merchants and case makers, and institutions connected to them: the Assay Office, and the Municipal School of Jewellery. A similar process produced a concentration of pen factories around Legge Lane.

Manufacturing began in houses or small workshops at the rear, some built over kitchen wings. By the 1830s combined houses and workshops were being built, a type that only died out *c.* 1880. During the later C19 domestic premises were rapidly converted. Rear 'shopping' wings and front extensions covered gardens, producing a tightly packed but small-scale industrial townscape. These simple brick structures with large iron-framed windows changed little throughout the C19. Many workshops and converted houses were let in small units, even single rooms, to specialist craftsmen; some still are. In the W part factories were developed in gardens, sometimes retaining the villas as offices. Elliott's button works of 1837 in Vittoria Street is probably the first

71. Nos. 13–15 Fleet Street, by Roger Harley, 1892–4. Interior

purpose-built factory in the Quarter, closely followed by Joseph Gillott's Victoria Works, which in 1853 produced 100 million steel pen nibs in a year. By the 1860s factory designs are of increasing architectural effect, at first by commercial architect-surveyors like *W.T. Foulkes*, but from the late C19 by more sophisticated local architects such as *William Doubleday* and *Arthur McKewan*.

In the early C20 factory planning became more sophisticated with e.g. T-plan factories with long workshop wings at right angles to front office ranges, giving maximum light. Constitution Hill and Great Hampton Street were largely rebuilt in the early and mid C20 on a larger scale than the rest. The local architect-surveyor *George E. Pepper* did several in Arts and Crafts or Baroque modes from 1909 onwards. Crowngate House of 1913–22 set a new scale, followed by large factories for e.g. the big firms of Lucas and Cannings during the 1930s.

After the Second World War the City Council planned reconstruction with large flatted factories housing many small businesses. Only one was built, the Hockley Centre, in 1970–1, and it failed to attract the craft firms which still dominated the industry. An alternative strategy of conserving the architecture and small-scale industries started from 1971 with designations of three small Conservation Areas, expanded in the 1990s to cover the whole Quarter. A comprehensive building study by English Heritage was published in 2002, when a Management plan was adopted to stop unsympathetic development. Residential conversions are currently the main threat to the jewellery industry's survival, with many appearing on the fringes.

a) From the City Centre to Caroline Street

We start at the junction of Great Charles Street and Newhall Street (*see* the Newhall Estate). NW down **Newhall Street** past vacuous mid-C20 blocks. Behind on the NE, the **Post Office Tower** (now BT) of 1963–7 by the *Ministry of Public Building and Works*, senior architect in charge *M.H. Bristow*, the city's tallest structure, but utilitarian compared with London's. On the SW, **Telephone House** of 1934–7, top floor of *c.* 1975. Here **Fleet Street** runs SW. On its NW side, flats by *Turner Woolford Sharp* of 2003–4. On the SE, Nos. 13–15 [71] of 1892–4 by *Roger Harley*, with rows of segment-headed iron windows, built as Newman Brothers' coffin-furniture factory and occupied by them until 1999, a remarkably unspoilt example of the typical late C19 factory of the area. Back to Newhall Street, on the NE side, **Brindley House**, straddling the Digbeth branch canal, by *D.K. McGowan*, 1967–8. On the SW the former **Science Museum** retains two bays of Elkington's factory of *c.* 1850, and a seven-bay late C19 range. On the NE a former printing works by *Cherrington & Stainton*, 1946–7, altered by *Mark Humphries*, 1987.

On the S corner to **Charlotte Street**, the **Queens Arms** pub by *Joseph Wood*,* delightful though old-fashioned for 1901. Projecting gables enclose first-floor canted bays with iron crestings. Rounded corner

---

*The pub architect whose business card of 'The Performing Ass-Quith' is amusingly illustrated in Andrew Saint, *The Image of the Architect*, 1983

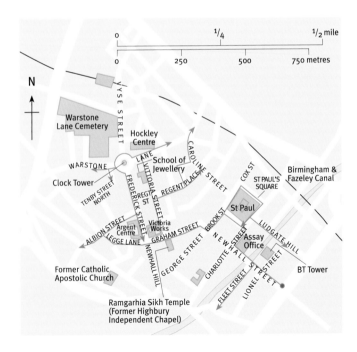

with big gold and brown terracotta panel, proudly displaying Mitchell's brewery's gold medals.

On the E corner, the **Assay Office**, for official testing and hallmarking of precious metal products. Originally established in 1773 in New Street following a campaign led by Matthew Boulton, and still the busiest assay office in Britain. It moved here in 1877–8, to the corner building by *A.B. Phipson*. Red brick with Darley Dale stone dressings. Grand but sober Italianate, with pilasters and a big centrepiece: projecting Tuscan porch and Corinthian aedicule with a segmental pediment; granite columns. Segmental windows, on the first floor with inset lintels supported on Corinthian columns. Royal Arms on top, enclosed in an extra storey by *Ewen & J.A. Harper*, 1914. In 1885 *Phipson* added a three-storey building to the SE, plainer. Between, an unfortunate mid-C20 brick loading bay. Many extensions, including *Harper* work of 1890, 1899, and 1907. Going NE down **Charlotte Street**, on the NW side Nos. 59–60, a warehouse of *c.* 1878.

Beyond, we enter **St Paul's Square**. Birmingham's only true Georgian square. In the centre, **St Paul's Church** [73, 74], the last survivor of the town's C18 churches. Built 1777–9 to designs by *Roger Eykyn* of Wolverhampton; the builders were *Standbridge & Co.* Upper part of the tower and spire added 1822–3 by *Francis Goodwin*, stonemason *Matthew Seaborne*. Bomb damage was repaired by *J.B. Surman*, 1949–51; much of the roof was replaced. The site, near the far NW end of the

72. Walk 2a

73. St Paul, St Paul's Square, by Roger Eykyn, 1777–9, upper part of tower and spire by Francis Goodwin, 1822–3

Newhall Estate, was given by Charles Colmore, undoubtedly to stimulate development. Eykyn's design was altered after criticism by Samuel Wyatt and a James Gibson of London. It is very much a pattern-book church of the period, heavily dependent on James Gibbs's St Martin-in-the-Fields and St Peter, Vere Street, London as published in his *Book of Architecture* (1728). The exterior is a heavy five-bay box with projecting pedimented square E chancel and w tower, and slightly recessed w corners enclosing porches. The stone said to be Bilston Rag. Rusticated quoins, and to N and s, two tiers of windows, with Gibbs-style blocked surrounds (round-headed above segmental), like T.F. Pritchard's St John, Wolverhampton of 1756–9. Big Venetian E window in a relieving arch. Pedimented doorways also with blocked surrounds. Cornice with massive consoles. Goodwin's work is faced in Tixall stone. His tower follows Eykyn's design in its two diminishing octagonal stages and spire, but its details are fashionably Greek: the lower octagon with Ionic columns set into the diagonals, and the spire delicately divided into four stages, the lowest with angle pilasters and all with tiny windows.

The interior, with Ionic arcades and an elliptical plaster tunnel vault, is equally Gibbsian. The aisles have groined vaults. The arcades stand on square piers which support the galleries, with their top mouldings continuing as the base moulding of the gallery fronts. w gallery with iron columns of 1779 in the centre, extended forward by *Hansom & Welch*, 1833, see the extra pair of columns in front. Elegant E window surround by *Samuel Wyatt*, 1791, with Greek Ionic half-columns and pilasters, and oval medallions. Its pediment is by *Surman*, 1950. Many original C18 **fittings**. Plain **box pews** with fielded panels, H-hinges and – a Birmingham touch – enamel numberplates. At the w end, **vicar's** and **churchwardens' pews** in elliptical coved recesses. Flanking the door, **beadles' seats**. – **Choir stalls** incorporating C18 panelling. – **Font**. C19. White Ionic capital, pink granite stem. Probably by *Thomason* who worked here in 1861 and 1884. – **Monuments**. The most delightful is around the s aisle E window, by *Peter Hollins*, to William Hollins and family. Carrara marble. Bust in Roman dress, tablets to the family with the 'fruitful vine' and 'olive plants' of Psalm 128, and delightful sculptured surround. All installed 1880 though the bust may be earlier. Contemporary **stained glass** by *Ward & Hughes*. – Going w, Richard Mico Wise d. 1826, sarcophagus on ornate lions' feet and an earthy cherub in the predella, by *Seaborne*. E wall of s gallery, Sarah, Eleanor and John Legge, d. 1805, 1807, 1824. Oval tablet with soul ascending to a heavenly crown, by (*William*) *Hollins*. In the NW corner several with weeping branches, e.g. William Redfern d. 1820 etc. by *P. Hollins*. Others by *J. Richardson*. Small tablets on the pier fronts. – **Stained glass**. The E window, the Conversion of St Paul, is an important piece of 1791, designed by *Benjamin West* and made

74. St Paul, detail of east window, designed by Benjamin West, 1791. Ananias restores St Paul's sight

by *Francis Eginton*. In the Baroque style West used for his paintings at Windsor Castle in the 1780s. The technique involves a double thickness of glass painted on inner and outer surfaces. – Nave SE, *Ward & Hughes*, *c.* 1880; the rest, mainly patterns, by *Pearce*, 1900–7. – N aisle, 2000, by *Rachel Thomas*. – **Organ** by *George Hollins*, 1838, reconstructed in 1927 when it was moved from the W gallery to the NE corner of the nave, with an additional case facing the gallery by *H. Ravenscroft Richards*. – **Royal arms**, W gallery, by *John Poole*, 1996, but of George III.

Churchyard laid out by the City Council 1895–6, retaining some early C19 tombs.

The original **houses** in the square are of three storeys, their Doric porches with panelled soffits and open pediments. The best survivors are Nos. 35–37 on the N side, with a small version of the bracket cornice on the church. Restored 1985 by *Associated Architects*. No. 35 has three bays still with exposed brick. Going clockwise, No. 34, the **St Paul's Club**, two original houses altered in the 1930s. Original doorcase, and early workshop wing behind in Caroline Street. No. 30 now includes three buildings: a swagger factory by *Marcus O. Type*, 1936, with giant arches, big end pediments and rusticated ground floor, but rather Arts and Crafts brick detail; a later C19 three-storey range with careful terracotta insertions in three-centred arches; and a fine though slightly dominating six-storey block by *Associated Architects*, 1993. Crisp grey metal-clad structure integrated by repeated horizontals in the ground-floor grilles, balconies and brise soleil. At the start of **Cox Street**, Nos. 36–37 of *c.* 1920, with a late Free Style giant arch and wavy parapet.

The E side starts with a nasty gap. Nos. 21–24 are of 1853 etc. for Goode & Boland, jewellers, reduced and stripped to imitate C18 houses. Then a pseudo-Georgian range by *Jacqueline Wall*, 1988. Nos. 12–14 are original late C18, similar to Nos. 35–37. Some original interior details, e.g. Adam-style cornices. No. 11 is mid-C19 classical, with five close-set bays. Doorcase with broken pediment and flanking windows. Nos. 11–14 reconstructed internally, with flats built at the rear by *Inston Sellers Hickinbotham* and *Baron Design*, 1983–7. The S side has some cheap 1980s Postmodern (No. 10 etc.). On the E corner of Ludgate Hill, No. 1, late C18, three bays. Unusual doorcase with heavy half-columns and husk garland frieze. Gutted 1981.

Ludgate Hill is lined by modest C19 industrial premises. The best group is on the E. No. 21 on the corner of **Water Street** is a warehouse of *c.* 1854. Two tiers of segment-headed windows in tall recessed panels, ground-floor openings also recessed in arches. Absolutely simple and functional, with just an Italianate bracket cornice. Slightly later six-bay rear extension. **Griffin House** is by *Holland W. Hobbiss* and *M.A.H. Hobbiss*, 1956–7. No. 17 on the corner of Lionel Street is by *De Lacy Aherne*, 1912, with impressive giant arches. Converted to flats with top structures and E extension 1997, by *Mark Humphries Architects*.

Back on the square, the SW corner of Ludgate Hill has a former bank of 1898 by *Sydney Allcock* with Jacobean entrance and oriel; flats by

Turner Woolford Sharp, 2005; then a late C19 generating station, converted to flats 2003 by *Nichols Brown Webber.* On the w side, Nos. 55–56 represents at least two original houses. Restored sashes, and on the Charlotte Street front, left, a Venetian window with Gothick glazing. Alterations by *H.W. Hobbiss,* 1934: the doorway below the Venetian window, big oval panel, much reconstruction to the square including the ground-floor arches, and cornice. Nos. 50–54 by *G.F. Hawkes,* 1902–3, functional brick with big cornices and banded pilasters. At the rear, shopping ranges with big windows flank a narrow courtyard. Refurbished well as offices by *Mark Humphries Architects,* 1989. No. 45, **Stevens Terrace,** is flats by *Associated Architects,* 1980–2. Big at six storeys, but the treatment, with narrow bays, recessed balconies and small oriels, is contextual and coherent. No. 42A on the corner of Brook Street is a paper warehouse of 1890 by *Roger H. Harley,* with giant pilasters. Converted to flats with an extra floor and projecting roof by *Associated Architects,* 1984. Facing us at the w end of the N side, a big functional job of 1934, rebuilt 1941–2 after bombing.

Now w along **Brook Street.** On the s, No. 11, a little Gothic warehouse of *c.* 1868. Opposite, the **Royal Birmingham Society of Artists'** gallery, a former warehouse by *Marcus O. Type,* 1912–13. Strongly articulated by recessed bays under segmental arches. Characteristic Type round windows. Bronze bracket lamp and plaques of 1912 by *Crouch & Butler* from the former gallery in New Street (*see* p. 111). Beyond, **Baker & Finnemore's** gentle Neo-Georgian factory by *Ewen Harper & Bro.* of 1911 and 1915 turns the corner N into **Newhall Street.** On the w here, Nos. 200–202 of 1900, then Nos. 204–206 of 1905, Free Style, big lunettes with bold sun-ray stone voussoirs. Both, surprisingly, by *F.H. Thomason.* The street bends w, becoming **Graham Street.** On the N, **Sovereign Court,** quite convincing industrial style by *Sinclair Architects,* 1990. More 1990s flats on the s, then the **Ramgarhia Sikh Temple,** built as the **Highbury Independent Chapel** in 1844. The only survivor of the city's larger C19 chapels. Classical front with projecting centre and tall round-headed windows arranged 1–3–1, divided by rusticated pilasters which rise rather awkwardly right up to the gable.

On the N side the block between Vittoria Street and Frederick Street is occupied by the **Victoria Works,** built for the pen-nib maker Joseph Gillott in 1839–40, perhaps by *Charles Edge* (cf. Elliott's button factory in Vittoria Street, p. 169). First the yard wall with plain pilasters and cornice, broken by a later C19 panel with a medallion of Queen Victoria under a big curved pediment. To the right, the curved metal roof of a block by *Mark Humphries,* 1989–90, an early example of High Tech style in the city. Going w, the factory itself, a dignified block with plain sashes and, on the second floor, small-paned iron-framed windows. Slightly recessed rounded corner, slightly projecting centre to Graham Street with restrained heavy stone entrance surround. Shallow plan with workshops lit from both sides.

75. Argent Centre, Frederick Street and Legge Lane, by J.G. Bland, 1862–3, detail

Across Frederick Street, the **Argent Centre** [75] was Wiley's pen works, by *J.G. Bland*, 1862–3. Huge for its date, nine bays by fifteen with a later N extension. Lombardic style, in bright red, white and blue brick and stone detail. The scale is well addressed by first- and second-floor two-light windows linked under relieving arches. The corner turrets originally had pyramid roofs. Again, a shallow plan with full-width workshops. Office conversion by *Bonham Seager*, 1993.

We continue W along **Legge Lane**, evocatively narrow, and lined by C19 pen and pencil factories, some ruinous. On the S, the former **Wellington Works**, mostly by *Thomas H. Mansell*, 1879, marked by segment-headed windows with red and blue brick voussoirs. On the N, No. 3 is a grand pencil case works by *Essex, Nicol & Goodman*, 1893, terracotta, with a big Jacobean shaped gable. Contrasting doorcases. No. 6 is two pairs of passage-entry houses and workshops by *William Tadman Foulkes*, 1885, very late for this combination. No. 7 is early *T.W.F. Newton*, 1887.

As the lane turns N, on the NE corner **Alabaster & Wilson's** jewellery factory. By *J.P. Osborne*, 1892; E extension 1899. Exceptionally well preserved. Good window heads, and moulded brick strings. Doorway with triplet lights above, under a pediment. Opposite on the SW the altered gable end of the former **St Paul's School** of 1869 by *J.A. Chatwin*, with brick lancets on the W side. In the SW corner, the entrance tower of Manton's **Union**, later **Gwenda**, **Works** of 1913 by *William Doubleday*. An eyecatcher in cream faience with big round entrance arch, foliage frieze, and battlemented top. Flat conversion 2003.

Beyond, N, a small square with, on the E, a former **Fire Station** by

T.G. Price, 1909–10. Bright red brick with bold stone dressings and Wren-style cupola. On the N, the sad wreck of the **George & Dragon** pub. Early C19, extended to its present length and fitted out as a pub by 1875.* Paired bracket cornice and Gothic canted bays. Just to the w, Nos. 103–106, a terrace of two pairs of passage-entry houses of *c.* 1855.

Now E along **Albion Street**. On the N, flats by *Bryant Priest Newman*, 2003. On the s, Nos. 62–65 is a factory by *William T. Foulkes*, 1883, with round-headed windows balanced by a heavy, attic-like top floor. Nos. 58–61 of *c.* 1839 are two pairs of passage-entry or 'three-quarter' houses with side entrances from a single central passage. Two-storey rear workshop ranges and canted bays to the street by *W.T. Orton*, 1900. Nos. 54–57 of 1837, similarly adapted. On the N, two Late Georgian survivors with rusticated ground floors. No. 33, two bays, has pilasters with Soanian incised panels. Nos. 34–35, set back, of four bays with side extensions, has a doorcase with Doric colonnettes, open pediment and wheel fanlight. Then on the s No. 50, a workshop of *c.* 1870. Gothic door with heavy traceried fanlight.

Beyond, on the sw corner of **Frederick Street**, No. 52 of *c.* 1866 with round arches retains fine glazing, especially the rear wing. On the E side, a little way s, Nos. 14–15, stucco Italianate of *c.* 1870. Unusual two-light windows with blind panels above decorated with circles, and many bearded head keystones. Nos. 19–20 are Edwardian classical by *T.G. Price*, 1908. Going N, No. 22 is a jolly Jacobean bank by *Hipkiss & Stephens*, dated 1901 in the semicircular gables. **Thomas Fattorini**, on the s corner of Regent Street, by *Mansell & Mansell*, 1894–5, in fine restrained Jacobean, with curly broken pediment to the N doorway. No. 25 on the opposite corner was the Berndorf Metal Co., by *Douglas J. Williams*, 1888–9. Impressively dour, with stepped segment-headed windows. Then a group of *c.* 1825–30. No. 26 has an Italianate ground floor, remodelled *c.* 1860 when it was bought by a goldsmith. No. 27 has a fine Greek Revival front with coupled Doric columns. Nos. 30 and 31 are contemporary villas, severe and cubic. No. 32 is a factory of 1914 by *Crouch, Butler & Savage*, in cream faience and green glazed brick (cf. their RBSA gallery in New Street, p. 111). T-plan with a long flat-roofed rear shopping wing. Two-storey N oriel.

On the w side, No. 48, a mongrel of *c.* 1870. No. 47 is a manufactory and house by *Foulkes & Ryland*, 1879, its projecting bays swept in below the dormers. No. 46, the **Variety Works**, by *Ewen Harper*, 1881, an even later house and factory, going Queen Anne. The first-floor cross-windows lit warehouse space, with living rooms below and bedrooms above. No. 45, set back, has a front of 1882 by *Ewen Harper* hiding a house of *c.* 1820, originally in landscaped grounds. No. 43 was a civic restaurant of 1949–50 by *W. Norman Twist*.

*The C19 interior was stolen *c.* 1995.

The crossroads at the N end of Frederick Street is the modern centre of the Quarter. Classical **Clock Tower** of 1903 commemorating Joseph Chamberlain's return from South Africa, explicitly imperialist in this Unionist city. Bracket lamps reinstated to the original design 1990. On the SE corner a mildly Baroque **Barclays Bank** by *Cossins, Peacock & Bewlay*, 1905. On the NE corner, the **Rose Villa Tavern** of 1919–20 by *Wood & Kendrick*. Brick and terracotta, Jacobean style, but sober and static compared to pubs of *c.* 1900. Big gables, dentil cornices, round-arched windows. The interior is confused by late C20 Victoriana, but its finest features are the painted glass in the bar, with orange and purple ships on green waves, and the tilework. The best of this is in the right-hand lobby and staircase hall: cornices with garlands, and an alcove with a fireplace and a framed tile-painting of maidens bearing flowers. On the NW corner, a bank by *Daniel Arkell*, 1892. Perhaps earlier C19, re-cast, and altered again in the late C20. Rich Romanesque doorway with statue of Banking in a niche, and carved tympanum.

Now a short detour W of the clock tower down Warstone Lane. On the N, the **gatehouse** of the **Church of England Cemetery**, 1847–8 by *Hamilton & Medland*. Puginian Gothic with its steep gable and stone oriel over the arch, but in beautifully toned Staffordshire blue brick. The chapel (demolished 1954) lay N, on the edge of a sunken amphitheatre, formed from an early C19 sandpit. Entrances to catacombs in its retaining wall. On the S, **Aquinas House** [76] by *Frederick Proud*, 1882. Corner office entrance with a diagonal spirelet. Impressive S factory wing with big paired round-headed windows, articulated by pilasters corbelled out into chimneystacks. Original iron-framed glazing. Iron-beam and shuttered-concrete floors, an early use of the technique. Later C19 factories continue down **Tenby Street North**, e.g. Nos. 8–10 by *Osborn & Reading*, 1879, and No. 20 by *William Doubleday*, 1898.

Now E down **Warstone Lane**. To the N the **Hockley Centre** (the 'Big Peg'), an eight-storey flatted factory of 1970–1 by *Peter Hing & Jones*. V-fronted projections very typical of the date. To its W the **Information Point**, an octagonal pavilion designed by students from the Prince of Wales's Institute directed by *Robert Adam Architects*, 1997. On the S side of Warstone Lane Nos. 35–39, **Northampton Parade**, a good range of *c.* 1850 on the SE corner of Vittoria Street. Two Venetian Gothic factories of *c.* 1870–1, Nos. 27–28 with fanciful window details, No. 29 more conventional, with juicy capitals and corbels. Now back and S down **Vittoria Street**. On the W the **Municipal School of Jewellery and Silversmithing** (now part of the University of Central England's Birmingham Institute of Art and Design). Founded in 1888, it moved here in 1890 when *Martin & Chamberlain* converted a goldsmith's factory of 1865 by *J.G. Bland*. This has an attractive Lombardo-Gothic front, its windows with insistent multi-coloured voussoirs. Bright tilework in first-floor tympana and cornice. Top storey of 1906 by *Cossins, Peacock & Bewlay*, who in 1911 built the massive S extension, in red brick

76. Aquinas House, Warstone Lane and Tenby Street North, by Frederick Proud, 1882

mottled with blue. Three wide bays with large windows between brick end towers with stepped tops. Minimal detail except for a rich but delicate stone cornice. Then in 1992–3 *Associated Architects* added a range further s, with brick piers and recessed metal windows echoing the 1911 design, and rebuilt much of the interior, creating a full-height atrium with gallery access to workshops enclosed by glazed screens. The long sides are linked by bridges with glazed brick floors. The reception area doubles as an exhibition space. It works well, combining enticing spaces with light and attractive workplaces.

Opposite, a Brutalist intrusion by *Dron & Wright*, 1965, in dark grey-brown brick with concrete slabs expressed as bands. No. 59 by *J.P. Osborne*, 1901, with large workshop windows. Opposite, s of the school, No. 68 of *c.* 1875 has round-arched first-floor windows with little tympana above the segmental window heads. The **Regent Works** on the NW

corner of Regent Street is an early purpose-built factory of 1837–8, probably by *Charles Edge*, for William Elliott, button maker.* Plain brick with slightly projecting centre and recessed rounded corner. Nos. 54–58 on the rounded sw corner by *Essex & Goodman*, 1904–5, has big windows divided by brick pilasters and a terracotta cornice. In **Regent Street**, No. 3 is an ornate Italianate factory of 1872.

Continuing down Vittoria Street, on the w side Nos. 48–52, early C19, retaining round-headed doorcases with incised decoration; a run mostly of bigger mid-C19 factories; and Nos. 22–24, a much-altered block of back-to-backs of *c.* 1840. Returning N up the E side, No. 33 of *c.* 1881 has the wall effectively cut back above the ground floor to create giant pilasters with rich Gothic capitals; Nos. 35–37 are quite grand 'three-quarter' houses of *c.* 1832 with a big Doric doorcase to the common entry, converted to a factory by 1860. On the SE corner with Regent Place a flatted factory, an interesting type, by *Thomas F. Williams*, 1879–80, with five separate entrances. Minimal classical detail above a rusticated and vermiculated ground floor. Nos. 51–53 on the NE corner is another altered pair of town houses of *c.* 1830.

Now E down **Regent Place**, with many good small factories. On the N, Nos. 12–14 of *c.* 1883, probably by *A.H. Hamblin*, in J.H. Chamberlain's Board School Gothic. No. 16 is a tall Free Style factory by *J.G. Dunn*, 1910. Giant arches, and Voysey-style piers rising above the

---

*Edge designed Elliott's house in Edgbaston, now demolished.

parapet. Entrance with prominent segmental pediment echoed in the
doors. It occupies the former garden of No. 20, a single-bay house of
c. 1824 with side entry doorcase. Opposite, No. 17 by *Martin & Martin*,
1905–6, simple brick with windows recessed in giant arches, showing
the influence of A.S. Dixon. Encased in it, part of a town house of 1824.
(In the rear yard a gas engine house of *c.* 1910–14, still housing the original engine.) On the N again, Nos. 22–26, houses of *c.* 1823–4 with heavy
Grecian doorcases. No. 32, **Squirrel Works**, another strongly three-
dimensional *J.G. Dunn* Free Style design, 1912–13, its square piers rising
clear of the cornice. Deep arched entrance set flush. No. 53, s, is a paper
warehouse by *J.H. Hawkes & Son*, 1906, restrained Free Style in brick
and orange-buff terracotta. Further E on the N side, Nos. 60–70, a factory of 1852–3. Nine-bay classical front, the end entrance bays slightly
wider, and with segmental pediments to the first-floor windows. String
course continuing across the mid-C19 block, left, suggesting it is
contemporary.

Back w, then N up **Regent Parade**. Ahead, the bulky rear of **Heritage
Court**, flats by *Lawrence & Wrightson*, 2001–2, corrugated and glazed
roofs. On the NE corner, No. 14 [77], a house of *c.* 1840 in finely laid
orange brick. The details, rubbed brick lintels and doorway with
recessed bolection-moulded surround, strongly suggest *Bateman &
Drury*. Rounded corner. No. 15 beyond, facing N, similar but altered.
Beyond, on the SE corner of **Caroline Street**, No. 65 of 1836, perhaps by
Fallows & Hart, built as house and factory for a silversmith, George

Unite. Three-bay front with centre angled to accommodate the curve of the street; solid Ionic porch. Going NE, No. 42 [78] on the SE has housed **Pickering & Mayell**, case makers, since *c.* 1900. Built as two houses *c.* 1826–7, a good example of houses taken over as workshops but retaining interior detail. One surviving Greek Doric doorcase with open pediment. Contemporary rear workshop wing along Kenyon Street.

The walk ends here. Return SE down Caroline Street to St Paul's Square. To start Walk 2b, continue across the square, down Ludgate Hill, and NE along Water Street to the start of Constitution Hill.

b) Constitution Hill, Great Hampton Street, and the Northern Jewellery Quarter

Constitution Hill and Great Hampton Street are the road NW out of Birmingham towards West Bromwich. The present wide straightened road dates from turnpiking in 1727. We start at **St Chad's Circus**, by St Chad's Cathedral, and go NW down **Snow Hill**. On the NE, **Focus Foyer** by *Ian Simpson Architects*, 1997–8; beyond, flats by *Associated Architects*, 1996–7. On the SW, No. 86, a cubic Neo-Georgian former Y.M.C.A. by *Harry Weedon & Partners*, 1952–3, incorporating part of the structure of a music hall of 1885–6 by *W.J. Ballard*; **Queens Chambers** by *J.H. Hawkes & Son*, 1902–3; and an Italian Renaissance former bank by *Dempster & Heaton*, 1892. Dominating the view, on the acute corner of Constitution Hill and Hampton Street, the stunning circular red terracotta tower of the former **H.B. Sale** factory [80], by *William Doubleday & James R. Shaw*, 1895–6. Eclectic Gothic with Spanish touches and an

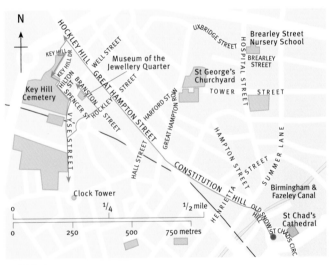

79. Walk 2b

80. Former H.B. Sale factory, Constitution Hill, by William Doubleday & James R. Shaw, 1895–6

almost oriental dome. Rich foliage band with raised lettering, and busts in roundels. In **Hampton Street** to its right a factory by *G.E. Pepper*, 1911, with bold giant arches. At the start of **Summer Lane** Nos. 391–396, picturesque Gothic by *J.S. Davis*, 1883. Opposite, Nos. 12–13 of 1844 retain at the rear Court No. 3, with four cut-down blind-back houses.

Now NW up **Constitution Hill**. On the SW, the **Bismillah Building** was Barkers' electroplating works of 1901–3 by *Newton & Cheatle*, a big Free Style block in red terracotta with brick infill. Huge central pediment, giant order, towers with segmental parapets and triangular pediments. Big, rather Baroque entrance. Converted to flats 1993–5. On the NE, Nos. 19–21 by *Henry R. Wintle*, 1881. On the corner of Henrietta Street an Italianate block by *William Davis*, 1881, with much yellow and cream glazed brick. The **Hen and Chickens** of *c.* 1875 on the opposite corner must be by *Davis* as well. Beyond, Nos. 31–51, wild Italian Gothic of 1881–2 by *J.S. Davis*. Canted bays like Nos. 391–396 Summer Lane, and a cornice with pierced stone discs. On the SW, the former **Taylor & Challen** works. Two Arts and Crafts factory blocks by *E.F. Reynolds*: a heavy, square showroom and office with stripped pilasters of 1919–21, and a single-storey showroom of 1915 with big pedimental gable, united by a giant arcade with characteristic imposts. Beyond, a functional block of 1938 by *Watson & Johnson* with stair-tower. Nos. 60–62 of *c.* 1822–3 was a japanning factory; simple handsome six-bay front. Original Royal Arms. Behind, a foundry of 1861 designed by *Joseph Taylor* and *S.W. Challen*. The restrained Queen Anne **White Horse Cellars** of 1890 is *J.A. Chatwin*'s only known pub design.

Further NW to the start of **Great Hampton Street**. On the NE corner the former **Gothic** pub of 1869–70, very Ruskinian. Pointed arches with voussoirs of red, white and blue brick, a little oriel, and steep dormers. Delightful octagonal turret and spirelet. Beyond, a pair of *c.* 1850, then the **Quality Works** of 1914 by *E.H. Wigley*, functional, minimal Tudor. Further along, No. 10, the **Sylva Works** (electroplaters), 1912 by *George E. Pepper*, free Baroque.

Opposite on the SW, the former **Cannings** factory, now **College of Law**, by *Peacock & Bewlay*, 1936, an impressive stripped block with a big rounded corner. Back on the NE No. 16, the excellent former **J. Ashford & Son** works of 1912 by *Arthur McKewan*, with Free Style end bays linked by a giant arch, contrasted with a Wren-style rusticated ground floor. T-plan with long rear wing. On the corner of Harford Street, the simple **Church Inn** claims, probably correctly, to be of *c.* 1840. Part of a Gothic refronting of *c.* 1880 on the NW. On the N corner, a **Lloyds TSB Bank** by *J.A. Chatwin*, 1899. Buff terracotta like a posh pub with a domed octagonal turret on a big lion's head and foliage corbel. Shaped gables pierced by chimneys. NE extension by *Associated Architects*, 1989–90. On the SW here, three former factories all by *G.E. Pepper*, 1919. Standard six-bay elevations with projecting ends, but varied treatment. **Clayton-Wright** is rather Arts and Crafts with tilework diamonds, and bold stone details, **A.J. Pepper & Co**. cream faience with coloured diamonds, **G.F. Westwood & Son** heavily Baroque. Then a former Lucas factory of *c*. 1926, converted to flats by *Nicol Thomas*, 2000–2.

On the NE, two early C19 buildings extended to the street over front gardens. No. 33 retains a Greek Revival front with fluted pilasters; No. 34, the **Lord Clifden** pub, has a façade of *c*. 1910 with semicircular window. Nos. 41–43, on the E corner to Hockley Street, Italianate of *c*. 1860 with a rich cornice.

On the N corner, the **Pelican Works**, an electroplating factory of *c*. 1868, with its eponymous crest. A tightly articulated Italian palazzo with arcaded ground-floor windows and close-set segment-headed lights above. Opposite, Nos. 85–87, *c*. 1850, with shops on former gardens. Nos. 83–84, **F.W. Needham's**, is Italian Gothic of 1871–2. Nos. 80–82, the **Great Hampton Works**, for buttonmaking, by *Yeoville Thomason*, 1872, also Italian Gothic, in a rich and very varied treatment. The capitals e.g. on the ground floor are simple imposts, on the first floor plain stone blocks edged in blue brick, and on the second floor foliage. Unified by continuous arcading with ornate brick voussoirs. Nos. 69–73, three separate early C19 developments, retain their domestic scale, set back behind former gardens. Nos. 71–73 are refronted, but Nos. 69–70, of 1830, retain simple lintelled sashes and doorcases with open pediments and incised ornament. Restored 1995–7 for the Birmingham Conservation Trust by *Frank Brophy Associates*. Long rear shopping wings of 1872–5 with iron-framed windows. Opposite, Nos. 55–56, a Greek Revival pair of *c*. 1820–3 with incised decoration on broad pilaster-like projections. Then the massive Nos. 60–64, **Crowngate House**. The corner block to Well Street by *J.G. Dunn*, *Dallas & Lloyd*, 1913, extended SE by *Dallas & Lloyd* 1919–22. Brick with terracotta bands and interpolated voussoirs. A grand version of the Squirrel Works (see p. 171) with giant arches and entrance bays marked by piers rising clear of the parapet, the entrance arches brought forward flush with the pier fronts. Above, chequer faience panels and little shaped parapets.

A left turn at the crossroads here leads to Vyse Street and the Museum of the Jewellery Quarter at the end of this walk.

Straight on, **Hockley Hill** starts on the N corner with a former bank by *Thomason & Whitwell*, 1892–3, NE extension 1901, stirring together French classical, Jacobean and Baroque. On the SW side altered early C19 buildings and the **Duke of York** pub, C18 refronted in 1859 with old-fashioned lintelled windows.* Beyond Key Hill, **Harry Smith Ironmongers**. Two early C19 houses flank a remarkable block by *Arthur Edwards*, 1913, clearly expressing its steel frame and quite functional except for the simplest dentil cornice. Good original lettering. **Gem Buildings** [81] by *Wood & Kendrick*, 1913, is equally impressive. Four

---

*Much of the contemporary gin-palace interior survived until stolen *c*. 1995.

bays with huge windows and just-classical tops to the end towers. Finally a Baroque **Post Office** of 1911. Down an alley to its left into **Key Hill**. In front of the stark rear elevation of Gem Buildings is the Nonconformist **cemetery** of 1835, with original railings and tremendous stone Greek domed piers by *Charles Edge*. We continue up **Key Hill Drive** to the left of the cemetery, with on the SE Nos. 5–11 of *c.* 1860, distinguished by lintels with inset decorative panels. At the far end an alley runs SE into **Hylton Street**.

This U-shaped street marks the start of a mid-C19 area of small houses and workshops on a grid pattern: Spencer and Branston streets run NW–SE across Vyse and Hockley Streets. There is a fairly consistent stylistic development from plain classical Georgian survival to increasingly decorative Italianate. Many industrial conversions with large added workshop bays, attics, and rear shopping wings. A scattering of later C19 and C20 purpose-built factories.

In Hylton Street Nos. 38–40 of *c.* 1866 is a well-preserved mid-C19 factory with three doorways for different occupiers. Going S, Nos. 16–24 of 1920 by *W.J. Davis* was an extension to Nos. 8–14 beyond, of *c.* 1880, with a round-headed arcade above iron-framed windows separated by pilasters, and much brick cogging. From 1916 W.H. Haseler Ltd and Liberty's store made 'Cymric' silver in partnership here. On the W corner to Vyse Street a good block of *c.* 1847–50 with Ionic doorcases. On the NE corner of Spencer Street, opposite, **Anvic House**, a pair of two-storey houses of *c.* 1850–1 with a third storey and E workshop wing, impressively glazed, with iron colonnettes, both of *c.* 1875.

Going S down **Vyse Street**, Nos. 37–38 of 1847, with four central doors in an Ionic surround, originally separate entrances to shops and living space above. On the E side Nos. 90–94 of *c.* 1864 with big Doric doorcases and dentil cornice. No. 94 has a contemporary workshop range to Hockley Street with a third storey added early, and a seven-bay extension of 1887. (Early surviving features include narrow ladder-like stairs, goods chutes, and round-headed side-hinged cast-iron windows.) No. 89, also of *c.* 1864, has a workshop bay of *c.* 1880 and glazed attic of *c.* 1900.

Now back NE down Hockley Street. On the corner of Spencer Street, **Plantagenet Buildings** of *c.* 1871, the most opulent Italianate design here: linked ground- and first-floor windows with canopied lintels, and a rich cornice with single and paired brackets and decorative frieze. In **Spencer Street** on the N, Nos. 93–107, modest mid-C19 houses and factories converted for the Duchy of Cornwall by *Derek Latham Architects*, 1989, into the **Jewellery Business Centre**. Entrance arch with sculpted gates by *Michael Johnson*, a tree with roots and branches in steel wire and strip.

Further down Hockley Street and NW into **Branston Street**. On the SW, Nos. 114–124, six survivors of seven houses of 1856–61. Refurbished in the early 1990s and rear wings demolished. On the NE Nos. 115–121 are four houses and workshops of *c.* 1857–8. On the s corner of Vyse Street, Nos. 75–79, the **Museum of the Jewellery Quarter**. A mildly Baroque red brick and faience factory of 1909 by *George E. Pepper*, with a workshop wing down Branston Street; s extension of 1914 also by *Pepper*, with round-arched openings. Museum conversion of 1990–1 by *Dyer Associates*, with new classical frontage further s by *Christopher Smith Associates*.

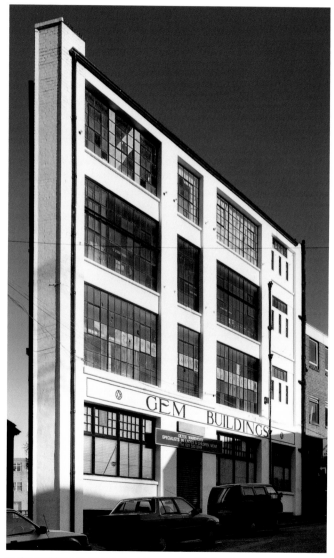

81. Gem Buildings, by Wood & Kendrick, 1913. Key Hill elevation

Other Buildings

Finally a scatter of buildings not covered above. **Summer Hill Terrace** facing Sand Pits on the s edge of the Quarter has No. 3, a five-bay villa of 1826–7 with Ionic porch, and *J.A. Chatwin*'s bold brick **Catholic Apostolic Church** of 1873, now Greek Orthodox, with an impressively tall interior. In **Camden Street**, running NW off the Parade behind Summer Hill Terrace, **Heaton House**, a detached villa of *c.* 1823 with a hipped roof, almost hidden behind C20 factories. In **Livery Street**, E of St Paul's Square and reached by Mary Ann Street or Cox Street, No. 45, the **Gothic Works**, a T-plan factory of 1902 by *Sidney H. Vaughton*, the front range in brick and terracotta with big mullion-and-transom windows.

On the E edge of the Quarter, reached from Great Hampton Street NE up Great Hampton Row from the Gothic pub, the churchyard of **St George's**. *Thomas Rickman*'s church of 1819–22, a landmark in the Gothic Revival, was demolished in 1960. What survives are his characteristic tapering octagonal cast-iron gatepiers (cf. Hampton Lucy, Warwickshire) and Rickman's **tomb**, by his partner *R.C. Hussey*, 1845. A big gabled superstructure, much battered and defaced. Further NE, reached N along Great Hampton Row and E along Uxbridge Street, **Brearley Street Nursery School** by *W.T. Benslyn*, 1938–9. Birmingham's first Modernist building. The wings look like 1965, with cantilevered concrete balconies and flying staircases. Floating top canopies, now glazed in. Only the central brick entrance hints at the real date.

Digbeth, Deritend and Eastside

The area covered is SE of the Bull Ring and Moor Street (the Inner Ring Road), N of the markets, and inside the Middle Ring Road on its E and SE part. Digbeth and High Street, Deritend, the road to Coventry and London, were built up by the later medieval period. The River Rea, dividing ancient Birmingham from Deritend in Aston parish, fed several mills. They have left their mark in street names such as Heath Mill Lane and Upper Mill Lane. The streets to either side of Digbeth were developed from the mid C18 with tightly packed houses and workshops. The widening of Digbeth and Deritend in 1953–5, and slum clearance from the 1950s, led to much rebuilding. The area was never fashionable or rich, and we go quickly from smart city centre into small-scale industrial streets. The new Bull Ring (*see* p. 85) has increased development pressure, and the Eastside development, around Millennium Point (*see* p. 190) will bring big changes.

a) Digbeth, Deritend and Fazeley Street

The start is the top of **Digbeth**, opposite St Martin's and Selfridges (*see* pp. 87–8). S side rebuilt after 1953, though the narrow block between Digbeth and **Moat Lane** to its S may represent C16/C17 encroachments on the lower part of the medieval market place. The N side retains the scale of the pre-1960s Bull Ring. Plain brick **Royal George** by *Kelly & Surman*, 1962–4. Behind it the former **London Museum Concert Hall** of 1863, the last survivor of the city's C19 music halls. Classical side elevation with windows in large recessed panels. Nos. 138–139 is by *S.N. Cooke*, 1936, with strip windows. No. 137 has an C18 front much rebuilt in 1947, retaining a good pedimented window. Inside, evidence of timber construction. C18 doors with broad plain architraves, and an early C19 stick baluster staircase. Nos. 135–136 of 1913 by *James Patchett* of Ombersley is late and crude but enjoyable Free Style: first-floor lunette, little oriels, green tiled frieze with the owner's name **G. Makepeace**, second-hand clothes seller. Then a former cold store [83] of 1899 by *Ernest C. Bewlay*, impressively functional with something of H.H. Richardson's Romanesque in its deeply chamfered paired windows with lunettes above. Opposite, **Wolverley House** of 1955–6 by *Bertram Baxter & Partners*. Porthole windows.

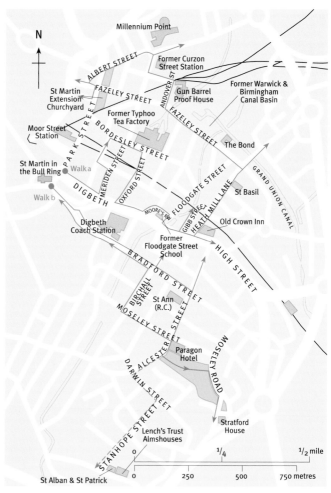

N

Millennium Point

Former Curzon
Street Station

ALBERT STREET

FAZELEY STREET

ANDOVER ST

Gun Barrel
Proof House

Former Warwick &
Birmingham
Canal Basin

St Martin
Extension
Churchyard

PARK STREET

Former Typhoo
Tea Factory

FAZELEY STREET

Moor Street
Station

BORDESLEY STREET

The Bond

St Martin in
the Bull Ring ● Walk a

MERIDEN STREET

OXFORD STREET

FLOODGATE STREET

GRAND UNION CANAL

St Basil

Walk b

DIGBETH

MOORE'S ROW

GIBB STREET

HEATH MILL LANE

Old Crown Inn

Digbeth
Coach Station

Former
Floodgate Street
School

HIGH STREET

BRADFORD STREET

BIRCHALL STREET

St Ann
(R.C.)

MOSELEY STREET

ALCESTER STREET

MOSELEY ROAD

Paragon
Hotel

DARWIN STREET

Stratford
House

STANHOPE STREET

Lench's Trust
Almshouses

0   ¹/₄   ¹/₂ mile

St Alban & St Patrick

0   250   500   750 metres

82. Walk 3

The **Police Station** is of 1911 by *Henry E. Stilgoe*, City Surveyor:
slightly uncertain Baroque with a picturesque corner turret. On the sw
corner of Meriden Street the former **Castle and Falcon** pub, brick late
classical of *c.* 1850. Alterations by *W.H. Ward* in 1907, including the corner with lunette and bands of blue and yellow brick. In **Meriden Street**
on the E a former garage of 1923 by *Harry W. Weedon* with big segmental
pediment. On the w the former Ash and Lacy works of 1905 by *J.G.
Dunn*; a long crisply articulated brick and terracotta range. On the sw
corner to **Coventry Street** a former garage with quadrant façade by
Bertram Baxter & Partners, 1955. w here, and up into **Allison Street**.
On the w a factory of 1888 by *James Moffat*, in a builder's version of
J.H. Chamberlain's Gothic, with decorative terracotta gable. Pointed

83. Former cold store, Digbeth, by Ernest C. Bewlay, 1899

windows with voussoirs of moulded bricks set on edge. To the N the blue brick railway viaduct of 1911–16 by the G.W.R. Superintendent Engineer *W.Y. Armstrong* (*see* Moor Street Station, p. 88). On its w side the contemporary former lower-level railway goods yard, an early reinforced concrete structure of 1912–14 on the *Hennebique* system. Impressive rows of piers supporting shallow segmental arches.

Beyond the viaduct on the E a former bottling factory by *Owen & Ward*, 1892, extended 1898–1900. On the sw corner with **Bordesley Street**, Nos 8A–10 of 1882–4 by *Jethro A. Cossins*, very progressive for its date and deeply influenced by Philip Webb. A blunt massive brick block of four tall storeys with steep, impressively corbelled gables and the sparest Queen Anne detail, e.g. the pilasters on the side elevation. The fenestration, shallow canted bays on decorative brackets below single tall casements, stresses the areas of brickwork. Opposite, on the NE corner of **New Bartholomew Street** the former Chamberlain and Hookham factory by *Arthur McKewan*: a functional block of 1913 with big steel windows, and sparing but effective Arts and Crafts detail: diapering, tile lintels, recessed tympana. E extension of 1927.

Now E down **Bordesley Street**. On the corner of Meriden Street the **Spotted Dog**, of *c.* 1810 with a later pilastered ground floor. Beyond, **Ladbroke House** of 1919–21 by *Ernest H. Wigley*. On the N the massive former **Ty-Phoo Tea Factory**, by *Harry W. Weedon & Partners* of Odeon cinema fame. First a plain extension of 1947, then the long central range in blue brick with stone dressings. Earliest the five w bays with sparing Neoclassical detail, e.g. the projecting pedimented ends, of 1929. Extended E by thirteen bays in 1937–8: an eight-bay, slightly Deco centre articulated by triangular giant brick piers, then five bays repeating the earlier work, making a symmetrical composition. Built-up attic with just a little fluting. Finally a block of 1949–50, still massive but

84. No. 58
Oxford Street,
by Buckland
& Haywood-
Farmer,
1911–12;
detail

emphasizing horizontals, with long thin canopies.

s into **Oxford Street**. Under the railway viaduct, a contemporary iron urinal in a recess on the E. Beyond on the w, No. 58 [84] is a fine Arts and Crafts factory of 1911–12 by *Buckland & Haywood-Farmer*. Three storeys of rough textured brickwork with simple windows, and a round-headed entrance doorway with decorative leadwork hood. Two-storey w wing to Coventry Street with effective blank upper floor articulated by shallow buttresses. The plan has workshops round a double-height space just like one of Buckland's school halls. On the E side opposite, the mid-C19 classical **Old Wharf** pub.

Returning s to Digbeth and turning E, No. 86 is a two-bay Gothic shop, slightly old-fashioned for 1890, by *Edward Mansell*. Its two-light windows imitate No. 85 next door, Bonser's Lion Warehouse of 1860 by *J.R. Botham*. An impressive, eclectic single-bay tower with a massive classical entrance and French truncated pyramid roof. The former **Old Bull's Head** pub was rebuilt c. 1880. The **Digbeth Institute** of 1906–8 by *Arthur Harrison* is Edwardian Mannerist, its classical elements used unstructurally to indicate the steel frame beneath. Doric columns support only draped female figures with musical instruments. Deliberate recessions between the canted bays above. Baroque centrepiece, and contrasting spiked central turret and Wren-style side cupolas. The steeply gabled **Big Bull's Head** was rebuilt in 1885, probably by *William Hale*, with canted bays effectively recessed between brick piers.

Across **Milk Street**, a crusty brick block of shops and warehouse of 1869 for Thomas Fawdry, restored in 2003 as part of a bulky creative arts centre development by *Nicol Thomas*. It incorporates the former **Floodgate Street School** behind, a fine *Martin & Chamberlain* job of 1890–1 in their later, more directly functional style. Huge windows under gables; on the N side, fronting **Moore's Row**, these are separated by buttresses with gabled tops enclosing open terracotta tracery. Large and small gables grouping well on the E. Strongly modelled ventilation tower, square with corner turrets.

s then E over the River Rea into **High Street**, **Deritend**, a medieval settlement in Birmingham manor but Aston parish. Its C15 chapel, on the s side, rebuilt in 1742, was demolished in 1947. An urban centre can still be felt here on the N. First, the former **Alfred Bird & Sons' custard factory**. Behind a vacant plot, a low sawtooth range of 1887 by *Thomas Naden*. Its tall chimney is of 1910 by *W.T. Orton*, who also did the main four-storey frontage, **Devonshire House**: six-bay centre of 1902 with buff terracotta arches and windows, ornate lettering and a rich shaped gable with a ship in tilework. Parapet cut out like a pie-crust, waiting for custard. Two plain bays of 1913 to the w, eight more of 1907–8 to the E, with functional later C20 rear extensions running down Gibb Street. Converted into studios, shops, and workshops, with an internal court-yard, by *Glenn Howells Architects*, 1994. On the E side of **Gibb Street** a *Howells* block of 1997–8: brick stair-tower painted blue, and a simple L-shaped block to its N delightfully treated with light oval plate-like bal-conies suspended from steel masts and a screen of rods and ties. Giant **statue** sprouting wire and plants, Green Man by *Tawny Gray*, 2002. On the corner of High Street, Deritend, Gibb Street, and Heath Mill Lane a former Lloyds Bank of 1874–5 by *J.A. Chatwin*. Domestic Gothic with power: a chunky stepped-up-and-down cornice and a four-lancet win-dow pushed into the gable. Parapet with beasties at the ends. To its N a former **Public Library** of 1866 by *Bateman & Corser*. A very ecclesias-tical Gothic design. Red brick with a little blue diapering, stone dress-ings and three-light Perp windows. Two gables to the street, the taller with two steps interrupted by a brick rectangle, rebuilt during repairs of 2003 by *Bryant Priest Newman*. Inside, four-centred-arched arcades, also Perp, and a complex roof.

Across Heath Mill Lane the **Old Crown Inn** [85], the only complete surviving medieval building of Birmingham (as distinct from farms and villages now within the city). Recent research by Stephen Price, Nicholas Molyneux and George Demidowicz has convincingly shown it to be the late C15 **Guildhall and School** of the Guild of St John the Baptist of Deritend.* The street front indeed has a civic air, with its close-studded and jettied first floor and central entrance, with a gabled oriel above on big brackets and attached columns. Original round-headed wooden windows to its sides. Ground floor underbuilt in brick in 1862

*Discrediting the traditional story of a pub founded in 1368. The decorative tie-beams (*see* below) are comparable to one at the Saracen's Head, Kings Norton, datable to 1492.

85. Old Crown Inn, High Street, Deritend, late c15

by *Joshua Toulmin Smith*, a local antiquary who saved the building and extended the E wing to the N. The great moulded bressumer supporting the first floor, faithfully restored by him, was removed in hamfisted alterations of 1998. Gabled cross-wings with important and unusual tie-beams decorated with blank arcading. The jetty continues down the w front. But the appearance is slightly misleading, as the right side was originally recessed, in the so-called Wealden arrangement. Evidence of this the surviving brackets supporting the wall-plate to the right of the oriel. A window here lit the schoolmaster's hall, with his parlour and other rooms in the E wing. The left side housed the school on the ground floor, and the hall above. At the rear, Toulmin Smith's N extension, reconstructed as bedrooms in 1998, when the rear entrance was added.

The porch leads to a cross-passage, much renewed. To its left, the bar, probably the former **schoolroom**, retains its beamed ceiling with a dragon (diagonal) beam supporting the SW corner. Bedrooms above incorporate stud partitions from the post-Reformation subdivision of the **guildhall**. Its roof survives above modern ceilings, with arch-braced collars and wind-braces. In one bedroom an C18 'buffet' corner cupboard. Inside the central oriel, a ceiling with original, early plasterwork: six-pointed stars and simplified fleur-de-lys, symbolizing the Trinity. On the right side the master's hall was divided horizontally in the C16, but retains its roof, with tie-beams, convex struts, and high straight collar. Smoke blackening suggests an original open hearth. The extra internal wall-plate is evidence of the Wealden arrangement. At the rear here, an early C19 stick-baluster staircase.

Further E four brick and terracotta shops by *J.H. Hawkes & Son*, 1906, and two more of the mid C19. Then the former **St Edmund's Boys' Home** by *Mansell & Mansell*. Two simple brick bays of 1912 fronting Deritend, then a bedroom extension with a wooden casement window, and a five-bay block of 1913–14 with hipped roof. Set back, the **chapel** of 1913 in Early Christian style, above a ground-floor workshop. Not quite as original as Dixon's or Ball's work (*see* St Basil, below) but with an impressive campanile, closely based on that at S. Giorgio in Velabro in Rome. The interior has an inserted floor, but retains a rich painted timber roof with king-post trusses on big consoles.

Beyond to the E, **High Street, Bordesley** starts. Bordesley was a medieval township in Aston parish. Two classical shops of *c.* 1860, and the **Rainbow** pub, rebuilt in Gothic *c.* 1876 with good detailing.

Back w and N up **Heath Mill Lane**. On the E side beyond the viaduct the former **St Basil's** church, now the St Basil's Centre, by *A.S. Dixon*, 1910–11, the finest example of his Arts and Crafts primitivism. Simple front of brick seconds, red with some burnt blue. Round arches, tile bands, bellcote and a little projecting baptistery. The Romanesque style seems to grow out of the functional buildings around it. The **interior** is more consciously Italian. Five-bay nave, infilled for offices in the 1980s. The arcade columns are granite monoliths, with cushion capitals painted with scenes from the life of St Basil by *Humphrey Dixon*. The E end remains intact, and is wonderfully evocative. Plastered walls, king-post trusses. Massive woodwork. *Dixon*'s **screen** has a dado with linen-fold panels, thick tapering square columns, and a heavy beam decorated with flower patterns supporting **rood figures** brought from Italy. Equally heavy **altar**. The **lectern** displays its construction. The apse has marble **panelling** recalling Lethaby, especially the inset **piscina**. Semi-dome with a **mosaic**. Patterned stone **floor**.

Further N, the **Forge Tavern** and the adjoining factory on the NW corner of Fazeley Street occupy the site of the medieval Heath Mill. To the N, in **Great Barr Street** remains of the never-completed Bordesley railway viaduct of *c.* 1852, a casualty of early railway competition. Beyond, a bridge of 1854 over the Warwick and Birmingham canal, by their surveyor, *Edward John Lloyd*, its shallow-arched span constructed entirely of large cast-iron plates. Panelled iron parapets. w down **Fazeley Street**. On the s a former **Unitarian Sunday School** of 1865 by *A.B. Phipson*, extended to the street corner in 1868. A small brick

86. St Gregory the
Great, Coventry Road,
Small Heath, by J.L.
Ball, 1910–13. Detail of
apse

Dixon's Birmingham churches, St Basil and St Andrew Barnt Green (1909 etc., Worcs.), are early examples of a brick round-arched style, by architects associated with the Arts and Crafts Movement. Behind a plain 1926–8 front, *J.L. Ball*'s St Gregory the Great, Coventry Road, Small Heath of 1910–13 is something of an urban equivalent to his friend W.R. Lethaby's church at Brockhampton of 1901. Its magnificent apse has random tile bands, and brick and stone diapering, like the work of E.S. Prior. *E.F. Reynolds* made his reputation with St Germain, Edgbaston (1915–17), a rough-textured basilica. His finest church is St Mary, Pype Hayes (*see* p. 293). His last, St Hilda, Warley Woods (1938–40), has a central plan.

Holland Hobbiss's churches are various and picturesque, with the feel of holiday postcards: from Germany at Christ Church, Burney Lane (1933), with its westwerk tower; from rural France at Holy Cross, Billesley Common (1935) with its belfry clambering up the aisle roof, from Romanesque Italy at Queen's College chapel (*see* p. 252). At St Francis' Hall, Birmingham University chaplaincy (*see* p. 246), he has been fishing on the Welsh borders.

Philip & Anthony Chatwin's St Faith and St Laurence, Harborne (1936–60) combines plastered Dixon arcades with Pype-Hayes-style cross-arches, and has an elegance different from either. *P.J. Hunt* was, unusually, an architect from a working-class family. He died at 43 from TB, in his parents' council house. His St Luke, Kingstanding (1937), now sadly mangled, was a cool design hinting at the Modern Movement.

temple, classical but with lancet windows. Beyond, the mutilated former **Chapel** of 1876–7 by *George Ingall*. A sharp gabled façade, divided by pinnacled piers. The triangle of **Floodgate** and **River streets** was the mill pond, drained in the mid 1840s. At its far s end the Italian Romanesque former **Medical Mission** of 1880 by *Edward Holmes*.

Back on **Fazeley Street**, N side, **The Bond** has a row of early C19 cottages with lintelled windows and simple doorcases. The site was a gasworks between 1837 and 1875, the cottage with a lunette window probably the works entrance. Right-hand cottage, by the present entrance, of 1898 by *Sidney H. Wigham*, who also extended its neighbours to the yard. To the N a big warehouse in alternating rows of red and blue brick, of 1884–6 for Fellows and Morton by the builder *Edwin Shipway*. Simple functional treatment, with segment-headed iron windows, and a partly surviving hoist over the canal to the N. Small canalside basin constructed *c*. 1890, and covered wharf with nice iron brackets probably of 1896 by *Wigham*.

Further w on the N side a large warehouse proudly inscribed 1935 and Fellows Morton & Clayton; by *Watson & Johnson*. Then the former **Warwick and Birmingham Canal basin**. The canal was cut here in 1796 but the L-shaped basin, infilled but recognizable, dates from *c*. 1840. No. 122 is the former canal company office and weighing machine keeper's house, of 1843–4 by *Edward John Lloyd*. Simple classical, with lintelled doorways and sashes, in fine plum-coloured brick. Also by *Lloyd* the basin entrance with big rusticated gate piers. Probably by him, Nos. 106–110, of 1850 for the Grand Junction Canal Co. Slightly later in style (*see* the pedimented doorcases) and in dark Staffordshire blues. Behind, a contemporary warehouse (gutted 2004). Behind the basin on the canalside, the so-called **Banana Warehouse** of *c*. 1850, with a covered loading bay over the canal supported on iron columns. Its w wall incorporates earlier fabric, probably of Pickford's warehouse of 1811–12. On the s side of Fazeley Street a factory of 1919–20 by *James & Lister Lea*.

N into **Andover Street** and E at the end under the railway into **Banbury Street**. At the end the **Birmingham Gun Barrel Proof House** [88]. A statutory institution, set up by an Act of 1813 to prove, i.e. test, barrels and completed guns. It is still governed by a Board of Guardians composed of master gunmakers, magistrates and councillors, and run by a Proof Master. Entrance range by *Jethro Cossins*, 1883. Simple Jacobean archway (raised in 1970). Caretaker's cottage to the N treated like a miniature C17 house with projecting gabled porch. The balancing s block links to the original building of 1813–14, running w–E. This is a delightful piece of vernacular classicism by *John Horton*, 'architect and builder Bradford St Derritend'. The centrepiece shows off slightly clumsily, but the effect is lovable: three-centred Doric entrance arch (infilled before 1833), big niche above with a splendid trophy of arms traditionally attributed to *William Hollins*, and a segmental gable with a clock. Five bays each side, the westernmost hidden by the 1883 work.

Sash windows with segmental lintels decorated with rosettes. The second bay from the E has a fine Birmingham-style Late Georgian doorcase with Doric half-columns, open pediment and five-petal fanlight, marking the Guardians' entrance. The symmetry is slightly misleading. Originally, the w side had four widely spaced bays, not five, forming 'dwelling houses' for the Proof Master and staff. *Bateman & Corser* made extensive but very tactful alterations in 1868–70 to turn it into workshops, re-spacing the old windows. The second ground-floor window w of the centre e.g. is theirs, with slight differences.

Single-pile plan. Inside the archway, reached through an office, a semi-oval staircase of 1869 leads to the Board Room, E. This has paired simple but handsome original doorways at each end, one blank, with fluted architraves. Heavy dado. Painted oval central ceiling panel of 1836 and another on the w wall of 1835, both by *Jno. Thorp* and copied from the façade sculpture. Marble fireplace probably of 1868–70. To the w, smaller but similar Finance Room; to the E, the Guardians' staircase with altered C19 handrail. The roof has kingpost trusses and diagonal struts.

87. Nos. 110 and 122 Fazeley Street, by Edward John Lloyd, 1850 and 1843–4

88. Gun Barrel Proof House, Banbury Street, by John Horton, 1813–14. Board Room

In the rear yard a simple covered way running N–S, with thin cast-iron columns, of before 1833. In the centre *Bateman & Corser*'s magazine of 1876; plain but of specially fired bricks closely jointed, for safety. To the W and S, extensions of 1868–70; short contemporary wing to the E. Beyond it, the original Proof Hole or proofing shed, rebuilt in tough simple Romanesque by *Charles Edge*, 1860. Inside, original iron deflecting plates below a special slatted roof, to diffuse blasts. Behind, remains of the original canalside wharf.

Now W up Banbury Street. On the corner of **New Canal Street** the terracotta **Eagle and Tun** pub by *James & Lister Lea*, 1900. Along to the N, the former **Curzon Street Station** of 1838 by *Philip Hardwick* for the London & Birmingham Railway, the first main-line railway in Britain. An austere square block, of fine ashlar. Its massively proportioned W façade has giant Ionic columns, an appropriate counterpart to the Doric of the demolished Euston Arch. Round-arched central doorway with finely sculpted shields of the London & Birmingham arms, and swags. First-floor windows with balustrades. The E elevation has attached giant Ionic columns. Inside, a dramatic full-height staircase hall with a screen of square piers on the ground floor and Greek Doric columns above. Several original doors with simple two-part architraves. Superseded by New Street (*see* p. 110) after 1854, used for many years as goods offices. A scheme by *Associated Architects* to convert the building for the Royal College of Organists, with an extra storey behind the parapet, and a linked concert hall to the N, was approved in 2003.

Opposite on the corner of Albert Street the **Woodman** pub of 1897 by *James & Lister Lea*. The first city pub to abandon the traditional pilastered ground floor. A simple but subtle elevation of alternating wide and narrow bays, the New Canal Street elevation slightly canted so that the building flows round the sharp corner. Arched windows, round on the ground floor, three-centred above. Inside, the Public Bar, wedge-shaped to fit the corner, retains its original bar back with round-headed panels of mirror glass, framed in marbled wood, and a bold bar front. *Minton* tiling here and in the Smoke Room.

On the N side here, **Millennium Point** of 1997–2001 by *Nicholas Grimshaw & Partners*, a design-and-build job with executive architects *Mason Richards*. A steel and glass shed, 165 metres (541 ft 4 in.) long, set back standoffishly behind a large brick paved space. The w half, **Think Tank**, the Museum of Science and Industry, is covered by tilting terra-cotta-panel sunscreens. An unmarked entrance leads into the atrium, the s part low and oddly angled, the N more dramatic, contrasting balconies linked by escalators with the big cantilevered **Imax Theatre**. Stainless steel and zinc panels give an overriding impression of grey. Confusing plan, with the main level and the museum entrance two floors up. The museum interiors are low, dark and claustrophobic, with heavy ducting and space that never flows. Galleried double-height machine hall at street level, but only accessible from above, and with rather contrived display structures. N front, reached through the atrium, quite different from the s, with the cylindrical theatre balanced by stepped floors to the w, confused by more grey cladding. Grand footway approach, oddly, from the NE.

w up Albert Street and s into **Park Street**. On the E the former St Martin's extension churchyard. On the w, **Freeman Street** was cut in 1728. The steeply gabled **Fox & Grapes** was built before 1731, perhaps by *Samuel Avery*. Altered in the 1860s, and again in 1925–6 by *H.W. Hobbiss*. Upper floors stuccoed to imitate ashlar, probably in the early C19. On the s a new scheme by *make* is proposed. Back N and w up Fazeley Street; in the **V** of Albert Street **Island House** of 1912–13 by *G.E. Pepper*. Mannerist, e.g. the reversed orders on the corner entrance: Ionic below, then Doric, then Tuscan.

b) Bradford Street and Highgate Park

The area s of Digbeth and Deritend, mainly the estate of Henry Bradford, was developed on a rectangular grid, starting in 1771 at the E end with Alcester Street, with Bradford Street, Cheapside and Moseley Street running parallel w towards the centre. By 1810 most of the plots were developed. Industry was there from the start and took over in the early C20. Wireworks were concentrated here. A few original houses survive, and some good terracotta pubs of around 1900. Many large mid-C20 factories, most now used for warehousing.

We start along **Bradford Street**. On the s, No. 32, by *James & Lister Lea*, 1891, was a hide and skin market, an important Birmingham trade. Big ground-floor arches and central pediment. On the NW corner of **Rea Street** the **Anchor** pub by the same, 1902. Simple exterior

89. White Swan, Bradford Street, by James & Lister Lea, 1899–1900. Interior

with arched windows. Public bar fittings also simple but remarkably complete. Bar front with chunky fluted pilasters; Jacobean-style bar back with Ionic piers and cut-glass mirrors. A rare surviving partition separates off the small bar. Diagonally opposite, a C19 office reconstructed in 1934 for Fisher and Ludlow, by *C.F. Lawley Harrod*; also his the three-bay factory of 1931 to the E. Beyond the River Rea on the S No. 54 by *J.P. Osborne*, 1908. Pedimented end bays and off-centre Baroque doorcase. Further up on the N, the **White Swan** [89], again by *James & Lister Lea*, 1899–1900. Public bar with panelled dado and *Minton* tiles, shell patterns on a plain background. Original bar front and back. The passage to the Smoke Room also has Minton tiles, particularly good, with an olive-brown dado and cream and green panelling above, divided by a band of wreaths and topped by a frieze of flowers in cream, green, orange, crimson and turquoise. In **Birchall Street**, N, **Park Works** by *J.G. Dunn*, 1908–9.

Back on Bradford Street, on the s the impressively large former brass foundry of Harrison & Co. by *Harrison & Cox*, 1908 (five E bays 1916–17, top storey 1924). Plain except for a central broken pediment. On its E side **Lombard Street**, with No. 30, a tiny house and workshop built in 1809 by *Thomas Lea*. On the NE corner of **Alcester Street** the big functional former Fisher & Ludlow No. 10 factory (car bodies) by *John Christie*, 1936. Beyond it in Bradford Street Nos. 234–236, the former Englands shoe factory, 1913 by *F.H. Thomason*, with giant arches. In Alcester Street to the N, a coffin-furniture factory of 1899–1900 by *F. Dennison* shows the persistence of the Georgian tradition.

We walk s, past **St Anne's** (**R.C.**) church of 1883–4 by *Albert Vicars*. Nave and aisles, and NW (ritual, actually SE) tower.* Early English style, in red brick with blue brick and stone dressings: old-fashioned but confident. Big Geometrical w window with many circles enclosing quatrefoils. The tower starts square and turns octagonal with diagonal buttresses to the belfry. Short spire with lucarnes on the diagonal faces, and sandstone banding. Inside, tall arcades with circular columns and arches with two chamfers; hoodmoulds with the Instruments of the Passion. Canted boarded roof supported by attached shafts on angel corbels. Lively tracery: E rose window, circular s aisle E window with a five-pointed star, very tall sanctuary lancets. Original **pews**, and chunky **confessionals** in the s aisle, also Gothic **altarpieces** in the aisles with lots of cusping and crockets.

Further s along Alcester Street, beyond Cheapside, the **Paragon Hotel**, built as a Rowton House (lodging house for working men) of 1903–5 by their regular architect *Harry B. Measures*. Bright red Ruabon brick. Picturesque skyline, with big shaped gables. Octagonal corner towers turning circular, with conical copper roofs and buff terracotta dragons holding shields by *Edwards* of Ruabon. Below, plain elevations with ranges of sashes, originally lighting 819 cubicles. Converted to a hotel *c.* 1990 and interiors lost. Behind in **Moseley Street** a former **police station** of 1877 by *Martin & Chamberlain*. Three tall gables split by tall corbelled-out chimneys (cf. their Telephone Exchange, p. 130). Terracotta panels.

Beyond the hotel, **Highgate Park**, laid out for the Town Council by *T.W. Coudrey* in 1876 with a fine avenue of planes and a lodge on the E side. **Statue** of King Edward VII by *Albert Toft*, 1913, moved from Victoria Square in 1951. A stiff standing figure in Coronation robes, carrying orb and (broken) sceptre. Bronze pedestal reliefs stolen, 1986.

Through the park to the E, up into **Moseley Road**. On its E side, a fine group of early to mid-C19 houses. No. 90 has a doorcase with segmental pediment and elegantly thin paired fluted Doric colonnettes. Of *c.* 1813, perhaps by *John Horton*, as the segmental lintels with rosettes are like the Gun Barrel Proof House (p. 187). No. 94 taller and Italianate,

*The church is orientated in reverse, E–w. This description uses ritual directions.

c. 1850. No. 102 has a good doorcase with open pediment and fanlight; plainer ones on Nos. 112 and 114. No. 106 is heavily Grecian: porch with square piers and acanthus capitals. Finally No. 116 has three semi-elliptical bays with rusticated pilasters, very Cheltenham Regency. Then a nicely contextual curving block by *Associated Architects*, 1993. Across a grassed space to the E, **Stratford House**. Dated 1601 on the porch lintel, which is also initialled ARB for Ambrose and Bridget Rotton for whom it was built. A timber-framed farmhouse in the West Midlands tradition, with characteristic decorative framing. Four gables. The left one is the parlour cross-wing. It projects slightly, and the smaller third one projects further, as a porch. The front, originally jettied, is largely underbuilt in brick. Herringbone framing on the first floor and square panels with quadrant bracing in the gables. Inside, the cross-passage has heavy ceiling beams and studding. Other details mainly early C19. Restored 1951–2.

Return to Alcester Street and w down **Moseley Street**, where Nos. 72–74, S, were three two-bay late C18 houses. **Small's Wireworks** have been there since *c.* 1878. Nice details, particularly on No. 74; window openings with segmental lintels, moulded keystones with rosettes, severe doorcase. On the NW corner of Birchall Street the **Market Tavern** by *James & Lister Lea*, 1899. Opposite at the start of Charles Henry Street a brick warehouse of 1884 by *Daniel Arkell*. Down **Birchall Street** to return to Bradford Street.

Finally a group reached from Alcester Street along Darwin Street and Stanhope Street. On the corner of Conybere Street, the church of **St Alban**, **Bordesley** [90].* A major late work of *John Loughborough Pearson*, 1879–81, complex in plan, masterly in construction, yet simple in detail. Nave with clerestory, transepts, chancel and E apse, all aisled. Built for missionary Anglo-Catholic priest brothers, James and Thomas Pollock, among working-class terraced housing demolished in the 1960s. Brick with stone dressings and a little diapering. The clerestory windows are paired lancets with circles above. Broad single lancets in the aisles. w front with octagonal turrets, rose window and small porch. The transept ends have smaller turrets. SW tower by *E.F. Reynolds*, 1938, massive and sheer with a saddleback roof, a reworking of his unexecuted design for All Saints, Four Oaks (1908).

The interior is vaulted throughout, in quadripartite ribs. These and the arcades are Bath stone, darkened by much incense. Complex arch mouldings with nice detail where they cross the pier shafting. Clerestory recessed behind high stone arches, with a triforium passage running all round. Pearson's use of the Golden Section in both plan and arcade elevation gives it his typical spacious and noble proportions, at

*Now St Alban and St Patrick, Highgate, reflecting another *Pearson* church nearby in Frank Street, 1896, demolished *c.* 1970.

once aspiring and profoundly restful. The closest parallel is his St Michael, Croydon. The s (St Patrick's) chapel is distinguished by dog-tooth ornament on pier and ribs. Its e end has a complex and intriguing spatial effect: a triple-arched vaulted stone canopy over the altar linked into the vaulting above by ribs leading to a boss with a pelican. The ambulatory, also vaulted, starts as the left bay of the triple canopy. w baptistery also canopied under the gallery.

Furnishings. Original low stone **screen** at the chancel entrance. Iron screen on it by *Pearson*, 1897; **choir stalls** also his. – **Rood beam** and **figures** of 1913, designed by *Frank Pearson*, carved by *Nathaniel Hitch*. The beam has vine trail and a Pelican in its Piety. From St Patrick's. – c18-style **pulpit** by *Romilly Craze*, *c*. 1960. – Octagonal **font** by *Pearson*, 1881. Of stone with bright red veins, perhaps Cornish? – Behind it a **fresco** of Christ with angels and children by *Clayton & Bell*, 1895–6. – s chapel **reredos** of beaten copper by *Myra Bunce* with painted panels by *Kate Bunce*, 1919; wrought-iron **railings** and **gates** by *John Goodman*, 1914. – n **chapel**,wrought-iron *Bromsgrove Guild* **screen** from St Patrick's, **panelling** of 1919 probably by *A.S. Dixon*. **Stained glass.** Central apse window by *Henry Payne*, 1904, bright green, red and gold, with sweeping angels' wings. Flanking it, two by *Sidney Meteyard*, 1926–7. *Clayton & Bell* glass in the ambulatory (single saints) and chapels (small scenes), all between 1883 and 1896. s aisle easternmost by *Morris & Co.*, 1909.

To the e, the **Lench's Trust Almshouses** by *J.A. Chatwin*, 1878–80. A delightful Queen Anne group, the first appearance of the style in Birmingham. Three ranges in an irregular U, with the warden's house in the centre facing the street. Brick with a few sandstone dressings. Steep little pediments with reliefs of flowers in vases, stepped-up window surrounds, and big keystones, all in moulded brick. Star-shaped chimneys, sadly cut down.

Behind houses to the s, the **Birmingham Central Mosque**. Building started in 1968 but was delayed by a shortage of money. Completed in 1982, with dome and minaret, by *William Copeland*.

Finally a brief note on the **Aston University**, n of the Digbeth/Deritend area, beyond Jennens Road, and e of James Watt Queensway. It began as the College of Advanced Technology, with buildings of 1949–55 by *Ashley & Newman* and 1957–65 by the City Architect, *A.G. Sheppard Fidler*. It became a university in 1966. A development plan by *Robert Matthew, Johnson-Marshall & Partners*, was adopted in 1967. Its most notable result was the Library, by *Sir Basil Spence, Glover & Ferguson*, 1972–5. The Lakeside flats along the Queensway are by *Feilden Clegg*, 1998–9.

90. St Alban, Bordesley, by J.L. Pearson, 1879–81. Interior

Walk 4.

Smallbrook and the Gough Estate

Smallbrook Street was built up in the medieval period as the start of the route sw from the Bull Ring. The Hill Street area to its N was built up by the mid C18, the areas w of Suffolk Street and s of Smallbrook Street (now Queensway) from the 1790s. The largest landowner was the Gough family; the Gooch and Inge estates were also involved. The construction of New Street station from 1849 cut the area off from the centre. Its extension s in 1881–5 included the cutting of Station Street, and caused substantial rebuilding. John Bright Street, cut in 1882, was not completely built up until around 1900. On the Gough Estate *James & Lister Lea* were very active in the late C19.

The area was badly bombed in 1940–1. Partly for this reason, the first stretch of the Inner Ring Road, Smallbrook Queensway, was con-

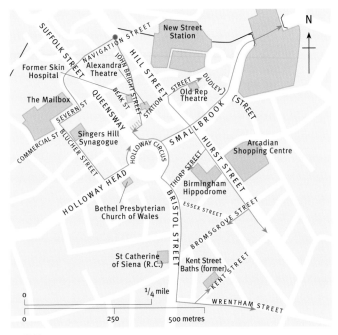

91. Walk 4

structed here in 1957–60. Decline came in the 1970s, but the area remained the city's 'theatreland', and developed as the gay quarter. Hurst Street was designated the city's Chinatown in the early 1990s, with much rebuilding. The construction of the Mailbox in 2000, the new Bull Ring to the E, and the tower at the w end of Smallbrook Queensway, are signs of increased pace here.

Sir Herbert Manzoni

Herbert Manzoni (1899–1972) was City Engineer from 1935 until 1963, in charge of all municipal works from road building to new houses. His achievements and his views have left an enduring mark on Birmingham. From his appointment he advocated redevelopment: 'proper zoning . . . the whole area must be new and it must look completely different'. The high densities required for rehousing dictated blocks of flats. The pioneering Emily Street scheme of 1939 by *Grey Wornum* and *A.C. Tripe*, a parallel to e.g. St Andrew's Gardens in Liverpool, was demolished *c.* 1972. He helped frame the Town Planning Act of 1944 which enabled comprehensive redevelopment nationally. The first high-rise blocks went up in Great Francis Street in 1954. The first Redevelopment Area, Nechells Green (Duddeston and Nechells), was approved in 1950 but not completed until 1972. Manzoni's greatest political ally was (Sir) Frank Price (b. 1926), Chairman of the Public Works Committee 1953–9, a young man committed to sweeping away the cramped housing in which he grew up.

Wide roads were advocated in William Haywood's *The Development of Birmingham* (1918), following the example of Corporation Street, and the Arterial Roads scheme of 1917 put improvement lines on major radial routes. But it was under Manzoni that the Inner Ring Road was planned from 1943 (Act 1946). Financial controls delayed the first section, now Smallbrook Queensway, until 1957–60. The complete circuit was opened by the Queen in 1971.

Major losses for the Ring Road included *Charles Edge*'s Market Hall, 1831–5, Central Library (*see* p. 77), *Jethro Cossins*'s Mason College, 1875, and Liberal Club, 1885, and *Essex, Nicol & Goodman*'s Central Technical College, 1895. But Manzoni had stark views on architecture, saying in 1957, 'I have never been very certain as to the value of tangible links with the past. They are often more sentimental than valuable . . . As to Birmingham's buildings, there is little of real worth in our architecture. Its replacement should be an improvement, provided we keep a few monuments as museum pieces to past ages . . . As for future generations, I think they will be better occupied in applying their thoughts and energies to forging ahead, rather than looking backward.' It is an attitude still alive in the city, ironically now aimed at buildings of Manzoni's time.

92. Rosebery
Buildings, John Bright
Street, by Marcus O.
Type, 1902–3

South and East

The start is the junction of Hill Street and Navigation Street, easily reached from Victoria Square or New Street. We walk s along **John Bright Street**. Cast-iron column with ball finial of 1908, from public lavatories in Hill Street. On the E, the uninspired **Gala Casino** by *Kelly & Surman*, 1963. On the w bulky flats by *B.L.B. Architects*, 2003–5, incorporate the façade of a hotel of 1899–1900 by *A.B. Phipson*: round arches with nice brick detail.* Then the brick and terracotta starts. The **Birmingham School of Speech and Drama** is the former Birmingham Athletic Institute, 1891 by *Ben Corser*, with windows linked vertically. Ground floor of 1950. Two buildings by *Marcus O. Type* mark the corners of Severn Street. **Geoffrey Buildings** of 1901–2, NW, has plain elevations but an original Free Style corner feature, a two-storey canted bay topped by a curved balcony, and a smaller oriel-like bay in front of the shaped gable. Recent appalling sign. **Rosebery Buildings** [92] of 1902–3, sw, was showrooms for the early car maker Heron, with workshop at the rear. A quirky, slightly sinister design with very free flat-topped gables, canted windows, and a corner turret with a sharp prow.

*Demolished 2002, a block of 1901 by *Frederick W. Lloyd* with a big shaped gable on the curve. An excellent landmark.

93. Former Futurist Cinema, John Bright Street, by Arthur Stockwell and Essex & Goodman, 1914–20

On the SE corner of Severn Street, **Cambridge Buildings**, 1884–5 by *Alfred Dickens Perry*, commercial Queen Anne with huge dormers. The former **Futurist Cinema** [93] is by *Arthur Stockwell* of Newcastle upon Tyne, started 1914, slightly simplified during construction by *Essex & Goodman*, and completed 1920. A classical, rather civic, design in pink-red brick and cream terracotta, a contrast with Birmingham work in the same materials. Open Ionic arcade above the entrance. Impressive blank rear elevation on Hill Street. Then the fifteen-bay Neo-Georgian **Borough Buildings**, 1909 by *Marcus O. Type*. English Garden Wall bond brickwork contrasting red stretcher rows and blue brick headers. Centrepiece with open pediment and oval window. The ground floor was another car showroom.

Opposite, the former **Skin Hospital** of 1887 by *James & Lister Lea* (the prominent date 1881 is that of the foundation). Its picturesque, asymmetrical Queen Anne front steps back to fit the narrow tapering site, like Webb & Bell's Law Courts (q.v.), then just being started. Concave leaded cupola over the entrance. Then a shop of 1898 by *Stephen J. Holliday* with a giant arch, and another by *Newton & Cheatle*, 1899–1900, early Neo-Georgian with an oval window to the chamfered corner. **Suffolk Place** runs W here to Suffolk Street Queensway. Visible across it, a Christadelphian meeting house of 1910–11 by *G.A. Birkenhead*, with Baroque doorcase.

Continuing s on John Bright Street, the **Alexandra Theatre**. The auditorium is on the E side. *Owen & Ward*'s original building of 1900–1 here was rebuilt in 1935 by *Roland Satchwell*. The site is constricted, and when the Inner Ring Road was built the opportunity was taken to build a new foyer and entrance, bridging the street: 1967–9 by the *John Madin Design Group*. Stylish glazed façade to Suffolk Street, now with a tacky fascia and canopy. The 1935 front to John Bright Street, with its circular turret, is pierced by the bridge and clad in silver panels. Doors with fan-pattern top lights. *Owen & Ward*'s office range survives at the rear.

Inside, *Satchwell*'s moderne interior is largely intact, refurbished in 1992 by the *Seymour Harris Partnership*. Crush bar with typical panelling and deep cove. A mirror-glass wall contrasts plain and bronzed panels. Tall, shallow auditorium, due to the site. Proscenium arch with bold plain and wavy mouldings running all round; similar balcony fronts. Deeply moulded, domed ceiling rose. *Satchwell*'s entrance foyer and staircase survive.

Beyond, the **Victoria** pub, of 1883 by *Thomson Plevins*, cheerful and eclectic. Ground floor altered probably by *Watson & Johnson*, 1908. Doorways with curly broken pediments, inset canted bays. Good ironwork grille with rosettes on the corner. We go up steps opposite into **Suffolk Street Queensway**, and turn s. On the E the forty-storey **Beetham Tower** by *Ian Simpson Architects*, under construction, 2003–5.* A sheer, utterly dominating, shape faced in fritted glass panels, some coloured pale blue curving disdainfully away from its neighbours to each side. It will include flats and a hotel. Then **Holloway Circus** with roundabout and underpass of 1964–8. On the w the **Sentinels**, two thirty-two-storey towers flanking **Holloway Head**, 1968–71 by *James A. Roberts* in association with the *City Architect*. Simple square shapes, totally dominating, with pale cladding. Battered dark brick bases, altered in the 1990s. To N and s bleak offices and car parks by *Roberts*, 1972–4, the s one incorporating a night club. By the s tower, the **Bethel Presbyterian Church of Wales** by *Roberts*, 1968. A complex and angular little design: triangular church on the first floor, with a copper roof, above a rectangular ground floor of hall, kitchen and caretaker's flat. The church interior is brick-lined, with a Parana pine roof. Traditional layout of pulpit behind communion table.

In the garden inside the **roundabout**, on the w side, mural of horse fair, 1966.† Landscaping by *Birmingham Design Services*, 1998, with a gloomy pagoda of grey granite made in China; being redone, 2005.

---

*Demolished for it the **Amalgamated Engineering Union** building, 1960–1 by *John H.D. Madin*. An elegant, deceptively simple façade of glazed panels and thin concrete mullions, with a recessed balcony. The full-height open staircase was supported on flying bridges and a single column.
†Currently in store, statue of Hebe by *Robert Thomas*, 1966, with pedestal by *L.A. Howles*.

From here **Smallbrook Queensway** runs E. The best piece of mid-C20 urban design in the city, and the only stretch of the Inner Ring Road built as a boulevard, rather than an urban motorway. Much of the effect is due to the S side. First the plain former **Scala House**, offices and cinema by *James A. Roberts*, 1962–4. Then a single six-storey block by *Roberts* of 1958–62 runs as far as the Bull Ring. Grand urban scale, and a good balance between thin concrete mullions, bands of windows, and relief panels. Projecting concrete trough uplighters give it excellent relief. In the centre a glazed section bridges Hurst Street on raking concrete piers.

Now S along **Horse Fair**. Only the E side survives. First, three survivors of four shops by *James & Lister Lea*, 1898–9. Vigorous terracotta street architecture, with big shaped gables and hints of giant arches, showing the influence of Martin & Chamberlain's No. 19 Newhall Street of 1896 (q.v.). Then a much altered C18 survivor (site lease of 1778). Casements with lintels, the top ones perhaps original. On the NE corner of Thorp Street, the former **White Lion** of 1896 by *J. & L. Lea* for Davenports Brewery. Brick with stone dressings, Elizabethan style: giant fluted Corinthian pilasters and a corner spirelet deriving from Burghley House.

Beyond Thorp Street the **Birmingham Royal Ballet** offices, probably by *Essex & Goodman*, 1905–6, altered. Large, mildly Postmodern block behind for studios and practice rooms by the *Seymour Harris Partnership*, 1990. The **Koh-i-Noor** restaurant was three shops of 1899 by *Ballard & Mantel* for Simeon Theodore King, grocer, whose initials appear in cartouches. Rather exotic Jacobean, e.g. the parapets of the bays with little cusped piercings. On the corner of **Essex Street**, shops and the former **Black Lion** pub by *Osborn & Reading*, 1879–80. Canted bays slightly recessed. Partly surviving shopfronts probably of *c.* 1900, perhaps by *Newton & Cheatle*. In Essex Street the **Queen's Tavern** by *J. & L. Lea*, 1894–5.

Now SW down **Bristol Street**. On the corner, a delightful block of 1890 by *Alfred T. Greening*. Wide brick pilasters with acroteria-like tops dying into a deep cove. Between them, tile bands and panels. Stone ground floor by *Peacock & Bewlay*, 1924. Then three little Gothic shops of *c.* 1880, two nastily rendered. **Alfred Allen's** has a big impressive concave gable which looks 1900 Free Style. Actually of 1926 by *T.D. Griffiths*. Original shopfront. Further down, **Bank of Cyprus**, a Neo-Georgian former Municipal Bank of 1929 by *W. Norman Twist*. Nos. 42–44, 1929 by *Cherrington & Stainton*, impressive Neoclassical rather than Neo-Georgian, has first-floor windows effectively set forward in stone architraves between brick pilasters. Behind modern glass, bronze **entrance doors** probably by the *Birmingham Guild*. Opposite on the W side, **St Catherine's** (**R.C.**) Church, 1964–5 by *Bernard James* of *Harrison & Cox*. Round nave, the first in the city to show the effect of the Second Vatican Council. Nicely balanced outside by a tapering campanile. Open-air pulpit with a charming canopy.

On the SE corner of Bromsgrove Street a fascinating group. From the left, No. 101, a rebuilding of 1897. Then Nos. 99 and 100, rare C18 three-storey survivors, probably of 1792–3. First-floor windows with typical segmental lintels with small keystones and stops. Then the **Wellington Hotel** [94], so named by 1818. The left part represents a house of *c.* 1792. Now stuccoed, a storey added, and a big wing built towards Bristol Street with a shallow bow and Corinthian pilasters. This looks convincingly Regency but is all of 1890–1 by *James & Lister Lea*, who also rebuilt the baker's shop to its right. (The 1792 lessee, Richard Avern, was a baker.) Ground floor by *J.P. Osborne & Son*, 1930. The bar has been gutted except for one cubic fireplace of 1930. Good billiard room of 1890 with coved ceiling and lantern.

Along Bristol Street an excellent group of four-storey shops all by *J. & L. Lea*, 1896–7, in brick and variously coloured terracotta. Nos. 76 and 78 have gables with fluted pilasters and segmental pediments (one missing); No. 80 is rather severe classical, with panelled pilasters and built-up gable; Nos. 82–90 have canted bays and windows with tympanum reliefs; Nos. 92–94 are the richest, with first-floor rounded bays in a golden terracotta arcade. Then a two-storey former bank of 1959 by *Yorke, Harper & Harvey*, partly bricked up. Nos. 98–100 by *J. & L. Lea*, 1899–1900, with blocked lintels and alternating steep triangle and semicircular pediments, form the corner to **Wrentham Street**. E down here. In **Kent Street**, N, Art Deco public baths by *Hurley Robinson*, 1931–3. Back in Wrentham Street No. 80 is a glass curtain wall factory by *Rudolf Frankel*, 1948. Added top storey to left end block.

94. Wellington Hotel, Bristol Street, c. 1792, extended by James & Lister Lea, 1890–1

Back to Holloway Circus and E along Smallbrook Queensway. On the N, beyond the tower, the former **Albany Hotel**, 1960–2 by *James A. Roberts*. Concrete frame rising clear at the top, brown brick facings. On the s the long Roberts block. **Hurst Street** runs s under its centre. On its w side, shops of 1899–1900 by *Cox & Silk*, with an octagonal turret, turning the corner into **Thorp Street**. Here on the N, the surviving front range of the **Warwickshire Rifle Volunteers' Drill Hall** of 1880 by *Osborn & Reading*. A typical two-storey Toytown castle. Entrance towers with arrow slits and chunky corbelled turrets, smaller Gothic gabled features, and occasional big dormers.

Back on Hurst Street, **Albany House** of 1963–5 by *Marshman & Warren*, a depressing dark aggregate slab. On the E a former W.H. Smith warehouse of 1956–7, by *H.F. Bayliss* of their architects' department. Beyond Ladywell Walk the **Arcadian** shopping centre by *FaulknerBrowns Architects*, 1990–2. Drum feature with free-standing columns and surrounding cornice. Inside, a Stirlingesque circular courtyard, but the overall effect is poor. Retained fronting Hurst Street, the **Old Fox** pub of 1892 by *J. & L. Lea*. Beyond it, *FaulknerBrowns'* façade breaks up the street front by curving recessions.

On the w side, the **Birmingham Hippodrome** [95] started as assembly rooms of 1895 by *Essex, Nicol & Goodman*. In 1899 *Frederick W. Lloyd* added the 'Tower of Varieties', a combination of stage and circus ring, to the rear. Its tower, a miniature of Blackpool's, lasted until 1963. The concern failed quickly and was reconstructed by *Lloyd* as the Tivoli Theatre in 1900. The auditorium was rebuilt again for Moss Empires in 1924–5 by *Burdwood & Mitchell*. In 1980–1 the *Seymour Harris Partnership* rebuilt everything behind the proscenium.

In 2000–1 *Associated Architects* in association with *Law & Dunbar-Nasmith* replaced the assembly rooms at the front with a new foyer and studios, and added dressing and rehearsal rooms to Thorp Street, N. At first sight a crisp, fashionable essay in slightly deconstructed Modernism; in fact, complex and subtle. A glass front wall between dark green slate-faced piers of unequal heights, a silver canopy and a big projecting panel to the left. Along Inge Street a long copper panel floating free of a dark metal-framed wall filled with orange unbaked terracotta tiles, rather Renzo Piano. All these materials well integrated, helped by the planar approach. The taller left pier and the projecting panel hint unmistakably at 1930s Odeons, just as the steel supporting structure inside the glass wall suggests C19 exhibition halls, and the contrast of copper and terracotta along Inge Street recalls the same combination on e.g. domes on a Frank Matcham theatre: a commentary on the architecture of entertainment. Real history survives in the side wall of the 1899 building along Inge Street, brick and terracotta with three-centred arched niches. Huge red metal flytower of 1980–1. Inside, the 1924–5 auditorium is chaste Neo-Roman, like e.g. the Palace Theatre, Manchester of 1913. Giant fluted Ionic columns enclose three

95. Birmingham Hippodrome, Hurst Street, front by Associated Architecs with Law & Dunbar-Nasmith, 2000–1

bays of boxes on each side, with big segmental pediments above. Long elegant single balcony.

Across Inge Street, a unique survival, the last group of **back-to-back houses** [96] in the city: three of them, Nos. 50–54, to Inge Street, and the entrance to **Court No. 15**, with a row of single pile 'blind backs', Nos. 55–63 Hurst Street. The site was leased by the Gooch Estate in 1789 but the earliest building, No. 50 Inge Street, was not erected until 1809, apparently as an ordinary house. Converted to a back-to-back pair *c.* 1821, and the others added between 1827 and 1831: first No. 52/2 Court 15 to its E, then No. 54/3 Court 15, and finally the Hurst Street terrace. Repaired and converted into a museum and holiday flats by *Derek Clarke* and *Bob Tolley* of *S.T. Walker & Duckham*, 2002–4, for the Birmingham Conservation Trust and National Trust.

The result is a three-storey L-shaped group. The small scale so close to the city centre is typical, and contrasts with e.g. Manchester. Vertical joints mark the phases. Fronts mostly Flemish bond, courtyard walls cheaper Flemish stretcher bond. The back-to-backs have one room on each floor, linked by newel staircases placed against the middle partition walls. Courtyard entry on Inge Street with a once-common Birmingham design of serif numberplate. Sash windows, some recessed, some flush in moulded frames. Typical Birmingham moulded lintels to the first-floor windows on Hurst Street. First-floor bay on the corner facing Inge Street. In the courtyard two reconstructed late C19 ground-floor canted bays with diagonal glazing bars. A few original fittings: part of a staircase in No. 50 Inge Street/1 Court No. 15, and stencilling restored from original evidence; rooms left unrestored in No. 2, with a surviving fireplace; staircase and partly tiled later C19 fireplace in No. 57 Hurst Street. At the rear of the courtyard, two much-rebuilt wash houses.

A few buildings worth mentioning further down **Hurst Street**. On the NW corner of Bromsgrove Street, the former **Australian Bar** by *J. & L. Lea*, 1897. Small Neo-Georgian extension by *Batemans*, 1930. W along **Bromsgrove Street**, the former **Rose & Crown**, 1900 by *William Jenkins*, with his favourite bargeboarded gables. Brick, four tall storeys. Further down Hurst Street on the W, a range of 1931 by *Alfred J. Dunn*, two storeys with pediments and banded piers, originally car show-rooms. On the E, the **Village Inn** is early C19, the ground floor rebuilt in 1887 by *C.J. Hodson* and altered recently. Large former Fisher and Ludlow factory of 1935 by *C.F. Lawley Harrod*, with long banded windows. At the corner of Sherlock Street the **White Swan**, early C19, completely re-cast by *J.B. Surman*, 1937.

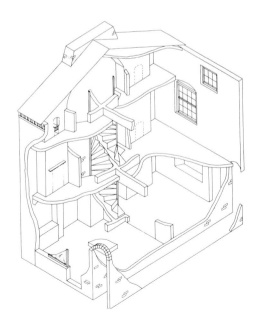

96. Nos. 50–54 and Court No. 15 Inge Street, 1809–31. Section drawing

Back to Smallbrook Queensway and N along **Hill Street**. On the W, the travertine-faced **Albany Banqueting Suite**, 1975 by *James A. Roberts*.* On the E, **Centre City**, a twenty-storey tower by *R. Seifert & Partners*, 1972–5. The cornice responds to its neighbours. Beyond on the SE corner of Station Street, the **Crown Inn**, stucco classical of c. 1881, probably by *Thomson Plevins*. Sober compared to his Victoria, with alternating single and triplet windows. Original ground floor with Corinthian pilasters. **Station Street** has New Street station on the N (see p. 116), with the *City Architect*'s twenty-storey residential **Stephenson Tower** of 1965–6. On the S the former **Shaftesbury Coffee House and Temperance Hotel**, a plain trabeated design by *J.P. Sharp & Co.*, 1890. C19 railway companies encouraged these near stations to cut drinking by staff and passengers. Further along the **Electric Cinema**, 1909 by *Bertie Crewe*, rebuilt 1936–7 by *Cecil E.M. Fillmore*. Refronted in 1981–2 and again in 2004. Inside a 1937 staircase. Then a former wine merchant, now a restaurant, of 1890–1 by *J.P. Sharp & Co.* A commercial mixture of pilasters, basket arches, and upcurving Baroque cornice.

The **Old Rep Theatre** is the best building in the street: 1912–13 by *S.N. Cooke*. (For the current theatre, *see* Broad Street, p. 145). Austere monumental-classic, fashionable for theatres c. 1910, cf. Albert Richardson's Opera House, Manchester. This is Greek drama, not a circus. Giant Ionic pilasters, delicately detailed, disappear into the tower-like end bays. Windows with heavy architraves and discs; Greek key and guilloche friezes. Semi-octagonal dormer like a lookout. Foyer and stairs have a heavy dado in brown and black marble contrasted with a delicate Doric entablature. Small auditorium with an extremely steep rake, because of the shallow site. Concave balcony with more Greek key on the soffit. Doric proscenium, austere and dramatic, with a huge frieze.

Finally the **Market Hotel** on the corner of Dudley Street. 1883 by *Plevins & Norrington*.† Warm orange brick with sandstone dressings and terracotta panels; a mixture of big bays with rounded ends and pilasters with foliage panels and little curly pediments. Built as part-hotel, part-warehouse for H.E. Jordan, pram maker: his initials and Plevins's appear on terracotta plaques.

Back to Smallbrook and E towards the Bull Ring. Beyond Centre City on the N, **Norfolk House**, by *Hurley Robinson & Son*, 1958–60, a convincing piece of its time: concrete-framed, with windows separated by green slate panels. Charming wavy canopy with circular glass light-holes. The E end office entrance is cantilevered over Dudley Street, described when built as 'a Venetian effect'!

---

*On the site of St Jude's church by *C.W. Orford*, 1850–1, demolished 1971.
†J.P. Norrington was the Borough Surveyor: interesting evidence of Plevins' many roles.

The Mailbox and Severn Street

From the junction of Hill Street and Navigation Street a second walk loops to Holloway Circus. In **Navigation Street** on the N, New Street Station **signal box** [97] by *Bicknell & Hamilton* with *W.R. Headley, Regional Architect, British Railways London Midland Region*, 1964–5. One of a series of boxes they designed for the West Coast electrification, cf. Rugby and Weaver Junction, Cheshire. Here the restricted site produced a compact, forceful four-storey structure, clad in massively corrugated rough concrete. Deep fascia above the control rooms. On the S side, lighting and paving by *Thomas Heatherwick Studios*; under the flyover, lighting of garlands and globes by *Mark Pimlott*, both of 2000–1 as an introduction to **The Mailbox**, immediately beyond. A former **postal sorting office** of 1970, the largest in England, by the *Ministry of Public Building & Works* in association with *Hubbard Ford & Partners*, reconstructed as shops, flats, and two hotels in 1999–2001. Lead architects *Associated Architects*, a design-and-build contract, with *Weedon Partnership* and *TCN*.

The front has real urban presence. It quotes no historical motifs but is irresistibly reminiscent of a huge Renaissance palazzo: stone base, red rendered elevation with tall windows hinting at pilasters, big central entrance up steps, dark metal and glass attic. Inside the impression is confirmed by a long narrow open courtyard, constrained by the steel grid of the sorting office. Supporting piers have dark metal framing and terracotta panels. At the w, escalators lead to a corridor and a canalside restaurant. This is a private palace; the public are kindly admitted, but it belongs to the people who shop at Harvey

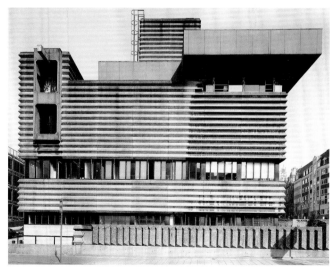

97. Signal box, Navigation Street, by Bicknell & Hamilton, 1964–5

98. Athol Masonic Hall (former synagogue), by Richard Tutin, 1827. Interior

Nichols. The s elevation still has dark aggregate and cast glass panels of 1970.

It faces **Severn Street**, laid out by the Gooch Estate in 1809. Its s side is of great interest. The **Athol Masonic Hall** [98] is a remarkable survival, a former synagogue of 1827 by *Richard Tutin*, the predecessor of Singers Hill (*see* below). Its modest classical front has pilasters, cornice, and low attic. Windows and brick panels of 1891 by *Essex & Nicol*, who also reconstructed the lobby. The main hall beyond is articulated by plain pilasters, above a high dado. Deeply coved ceiling. At the s end the former **Ark**, a handsome Greek Revival niche with Doric columns *in antis* and a rich entablature with palmettes. At the rear, a Banqueting Hall added for the freemasons in 1871 by *Henry Naden*. Opulent ceiling with beams supported by big consoles. At each end a fireplace with a shouldered lintel, and a large mirror above framed by Corinthian columns and a segmental pediment. The decoration includes five- and six-pointed stars, suitable for a lodge with many Jewish members.

Further w, the former **Severn Street School**. The first Nonconformist school in the town, started in 1809. The First Day School founded here in 1845 was the epitome of the civic gospel.* First the former playground wall, and behind it the original 1809 building, reconstructed and extended upwards in 1851–2. A massive ten-bay, two-storey block. Impressively industrial appearance. Red brick, blue brick dressings, iron-framed windows. Big cornice, raised centrepiece with 'BRITISH SCHOOL' cut in the frieze. Cast-iron columns inside. To its w an extension of 1869–70 in similar materials by *Yeoville Thomason*, linked by a wooden bridge. Upper classroom with a good clerestory roof. Now partly hidden by a *Martin & Chamberlain* block of 1879–80, excellent Italian Gothic in red brick with terracotta decorative panels. Its street front has a central gable rising from a hipped roof: cusped round window above three transomed lancets. Large upstairs classroom with a complex and beautiful roof: tie-beams, arch braces, Gothic arcading, and end braces supporting the purlins at the hips. Staircase in quarter-round w projection. Beyond to the w, a three-storey house of *c.* 1809 with simple doorcase. Inside, original six panel doors.

s into **Blucher Street**. On the E, **Singers Hill Synagogue** [99] (Birmingham Hebrew Congregation), 1855–6 by *Yeoville Thomason*. The earliest surviving so-called 'cathedral synagogue' in Britain. Italianate, in red brick with dark stone dressings; paired round-headed windows and big bracket cornice. Entrance front with a triple arcade and a rose window in the gable, delightfully recessed behind wings. The blunt parapet of the arcade probably of 1937, when the whole gable wall was rebuilt one bay w by *Harry W. Weedon & Partners*, to increase capacity. Oscar Deutsch, for whom Weedon designed Odeons, was president of the synagogue. In the wings, round-headed doorways with leaded hoods of 1957–9 by *Cotton, Ballard & Blow*, part of alterations for a children's synagogue, N, and washing areas, s. *Thomason*'s side elevations have two tiers of windows in shallow round-headed blank arches (cf. the Law Society, Temple Street, p. 121). On the s, beyond the synagogue, the former **Jewish School**, also *Thomason*. The w part of 1862, originally of two storeys. In 1884 the top storey was added, a first-floor Council Room formed, marked by round-headed windows, and the two-storey E block built.

Sumptuous interior. Seven-bay arcades with Corinthian columns above the galleries, and square piers, with very Byzantine leaf capitals, below. The treatment owes as much to Wren, e.g. St Andrew Holborn, as to Italy. Barrel vault with Thomason's interlaced heart ornament on the ribs. Apsed E end, beyond a grand arch with paired attached piers

*It was a Quaker Sunday School, founded by the merchant and peace campaigner Joseph Sturge to teach adults and poor children. Its leader for many years was Alderman William White, chairman of the Improvement Committee which built Corporation Street. George Cadbury taught here from 1859, and in 1903 recorded meeting five former mayors at the teachers' Sunday breakfast.

99. Singers Hill Synagogue, Blucher Street, by Yeoville Thomason, 1855–6. Interior

supporting free-standing columns; modern Ark. The rich mid-C19 impression owes much to the two tiers of original gilded metal **chandeliers**. Galleries reconstructed and ground floor reseated by *Weedon* in 1937, retaining ornate C19 supporting trusses. His w extension contains a deep gallery. – **Bimah** (pulpit) of 1988 using C19 pieces. – **Stained glass.** An unusual series of *Hardman* windows, mostly of late 1940s–1962; some later windows upstairs (dates commemorated 1975–6). They are figurative and mildly Expressionist, but all faces are concealed, e.g. the dramatic Moses with the Tablets (upper level, s). A series of Jewish festivals (lower level, N). Fascinating social documentation, e.g. the Exiles Return to Israel (lower level, s). Behind, *Thomason*'s school **hall** of 1862 with blank arcading, reconstructed as a social centre in 1934 by *John Goodman*, who also refitted the Council Room in a solid, mildly streamlined way.

In Commercial Street, opposite, a Gothic factory of 1872 by *Thomason*. Further along Blucher Street, on the w the **Craven Arms** pub of 1906 by *Arthur Edwards*, with splendid terracotta: blue ground floor, golden-brown Holders Brewery plaques above. Gutted 2005. Continuing s down the hill, on the w, a former furniture factory by *J. Seymour Harris & Partners*, 1954–5, good Festival of Britain style, with glazed curtain walling, rubble-stone-faced basement with glass-block windows, and brick staircases with projecting headers. Opposite, **Trefoil House**, with a big semicircular bow, by *Holland W. Hobbiss & Partners*, 1962. On the corner of **Holloway Head**, **Lee Bank Business Centre** is a City Council flatted factory of 1957–8 by *Philip Skelcher & Partners*. E from here to **Holloway Circus** (*see* p. 200).

Outer Areas and Suburbs

Edgbaston: the Nineteenth-century Suburb

'Unquestionably the most important suburb of Birmingham, the favourite place of residence for the professional men, merchants and traders of the busy town which it adjoins.' So said the first issue of *Edgbastonia* magazine, 1881. It is still largely true. Edgbaston is a middle-class suburb unique in Britain in size, closeness to the centre, the low densities of its wealthiest roads, and the way it was developed by the Gough-Calthorpe family. In David Cannadine's words, 'The town obtained its suburb under aristocratic auspices, and the landed family drew its income largely from urban revenue.'

Sir Richard Gough bought the estate in 1717, and his grandson was created Lord Calthorpe in 1796. A few leases were granted from 1786 in the triangle between the Hagley and Harborne roads, nearest the growing town, but it was George, 3rd Lord Calthorpe, who started replacing agricultural tenants with 'gentlemen and tradesmen' in 1810. Between then and 1814 Calthorpe, Frederick and George roads were cut, near Five Ways, and Wellington and Sir Harry's roads off the Bristol Road. The area between Hagley and Westbourne roads followed after 1820. Early C19 booms and slumps meant that many roads took years to complete. Wellington Road e.g. was almost empty, except the E end, until the mid 1830s. The early 1840s saw very few new leases.

The first agent, John Harris, started the policy of attracting the wealthiest by 'acquiring a reputation for giving every indulgence and attention' to lessees: 'those people who, having acquired a moderate competence, wish to retire to a small country house, and therefore take just as much land as would be sufficient for the purpose'. Many local builders, however, developed several plots in succession. They also built, in bigger blocks, artisans' houses on the edges of the estate, e.g. in Sun Street and Balsall Heath Road. Increasingly through the C19 a horseshoe-shaped area of lower- to middle-middle class roads, such as the Frederick and George roads area and the district SE of Bristol Road, protected the upper-middle-class core. The 3rd Lord was a devout Evangelical, related to William Wilberforce, and he encouraged charitable and educational institutions: the Deaf and Dumb Asylum in 1814 and the Botanical Gardens in 1831.

Development moved SW with Arthur Road, started in 1848, and Ampton Road in 1850. The 1880s building boom saw a start on the

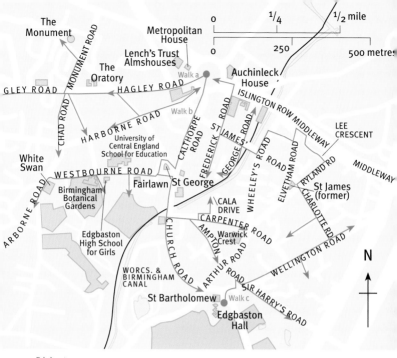

100. Edgbaston

Somerset and Farquhar roads area, but after this the area failed to equal
the growth of rival areas like Moseley and parts of Kings Norton. The
estate passed in 1910 to the Anstruther-Gough-Calthorpe family, and
some land sales began: to the University, and in the 1930s to the hospitals board and King Edward's School.

Houses are mostly detached, with some semi-detached pairs. Larger
plots have ample, well-treed grounds. Only in the earliest development,
e.g. the city end of Hagley Road, are there terraces. The estate is a
wonderful display of C19 domestic architectural styles. The 3rd Lord
Calthorpe's conservatism can be seen in the long survival of the
classical tradition. The earliest houses seem to be builders' designs, in
the Wyatt-influenced local Georgian. Greek Revival appears c. 1820, and
stucco often covers brick. Proportions become taller and more dominating. Ground floors are frequently rusticated; sometimes there are
pilasters above. *Charles Edge* probably introduced c. 1830 Soane's language of cut-back wall planes, and then the Neo-Palladian manner used
by C.R. Cockerell. *John Fallows* used Soane's incised ornament,
'Graeco-Egyptian' with tapering architraves, and also picturesque
Tudor. Neo-Palladian develops into Victorian Italianate. From 1840
Frederic Fiddian, *Samuel Hemming* and others adopted first a heavy,
severe manner, then an increasingly rich one with ornate detail,
especially cornices. They were developers as well as architects, as
slightly later was *Yeoville Thomason*, who introduced brick 'Lombardic'
polychromy. *J.J. Bateman* introduced c. 1845 the rural Italian villa,

asymmetrical with a low tower, deriving from Nash and J.B. Papworth's *Rural Residences* (1818). *J.A. Chatwin*'s work looks Victorian from his very first design, Nos. 38–39 Frederick Road, 1850. In the 1850s he used a wild Jacobean, perhaps inspired by *S.S. Teulon*, whose rogue-Gothic St James of 1852–3 is now flats. Full-blown domestic Gothic Revival arrived as late as 1855 with *J.H. Chamberlain*'s No. 12 Ampton Road, which shocked contemporaries. Around 1900 *W.H. Bidlake, J.L. Ball* and others designed several fine houses in the Edgbaston Park Road and Farquhar Road area, Arts and Crafts-influenced (for these *see* p. 250 etc.).

John Madin's plan of 1957 (*see* topic box, below) successfully maintained the estate's character in the later C20. At the start of the C21, the greatest threat is commercial redevelopment, with proposals for e.g. Edgbaston Shopping Centre and the Chamber of Commerce site very damaging to Madin's plot densities.

Madin's Edgbaston Plan of 1957

The Calthorpe Estate faced serious problems after the Second World War. The largest Victorian houses, built for families with servants, had become uneconomic; and nearest the centre, around Five Ways, many had become offices. The Estate wanted to increase commercial revenue, and attract middle-class families and single residents, but retain the character of the area. In 1957 Sir Richard Anstruther-Gough-Calthorpe commissioned the young *John Madin* to replan the Estate.

Madin's imaginative scheme zoned the Five Ways area for offices, with high-rise blocks, but a maximum of one-third plot coverage. It is a plan firmly in the central tradition of C20 Modernism. The rows of office towers on Hagley Road recall schemes such as London's Route XI, but with extensive landscaping which cleverly disguises car-parking areas. Further s and w, C19 mansions were replaced by closes of detached houses, and high-quality groups of low- and high-rise flats, e.g. Stonebury, Norfolk Road, Cala Drive (*see* p. 228) and Warwick Crest (*see* p. 227). They use a simple language of brick and tile cladding. Again there is generous landscaping, often retaining old garden walls and gatepiers. Two shopping centres, the Eastern and Western 'Hearts', were built at the junction of Carpenter Road and Wheeleys Road, and on Harborne Road opposite the White Swan. The plan is a perfect example of what Pevsner described, referring to Gropius & Fry's Impington Village College, Cambs., as 'austerity of forms, but . . . humanizing . . . these forms by their free and happy grouping and their placing amid lawn and trees'. The residential areas remain popular after forty years, but a recent change of policy by the Estate threatens the office area with intensive redevelopment.

a) Hagley Road and Harborne Road

We start at **Five Ways**. Roundabout and underpass of 1969–71. Clockwise from the N (Ladywood Middleway), the **Broadway** complex by the *John Madin Design Group*, 1973–6, brick-faced, typical of their later work. Across Broad Street, **Auchinleck House** by *J. Seymour Harris & Partners*, 1961–2, has a commanding fourteen-storey tapered end towards the junction, topped by a wavy canopy. Refaced 2000 by *Ove Arup & Partners* with mural by *Bruce McLean*. **Lloyds Bank** by *P.B. Chatwin*, 1908–9, is effectively treated as two sides of a square Palladian villa, with a giant Ionic order and open central pediments.

No. 60 **Calthorpe Road** [101], in the fork with Harborne Road, is of 1814–15 by *George Jones*, builder, for himself. A catalogue of good local Late Georgian details: porch with quadrants, flanked by windows with fluted pillarets; tripartite window above divided by slim fluted pillarets; *oeil-de-bœuf* in the pediment. Later C19 wings removed. Rear extension by *JMDG*, 1970–1. In front a late C19 Gothic **clock**. Across Harborne Road the huge Neo-Georgian **Marriott Hotel** by *Cotton, Ballard & Blow*, 1958–60, built for Tube Investments. In front, **statue** of Joseph Sturge by *John Thomas*, 1859.

At the NW corner the nineteen-storey **Metropolitan House** [102], 1972–4 by the *John Madin Design Group*, breaking the conception of square towers with wings offset from a central core, and canted glazed corners. Behind in Ladywood Middleway, the former **Lench's Trust Almshouses** of 1858 by *Hornblower & Haylock*, Tudor with shaped gables.

101. No. 60 Calthorpe Road, by George Jones, 1814–15

Metropolitan House starts **Hagley Road**, with mid-C20 towers of Madin's plan, mostly seventeen or eighteen storeys, interspersed with Georgian survivors. On the N, intrusive **Tricorn House** by *Sidney Kaye, Eric Firmin & Partners*, 1973–4, then **Hagley House** by *Madins*, 1963–5, exposed concrete structure and glass mosaic facing panels. On the S, **Edgbaston Shopping Centre** by *T.P. Bennett & Son*, 1964–6; No. 54 by the *JMDG*, 1974–6; **Lyndon House** by *Madin*, 1962–4, its mosaic now replaced by render. No. 64 of 1795, by the builder *Charles Surman Smith*, is the earliest survivor of the Edgbaston development. Doric porch, flanked by triplet windows with thin colonnettes. On the N Nos. 93–95, early C19, have Tuscan porches with garland friezes. Nos. 97–107 [103], a terrace of six, and No. 109 beyond, are part of a symmetrical scheme of 1819–20, unusual for Edgbaston; the balancing left-hand terrace was never built. Developer *John Harris*, plumber; *Thomas* and *Joseph Bateman* acted as surveyors and probably designed them. Handsome Greek Doric doorcases (No. 109); giant pilasters above, early for Edgbaston. Façaded by *JMDG c.* 1971. No. 111 by *Harry Bloomer & Son*,

102.
Metropolitan
House, Hagley
Road, by the
John Madin
Design Group,
1972–4

103. Nos. 97–109 Hagley Road, probably by Thomas and Joseph Bateman, 1819–20

1965, has a low circular forebuilding and office block behind. Nos. 119–121, early C19 with handsome semicircular bays. No. 123 of 1965–7 was the *John Madin Design Group*'s own offices, brown brick with long horizontals balanced by Louis Kahn-style stair-towers. The **Plough and Harrow** is by *John Fallows*, 1832–3, in Tudor Revival for Lord Calthorpe, who disliked it as 'ultra-gothick'. Orange brick with eroded pink sandstone dressings. Three s gables, the central one shaped. Big cusped mullion-and-transom windows. The w side has a two-storey entrance with shaped gable, and flanking gables pierced by chimneystacks. Large later C19 E extension. Charming bargeboarded **stables** of *c.* 1825, classical in form but with Tudor detail. Cupola with boar's-head weathervane.

On the s side beyond Highfield Road No. 76, Early Victorian with a Tuscan porch. Then Nos. 78–84, pairs with central bargeboarded gables, and Nos. 86–92, linked pairs. Doorcases with fluted pillarets similar to Nos. 97–107, so perhaps by *Thomas* and *Joseph Bateman*. On the N side **Newland House** by *J.P. Osborne & Son*, 1962–4.

Then on the N side the **Oratory** [104]. John Henry Newman established the English Congregation of the Oratory of St Philip Neri in 1849, at first where St Anne's Deritend now is (*see* p. 192). The Edgbaston site was bought in 1850. The buildings are tremendously Italian, befitting a Counter-Reformation order. Newman thought Pugin a 'bigot' and loved classical architecture, writing, in 1850, 'Now is not a *dome beautiful*, "poetical and solemn"? Is not a row of pillars beautiful? By my taste they are as beautiful, nay more so, than any thing in Gothic.' He lived here even after he was made a Cardinal in 1879, until his death in 1890.

The street front, in red brick with stone dressings, starts with the **Oratory House**, a sober Renaissance palazzo by *Terence Flanagan*, 1851, with just a Michelangelesque doorcase and string course with Vitruvian scroll moulding. To its W the former **School Hall**, by *Henry Clutton*, 1861–2, beautiful Italian Romanesque, with arched windows above a blank ground floor. The entrance here leads into *Clutton*'s cloister of 1872–3, strikingly treated with stone bands reinforcing the brick vaults, and short columns on high tapering bases. The side against the school, never completed, has part arches supporting a corridor.

Opposite, the cloister runs behind the façade of the **Church**. Newman obtained drawings in 1851 from a French architect, *Louis Joseph Duc*,* and had a model of a basilica made. A temporary church of 1853 by *Flanagan* perhaps incorporated some of these ideas. In 1858 *John Hungerford Pollen* added a small s chapel and the St Philip's Chapel beyond it. The present church by *E. Doran Webb*, 1903–9, built as a memorial to Newman, reflects his tastes and early ideas. Latin-cross plan with seven-bay basilican nave, short transepts, dome on pendentives and apsed sanctuary. Sumptuous materials: arcades of pink Breccia marble on green Swedish marble bases; sandstone Corinthian capitals and continuous cornice. Corinthian pilasters on the aisle walls. The barrel vault with big dormers defines an impressive but static space. The W gallery and the side chapels betray Webb's preference for English prototypes, slipping into English Jacobean, with chubby part-fluted columns, moulded arches, and bulgy balustrade. Domed NE chapel (**Shrine of St Philip**), by *G.B. Cox*, 1927, with columns of red Languedoc marble. Simple SE **chapel**. Beyond it, **St Philip's Chapel** by *Pollen*, 1858. Triple-arched entrance screen.

What distinguishes the church are its **decoration** and **fittings**. Marble everywhere, richest in the sanctuary which has red African and green Mexican onyx. Only the finest pieces can be listed. – **High Altar** by *Dunstan Powell*, 1899, red marble, with curved ends and supporting cherubs. – **Baldacchino** by *Sensi* of Trastevere. – Apse **mosaic** of the Coronation of the Virgin. – **Choir gallery**, s transept, by *Sensi*. – N transept **altar**, C17, brought in 1911 from Sant'Andrea della Valle in Rome. Statue of the Virgin, French C20, in a niche by *F.A. Walters*. The Siberian onyx columns were intended for Westminster Cathedral. – **Altar rails** here and in the sanctuary also from Sant'Andrea. – **Pulpit**, 1911. – **Font** by *Dunstan Powell*, 1912. Oval alabaster basin carved by *Bridgemans*, bronze cover with St John the Baptist, made by *Hardmans*. – SE chapel **altar** by *Pollen*, 1858. – **Altarpiece** in St Philip's Chapel by *G.G. Scott Jun.*, 1880. Chellaston alabaster, with angels supporting the central frame.

*Not, as was long thought, E.E. Viollet-le-Duc. The church faces N but ritual directions are used here.

104. Oratory Church, Hagley Road, by E. Doran Webb, 1903–9. Interior

The **Oratory House** has Renaissance details matching the exterior. Panelled **refectory**; cornice decorated with anthemia and corner pulpit. Cardinal Newman's **study** is preserved intact. The finest room is the **library**, by *Pollen*, above his St Philip's Chapel. Long and narrow, with low clerestory lighting, continuous iron **gallery**, and original **seating**.

Continuing w along Hagley Road, **St Philip's Sixth Form College** by *Paul Bonham Associates*, 1968–9. **Windsor Terrace** of 1845, perhaps by *J.R. Botham*, runs N. Stucco pairs with ground-floor windows in shallow reveals. Further w, mid-C19 shops, ending in the **Ivy Bush** pub on the NE corner of Monument Road, reconstructed 1929, probably by *J.P. Osborne & Son*. **Monument Road** itself has early to mid-C19 houses, and further N **The Monument**, or **Perrott's Folly**, an impressive Gothick tower of 1758. Massive two-storey base chamfered into a slim five-storey octagon with pointed windows, stone battlements and circular stair-turret.

Back on Hagley Road the N side has late C19 shops: Nos. 189–195 by *Bland & Cossins*, 1882, severe Queen Anne, and Nos. 197–199 by *Radclyffe & Watson*, 1888–9, rich Jacobean in brown terracotta and red brick, with giant fluted Ionic pilasters. **St Chad's Court** by *Diamond Partnership*, 1990–1, engulfs a good five-bay Late Georgian house with unusual detailing, e.g. the windows with side panels. No. 215 is a three-bay early C19 house with a mid-C19 right-hand bay and heavy porch. Original doorcase repositioned, facing Stirling Road.

Beyond Stirling Road the **Warwickshire Masonic Temple** by the *John Madin Design Group*, 1970. A blank brick block sculpturally treated, the piers recessed between panels above, but splaying out below, where the panels chamfer inwards. Further w, the **Thistle Hotel**, a circular 'Dekotel' with lower-level car parking, by *Duke & Simpson*, 1970–1.

Back E along the S side and first down **Chad Road**. On the NW, Italianate villas of *c.* 1850; Nos. 8 and 9 a mirrored pair probably by *J.J. Bateman*. On the SE side Nos. 16–17, 1853 by *Deakin & Phipson*. No. 15 of 1838 must be by *Charles Edge*, who did similar contemporary houses in the road, now demolished. A good three-bay villa. Slightly projecting centre with Doric porch. Back and into **Vicarage Road**. Nos. 3–8, E side, are of 1838–40. No. 3 particularly attractive, with incised pilasters and iron veranda.

Back E along Hagley Road and SE down **Highfield Road**. On the SW a pair of 1838 have pediments and side consoles, and iron verandas. On the NE a Greek Revival villa of *c.* 1830. On the N corner with Harborne Road the **Birmingham Chamber of Commerce**, by *Madin*, 1959–60. Edgbaston's first tall post-war building. Four-storey block for the Chamber itself. Recessed ground floor with green Serpentino marble piers and blue and grey facings. Mullions of cream Travertine with Serpentino fillets. The w end cleverly disguises differing floor heights. Linked by a bridge, infilled by *Associated Architects*, 1996, to a simpler eight-storey block with aluminium mullions and a framing Travertine band, forming a T-shape. The foyer retains a *John Piper* mosaic: bright greens, yellows and oranges on a background of black and dark green with a little blue [105]. Rough-textured finish with gloss-fired tiles set proud. An urban landscape, perhaps, with tall towers. Highfield Road to the s has consistent, mainly semi-detached villas of 1830–45.

In **Harborne Road** to the sw, No. 89, roguish Jacobean revival of 1851 for the builder George Branson, almost certainly by *J.A. Chatwin*. Entrance with alternating banded Ionic columns, canted bay above, flanking square bays with V-shaped central projections. Opposite, houses of 1825–9, Nos. 38–40 with Doric doorcases, No. 46 particularly attractive in orange-red brick. Delicate doorcase with incised pilasters and lintel.

Now NE along Harborne Road back to Five Ways. On the N, **Neville House** [106], by *Douglas Hickman* of the *John Madin Design Group*, 1975–6. A beautifully crisp Miesian glass box, the ground floor recessed behind piers, on a chamfered base of small square rough-textured stone. On the s, pairs of 1876–7 built by *John Barnsley & Son*.

105. Birmingham Chamber of Commerce, Harborne Road, by John H.D. Madin, 1959–60. Detail of mural by John Piper

106. Neville House, Harborne Road, John Madin Design Group (Douglas Hickman), 1975–6

b) Calthorpe Road and Carpenter Road, south to the Old Church

Calthorpe Road runs sw from Five Ways. On the SE, No. 12 by *John H.D. Madin*, 1961–2, an elegant slab running NW–SE linked to a lower block extending SW. Dark marble-clad verticals and restrained mosaic panels. Characteristic recessed entrance. Well refurbished in 1999 with new recessed equipment floor. On the NW, the horrible **Apex House** development by *Hitchman Stone*, 1990. Then semi-detached pairs of 1876 etc. built by *John Barnsley & Sons*, the central one removed for an inert office scheme by the *Weedon Partnership*, 1988.

On the SE beyond St James Road, detached villas of *c.* 1815–20. No. 19 has a later C19 porch and open arcade, No. 20 a big doorcase with incised ornament, and windows in segment-headed recesses, No. 21 a doorcase with open pediment, No. 22 a more unusual one with banded Doric columns and vestigial pediment. Later C19 bays. No. 23 is an elegant picturesque Italian villa deriving from Nash. **Greenfield Crescent**, developed in 1875–7, runs N here. On the SW corner, No. 19, almost certainly by *J.H. Chamberlain*, with foliage panels above the ground-floor windows, and a gable with bargeboards bracketed off the top lintel. Houses beyond mostly by *Henry Naden*; nice bargeboards on Nos. 12–15. On the E, Nos. 1–2, probably by *G.I. Haylock*, Jacobean hinting at Queen Anne, with little pediments to the canted bays.

Continuing sw down Calthorpe Road, Nos. 24–27 on the SE have Doric porches with correct triglyphs. On the NW good pairs of *c*. 1830, especially Nos. 41–42 with incised giant pilasters set short of the corners. No. 36 of 1830 by *John Fallows* is a three-bay 'Graeco-Egyptian' villa with single-storey wings. Fluted baseless Corinthian columns to the porch, similar capitals to the first-floor pilasters. Tapering window architraves. A careful balance of horizontals and verticals. No. 35 [107], of 1829 by *Fallows*, faces sw. At first sight cool Greek Revival, with full Doric portico and deep attic, but the detail is restless. The upper windows break the cornice (perhaps an alteration, but the mouldings return); the lower have segmental heads clamped between the paired pilaster strips. Round-headed lancets flank the entrance. Opposite on the SE, No. 31, now the core of **St George's School**, of *c*. 1830 by *Fallows*. Round-arched windows below, Egyptian above. Extended NE by *J.A. Chatwin*, 1893, a section with a parapet and then a small hipped roof, and further. Rear hall by *Jackson & Edmonds*, 1961. Low junior school block with small monopitch by *Kelly & Surman*, 1971.

St George's church stands prominently on an island site in the angle between Highfield and Westbourne roads. Grey-brown Alvechurch sandstone. Six-bay nave and aisles by *J.J. Scoles*, 1836–8, chancel by *Charles Edge*, 1855. In 1884–5 *J.A. Chatwin* built a new, bigger nave and s aisle, making the original nave his N aisle. His SE tower remains a two-storey stump. Edge's octagonal NE turret is overwhelmed by the new

107. No. 35 Calthorpe Road, by John Fallows, 1829

nave. Scoles's N elevation has typical 1830s big lancets, thin uniform buttresses, and corbelled parapet. Chatwin tactfully repeats this on the s, but adds a clerestory of sharp paired lancets with trefoiled heads. His E window has five grouped lancets in a single arch. His w front has very plain lancets and an ornate rose window (but has lost its pinnacles). One tall 1838 pinnacle remains poignantly at the NW.

The **interior** is unexpectedly good. Scoles's work is tall and airy. His surviving N arcade has very thin circular piers with four attached half-shafts. Panelled canted ceiling. Edge's former chancel arch follows Scoles's C13 style with richer mouldings, including filleted shafts. N and w galleries with E.E. arcaded fronts probably by *Edge*, 1856, the N infilled for meeting rooms. Chatwin makes a virtue of necessity by raising his new clerestory above the older work. The result, with C13-style four-shaft arcade columns, is nobly proportioned. It recalls Gilbert Scott, and the wide tall E bay parallels Scott's favourite church, All Souls Haley Hill, Halifax. Wall-shafts between the clerestory windows end on leaf corbels just above the arcade piers. Mannered details: the easternmost wall-shaft ends in a curl of stone across the arch mouldings, the chancel arch has corbels with shafts stepping curiously inwards.

The wide E nave bay is a preaching space, confirmed by *Chatwin*'s open stone **pulpit** of 1885. Circular top linked by ribs to a polygonal base. Alabaster cresting. Matching low **screen**. – **Choir stalls** and **clergy stalls**, typical *Chatwin* of 1888–9 with scrolled tops and carvings of angels and Evangelists, made by *Bridgeman*. – Mosaic **chancel floor** with Evangelical symbols and Agnus Dei in roundels. – Big wooden **reredos** by *P.B. Chatwin*, 1903, also made by *Bridgeman*. – Oak **screen** to the N (Lady) chapel by *P.B. Chatwin*, 1905–6. – **Organ**, chancel s, by *Brindley & Foster*, 1890. Case with delicate trumpeting angels. – Good late C19 **stained glass**. Of 1888 the E window, *Burlison & Grylls*; Chancel s, *Heaton, Butler & Bayne*; s aisle from E, Resurrection, *Burlison & Grylls*; Life of Hannah, *Hardman*; Suffer little children, *Heaton, Butler & Bayne*, with Jacobean architectural surround. Similar surrounds to the next two, by the same firm, 1891 and 1892. w window, *Dunstan J. Powell*, 1898, made by *Hardmans*, a forest of intricate leading surrounding the figures. N chapel E, *Kempe*, 1903, with powerful figures. Also his the N lancet, 1907. – **Royal arms** of 1841, carved wood, w wall, signed *G.R. Collis*. – **Memorials**. Alabaster **war memorial** tablet by *P.B. Chatwin*, 1919, w end, N wall. Opposite, circular metal tablet to James Dixon d. 1916, by *A.S. Dixon*. s aisle, E wall, Raymond Lodge d. 1915 by *Oliver W.F. Lodge*. Alabaster tablet, tiny putti.

At the start of **Highfield Road** No. 21 by *Norris & Stainton*, 1961. w of the church, surviving early C19 gatepiers of **Mariemont**. Buildings under construction here for the University of Central England by *Associated Architects*, 2004.

Here there is an optional walk w down **Westbourne Road**, to the Botanical Gardens and beyond. On the s, No. 5 of 1827, set back behind trees. Then **St George's Close**, developed by *Madin* in 1959–62. First two blocks of three-storey flats, one with a characteristic full-height canopied recess for staircase and balcony. Then a retained Gothic lodge of *c.* 1870. Landscape with mature trees.* To the SE No. 20, **The House**, a Regency villa reinterpreted in mid-C20 blue brick, perfectly square with an exposed concrete floor slab, pyramid roof and central chimney.

Back on Westbourne Road, on the N, the **University of Central England School of Education** by *A.G. Sheppard Fidler*, 1957–8. Then the former lodge to **Oakmount**, dated 1879 and inscribed REC, for Richard Chamberlain, Joseph's brother. Almost certainly by *J.H. Chamberlain* and showing a move towards Shaw's and Nesfield's Domestic Revival. The roof folds over the hipped W gable, with its canted bay and tiny traceried window above between half-timbered panels, SW porch, and chamfered NW projection. Big chimney with flutes twisted halfway up.

On the S, the remarkable **Ravensbury** [12, 108] of 1935 by *T.M. Ashford*, assisted, it is said, by the young *Robert Furneaux Jordan*. Tudor Revival collides with Art Deco. Conventional H-plan with end gables, but the smooth expanses of maroon brick are relieved by an abstract pattern of protruding headers. Deep central eaves with big soffit discs. Garden front with full-height timber windows and a jolting central chimney with Art Deco sundial. Below its terrace, a formal garden with central canal, running to a boldly treated arch. Inside, the narrow full-height galleried **lounge** has a heavy beamed ceiling and stair-rail, and a primitivist stone fireplace with stubby twisted Ionic columns, zigzag-pattern lintel, and tapering hood. First-floor **bathroom** with black-tiled walls and black floor with inset stainless steel circles and waves. To the W, **Bevan House**, by *Associated Architects*, 1998. Beyond, **Edgbaston High School for Girls**, *H.W. Hobbiss & Partners*, 1960; alterations by *S.T. Walker & Partners* from 1991.

*No. 15 to the SW, *Madin*'s own house, was nastily rebuilt in 1991.

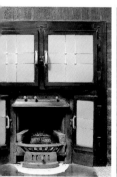

108. Ravensbury, Westbourne Road, by T.M. Ashford, 1935. Details

109. Cottage, Botanical Gardens, by Edge & Avery and S.S. Teulon, 1846–8

Next the **Botanical Gardens**. Laid out 1831–2 in the grounds of the villa **Holly Bank** of 1822, now engulfed by later buildings. The original garden design by *J.C. Loudon* partly survives. **Entrance lodge** of 1831 by *Rickman & Hutchinson*, heavily altered. New **entrance** of 1986–7, when much rebuilding was done by *Peter Hing & Jones*. Arches mimicking the Terrace Glasshouses (*see* below). Inside, going s, the **Tropical House**, reconstructed 1991 by *Peter Hing & Jones*, incorporating the remains of *Charles Edge's* **Lily House** of 1852. Beyond, the **Sub-Tropical House** is the remaining part of *F.B. Osborn's* **Palm House** of 1871. It lost its clerestory in a gale in 1967, but retains a three-bay square cast-iron arcade with round arches and twisted columns. Outside, on the s side, thin Corinthian pilasters. To the w, the **Terrace Glasshouses** of 1884, designed and made by *Henry Hope & Sons*. Tall round-arched central feature with original petal tracery. Behind, decorative chimneystack or 'Smoke Tower' by *Osborn*, *c.* 1884. To the E, *Peter Hing & Jones'* **Pavilion Restaurant** of 1990.

The **gardens** have a main lawn and, beyond it, curving paths sloping downhill, part of Loudon's 1831 design, conserved after a report by *Mary Mitchell* in 1978. To the s, sandstone bowl **fountain** of 1850 by *Charles Edge*, and hexagonal **bandstand** by *F.B. Osborn*, 1873 with columns like the Palm House. To the SE, eyecatching **aviary** of 1995 with four domed flights surrounding a central lobby with tall square cupola and finial. Concept by *Ian Morris*, design by *Ken Fairbairn* of *Peter Hing & Jones*. To the sw, a **gazebo** of *c.* 1850 rebuilt here in 1994. In the Herb Garden in the far sw corner, a **cottage** [109] with a complex history. In 1846 *William Burn* made designs, then *Edge & Avery*, and the T-plan with canted s bay is theirs. With foundations laid, Lord Calthorpe brought *S.S. Teulon* in, and the superstructure is his, of 1847–8, recognizable by determinedly shaped gables and mullion-and-transom windows, some stepping up in the centre. Scissor-truss roof in the s wing.

The cottage originally stood in the **Guinea Gardens**, which remain s of it, reached separately from Westbourne Road, w. A unique survivor of the C19 plots of allotments which surrounded the town, many with summerhouses where families spent days out, as well as growing flowers and vegetables.

On Westbourne Road, w of the access road, No. 15, severely beautiful Queen Anne by *Jethro A. Cossins*, 1881–2. Front sharply defined by the bold chimney, left, and two contrasting gables, the first sheer with a projecting segment-gabled wooden porch, the second hipped with a dormer and large canted bay. Hipped gable and dormer echoed in the coach-house, left. No. 16 is a Gothic lodge of *c.* 1870, to **Westbourne Manor**, a large restrained Italianate villa of 1839 with big canted bays. Beyond in **Harborne Road**, the former hamlet of **Goodknaves End** is marked by the **White Swan** pub, which may hide earlier fabric behind its mid-C19 gables and Tudor casements. Opposite, the western 'heart' of *Madin's* plan, houses and shops of 1969–73.

Now back E to St George's, and s down **Church Road**. The E side starts with **Beechwood House** of 1823, now linked to **The Chains**, by *Oliver Essex* for himself, 1894. Domestic Revival with a Rococo terra-cotta name plaque. Next, a fine villa of 1818. Rusticated ground floor with sashes in round-headed recesses. Doric porch with paired columns. Two full-height semicircular bows behind. N and s extensions of 1898–9 by *F.B. Osborn* for the former **Royal Institution for Deaf and Dumb Children**, the latter with an attractive Venetian window breaking into the pediment. Many C20 additions.*

The w side starts with No. 53 by *Hobbiss*, dated 1935. **Hallfield School** occupies **Beech Lawn**, an ornate villa of *c.* 1860. Piquant Gothic **lodge**, perhaps by *Teulon*. Opposite, No. 7, *c.* 1830, altered 1937.

Now E down **Carpenter Road**. On the N side a fine stucco group: Nos. 3–6, begun 1834, Nos. 7–14, of 1844–52. Nos. 4–5 [110] still Regency with delightful concave-roofed iron porches. No. 7 is builder's Soane, perhaps by *John Fallows*. No. 12, with Ionic porch and segment-headed windows, is by *D.R. Hill*, 1849. On the s two houses of 1865: No. 51, chunky picturesque Tudor by *J.J. Bateman*, No. 50, brick Gothic by *J.H. Chamberlain*. Stone blind arcade continued as the open cusped arches of the porch. On the corner of Arthur Road, **Warwick Crest**, a light sixteen-storey block by *J.H.D. Madin & Partners*, 1962–3, faced in blue brick and mosaic.

*The Institution's main building of 1859 by *F.W. Fiddian* (replacing a Gothick original of *c.* 1812), and *Rickman's* Master's House, Tudor Revival of 1829, lay to the SE. Demolished *c.* 1960.

110. Nos. 4–5 Carpenter Road, 1834

Between Nos. 11 and 12, **Cala Drive** runs N. Distinguished infill by *Madins*', 1962–3. Detached houses step in and out downhill [111]. At the bottom, a footpath into **Estria Road**. Terraces and two-storey flats, with typical Madin recessions, here for open balconies and porches. Grey-buff brick and dark hexagonal tile-hanging. Brick piers support lapped timber roof canopies. The blocks are square, occasionally stepped; the roads and treed lawns curve round them. The influence of Span is clear, but so is e.g. the Harvey of Bournville Tenants' Estate (*see* p. 266).

Back and SE down **Ampton Road**. No. 12 [4] is *J.H. Chamberlain*'s first house, built for his uncle's partner Eld in 1855. The first High Victorian house in the town, inspired by Butterfield and Continental sources. Insistently vertical among low, spreading villas. Red brick with lots of yellow and blue patterning, and Bath stone dressings. The SE

111. Cala Drive, by John H.D. Madin & Partners, 1962–3

front has a tall gable with a two-storey canted bay, balanced by a short
wing with segmental windows above lancets. Big gabled door hood in
the angle. Quoins with inset colonnettes. Contemporary stables to E.
Well-preserved interior. A square lobby leads to a dizzily tall stair hall
with a ceiling on brackets and big central skylight. Iron balustrade with
ivy leaves below the rail and supports with paired twisted and plain
colonnettes. Tiled floor. The main rooms have marble fireplaces with
ivy and shamrock leaves, and matching cornices.

Beyond it two more Tudor villas by *Bateman*. No. 11 of 1855 has been
roughcast, and has a square bay of 1911. No. 10, dated 1860, shows off its
ample stone dressings and wavy bargeboards. No. 9 rich Italianate, also
No. 7 on the w. The **Walker Memorial Hall** was the parish school. Low
Tudor ranges of 1847 etc. No. 18, the slightly later schoolmaster's house,
is probably by *F. W. Fiddian*. Rogue Gothic with cusped arched windows
outlined in blue and yellow brick. N extension with inset porch. On the
E, Nos. 5–7 pre-date the estate development: C18 cottages re-cast *c.* 1840
with slight Tudor details and porches with finials.

Back N and w to Church Road, then s. On the w, No. 45, *c.* 1828. Later
square bays. Beyond, the University's Vale site (*see* p. 253). On the E, No.
11 by *Buckland & Haywood*, 1936–7. An austere cubic brick block with
metal windows and (formerly) a tilted glass canopy. Shaped gatepiers
(garden with fountain by *Bloye*). No. 12 is Greek Revival of 1827 with
mid-C19 alterations. No. 13, **Lawnfield** [112], 1855, built by *John Barnsley*,
is very rich Italianate with a Corinthian porch, triplet windows under
lintels, strongly modelled cornice. No. 14 of 1850 is late Greek, with a
Doric porch facing N. On the w, two grand C19 gateways and Nos. 33
and 34, lodges of *c.* 1850.

At the crossroads **Arthur Road** runs E. On the N, No. 1B, **Edgbaston Vicarage**, by *Holland W. Hobbiss & Partners, c. 1967*. Beyond, Nos. 1 and 2 of 1849–51, almost certainly by *F.W. Fiddian* (cf. No. 43 Wellington Road, p. 233). Back to the crossroads and S. On the W, the entrance to **Edgbaston Hall** [113], now a golf clubhouse. Wall and brick **lodge**, probably of 1850 by *S.S. Teulon*. Simple sashes and big door hood on blunt consoles echoed by projecting curved bases. The hall itself was rebuilt by Sir Richard Gough in 1717, perhaps by *Francis Smith*. Plain five-bay SE front. Three storeys, brick, in old-fashioned English bond, with grey stone quoins and lintels. Simple dentil cornice and parapet. An unusually early instance of a *piano nobile*, its windows enlarged in the C19. NE wing of 1751–2 by *William & David Hiorn*, similar but with rubbed brick lintels. Central porch with pierced brick parapet, part of alterations of 1852–3 by *Sir Charles Barry*. The doorcase is the original, moved forward: grey stone Doric half-columns and sandstone entablature. Canted SW bay of 1852–3, heightened 1937 by *Harvey & Wicks*.

Through the porch into the **entrance hall**. Fine **staircase** of 1751–2 by the *Hiorns*, U-shaped, in three flights, with twisted balusters and swept-up corners marked by little fluted Corinthian columns, and matching pilasters to the dado. Contemporary arch leading NW on the first floor, with panelling and fluted pilasters. C18 full-height panelling in the **Calthorpe Room** (ground floor, E), and in the **snooker room** upstairs. Some reworking, probably by *Harvey & Wicks* in 1937, when *William*

112. Lawnfield, No. 13 Church Road, by John Barnsley, 1855

113. Edgbaston Hall, staircase by William & David Hiorn, 1751–2

Bloye also worked here. The **lounge** beyond the hall, and the **Members' Library**, have refined Jacobean panelling and fireplaces, probably early C20. The **Ladies' Lounge** (NE wing) has good *Hiorn* fittings: doorcases with eared architraves and pediments, dignified fireplace.

On Church Road beyond the hall entrance, **St Bartholomew's (Edgbaston Old Church)**. The first impression of a charming, low medieval fabric is misleading. A church existed by 1279. A N aisle was added *c.* 1500, a W tower in the early C16. Severe Civil War damage took years to make good (briefs of 1658 and 1684). The upper part of the tower was rebuilt. In 1810 the N arcade was removed and the space roofed in a single span. In 1844–6 *Harvey Eginton* raised the walls, replaced windows, and built a new N porch and vestry. In 1850 *S.S. Teulon* proposed complete replacement by a hall church with unusual extra outer passage aisles. Instead a S aisle was added in 1856 by *F.W. Fiddian*, assisted by the young *J.A. Cossins*. In 1885–6 *J.A. Chatwin* built a new chancel, N chapel, N arcade (re-dividing the old space), and SE organ chamber, and raised the nave walls further to form a clerestory. Finally in 1889 *Chatwin* added an extra outer S aisle.

So our first sight is the much-patched medieval stonework of the N wall, with *Eginton*'s simple porch and vestry, walling above the string course, and typical 1840s two-light Perp windows, themselves much renewed. C15 N doorway. Above, an oval plaque, probably C17, mysteriously inscribed '777'. Two-stage tower, divided by a string course. W window with irregular Y-tracery, probably of *c.* 1300, reassembled badly here in the C17. Large basic pointed C17 belfry windows, and small pinnacles which look C18 Gothick. w door of 1885. *Chatwin*'s work respects the Perp style and low proportions, echoing late medieval North Country churches. Big six-light four-centred E window with two smaller four-centred arches in the tracery. The N chapel has *Fiddian*'s E window of 1856 repositioned, with an unusual eight-cusped vesica. Chatwin's N windows follow Eginton's. Clerestory with paired lights. Small sw hall by *Anthony Chatwin*, 1969, linked by a canopy.

The **interior** is nearly all *Chatwin*'s, but influenced by *Fiddian*'s s arcade, Georgian Perp survival with thin four-shafts-and-hollows piers. Chatwin's N arcade, tactful as ever, follows it but with slightly different capitals. His outer s arcade similar. His wide and low chancel arch and stepped segmental N and s chapel arches are heavier, typical late C19, on rich leaf corbels. Camber-beam nave roof. The interior is faced in beautiful pink-grey sandstone ashlar. *Fiddian*'s s aisle roof survives, collar-beam trusses with many stop-chamfers. Late medieval tower arch with clumsy quarter-rounds and one deep hollow moulding.

Complete C19 **fittings**. Typical *Chatwin* **choir stalls** of 1885 with scrolled ends, here supporting Evangelical symbols. – Contemporary **pulpit** with traceried panels, **pews** and **reredos**. – **Font**. Octagonal, limestone, Perp style, by *Eginton*, 1846. – s chapel **screen** and **reredos** by *Holland W. Hobbiss*, 1932. – **Stained glass**. E window incorporating two three-light windows of 1859 from the former s aisle, by *J. Hardman Powell*, in hot colours. Chancel N and s by *Hardman*, 1886. N chapel E, the former E window, by *Hardman*, 1859. More by them in the N aisle, 1887. Its w window by *Kempe & Co.*, 1909. Outer s aisle, window to Edwin Gwyther d. 1871, probably designed by *Chatwin*, and made by *Hardman*.

Monuments. A selection. N aisle from E. Sir Richard Gough d. 1727. Ionic aedicule in two shades of grey marble, heavy fluted base. Perhaps by *Francis Smith*. – Sir Henry Gough d. 1774. Conventional tablet with urn above. Nice cherub in the predella. – 1st Lord Calthorpe d. 1798, by *King & Sons* of Bath. Two oval tablets in a marble surround, with a weeping woman against an urn above. – Frances, Lady Calthorpe d. 1827. Chunky Greek Revival. Tall urn in semicircular-headed surround with key ornament. – Over the door: William Kimberley d. 1846 by *Peter Hollins*, Alice Kimberley d. 1833 in childbirth, by *John Bennett*. – s aisle, from E. Gabriel Jean Marie de Lys d. 1831 by *P. Hollins*. With bust. – Samuel Wheeley d. 1831 by *Bennett*. – William Withering, the discoverer of digitalis, d. 1799 by *William Hollins*. Oval tablet with, in the base, a most lifelike snake twisting round a branch and a sprig of foxglove. – Joseph Ledsam d. 1816 by *William Hollins*. Elegant tablet with reeded border. – w wall, Henry and Sarah Porter, d. 1710, 1724. Lead tablet.

The **churchyard** has good C19 tombs w of the tower. By the porch, William Alexander Harvey, the architect, d. 1951 and his wife Hannah, by *H.G. Wicks*. Ribbed urn.

c) The Old Church north to Five Ways, via Wellington Road and Charlotte Road

Opposite the church on the N, a bungalow with monopitch wings: *John Madin Design Group*, 1980. To the E the **Priory School**, an elegant five-bay villa of 1829; its single-bay pedimented centre with Corinthian columns suggests *Charles Edge*. To its left, a sympathetic but slightly larger five-bay block of 1878–9 by *T. Chatfeild Clarke* of London. To the right a big mid-C20 block with Gothic windows. Entrance hall grandly re-modelled by *Martin & Chamberlain*, 1890. **Ampton Road** (SE end) runs NW here with big stucco villas of *c.* 1852–3. Opposite, **Sir Harry's Road** runs SE. Beyond the school grounds on the SW side, Nos. 12 and 11 of *c.* 1852–3 by *F.W. Fiddian*, Italianate with rich bracket cornices. Then two by *Samuel Hemming*; No. 10 of 1852–3, stucco, with much frilly anthemion decoration, and No. 9 of 1854–5, brick with an emphatic asymmetrical bay.

Now E down **Wellington Road**. On the N, villas of 1847–50. The finest is **Beech Mount**, with projecting centre bay, giant Corinthian pilasters and 'debased' details e.g. consoles sprouting from mullions and supporting a string course. On the S, Nos. 54–57 of 1936–8, No. 56 by *Holland W. Hobbiss* in his King Edward's School Tudor style. On the N again No. 44 of 1845, and No. 43 by *F.W. Fiddian*, 1840, severe. Pedimented doorcase with an exceptionally heavy lintel. Later C19 bays. Then on the S three large houses of 1828–30. No. 58 has incised pilasters and an off-centre pediment; No. 60, set back, with pilasters and cornice. No. 61, **Fieldgate House**, has Corinthian pilasters with tall single-tier capitals. Its porch suggests *John Fallows*. Later C19 octagonal extension. Here a drive runs S, dividing into three. To the W, **Spring Folly**, a mid-C19 sham ruin. Continuing S, **Highland Lodge** [114] of *c.* 1830 with elegant shallow bays, then a lodge of 1864 by *J.J. Bateman*, and, set beyond a small lake, **Spring Cottage**. Nucleus of before 1827, but the long range with shallow bow of after 1855, probably also *Bateman*.

Back to Wellington Road and E. On the S, No. 63 of 1845–7, almost certainly by *J.J. Bateman*, is a rural Italian villa of the Nash or Papworth type with a three-storey tower, right. Linked architraves with panels of foliage and little supporting consoles. On the N here behind a wall, No. 39, **Apsley House**, 1836, probably by *Charles Edge*, who added the Ionic porch in 1850. Nos. 34–35 are old-fashioned for 1850–1, with channelled rustication and pilasters above. Opposite, No. 68 by *E.C. Bewlay* of *Cossins, Peacock & Bewlay*, 1913. His own house. Arts and Crafts Neo-Georgian with a shell-hood doorcase.

No. 28, N, begins a line of stucco villas mostly of 1844–7, which continues past Charlotte Road and into **Spring Road**. On the S opposite, No. 73 of 1816, a large house facing E, behind a stable wing with Tudor cupola. Later C19 Gothic lodge. Then a group of 1815. No. 74 has a Greek Doric doorcase, inside a later Roman Doric porch. Nos. 76–77 have Doric doorcases and little tympana over the windows,

114. Highland Lodge, Wellington Road, *c.* 1830

No. 78 a doorcase with fluted pillarets in a moulded surround. Finally the ornate No. 82, *c.* 1860, with a Corinthian porch with vermiculated rustication.

Now back w, and N down **Charlotte Road**. Good stucco villas of 1847–9, etc. (more in **Gough Road**, running w). Nos. 13–14, on the w, are a mirrored pair of rural Italian villas with low end towers by *J.J.*

Bateman, 1851, Nos. 17–18 a brick 'Lombardic' pair by *Yeoville Thomason*, 1853–4. No. 20, a large villa with Palladian alternating pediments, starts a line running w down **Pakenham Road**.

On the NW corner of the crossroads here, the former **St James's church** by *S.S. Teulon*, 1850–3. Redundant from 1973, converted to flats 2003–4. Lord Calthorpe was considering a new church in 'Middle-aged Gothic' in 1846, when *R.C. Carpenter*, *F.W. Fiddian* and *Charles Wyatt Orford* made designs. Teulon's early suggestions have an aisled nave with a sw tower or a belfry and catslide roofs. His final drawings are dated 1850. Not his wildest design, but there are many original touches. A simple cruciform preaching church, without aisles. E end above a basement, due to falling ground. SE organ chamber and vestry by *Thomas Naden*, 1886. Teulon's tower rises between it and the s transept, tapering into an octagonal belfry with alternating one- and two-light windows, and a short spire with lucarnes. Big sheltering roofs, especially over the nave, which has conventional dormers and additional triangular ones above (more added 2004). s porch. The five-light Dec E window prepares you for the ingenious transept roses. The s has two huge quatrefoils, set at forty-five degrees to each other, so eight even points touch the edge. Eight spokes radiate from the middle. The N has trefoils set at sixty degrees, so six points and six spokes. w window a spherical triangle. Two-light nave windows (sills lowered 2004).

Interior now heavily sub-divided. *Teulon*'s roof survives, the nave trusses alternating scissors with complex hammerbeam and double-collar structures, the lower collar arch-braced, and big cusped hexagons between the two. The crossing has hammerbeams set diagonally supporting central collar-beams, the lower one projecting to form the transept ridges. *Naden*'s organ chamber has a two-bay arcade with pink granite columns. Open stone trefoils in the arches. Below to the sw, Neo-Georgian vicarage of 1911–12 by *C.E. Bateman*.

Now E down **Ryland Road**, with modest terraces just outside the Calthorpe Estate. The s side is of 1845–54. Nos. 66–69 of 1854 are pairs of single-pile passage-entry houses, with rear houses reached through the passages. Nos. 78–79 have good doorcases with fluted surrounds. The N side was started in 1832. Nos. 37–42, a single terrace, have pilasters, vestigial centre and end pediments, and Egyptian-style tapering doorcases. Nos. 33–36, another passage-entry pair with panelled entry. NW up **Lee Crescent**, open on the NE. A delightful group villa terrace [115] of *c.* 1830 climbs the hill. Doorcases with panelled soffits and fluted surrounds. Nos. 47–49 grander with fluted pillarets and sashes in segment-headed recessed panels, Nos. 43–46 with incised panels and first-floor pilasters. Then two big passage-entry pairs: the entry doorcases have fluted pilasters on Nos. 39–40 and paired pillarets on Nos. 37–38. Nos. 35–36, **Wineyford Brown's Building**, dated 1830, shows a step beyond passage-entry layout, with close-set doors. Nos. 31–32 similar. Finally No. 30, detached, facing SE.

115. Lee Crescent, villa terrace, c. 1830

We walk NW here, then SW into **Elvetham Road**. On the NW, **Leofric Court** by *Hickton Madeley*, 1982–3, with double-level balconies on light timber supports. Now NW along **Yew Tree Road**, its contrasting sides showing the difference between the late 1830s and 1850s. The NE has modest brick pairs [116] by *Bateman & Drury*, Nos. 2–5 of 1836–8 and Nos. 8–9 of 1841. Round-arched doorways and lintels in rubbed brick. Doorcases with flattened fluted pilasters, and teardrop fanlights. Breaking the row, Nos. 6 and 7 of *c.* 1834, stucco cottages with arched bargeboards. The SW starts with No. 14, tall Gothic of *c.* 1872, with frilly bargeboards and porch brackets. Then big stucco and brick classical pairs of 1853–5 with Italianate detail. Left at the far end into **Wheeley's Road**. On the left, Nos. 57–64, heavy stucco pairs, and Nos. 65–66, 'Lombardic' red and blue brick, all of *c.* 1858–60 by *Thomason*. Again a contrast with earlier, more modest stucco houses opposite. Nos. 17–18 here are of 1829 with first-floor Ionic pilasters. No. 19, contemporary, has a good reeded doorcase, now blocked. No. 22 of 1819 has another.

We reach **St James Road** again with **The Round House** facing us on the W corner. Its circular central block of 1818 was built as a garden house. Nash-style conical roof and deep eaves, Gothick windows in both floors. Turned into a residence *c.* 1827 with flanking blocks to either side, the S one retaining a Tudor-style window. Walking NW across the railway, on the NE gross flats by *Temple Cox Nicholls*, 2000–2. Then the crossroads with George Road, with the **Friends' Meeting House** [117] by *William Henman*. Dated 1893. *Rundbogenstil* in brick with stone dressings. Heavy pedimented entrance on the SW angle with a big arch and short fat columns. Rich leaf capitals. The main block runs N–S, with a lower W wing lit by a Venetian window in the end gable.

Here we reach some of the earliest development of the suburb. First NE up **George Road**. On the SE an unusual Greek Revival villa of 1827 with recessed centre and doorcase with simplified Tower of the Winds capitals. Garden front, SE, with giant pilasters. Then two pedimented villas of *c*. 1833. Further up, Nos. 43–44 of 1830, probably by *Bateman & Drury*, have rubbed brick lintels and arched doorways. Doorcases with bolection mouldings. Nos. 45–46, a contemporary three-storey pair. Opposite, a good group of 1820 including a pedimented pair. Doorcases with Tuscan columns. (An optional walk from here SE down Islington Row and S into **Enfield Road** for the Neo-Norman former **Vestry Hall**, 1848 by *F. W. Fiddian*.)

Then back down **George Road** and SW across St James Road. On the SE, a stucco villa and terrace of three of *c*. 1820 with fluted Tuscan columns to the doorcases. Beyond No. 29 of 1818, tall, its porch *c*. 1830, probably by *John Fallows*, and No. 28 of *c*. 1828. Opposite, No. 22, a stucco villa facing SW. Its history is complex. *Hansom & Welch* built a house here in 1833 but went bankrupt before they signed the lease: either this or, more likely, that adjoining to the NE, now demolished. By 1836 both plots were developed. No. 22's façade, with its recessed centre and small pediment, resembles others associated with *Charles Edge* (e.g. Apsley House, Wellington Road; No. 15 Chad Road), and seemingly derives from C.R. Cockerell's Langton House, Dorset, of 1827–32. No. 23, **The Bothy**, was its coach-house and stable, plus a central projecting garden room with canted bay. Tudor Revival of *c*. 1860, all bargeboarded and battlemented.

116. No. 4 Yew Tree Road, by Bateman & Drury, 1836–8

Back and NW up St James Road to **Frederick Road**. Turning SW, on
the SE a good group all of 1828 [118]. Nos. 19–20 dated. Nos. 21–26 are
consistent semi-detached pairs, with simple side entrances and early
bays. No. 29 a big rendered villa of *c.* 1830. Beyond, down a drive, three
Classical Revival houses by *Sinclair Architects*, 1994. Returning NE, on
the NW, Nos. 31–34, two pairs of 1844–6 with Greek Revival detail, No.
32 tactfully extended in 1866. Then two pairs of 1850. Nos. 35–37 are
Italianate. Nos. 38–39, more obviously Victorian with heavy decorative
door heads and arched windows, are *J.A. Chatwin*'s first design, before
he trained with Barry.

Across St James Road, a good stucco villa, set back, of 1826. Then Nos.
42–44 of 1853, similar to Nos. 38–39, perhaps also *Chatwin*. Opposite,
No. 16 by *Madin*, 1957, a simple handsome statement with cantilevered
Travertine first floor. Characteristic recessed entrance, with a fluted pier
cut back at the top, and free-standing patterned slate slab. Nos. 14–15 of
1822 have good doorcases. Dominating its neighbours, **Five Ways
Tower** by *Philip Bright* of the *Property Services Agency*, 1979, a twenty-
three storey James Stirling-style tower and two-storey podium. On the
N opposite, Nos. 45–49 of 1839–45. The first four stuccoed; No. 49 has
exposed brick, a crisp doorcase, and lintels breaking forward in the centre. No. 52 is heavy Gothic of *c.* 1870. Here we reach **Islington Row**, with
on the S corner, **Five Ways House** by *Eric Bedford* of the Ministry of
Works, 1956–7. We walk NW back to Five Ways.

Buildings further West

Lastly, a brief mention of the late C19 W part of Edgbaston, with important Arts and Crafts houses of *c.* 1900. St **Augustine's Road** runs N from Hagley Road, with on the W Gothic villas by *J.J. Bateman*, 1872–4, to *J.A. Chatwin's* confident **St Augustine** of 1868. Superb tower and spire of 1876, with an encircling corona, inspired by Patrington, Yorks. In **Rotton Park Road** just to the E, Nos. 17–19, by *J.L. Ball*, 1894–5, an absolutely simple brick pair with casement windows. Further W, equally simple No. 415 **Hagley Road** also by *Ball*, 1902–3. Further W, **Barnsley Road** is all by *Ball*, 1898–1900. At its N end the former **Methodist church** by *Ernest Barnsley* and *Ball*, 1889; chancel by *Ball*, 1901, in Lethaby mood. In **Norfolk Road** running S from Hagley Road, massive **Blythe Court** by *Buckland & Haywood-Farmer*, 1911–13. By the same partnership Nos. 15–21 **Yateley Road**, No. 21 of 1899 especially fine; doorway with carved frieze (Buckland's own house). Far W in **Woodbourne Road**, No. 25 by *C.E. Bateman*, 1897–8. Finally, far SW in **Hintlesham Avenue**, off Metchley Lane and nearly in Harborne, the Frank-Lloyd-Wright-inspired No. 23 by *Robert Townsend*, 1955.

Edgbaston:
the University Quarter

Including descriptions by Ian Dungavell (Webb & Bell) and
Elain Harwood (post-war University and Barber Institute)

Birmingham University is one of the great Victorian provincial foundations, comparable with those at Manchester and Liverpool. It is a
complex of exceptional interest, with the original buildings by *Aston
Webb & Ingress Bell* of 1900–9, good 1930s work, and 1960s developments by firms such as *Casson, Conder & Partners*, *Arup Associates*,
Howell, Killick, Partridge & Amis, and *Chamberlin, Powell & Bon*. This
account includes nearby early C20 Arts and Crafts houses, many now in
University use, and institutions, such as King Edward's School.

The University started in Edmund Street as Mason College, a science
college founded in 1880.* It became Mason University College in 1898,
and received its charter in 1900 with Joseph Chamberlain as first
Chancellor. 'What we want to begin with is brains and not architecture,'
he told the steel magnate and philanthropist Andrew Carnegie. But
Carnegie thought differently, and the £50,000 he offered to establish a
'first class modern scientific college' on the model of Cornell University
was conditional on new buildings being erected.

In 1900 Lord Calthorpe gave a 25-acre (10-hectare) site on the
Bournbrook side of the Edgbaston Estate, about three miles s of the
centre. As architects Chamberlain chose *Aston Webb & Ingress Bell*.
They had both local and national work in their favour. Their Victoria
Law Courts on Corporation Street (*see* p. 74) had earned the city more
praise than any other building of the previous twenty years, and they
were engaged in new buildings for the Royal Naval College, Dartmouth
(1898–1904) and the Royal College of Science at South Kensington,
London (1898–1906). The new campus was opened on 7 July 1909 by
King Edward VII, though several buildings had been already occupied
for a couple of years.

The site falls about 30 feet (9.1 metres) from N–S, so the architects
placed their buildings on two terraces with a drop of 16 feet (4.9 metres)
between. The basic plan [120] was D-shaped, with the incomplete
straight side running E–W along University Road. The convex side faced
s, straddling the drop, from which on the lower side radiated two-storey
T-shaped teaching blocks (of which only three of the intended six were

*Its Gothic building by *J.A. Cossins* was demolished in 1964.

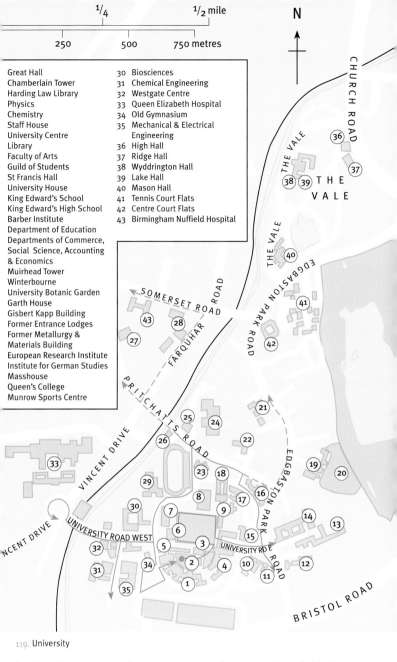

Great Hall	30 Biosciences
Chamberlain Tower	31 Chemical Engineering
Harding Law Library	32 Westgate Centre
Physics	33 Queen Elizabeth Hospital
Chemistry	34 Old Gymnasium
Staff House	35 Mechanical & Electrical
University Centre	Engineering
Library	36 High Hall
Faculty of Arts	37 Ridge Hall
Guild of Students	38 Wyddrington Hall
St Francis Hall	39 Lake Hall
University House	40 Mason Hall
King Edward's School	41 Tennis Court Flats
King Edward's High School	42 Centre Court Flats
Barber Institute	43 Birmingham Nuffield Hospital
Department of Education	
Departments of Commerce,	
Social Science, Accounting	
& Economics	
Muirhead Tower	
Winterbourne	
University Botanic Garden	
Garth House	
Gisbert Kapp Building	
Former Entrance Lodges	
Former Metallurgy &	
Materials Building	
European Research Institute	
Institute for German Studies	
Masshouse	
Queen's College	
Munrow Sports Centre	

119. University

built) and the Great Hall at the centre. At the semicircle each block meets a domed square pavilion with small domed corner turrets. The semicircle housed offices served by a spine corridor, two storeys high on the N side, three storeys on the S. The plan was adapted from pavilion hospitals, the curved spine achieving maximum light and ventilation

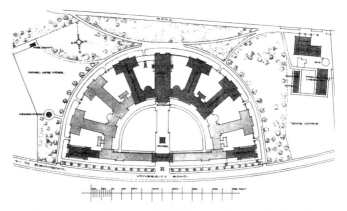

120. Birmingham University, by Aston Webb & Ingress Bell, 1900–9. Plan from *The Builder*, 1907, with executed blocks shown darker

with a minimum distance between individual buildings. But Birmingham was also the first formally planned British university, influenced by the Beaux Arts layouts popular at American colleges in the 1890s.

Interwar developments included *Holland W. Hobbiss*'s Guild of Students building and Queen's College, and *Robert Atkinson*'s masterpiece, the Barber Institute of 1936–9. *William Haywood* of *Buckland & Haywood* made plans to expand Webb & Bell's scheme in the same Beaux Arts manner, but little was done. *Verner O. Rees* was appointed in 1945 to prepare plans for bringing the remaining faculties to Edgbaston. He produced two schemes. One continued Webb's symmetrical plan and grand axis, but the selected one blocked it, to lasting regret, with the library and arts faculty buildings. Funding for these was secured only in 1955. Meanwhile, science buildings proliferated haphazardly around the w and s, as surviving Orlit huts testify. (Birmingham was one of the universities selected for expansion in technical subjects in the early 1950s.)

In 1957 the University asked *Sir Hugh Casson & Neville Conder* to prepare a new development plan. Casson & Conder had won a limited competition for the new arts area at Cambridge, and at that moment were the leaders in campus design. They organized the teaching area into informal squares, with additional blocking buildings that enclosed views and kept out traffic. The University had meanwhile acquired the land stretching N, providing a remarkably extensive campus for a university in an industrial city, and here larger buildings were set on either side of a new ring road. In 1960 the University committed itself to expand to 7,500 students in a decade, and Casson & Conder revised their plan in 1963 to include a tall tower (Muirhead Tower). Some of the new buildings were by the firm, but what makes Birmingham exceptional among the red brick universities is the employment of so many other major Modernist practices: only Oxford and Cambridge boast greater selections. The pity is that not every building was constructed, or completed as intended, while others have been altered or demolished. As a concentrated experience of 1960s university architecture, however, Birmingham remains hard to beat. Recent developments have sought to fill gaps on the periphery.

The Original Centre

It is difficult to describe the University in a manner that will make perambulation easy, partly because of the piecemeal plan and partly because one has to start at the centre and fan out. The picturesque and romantic skyline of the first phase is best appreciated from the s, the viewpoint of most students as they arrived at Bournbrook on trams from the city. Sir Hugh Casson found it 'impossible not to admire' and wrote that 'from certain aspects and in certain lights [it] can even look as magical as the domes and spires of Istanbul or Moscow'.

It is best to start a detailed tour with the original physical and ceremonial centre, **Chancellor's Court**. Had the plan been completed, this would have been the closest thing at Birmingham to an Oxbridge quad. However, both in style and plan Webb & Bell's buildings deliberately distance themselves from Oxbridge colleges, as something different was felt to be required for the first English university primarily devoted to science. The red bricks, stone stripes and saucer domes would have called to mind Bentley's Westminster Cathedral, London (1895–1903), a building whose Byzantine style avoided any appearance of rivalry with Westminster Abbey nearby, and thus solved a similar problem. The style was much promoted by W.R. Lethaby, who thought it rational and universal in character, and the University buildings also play with the geometry of squares and circles, cubes and hemispheres, perhaps inspired by Lethaby's *Architecture, Mysticism and Myth* (1892).

At the centre of the s side is the **Great Hall**. The entrance pavilion is square, of three storeys, surmounted by an octagonal drum which supports a ribbed dome and tiny lantern. Square turrets at the corners, capped by hemispherical ribbed domes and a great round-arched mullioned window. In its spandrels, the arms of the Midland counties the University aimed to serve. Above, in a ceramic frieze by *Robert Anning Bell*, the enthroned goddess Learning hands the wreath of scholarship to the new University, represented by a kneeling man in modern academic dress. Over the doorways a pantheon of immortals carved *in situ* by *Henry Pegram*: Beethoven, Virgil, Michelangelo, Plato, Shakespeare, Newton, Watt, Faraday, Darwin; a fusion of arts and sciences with the most famous Midlander at the centre.

The Great Hall itself cannot be seen from this side, but from the s it is evident that its distant ancestor is the type of grand late medieval building with end gables flanked by corner turrets, such as King's College Chapel, Cambridge. Stepping inside you come first to the

121. Chamberlain Tower, Birmingham University, by Aston Webb & Ingress Bell, 1900–9

domed and galleried Entrance Hall, a 50-ft (15.2-metre) cube topped by a hemispherical dome of 50-ft diameter, recently painted with rather heavy *trompe l'œil* coffers. Geometric patterned floor of Pentelikon and Sicilian marbles. The hall itself is 150 by 75 feet (45.7 by 22.9 metres), which is, as contemporary accounts were keen to point out, larger than Birmingham Town Hall. The passages at ground and first floors are vaulted transversely, and the gallery balustrade and pilasters carrying the ceiling ribs are of buff terracotta. The barrel-vaulted ceiling has plaster enrichments of the city and university arms by *George Bankart* of the *Bromsgrove Guild*. The stained-glass window designed by *T.R. Spence* celebrates major benefactors alongside an uneasy choice of figures emblematic of pure and applied knowledge.*

The pavilion fronts to the teaching blocks are similar to that in front of the Great Hall, but of two storeys only, with round corner turrets, their ground-floor windows originally lighting lecture rooms. Libraries above were top-lit by Diocletian windows in the octagonal drums of the domes. Ceramic friezes by *R. Anning Bell* represent in contemporary

*To the s, across the playing fields, at the Bristol Road entrance, *Webb & Bell*'s **South Lodge** faces Bristol Road.

costume Midlands trades and industries. The linking curve is of two-storey offices with recessed windows under segmental heads pulled together by stone string courses at the level of the tops and transoms of the ground-floor windows. The teaching-block floors were unencumbered by columns, creating flexible spaces that could be partitioned as required.

The **Chamberlain Tower** [121] is in front of the Great Hall, a tall detached campanile which serves as a landmark to emphasize the existence of the University, and which was described in the *Birmingham Daily Post* as 'the intellectual beacon of the Midlands'. This has no stylistic connection with the buildings around it, though it too is of Accrington red brick. For it was Joseph Chamberlain and his wife who, during an Italian holiday, had settled on the Torre del Mangia at Siena as a suitable model for Birmingham. Webb & Bell obligingly did as they were told, though it is not an exact copy.

The incomplete long straight wing along University Road is also of red brick with Darley Dale stone dressings. Above the arcaded entrance loggia at the centre is the **Harding Law Library**. The w end originally housed the chemistry department, the e physics.

Webb's semicircle was infilled with less style for science, first on the w by *Maurice Webb*, 1935–7, with, filling in behind, the **Hills Chemistry Block** by *Wornum & Playne*, 1955. On the e, detached sections of hemicycle and of the straight wing, the **Poynting Building**, both by *Webb*, were linked by **Physics West**, 1957–9 by *Verner Rees, Laurence & Mitchell*. To their n, the same firm's **Watson Building** for mathematics, 1958–61. Behind Physics West, linked by a bridge, their **Physics East** of 1965–7 in a plain modern style. Behind it the **Radiation Centre** of 1968–71 by *Devereux, Mitchell, Price & Davis*.

Back to Chancellor's Court and n, we enter **University Square**, the centrepiece created by *Casson & Conder* that gave a grassy heart to the campus. On the w side is the **University Centre** and connected **Staff House**, stepped forward and with a small hexagonal office in the glazed link. All by *Conder*, 1958–62. The two are very different: in the University Centre, for students, concrete horizontals and plate glass predominate, clearly dividing the elevation into five bands, while the chief features of the green-rendered staff house are vertical windows in broad painted architraves. The uppermost floor contains guest rooms. Both interiors much altered. The University Centre was remodelled with shops in 1991–2, but a cantilevered stair survives, floating free of the timber-lined walls, its skylight part-concealed by a thin concrete canopy that completes the ethereal sensation as you ascend. Similar timber lining in the Staff House refectory. Trite yet disturbing sculpture by *Bernard Sindall* of a nude in a hat, presented 1974.

On the n side is *Verner Rees's* **Library** of 1957–60. Five storeys with red brick piers hinting at pilasters, and a recessed band as cornice, on a heavy podium. It blocks the formal avenue on the axis of Chancellor's

Court, to the former main entrance in Pritchatts Road (*see* p. 251). In front, **sculpture**: Ancestor 1 of 1970 by *Barbara Hepworth* (cast 1971), part of the Family of Man series. On the E side, the spreading four-storey **Faculty of Arts**, by *Verner Rees, Laurence & Mitchell*, 1961. Red brick, but less emphatic, with a prominent copper attic.

Walking E under the bridge between Arts and Physics, on the s side, facing Edgbaston Park Road, the **Guild of Students** building by *Holland W. Hobbiss*, 1928–30. E-plan front, with three big gables, inspired by Midlands manor houses. Brown brick with red relieving arches and stone dressings. A chimney out of Nesfield's Kinmel Park breaks the symmetry. Central plaque by *William Bloye*. The back has giant Ionic pilasters of the Kirby Hall type. Extensions by *Holland W. Hobbiss & Partners*, 1948–51 and 1960, form three sides of a quad surrounding the **Mermaid Fountain** by *Bloye*, 1960. Inside, an impressive staircase leads to the **Debating Hall** with a complex timber roof, each truss with hammerbeams, two collars, king-strut, and curved braces. To the s, **St Francis' Hall**, the University chaplaincy. First an octagonal building of 1968–9 by *Hobbiss & Partners*. Behind, the original *Hobbiss* building of 1936, its short 'nave' and low tower, gabled N–s, probably inspired by the church at Michaelchurch-on-Arrow, Radnorshire, near where he fished. Behind was a multi-storey **car park** of 1964–5, the result of a traffic survey made as early as 1962. By *Casson, Conder & Partners*, with separate entrances for staff and students, partly set into the ground and with student tennis courts on top.

Opposite the Guild, **University House**, originally for women students, by *Buckland & Haywood-Farmer*, 1908, friendly Arts and Crafts Neo-Georgian with linked stone windows, in the Newnham tradition. Big boxy extension by *Architects' Design Partnership*, 2003–4.

King Edward's Schools and the Barber Institute

To the N, grouped with the University, **King Edward's School** for boys and **King Edward's High School** for girls, by *Holland W. Hobbiss*, 1937–47. The boys' school was founded in 1552 in New Street, rebuilt there in 1731–4 and again splendidly in Tudor Gothic by *Charles Barry*, 1833. **Foundation Offices** flanked by square Nesfield-type lodges, their linking archways sadly removed. The **Board Room** has a marble chimneypiece of 1747 by *Peter Scheemakers* with crisp flowers and garlands, crowned by a bust of Edward VI. At the top of the drive the unfortunate **Design Centre** by *Mason Richards*, 1987. Beyond, *Hobbiss*'s school buildings. They form a loose, subtly related, brown brick group, with stepped buttresses and big metal classroom windows, pulled together by steep Lutyens-style roofs. The fenestration of **Big School** is a perfect example of Hobbiss's skill: full-height stone oriel, and tall windows under relieving arches, balanced by the long row of ground-floor triplets. Oak hammerbeam roof. Chief Master's **chair**, canopied Gothic by *A.W.N. Pugin*, 1833, inscribed Sapientia. **Dining hall** with segmental barrel vault and stained-glass coats of arms by *Moira Forsyth*, 1947. **Swimming pool**, now covered, with a deliberately primitive open loggia recalling Gimson. The upper corridor of *Barry*'s school was re-erected as a detached building with a brick skin by *Hobbiss*, and converted into a **chapel** in 1952–3. The beautiful interior is Perp, in Darley Dale stone, with a lierne vault. Four-light windows in arched reveals, their mullions integral with the stone panelling. Details by *Pugin*. Also his, heraldic **stained glass**. **Benches** made by boys, designed by *J. Bruce Hurn*; his **reredos**, an Expressionist Crucifixion, sadly overpainted in sugary blues. **Music school** by *J.P. Osborne & Son*, 1964. Saw-tooth walls, Coventry Cathedral style.

Across the road from the schools, the Barber Institute. In front, bronze equestrian **statue** of King George I. Commissioned in 1717 by the City of Dublin and installed there in 1722. Bought in 1937 by Prof. Thomas Bodkin, the Institute's first director. Attributed to *John van*

122. Barber Institute, by Robert Atkinson, 1936–9

Nost the Elder, though probably executed by his assistants *Andrew Carpenter* and *Christopher Burchard* after his death. Obviously influenced by the famous antique statue of Marcus Aurelius now on the Capitoline Hill in Rome. The heavily built king is in contemporary armour, but wears a laurel wreath.

The **Barber Institute** [122] itself is of 1936–9 by *Robert Atkinson*. Shortly before her death in 1933, Lady Barber offered to fund a building for the visual arts and music; she and her husband Sir Henry Barber (1860–1927) were long-standing patrons of the University. Atkinson was appointed in 1934; as an architect straddling modern and traditional tastes, and a noted connoisseur, he was an impeccable choice. Following the appointment of the first director, Atkinson's plans were modified to give more space to arts than to music. The final form is a central music auditorium ringed by libraries, a ground-floor lecture hall, and an imposing sequence of top-lit galleries above. Brick dominates over stone, to be more in keeping with the neighbouring Guild of Students, with a plinth of Darley Dale stone. The styling owes much to Atkinson's growing fascination with Scandinavian classicism and also to the Boymans Museum, Rotterdam, which he visited in 1935. *Rosemary Stjernstedt* was his principal assistant. Heraldic shields, and relief panels of a laurel branch, palm leaf, lyre and torch designed by *George Atkinson* (no relation) and executed by *Gordon Herickx* of Birmingham Sculptors, Moseley. The Boymans Museum also inspired the gallery interiors with their hessian wall coverings and picture rails. The auditorium, panelled in Australian walnut with a proscenium of satin inlaid maple, demonstrates Atkinson's skill in decoration: a fusion of classical, Deco and Adamesque. The Institute is his finest surviving work and an exemplar of the influence of North European classicism in 1930s Britain. Only the glass roof by *Bickerdike Allen*, 1986–9, intrudes.

Buildings Further North

The best of the 1960s buildings were laid out along the ring road N of the Barber Institute. Walking N, facing us the businesslike **Department of Education** by *Casson, Conder & Partners*, 1966–7. To the W, the Ashley and Strathcona buildings, now the **Departments of Commerce, Social Science, Accounting and Economics**, were early post-Casson & Conder realizations, in 1961–4. They were also early in the career of *Howell, Killick, Partridge & Amis*, appointed following their succès d'estime in the competition for Churchill College, Cambridge. The five-storey **Ashley Building** [123] brought together previously scattered departments, deliberately setting all sixty-nine tutors' rooms around a single atrium, through which coils a circular stair. It is the single best 1960s space in the University, rough but full of panache. The exterior is clad in the full-height pre-cast panels that HKPA were among the

123. Ashley Building, by Howell, Killick, Partridge & Amis, 1961–4. Staircase

124. Muirhead Tower, by Philip Dowson of Arup Associates, 1968–9

first to use, while still working for the London County Council at Roehampton; here with distinctive projecting sills designed to throw off rainwater. Next to it is the two-storey **Strathcona Building**, a long curving tail designed to avoid a straight corridor, built of concrete blocks and housing lecture theatres and seminar rooms. Behind, the mammoth **Muirhead Tower** [124] for Arts, bridging the ring road (a location regretted by Conder), by *Philip Dowson* of *Arup Associates*, 1968–9, variously loved or loathed. A 'dark' floor of laboratories or lecture halls for every two glazed floors, and a large hall in its sloping underbelly.

Further N up **Edgbaston Park Road**, the University occupies two important Arts and Crafts houses. On the E, **Winterbourne** by *J.L. Ball*, 1902–4, for J.S. Nettlefold. His finest house, a long low range with gabled porch and staircase projections. Strongly influenced by Lethaby but with an angular, rectilinear character of its own. The length reflects its planning with a single range of rooms and a long, wide hall and first-floor landing. The angularity is pointed up by massive platbands which continue the eaves line across the gables. Casement windows set flush.

The garden front has end gables linked by a long cross-range, with a ground-floor loggia. Inside, the hall has a three-centred barrel vault and fine plasterwork by *George Bankart*. sw annexe by *Madins*, 1966. Good early C20 gardens, now the **University Botanic Garden**, including a Japanese garden with tea house and bridge. On the w, **Garth House** by *W.H. Bidlake*, 1901, for Ralph Heaton of the Birmingham Mint. A sharp contrast to Winterbourne. Red-blue brick below and roughcast above give it a gentle, fresh quality and disguise the power of its refined vernacular features. Muthesius illustrated it in *Das englische Haus* (1904–5) and noted Bidlake's naturalness and simplicity. Its seemingly random elevations are in fact carefully integrated, e.g. the garden front, s, with its big bay and paired gables balanced by a big chimney which encloses a little window. Its apparently rambling S-plan is carefully arranged round a low tower (with altered top) and the entrance hall, with its shallow barrel vault and open screened staircase. Casement windows quietly stress the transoms. The roughcast suggests Voysey, but his distinctive manner is only evident in the coach-house range with its eyebrow arch and tapering chimney.

Back and nw up **Pritchatts Road**. On the ne, the **Gisbert Kapp Building** for Electronic, Electrical and Computer Engineering, 1964–8 by *Denys Hinton*. Opposite, the **J.G. Smith Building**, 1975–6, by *Casson, Conder & Partners*, for Urban and Local Government Studies. Beyond it the former main entrance, with *Buckland & Haywood*'s subtly curved **lodges** and enclosing walls of 1930, and gates by the *Birmingham Guild*. Across the road, the Interdisciplinary Research Centre has built the cool **Net Shape Building**, 1996–8 by *Architects' Design Partnership*, and has taken over the adjoining **Metallurgy and Materials Building** of 1964 by *Philip Dowson* of *Arup Associates*. This has four linked laboratories designed to be extremely flexible internally and to provide a 'wall' at the campus edge, defining the greensward within. It was the first major building in England to use a 'tartan' grid to incorporate servicing, a concept developed in the United States by Eero Saarinen and Louis Kahn. A column is placed at the corner of each pre-cast section, giving four columns internally where the corners join, allowing space for services and ventilation shafts between them. These nodes are expressed externally by little roof vents. **Plasma Laboratory** behind by *Arup Associates*, 1970. Further behind, in Elms Road, the **Computer Centre**, 1972–4 by *Casson, Conder & Partners*. Across Elms Road the **European Research Institute**, 2000–1 by *Feilden Clegg*, purple brick and prominent sunscreens. To the nw, No. 32 by *Harold S. Scott*, 1936–7. Opposite, the domestic-scaled **Institute for German Studies** of 1994 by *Rathbone & Taylor*, its entrance in Hobbiss revival.

An optional excursion here, across the railway. First, nw and n up **Pritchatts Road**. On the w, two houses by *E.F. Reynolds*, No. 13 of 1927 with inset towers, and No. 11 of 1926. Then No. 9 by *Cossins, Peacock & Bewlay*, 1905–6, a smooth version of Arts and Crafts radicalism. On the

E, the **Masshouse**. The front block is late C17 in appearance, with hipped roof, dentil cornice, and big platband. It was, however, probably added to an existing farmhouse in 1722, for a Franciscan school which started here in 1723. Later C18 sashes. Projecting central entrance with early C19 doorcase. Alterations by *S.T. Walker*, 1932–3. (Interior with original six-panel doors, and upper part of staircase; fireplace by *A.S. Dixon*, brought from Chad Road.) Then back and NE up **Farquhar Road** through good early C20 houses, e.g. No. 81 by *Harry Weedon*, 1926, and the finest, No. 79 by *Bidlake*, 1914, tightly composed with three unequal gables. On the corner of Somerset Road, **Queen's College**. Neo-Georgian residential block and lodge of 1929–30 by *Hobbiss*, and his brick and tile textured Romanesque **chapel**, begun 1938 and completed 1947.* Tympanum by *Bloye*. Later residential blocks by *JMDG*, 1972 etc. In Somerset Road itself No. 24 by *Ball*, 1906, now part of the Nuffield Hospital, and opposite, No. 25 and its lodge, Jacobean by *J.A. Chatwin*, 1861.

Back past the Institute of German Studies and then s down a footpath alongside the sports fields. At the far end, the **Munrow Sports Centre**, begun in 1963 to the designs of *Chamberlin, Powell & Bon*, but never completed. Phase One contains a sports hall and gymnasia, with the humped shell-roofs in which the practice delighted *c.* 1960. Swimming pool added 1976, squash courts 1978, the entrance and bar remodelled in 1991, and a **gymnastic centre** by *Henry Boot Design and Build* added 2001. A ramp leads to sublime rooftop shapes.

Walking further s, on the w side of the University Road a gross Post-modern addition of 1999 for **Geography, Earth and Environmental Sciences**, by *Martin, Ward & Keeling*. Behind it, Biosciences of 1960 by *Playne & Lacey*, its ten-storey tower strongly modelled, with the ninth storey projecting. Otherwise, panels with bold pebble aggregate, and projecting end window. Across University Road West the **Haworth Building** for Chemistry, also by *Playne & Lacey*, built a little earlier, 1957–61. Lower, with gently modern foyer. w and s down South West Campus to the **Chemical Engineering department**. A block of 1954–6, with another, behind, of 1925–6, both by *Hobbiss & Partners*, and traditional. Mostly of three storeys. Link between them by *Corstorphine & Wright*, 2003. Addition for **Biochemical Engineering** of 1955–7, extended 1987–8 by *David Rathbone*. At the foot of the hill is the **Civil Engineering Court**, completed 1963 by *Playne & Lacey*. Pleasant and suitably efficient-looking. The taller extensions are Derwent units of 1968.

Back to University Road West and w again, past **Chemistry West** by *Arup Associates*, 1973, to the **Westgate Centre**, marking the entrance to the campus from University Station. On the s, **Computer Sciences**, on the N, **Learning Centre and Primary Care**, both by *Architects' Design*

*Important in the history of liturgy, as the first English ecclesiastical building with a forward altar for celebration facing the congregation.

Partnership, 1999. Between them *Eduardo Paolozzi*'s giant **sculpture** of Faraday, a gift of the artist commemorating the University's centenary, 2000. To its s, **Public Health**, 1996–8 by *Martin, Ward & Keeling*, and **Occupational Health** by *L.J. Multon*, 1981–2.

To the NW beyond the railway, the **Queen Elizabeth Hospital** complex by *Lanchester & Lodge*, 1934–8. Three pale buff brick blocks set behind one another: the University Medical School, the hospital proper, and a nurses' home at the rear. The largest British medical development of its time, co-ordinating many services on one campus. Formal Beaux-Arts plan (cf. Lanchester's Cardiff City Hall) centred on a tall stepped-up tower. The architects' response to cost constraints was a design 'devoid of mere ornamentation, reliance being placed on mass and line'. The Medical School has an austere framed entrance, with a sculptured panel of Aesculapius bearing the city arms, by *Bloye*, 1938. To either side, the façade plays with recessed planes. Prominent to the NW, **Institute of Biomedical Research**, orange brick. By *RMJM*, 2003.

Back to the ring road by the Haworth Building. To its s the **Old Gymnasium** of 1939–40, restrained yet subtly elegant. Then the large **Mechanical and Electrical Engineering departments**, built in stages by *Peacock & Bewlay*, 1951, 1954 and 1957. Additions by *Peter Neale* of the firm, 1962, three storeys, red brick and stone dressings, plain but still traditional. Solid centrepiece with a big frame, recalling the Medical School. **Sculpture**: frieze with lightning shot through a cogwheel, representing the two departments, and two groups of male students with their tutors, hieratic figures but in contemporary dress (including a duffel coat), by *Bloye*, unveiled 1954. Inconspicuous to the NE, Wrestlers, **sculpture** by *E. Bainbridge Copnall*; 1950, sited 1974. From here we can return E to Chancellor's Court.

The Vale

A final excursion can be made, about one mile N, to **The Vale**. *Casson & Conder*'s first commission at the University, in 1956, was to produce a layout for a new residential area. In 1951 Birmingham had only one purpose-built hall of residence, University House, and the highest number of students in private lodgings of any provincial university. Seven acres (2.8 hectares) were given by the Calthorpe Estate to build more halls in 1948–9, and by 1954 the University was in negotiation for another 110 acres (44.6 hectares) to consolidate its holdings. This included a site of 45 acres (18.2 hectares) dominated by three large early C19 villas N of the main campus, which was secured in 1955.

The Vale site was, in the words of Casson & Conder, 'a mature, gracefully contoured and planted piece of parkland', which they recommended should be developed 'in the tradition of the English picturesque movement of the eighteenth century, but recreating it in contemporary terms'. The villas were demolished and their grounds overlain by new landscaping mounded to shield the surrounding buildings to the NE and which turned the low-lying damp centre of the site into a lake. **Bridge** by *Neville Conder*. The new parkland reflected that of Edgbaston Hall opposite, and was intended to complement the 'green and gracious' Calthorpe Estate generally. Victorian exotics were enhanced with additional planting by *Mary Mitchell* to create a masterful piece of C18 landscape revivalism. Halls of residence were set around the edge to encroach upon this swathe as little as possible. A central service court intended N of the lake was never built. Instead three pairs of halls, each sharing a common kitchen, were designed to Casson & Conder's briefs. **Chamberlain Hall** comprises a twenty-two-storey tower, originally **High Hall**, by *Harvey & Wicks* with *Jackson & Edmonds*, 1962–4, with a lower range, originally **Ridge Hall**, alongside – eyecatchers closing the view from the lake and best seen from a distance. On the N they face Church Road (p. 229). To the w, **Wyddrington Hall** and **Lake Hall**, from 1998. **Shackleton Hall**, was built in 1963–6 by *H.T. Cadbury-Brown* and remodelled 2003–4 as student flats by *Barton Fellows*, after a scheme for new buildings by *Temple Cox Nicholls* that would have encroached on the landscape was abandoned. **Mason Hall**, originally Mason and Chad Halls, is by *Tom Mellor & Partners*, 1964–7; staff accommodation by *F.W.B. Charles*, 1964. Students now prefer flats to halls of residence, but architecturally these are unexciting: **Maple Bank** flats by *Mial Rhys Davies*, 1976–7, **Tennis Court** flats, *Danks Rawcliffe*, 1981–8, and **Centre Court** by *Benniman Design and Build*, 1990–1.

Bournville

Bournville is a model village, now a garden suburb, created from 1894 by the Quaker chocolate maker George Cadbury (*see* topic box). It follows Bedford Park in London (begun 1875) and Port Sunlight, Cheshire (begun 1888), but comes before the work of Ebenezer Howard and the Garden City movement, which starts with Letchworth, Herts., in 1903. It is particularly important as a social experiment and example; it was planned as a model for progressive private housing development. New Earswick, near York, was developed from 1904 by the Rowntree family to designs by *Parker & Unwin*, with advice from Cadbury, and closely following the Bournville model. It had Continental influence too, through Hermann Muthesius's *Das englische Haus* (1904–5).

In 1879 George and Richard Cadbury moved their factory to a country site three miles sw of central Birmingham, between Selly Oak and Stirchley. They named it Bournville, because French chocolate was highly prized. It was laid out spaciously, and surrounded by recreation grounds. A few typical late C19 houses, designed by *George Gadd*, were built for senior workers (dem.). But most employees had to travel from Birmingham, until in 1893 George Cadbury bought 120 acres (48.6 hectares) next to the factory, to develop for housing.

The estate **layout** was designed in 1894 by a Quaker surveyor, *Alfred Pickard Walker*, who was also responsible for the first houses, in Mary Vale Road (q.v.). Then in 1895 Cadbury appointed *William Alexander Harvey*, a pupil of W.H. Bidlake's, aged only twenty, as architect. He was inexperienced, his only completed work a terrace in Stirchley, and he had a tight budget. His first **houses** are still breaking free of late C19 conventions, and some still have the 'tunnel back' plan of Victorian terraces, with a rear kitchen wing. But by 1897 he was designing cottages, under Cadbury's influence, with small rear scullery wings, and by 1900, in Sycamore Road, completely rectangular plans, with the kitchen and third bedroom within the block to allow more light into the main rooms. Influenced by the Arts and Crafts Movement, his designs use simple traditional forms, and avoid self-conscious styles. They are of brick, occasionally roughcast, with hipped roofs, overhanging eaves, and most often casement windows. From about 1898 he used timber framing, increasingly structurally, for e.g. porches. His later work, such as the Bournville Tenants' Estate (*see* p. 266), is in a slightly heavier

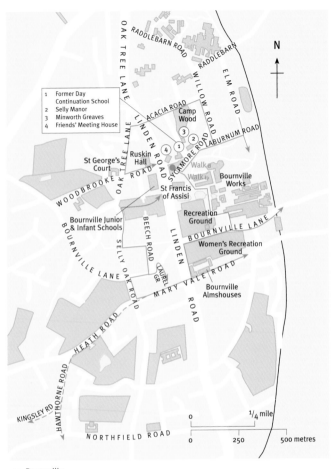

125. Bournville

manner, with dentilled eaves and big Tudor or arched chimneys.

Harvey could hardly avoid imitation when designing so much so quickly, and few have committed architectural petty larceny so often but to so much effect: Edgar Wood at the Friends' Meeting House, Harrison Townsend at the mission church, Shaw, Voysey and Bidlake in details of the houses. The *Architectural Review*, reviewing Harvey's 'Bournville: The Model Village and its Cottages' (1904), praised it highly while commenting that 'in some of the houses one can scarcely see the architecture for the "features"'.

Development started from the s end of the estate at Mary Vale Road, and the N end at Raddlebarn Road. By 1900, when Cadbury set up the Bournville Village Trust (*see* topic box, above) there were 313 houses. In 1904 Harvey resigned to go into private practice, though he was still employed to design the public buildings round the Green, started in

George Cadbury and his Social Vision

The brothers George (1839–1922) and Richard (1836–1899) Cadbury came from a Quaker family with a tradition of public service. Their grandfather Richard Tapper Cadbury (1768–1860) was the last Chairman of Birmingham's Street Commissioners before their absorption by the Town Council in 1851. George Cadbury was a deeply religious man; his friends called him a 'practical mystic'. 'Religion,' he said, 'does not consist in outward show or outward profession, but in feeding the hungry, giving drink to the thirsty, and taking in the stranger.' He knew working-class conditions at first hand from teaching at the Severn Street school (*see* p. 209). He was interested in many social issues apart from housing, campaigning nationally on the issue of 'sweated' labour, and in favour of temperance.

Cadbury started at Bournville as his own developer, selling houses on long leases. When it became clear that many could only afford tenancies, the Bournville Village Trust was set up in 1900. It has always been quite separate from the factory, and even in the early years less than half the residents worked there. It was intended as a model for private development, so tenants paid an economic rent. There has always been a deliberate mixture of owner-occupied and tenanted properties. Early tenants paid between 4s. 6d. and 12s. per week, within the means of at least skilled artisans. Early records show carpenters, brassworkers, a blacksmith and an engine driver. Cadbury was directly involved with planning the estate. He wanted the maximum air and light in houses, and so Bournville was given wide roads, and large plots of which houses covered only a quarter. They were designed in groups of no more than four to give an open and diverse appearance, avoiding the monotony of terraced housing. Gardens were laid out and planted with fruit trees ready for the new occupiers.

Cadbury understood the dangers of the kind of paternalistic control exercised by Lever (Lord Leverhulme) at Port Sunlight. He encouraged the formation of village councils covering Bournville Village and Weoley Hill, and intended the Trust to move towards electing trustees.

1905. His successor *H. Bedford Tylor* left in 1912, when the Trust closed its direct building operation. By 1914, with the original village nearly complete, the estate had 894 houses. Later developments to the w and sw include some by independent societies using the Trust's architects: the Bournville Tenants' Estate of 1906–13, and the Weoley Hill Estate of 1915–39. The Shenley development of 1950–65, w of Weoley Hill, was built in partnership with the City Council. Tylor's successor *S. Alex Wilmot* specialized in planning, and most of the important interwar buildings were by his assistant *John Ramsay Armstrong*. The Trust's design approach has remained simple and traditional, and hardly influenced by the Modern Movement. Old trees, hedges and lanes, such as Oak Tree Lane [125] (*see* p. 263), have been retained, and consistency achieved by careful control of materials and details such as window design. By 1999 there were 7,600 houses on the estate.

a) The Green and the Roads to the North

We start in the centre of **the Green** with the octagonal **Rest House** of 1913 by *W. Alexander Harvey*, based on the C16 yarn market at Dunster, Somerset. Paid for by Cadbury's workers to mark George and Elizabeth Cadbury's silver wedding. Its continuous canopy, gables and lantern create a strong presence among the grass and trees. Inside, a painted roof rises from crenellated capitals and the lantern has pendants with balls. Carved plaque with Commonwealth shields and luxurious foliage, by *William Bloye*, 1932.

On the N the **Friends' Meeting House** [126] by *Harvey*, 1905. Big central gable and wings running out at forty-five degrees, a round-arched entrance, and an octagonal stair turret with candle-snuffer roof. This is a domestic version of Edgar Wood's First Church of Christ Scientist, Manchester of 1903–4 (Wood lectured in Birmingham in 1904). Subtle contrasts of materials: deep red brick with dressings in limestone and rich veined brown ironstone. A band of limestone windows runs across the front and the right wing. The entrance breaks this band but has limestone abaci. Shaped window lintels and sills, to act as hood- and dripmoulds. The gable end of the S wing, facing the Green, has a niche with a bust of George Cadbury by *Francis Wood*, 1924, surveying his creation. Simple undivided interior, dominated by a roof with huge cruck-like arched trusses springing from ground level, linked to the wall-plates by horizontal braces resembling hammerbeams. W gallery. N extension by *BVT Architects*, 1970.

Going anticlockwise round the Green, **Ruskin Hall** by *Harvey*, 1902–5, was the village institute. Conceived as a national memorial to John Ruskin, inspired by his friend J.H. Whitehouse. The original part is the big gabled N wing and the range running S with big swept roofs broken by small dormers. Entrance under a smaller gable. Restrained Tudor details, some slightly wilful, e.g. the peak in the bay window parapet. S wing with effective three-storey cross-gabled corner tower by *Harvey & Wicks*, 1928. NW extension by *Harvey & Wicks*, 1956, extended E, with another gable to Linden Road, by *BVT Architects*, 1966. Moulded plasterwork in the Library. Staircase with twisted iron uprights and a tapering wooden post with a band of rose decoration. Refurbished by *Associated Architects*, 2002, with glazed infill on the W.

Across Woodbrooke Road to the S **Bournville Junior School** by *Harvey*, 1905. A complex design of calculated contrasts. The focus is a powerful stair-tower in brick with stone dressings, the tallest accent on the Green, topped by the open lantern and ogee dome of the **Carillon**,

126. Friends' Meeting House, the Green, by W. Alexander Harvey, 1905

1934. Its bluntness is relieved by window bands and small delicate late Gothic elements, e.g. the oriel window with carved corbel. The massive brick and stone language continues through the main hall, aligned N–S behind and marked by a flat-topped turret, and the NE and NW entrances. The doorways have heavy foliage blocks interrupting delicate arch mouldings which die unnoticed into the jambs. The carving is by *Benjamin Creswick*. This massive architecture contrasts with gabled classroom blocks in a much lighter style with big white-painted mullion-and-transom windows. The hall has a massive, heavily pegged roof with two collar-beams, the lower with arched braces which rise from corbels. Vertical struts linking the collars, and big wind-braces. The upper wall panels between the trusses are filled with frescoes of

Biblical scenes by *Mary Creighton McDowall* and *Mary Sargent Florence*, 1914. Light colours, rapid sketchy handling. Architecture divides panels into separate scenes. Sargent Florence's figures are small, lost in space: McDowall's heavier, almost prefiguring Stanley Spencer – Bournville buildings appear in some scenes.

To the s the **Infants' School** by *Harvey*, 1910. A simpler design, tied together by tall windows rising into gables and dormers. Timbered bays used as discrete elements in Harvey's mature way. A touch of power in the s entrance, its gable clamped between buttresses, and a big chimneystack with star-shaped chimneys.

Across Linden Road on the e, **St Francis of Assisi**, the parish church, by *Harvey & Wicks*. At the n the mission church of 1913, now the church hall. Simple Italian Romanesque with low broad roof and round-arched entrance with stone columns, recalling Harrison Townsend's mission church at Blackheath, Surrey of 1895.* To the s the aisled basilican church, planned in 1913 but not built until 1924–5, also Romanesque, and linked by a rear cloister of 1937. The handling is more self-conscious than A.S. Dixon's or J.L. Ball's, e.g. the parapet arcading, w rose window, and apse with stone arcading. The blocks at the gable ends have cogging framed in plain brickwork. A campanile planned for the junction of church and cloister was never built. n and s porches of 1933. The n has a contemporary tympanum by *Bloye*, of St Francis's Sermon to the Birds, with flowers and trees forming wooden mullions separated by glass; the s tympanum is by *John Poole*, 1964, of St Francis' Canticle of the Sun. The cool rendered interior has arcades of Cornish granite columns. se chapel by *Selby Clewer*, 1965–6.

Along the se side of the Green, shops of 1905–8 by *H. Bedford Tylor*. Oversailing timber upper storey with quietly asymmetrical gables. Angled ne porch balancing **Lloyds Bank** also by *Tylor*, 1908: slightly louder in pinky-red brick and brown ironstone. Carved name and bee-hive symbols to the entrance door, and original glass.

On the n side opposite, the **Day Continuation School** of 1925 by *J.R. Armstrong*. Brick and stone dressings. Alexandra Wedgwood noticed how it is 'rather like Lutyens'. At first sight a long, symmetrical Neo-Georgian range: two-storey centre, gabled end pavilions with canted bays. Walking e there is a two-storey gatehouse with big sloping buttresses, an effective landmark, and set on an acute corner. This reveals itself as the centrepiece of the composition, with a second, identical range running n along Maple Road. Through the archway, projecting ranges face you at angles, their entrances with stone and tile diapering. Refurbished by *Associated Architects*, 2002. Open wooden walks glazed in, and a new workshop block with a grey metal monopitch.

Across Maple Road to the e, two houses re-erected from elsewhere by George Cadbury to add historic interest to his village: early examples

*Illustrated in Nicholson and Spooner's *Recent Ecclesiastical Architecture* of c. 1911.

127. Selly Manor, Sycamore Road, c15–c17, reconstructed 1912–16

of this kind of re-creation. Both were partly reconstructed by *Harvey & Wicks*, using other contemporary material. **Selly Manor** [127], from Raddlebarn Road, Selly Oak, was rebuilt here 1912–16. Three gabled bays of timber framing face Sycamore Road. Projecting c15 w wing of two storeys, close-studded and jettied to the first floor. On its w side is a projecting gabled porch, with stairs to the first floor reconstructed from a David Cox watercolour. Blocked external door at first-floor level. Early c17 brick chimneystack with star-plan decorative chimneys. The central block, on the site of the open hall, is of *c.* 1600 and has the largest gable. Close-studded framing with contemporary herringbone brick-nogging. The original main entrance opens here into a lobby against the chimneystack. The E wing, originally c16, has been reconstructed in square framing. The first-floor interior of the w wing has plaster between the joists, and the central roof truss, which has been cut to afford access, resembles a hammerbeam. There is evidence for a partition on this line on both floors. Good wind-braces. The central block and E wing have roofs with tie-beams and raking struts. The E wing has been reconstructed without a floor. To the N, **Minworth Greaves**, re-erected here 1929–32. Its three bays incorporate a two-bay, c14 or c15, hall of cruck construction, originally with a c15 box-framed cross-wing. Only the wall framing and the crucks are original. The middle bay is all c20, and both the intermediate trusses.

Continuing NE up **Sycamore Road**, a stretch all by *Harvey*, 1902. On the SE, Nos. 17–21 have simple brick three-storey elevations but unusual plans: set below the road, with first-floor doors reached by bridges. Nos. 13–15, part rendered, contrast curved ground-floor bays

128. Nos. 10–12 Sycamore Road, by W. Alexander Harvey, 1902

with little canted ones in the gables on shaped brackets. Nos. 9–11 are a dormer bungalow pair with a big swept roof, long dormers, tall tapering chimneys, and eyebrows over the doors: a dramatic little design, reused with slight variations. Nos. 5–7 are a small plain pair with flatheaded semi-dormers and round-headed doors. They start a group which is a good example of Harvey's way of varying essentially similar houses, sharing the same simple cottage plan with three pairs opposite on the NW. These are particularly important historically because they are illustrated in Muthesius's *Das englische Haus*: Nos. 30–32 with eyebrow dormers, Nos. 26–28 with gabled semi-dormers and windows linked to front door canopies, and Nos. 22–24 with the same dormers as Nos. 5–7 but plain doors with tiny canopies. Unfortunate extension and windows on No. 32.

Continuing NE, still *Harvey* work of 1902, two grand three-storey designs, carefully placed to form an accent at the sw end of a triangular green at the junction. Nos. 14–20 are a U-shaped block with tall end gables separated by a big sweep of roof, a special version of a design used several times. Nos. 10–12 [128] are a unique 'Dutch' pair with lots of arty details: stepped gables, little Venetian windows over canted bays, timber corner porches below dormers with very concave little leaded roofs. The green has a **war memorial** of *c.* 1920.

E along **Laburnum Road**, *Harvey* work of 1901–2. On the N, No. 32 emphasizes the corner by a two-storey canted bay under the gable, and timber porch with convex braces. Nos. 28–30 are another small cottage variation: square bays and timber gabled dormers. Nos. 24–26 is a quiet but radical Arts and Crafts design in thin handmade maroon-grey brick. Gables with tumbled-in brickwork and stone copings; stepped stone-capped chimneys with side smoke holes. On the s side **Holly**

Grove. The w side by *Harvey*, 1900–1, decidedly picturesque: Nos. 1–4 have a timber N gable end and a Voyseyish rendered S one; Nos. 5–6 a slate-hung first floor swept over the brickwork below, and slightly tapering side porches. Lastly Nos. 7–10, Voyseyish again, even to the shutters with heart-shaped piercings, but with a continuous first-floor bressumer on brackets. Back and across Laburnum Road, **Elm Road** runs N. On the w Nos. 92–94, part of the Holly Grove group, with low end gables. Ground-floor windows in deep reveals. No. 90 has diagonal buttresses and a semicircular porch hood on rich consoles. Beyond, simple terraces of four built from 1898 and let at modest rents, e.g. Nos. 73–79, E, by *Tylor*, 1907.

Back to the triangle and N up **Willow Road**. Again *Harvey* work of 1902 etc. Simpler pairs but much quiet interest, e.g. Nos. 57–59, E side, with shaped gables; Nos. 52–54, w side, with chimneys in fours set diagonally. Nos. 37–39 have a single big gable, a builder's motif transformed. The corners of **Acacia Road** marked by No. 30, SW, with a timber gable supported on typical *Tylor* big stepped brick brackets, and Nos. 26–30, NW, by *Harvey*, a simple three-storey block of four with end gables.

Along Acacia Road, on the S, Nos. 1–7 by *Harvey*, 1898, rendered with shouldered dormers, and Nos. 9–11 by *Tylor*, 1906–7, showing his simple, rather angular style. The best block here is by *Harvey*: Nos. 12–18, N, *c.* 1900, a beautifully simple and economical version of the three-storey U-shaped design: plain casements with relieving arches over the first-floor end windows and curved ground-floor bays. Stepped stone-capped chimneys. Then 1960s bungalows in **Camp Wood Close**. Nos. 36–42, further w, by *Harvey*, have slightly projecting gables with chamfered corners, marking the junction with Maple Road, running S opposite. His contemporary part-rendered Nos. 15–17 (SW corner) have a similar gable. At the start of **Maple Road** Nos. 1–5 by *Harvey*, 1903–4, three storeys, with differing Venetian windows.

Further w we reach **Linden Road**. The corners are marked by a group of three cottages by *Harvey*, 1903, across the NE angle, and Nos. 19–21 and 23–25 on the SE by *Tylor*, 1905, big rendered carefully asymmetrical pairs. On the w side Nos. 24–26 [129] by *Harvey*, 1898, important because No. 24 was Harvey's own house. A low spreading U-shaped pair. His developing feeling for timber is shown in the partly structural end gables with small canted bays on brackets underneath, and the pent-roofed porches in the internal angles, with tiny rooms above. Low sloping diagonal buttresses. Nos. 22–24 to the N a simpler version.

Between them we take the footpath to **Oak Tree Lane**, and turn S. On the w side bungalows in **Westholme Croft** of 1957 etc. On the E, Nos. 139–141 and 143–147 by *Tylor*, 1908, the last with a big stepped staircase window spoilt by a S extension. On the w two exceptional, large single houses. No. 168 by *Harvey*, 1908, is a big L-shape, rendered, with carefully random fenestration and brick chimneys. Angled porch with rich consoles. No. 172 by *Harvey*, dated 1907, is a smaller brick L-plan with a

129. No. 24 Linden Road, by W. Alexander Harvey, 1898

typical little oriel window, diamond-paned casements, and a timber porch in the angle. Detached cross-gabled garage by *Harvey*, 1909, with a very Herefordshire lantern and a round-arched entrance. No. 174 of 1910 has nicely grouped gables. On the NW corner to Woodbrooke Road is **St George's Court** by *J.R. Armstrong*, 1924–5, flats for single professional women. A U-shaped Neo-Georgian range, plain except for pairs of porthole windows. Quoins marked by recessed brick bands. In the S continuation of Oak Tree Lane, on the E, Nos. 165–181 by *Tylor*, 1911, a U-shaped court, well grouped with a dominating N gable.

Along Woodbrooke Road to the E. On the N, two U-shaped ranges of bungalows by *Tylor*, 1909. The W one has timber porches with catslide roofs. Opposite on the SE corner of **Thorn Road**, a pair by *Harvey*, 1903, a central gable with Venetian window between chamfered piers. Darker, higher quality red brick than usual, also used to the E on his contemporary Nos. 1–7, similar but with square piers. Beyond these we reach the Green.

b) The Factory, and Houses South of the Green

We start from the Green, S between Lloyds Bank and the shops (following the signs marked 'station'). This leads through the buildings of the **factory**, basic classical with plain pilasters and a big dentil cornice, of 1908 etc. At one place a glimpse of the **recreation ground**, W, of 1896, with *Tylor*'s **pavilion** of 1902, picturesque half-timbering with a turret like that on the Meeting House. To the E of the ground a more decorative factory block with canted Tudor bays and Venetian windows.

Alterations by *Stanton Williams*, 2004–5. (A bronze of Terpsichore by *William Bloye*, 1933, is currently in store).

We emerge onto **Bournville Lane**, by the **Baths** of 1902–4 by *G.H. Lewin*, the factory's architect. An original and picturesque Free Style design. Brick with stone dressings and footings. Plan and handling suggest a progressive Nonconformist chapel: a 'nave' running N–S with a big shaped gable and a round-headed window with blunt tracery, and a cross-gabled w 'aisle'. SE tower with long sloping buttresses enclosing tall windows with alternating brick and stone sections to their arches, and an octagonal top with full-height flat-topped angle buttresses, and an ogee lead cap with a delicate weathervane. Below the main gable window a large carved panel by *Benjamin Creswick*, with his distinctive heavy and luxurious foliage; being refurbished, 2005. In the w wall **datestone** of one of the original works cottages, 1879.

On the s side opposite, a lodge of 1895 by *A.P. Walker*. E of it a block of 1959 by *Cadbury Bros' Architects' Department*. Also by them on the N, a seven-storey block with a wavy roof of 1963–4. Beyond it, a surviving early factory range with oversailing half-timbered upper storey. **No. 1 lodge** at its w end has a hexagonal roof with gabled projections.

We return w. On the s, the **Women's Recreation Ground** has the brick wall of Bournbrook Hall and, set back, a tall brick pavilion with delicate lantern. On the NW corner of the crossroads with Linden Road, the **Old Farm Hotel**, a farmhouse remodelled by *Harvey*, 1900, originally as a Temperance inn. Altered, but retaining his E front with grouped gables, bay and corner porch. To the N, early pairs by *Harvey*, 1897, the semi-dormers on Nos. 88–90 with segmental pediments.

Now s up **Linden Road**. On the w side early estate houses. Some, such as Nos. 124–126 and 132–134, are simply local builders' designs. Nos. 128–130 are *Harvey*'s earliest design, of 1896, still tunnel-backs, and with conventional square bays (originally balustraded) and moulded jambs to the windows, but handled much more simply than their neighbours. On the E three-storey pairs with end gables of 1898. On the NW corner of Mary Vale Road, shops and flats by *Harvey*, 1897–8, with timber gables and oversailing upper floors on brackets with grotesque heads carved by *Benjamin Creswick*. Slightly overloaded compared with his mature work. On the NE corner the **Bournville Almshouses** of 1897 by *Ewen & J.A. Harper*, given by Richard Cadbury. Single-storey cottage pairs and longer ranges, linked by walls and gates round a large grassed quadrangle. In a Late Victorian Tudor style reminiscent of John Douglas, untouched by the Arts and Crafts Movement. Half-timbered gables and canted bays with ogee lead roofs. Gatehouse-like entrance on Mary Vale Road with domed octagonal corner turrets to the porch and above to the main gable. Solid panelled entrance hall. Beyond to the E in **Mary Vale Road** more early three-storey pairs of 1898. The s side is early C20, by a good commercial developer, *Grants Estates*. Conventional tunnel-back terraces with square bays, and doorways with shaped pediments, a telling contrast with Bournville.

Back across Linden Road and w along Mary Vale Road. On the N, Nos. 222–232 are the earliest houses on the estate, by the surveyor *A.P. Walker*, 1895. Conventional Late Victorian, with awkwardly hipped roofs, one with tile-hanging. Nos. 234–236, a pair of shops by *Harvey*, 1899, show him trying out Voysey's manner: rendered, with big sloping buttresses contrasted with shallow bows to the shopfronts. No. 246 onwards are pairs by *Harvey* of 1896, with shouldered plain gables. Nos. 270–272 by *Harvey*, 1899, another Voyseyesque design, with long dormers cut into by the eaves. *Harvey*'s No. 274, 1896–7 for J.H. Whitehouse, turns the corner into Selly Oak Road. An eyecatcher with clashing s and w gables, the former sweeping down to enclose the porch. Carefully placed small bay, w.

N along **Selly Oak Road** and E into Bournville Lane, with more early *Harvey* work, the best ones of 1901: Nos. 97–99, N, and Nos. 80–86, s, dormer bungalow pairs with big central chimneys, all slightly different. In the short **Laurel Grove**, s, No. 3, with gabled timber upper storey and porch with shaped parapet: built as washing baths by *Harvey*, 1896–7, for early residents without their own. **Beech Road** runs N here with more early pairs by *Harvey*, the best Nos. 14–16 of 1897–8. A footpath E between Nos. 11 and 13 leads back to Selly Oak Road. The wide central green here has been infilled by 1960s bungalows. On the E side U-shaped courts and a stepped-up terrace, Nos. 55–65, by *Tylor*, 1910; on the w, terraces of four and a pair by *Harvey*, 1902–3, obviously on a budget. Going N, a terrace of pre-Bournville houses, one dated 1879, makes a sharp contrast. Opposite Hay Green Lane we enter the park on the E and walk through back to the Green.

The Bournville Tenants' Estate

This was developed between 1906 and 1914, and all designed by *Harvey*.* A mile sw of the Green, reached from Mary Vale Road w along Heath Road, then sw down **Hawthorne Road** to the triangular green at the junction of Kingsley Road. The houses here are mainly of 1907–9. On the E side, pairs and groups of three, stepping forward and back, some partly rendered. Steep gables with dentilled eaves resting on slight capitals suggesting open pediments. Nos. 26–28 have vestigial pilasters. On the sw side, angled groups of 1912–13, the last houses on the estate. Going s down Hawthorne Road, houses of 1907–9. Nos. 11–13, w, stand out, with arched central chimney, chamfered side projections for staircases, and concave, lead-roofed porches. Canted bays, repeated on Nos. 7–9, w, and Nos. 8–10, E. On the corners of **Northfield Road** two complex groups of three. Each has a timber gabled projection, a steep brick gabled wing with an inset two-storey flat-roofed porch, and further s a timber porch with big brackets. The E terrace (Nos. 2–6), has recessed

*Except for two pairs by the Estate Company's secretary, *David Glass*, on Woodlands Park Road.

brick quoining and an arched chimney; its twin has diagonal stacks. More houses E and W on the N side of Northfield Road.

Kingsley Road has long terraces of 1908–10, with varied fenestration. Nos. 51–57 are the show job here, rendered and with a centrepiece of two gabled timber projections linked by a balcony. Nos. 43–49 have big diagonally set chimneys on the SW gable. Nos. 48–54 on the N have eyebrow dormers, Nos. 35–41 on the S a wide segmental porch, Nos. 19–25 and 11–17 dentilled gables and rows of big dormers. The corners to **Woodlands Park Road** have terraces of 1907–8, with two-storey canted bays in the gabled projections. The N one steps down the hill. Just N in Woodlands Park Road, on the E, a public hall by *Harvey, c.* 1913. Timber construction and, a rustic Baroque doorcase with segmental pediment. Oculus above.

The estate has a quiet purity of design, which makes the spread of plastic windows especially damaging.

Selly Oak Colleges

These are a loose federation of higher education institutions, many of them denominational, which started in 1902 with George Cadbury's development of Woodbrooke (*see* below) as a Quaker college. Reached from the Green N up Linden Road, W via Langleys Road (past **Selly Oak Methodist Church**, 1965–6 by *Hulme & Upright*), and along **College Walk**. On the N, the **Asbury Memorial House** of 1926 by *Beresford Pite* and *Arnold Silcock*. Important because of Pite's lifelong concern with mission buildings. 'In all Pite's architecture,' says Brian Hanson, 'there is always something highly charged straining to express itself through a carefully contrived simplicity,' and this bulky block, with canted bays rising into a big mansard roof, seems to push out toward us. The grand motif, the pair of chimneys set at forty-five degrees, expresses a cunning arrangement of corner fireplaces inside.

At the far end, SW down **Bristol Road**. On the SE side the **George Cadbury Hall** by *Hubert Lidbetter*, 1926–7. Portico with paired Doric columns and a big steep roof not expressed inside. The **Rendel Harris Memorial Library** is by *J.R. Armstrong*, 1931, smaller but massive Neo-Georgian, its raised centre with a vestigial pediment clamped between hipped wings. Further SW the drive to **Fircroft College**, with on the corner No. 1022, brick and render by *Harvey*, 1901. The college buildings were **Primrose Hill**, George Cadbury Jun.'s house, a major Arts and Crafts work by *Harvey* of 1901, confused by later additions. The main block running NW–SE has simple, blunt chimneys and stone mullion-and-transom windows. Two projecting bays have gables with shaped stone copings (cf. Nos. 24–26 Laburnum Road, p. 262). Entrance, right, with a Lethaby-style segmental door hood. The garden front has full-height canted bays. Contemporary timbered coach-house wing, originally separate. *Harvey* extended the house SE in 1909, and linked it to the wing with a charming timber overhang on long brackets, 1911.

Further sw on Bristol Road, **Woodbrooke College**, with semi-detached lodges by *BVT Architects*, 1924. A grand early C19 country house, much altered. The sw garden front survives: seven bays of giant Corinthian pilasters, small central pediment. Six later C19 bays, left, with a three-bay attic which knocks the composition off-centre. Major extensions by *BVT Architects*, 1960–1: a long wing running NE, and more at the rear with a tall tapering chimney.

Now across Bristol Road. **Witherford Way** is the start of the **Weoley Hill Estate**, by *BVT Architects*, begun 1915. Rendered terraces, here going slightly classical, with pedimented centres. Back NE up the hill, first the drive NW into **Westhill College**. E-shaped main block (now **Archibald House**) by *Harvey & Wicks*, 1914–15, showing the influence of Lutyens: Wren-style three-storey central porch, its doorway with a big curly pediment, main block articulated by giant arches with the upper storey partly open, mansard roofed wings. Garden front with an impressively piled-up centre. To the NW, **Barrow Cadbury House** by *Clifford Tee & Gale*, 1961, has a circular porch supported on a central pier, with a little flying staircase. Further NW the former principal's house, **No. 12 Fox Hill**, by *Harvey & Wicks*, 1922–3. A small but exquisite Arts and Crafts L-plan house with Neo-Georgian details, in the manner of Ernest Newton or Baillie Scott. Doorcase flanked by round windows, sumptuous Venetian window with relieving arch to the garden. Back down the drive and NE, we reach **Kingsmead Close**, student residences by *Harvey & Wicks* grouped along the sides of a large green. The sw side has three linked cottage-style blocks, not quite symmetrical, of 1912–13. The NE side has a similar block of 1915, and to the SE of it, a rather heavy Neo-Georgian block of 1911–12. Further SE an eight-storey block by *Clifford Tee & Gale*, 1962. Further sw, their contemporary **chapel**. To the NE, the bulky **Orchard Learning Centre** by *Ahrends Burton Koralek,* 1996.

Weoley Park Road to the NE has the Baptist **International Mission Centre**, a Victorian house extended by *Harvey*, 1912, with a prominent stair-tower. To its w a picturesque early C19 cottage.* Further w, the **College of the Ascension** of 1928–9 by *Christopher Wright*. Domestic lodge house and ranges in maroon brick; chapel with tower nave.

Outliers

On the Weoley Hill Estate in Bryony Road, **Weoley Hill United Reformed Church** of 1932–4 by *J.R. Armstrong*, with a big stepped Scottish gable front and simple arcades inside.

In Cotteridge, s of Bournville down Linden Road and Watford Road, the **Friends' Meeting House** of 1962–4 by *Harry Harper* of *Clifford Tee & Gale*, combines Modernism and the gentle Bournville approach. Single storey, buff brick, low-pitched V-roof. L-plan facing a rear lawn, always felt through large windows.

*On the N were the former **Middlemore Emigration Homes**, a severe Neo-Georgian U-shaped block of 1928 by *Buckland & Haywood*. Demolished 2004.

Hall Green

Birmingham's interwar prosperity means that it has delightful and high quality Dunroamin, and this excursion centres on some of its good 1930s commercial housing – the world of Alan A. Jackson's *Semi-Detached London* and the Avenue novels of R.F. Delderfield. Typical of Birmingham suburbia are its layout with the large dual carriageway of Fox Hollies Road, the presence of earlier, rural, buildings, and the many trees which line its roads. It was designated a Conservation Area in 1988 as a good example of the period, but this has not prevented many replacement plastic windows and doors. The area desperately needs action before all its original details are lost.

We start on the corner of Fox Hollies Road and School Road, with the **Church of the Ascension** [131], or **Job Marston's Chapel**, now the parish church. Marston left £1,000 for this 'handsome convenient firm and durable chappel'. Designed by *Sir William Wilson* of Sutton Coldfield, and built by *William* and *Francis Smith*. Dated 1703 in a plaque over the w door carved by *Wilson*. Transepts and chancel added 1860 by *J.G. Bland*, builder *Samuel Briggs*.

The c18 nave and w tower are slightly toy-like and of great charm. Red brick laid in Flemish bond, with stone dressings. Four-bay nave

130. Hall Green

articulated by Doric pilasters – a very early use of these on a church – on pedestals; full entablature with pulvinated frieze, and balustrade. The classical treatment is applied to a building slightly too small for it; Wilson, a mason and sculptor turned architect, was showing off his knowledge of the orders (cf. his own Moat House, Sutton Coldfield). On the s side, **sundial** inscribed *Joseph Peter*, 1766. The w tower has brickwork patterned with burnt headers; the bricklayer, *John Lee*, cut his name on a brick. Its N and s sides have oculi. Above, two octagonal stages and a copper dome. The 1866 E parts are remarkably tactful, distinguishable by slightly larger, darker orangey bricks, and a blue brick English bond plinth. Plain walls with more oculi, and hipped roofs. **Interior** quite plain, with a coved ceiling, continued in the C19 parts.

Fittings. **Box pews**, C18, cut down; 1860 ones in the transepts. The originals have fielded panels. – **West gallery**, C18 but extended in the early C19 on iron columns. – **Galleries** N and s of 1860, on iron columns with leaf capitals. – **Pulpit**. Octagonal C18 top, ornate Victorian brass stair-rail, base probably C20. – **Font**. Small, alabaster, 1933. – **Communion rail** and **clergy seats** of 1932 by *Percy Yabsley*, with balusters. **Choir stalls** probably also his. – **Benefaction board**, s wall, a good piece dated 1703. Job Marston's arms in a top projection. – His **hatchment** opposite. – **Pew allocation boards**, C18. – **Royal arms** on the w gallery front, 1828 by *J. Thorp*, 'Herald Painter', with a bear-like lion. **Stained glass** of 1866 in the E, N and s chancel windows. In the E window, the risen Christ in a mandorla with soldiers below.

Original brick **churchyard wall** with big half-round sandstone copings. A number of table tombs, the best Mary and Benjamin Steedman d. 1826, 1840, tapering, with gadrooned corners. To the w a brick **hall** of *c*. 1910, with entrance block of 1932 by *Batemans*.

Diagonally opposite the church, the **Charles Lane Trust Almshouses** of 1937 by *J.B. Surman*. Conventional Tudor, but the beautifully austere and subtle handling hints at the coming Modern Movement. Warm brownish brick laid in Monk bond, with stone dressings. Single-storey blocks, irregularly shaped, with hipped roofs, arranged in a horseshoe group round a grass court. Very slightly canted gabled bays, and dramatic chimneys alternating between pairs set diagonally and big blocks with patterns of projecting headers. Good original lamp standards.

Now E down **School Road**. *H. Dare & Son* [132] were the best commercial house builders in interwar Birmingham. They advertised 'Dare's Distinctive Houses' on their 'Severne Estate' in 1933. The houses here, and down **Studland Road** to the N and **Miall Road** curving s through to **Lakey Lane**, are all *Dare*'s, built 1933–6, roughly from s to N. Nearly all are semi-detached, and have big round two-storey bays, mostly under square gables. Many deep round-arched porches. Red brick varied by purple-maroon Staffordshires. Much variation in e.g. the small bedroom windows: some plain, some little canted oriels, some dormers set in catslide roofs, a Dare's trademark. Lots of quiet

131. Church of the Ascension, Hall Green, by Sir William Wilson, 1703

curves: the bays splay out above the lower windows, as do some of the oriels, and the catslide roofs sprocket at the bottom. The side roads are similar. Dare's offered customers the option of moderne, or 'suntrap' designs, but Birmingham conservatism is demonstrated by the fact that only one such pair was built here, Nos. 144–146 **School Road**. Curved windows, with original glazing in No. 144, and stepped lights to the small bedroom, continued round the sides. On the N side of School Road Nos. 168–190, a row of shops by *Dare's*, 1935, pure Metroland with huge steep gables and lots of fake half-timbering. Nos. 59–61 Miall Road have windows still painted in a traditional way with black mullions and transoms enclosing white frames, and 'home-made' wooden porches.

Opposite the shops on the SW corner to **Shirley Road** the **Three Magpies** pub (or 'The Maggies') by *E.F. Reynolds*, 1935. A bold response

132. Miall Road, Hall Green, houses by Dare's, 1933–6

to this conservative area, in a brick style influenced by Dudok, treated in Reynolds's massive and austere way. Square block with Public Bar and landlord's flat above, the entrance on the right side; lower wing, left, with ground-floor cellar, and smoke room and lounge beyond, entered round to the left. This unusual plan allowed the owners of the Dare's houses, the higher-grade clerks and the foremen from the Bakelite factory, to take their wives for a drink without seeing men in overalls. The unifying motif is a thick pier with a bullnose front. It divides the strip windows of the bar, and appears in the thin tower with a ball and cap on top. The **public bar** retains its wooden bar back, divided by similar piers. The **smoke room** and **lounge** are now one room; the large semicircular window is an expansion of the bullnose motif. It faces the bowling green and its **pavilion**, again with bullnose piers.

One further sortie, s from the church down **Fox Hollies Road**, past No. 592, the **vicarage**, by *Philip & Anthony Chatwin*, 1953, to **The Hamlet**. C19 Domestic Revival houses, in a rather George Devey manner with tile-hung upper floors on big brick brackets, casement windows, half-timbered gables, and star-shaped chimneys. By a local builder, *Frederick Daniel Deebank*, for John Simcox, who owned Stratford House, Bordesley (*see* p. 193), hence the liking for half-timbering. Several are dated 1883. The best are No. 38 on the corner of **Hamlet Road**, and further s Nos. 653–655 and 657–659, the latter dated 1892. On the corner of Hamlet Road and Stratford Road, the **Friends' Meeting House**, in a similar style. Opposite, the **Junior School** by *Arthur Harrison*, 1892–3, in more developed Queen Anne.

Excursions

Aston Hall and
Aston Parish Church

Aston Hall
by Oliver Fairclough

The only major Jacobean mansion in the old county of Warwickshire, Aston Hall is now a stranded relic of Birmingham's rural past, prominently sited on a ridge overlooking the road between Birmingham and Lichfield. The house was begun in 1618 by Sir Thomas Holte (1571–1654), a landowner with Court connections, and despite alterations c. 1700, it remains substantially as completed in the 1630s. In 1656 Sir William Dugdale called Aston Hall 'a noble fabric . . . which for beauty and state much excedeth any in these parts'. Its exceptional height, elaborate articulation and strict symmetry, and the dramatic skyline of lead-capped turrets and shaped gables, recall such great Jacobean contemporaries as Hatfield (Herts.), Blickling (Norfolk), Charlton Park (Wilts.), and Holland House in London. The plan is derived from drawings supplied by *John Thorpe*. Thorpe is best known as a surveyor, rather than as a designer of houses, but the ground- and first-floor plans for Aston Hall (in his 'Book of Architecture', now in the Soane Museum, London) are clearly design proposals, rather than survey drawings.

The last of Holte's descendants to live at Aston, Sir Lister Holte, died in 1770, and the estates were dispersed in 1817. From 1819 Aston Hall was occupied by James Watt Jun. (1769–1848), son of the great engineer (for whom *see* topic box p. 287). Watt used *Richard Bridgens*, who had worked for George Bullock at Battle Abbey and at Sir Walter Scott's Abbotsford, to design antiquarian furnishings for the house. Much of Aston Park was developed in the 1850s, and Aston Hall was saved from demolition by a Birmingham working men's committee which, as the Aston Hall and Park Co., opened it as a museum of curiosities and place of entertainment, 1858–64. The house, together with a remnant of its park, was then acquired by Birmingham Corporation (becoming the first major historic house in Britain to pass into public ownership), and is now a branch of Birmingham Museums and Art Gallery.

Exterior. The house chiefly consists of a main block facing E with two projecting wings enclosing a forecourt. It is built of red brick, in English

133. Aston Hall, by John Thorpe, begun 1618. Entrance front

bond, with a diaper patterning of blue-grey bricks. Its stone dressings (originally pale grey sandstone, but almost entirely renewed) include facings and quoins at the corners, string courses at the level of the window heads, strapwork cresting, and ball and spire finials. The middle five bays of the E (**entrance**) **front**, corresponding to the hall and three chambers on the floor above, break forward slightly from the flanking bays, where the two stairwells are lit by transomed windows of different sizes. This projecting hall-block has a balustrade parapet and, despite its three-light transomed windows, it has a more classical feel than the rest of the E front. Entry is through a central doorway, rather than a screens passage at one end of the hall. This would have been a markedly progressive arrangement in the 1620s, and Aston Hall has been regarded as a transitional building, Jacobean in appearance, but with a centrally entered hall intended for display rather than use. However, recent research established that this part has been refaced, probably in the mid C17, replacing a porch at the lower end of the hall and an upper-end bay window, as indicated by Thorpe. The stone doorway appears to be the original, widened and reset. The round-headed entrance is flanked by Doric columns. An inscribed panel above states that the house was begun in 1618, occupied in 1631 and completed in 1635. This sits a little uncomfortably below a broken pediment which seems more Mannerist than the surrounding ornament. The roof-line is enlivened by four shaped gables with pinnacles, and by a tall central tower with an elaborate ogee and square-dome cupola (the clock was added 1867). The house was largely re-glazed in the C18 with octagonal panes in wooden frames, similar to those used by William Kent at Rousham (Oxon.), and some of these survived late C19 'releading'.

Aston's projecting **wings**, a conservative feature and longer than those of many late Elizabethan and Jacobean houses, give an impression of depth and recession, emphasized by long walls flanking the forecourt. A square stair-turret projects from the inner face of each wing.

Slightly lower than the central tower (rising two storeys above the second floor, rather than three), these turrets have simpler lead ogee cupolas. At ground level each has a doorway flanked by flat fluted pilasters, with a shell tympanum. The more ornate first-floor pilasters are ornamented with masks. These are recent replacements, but their form is recorded in early views. On either side of the turrets transomed windows below a shaped gable look into the forecourt. The wings end in three-sided bay windows with strapwork cresting.

Originally the ends of the wings were only one bay wide above the ground floor. Some time around 1700, these were extended outward over a single-storey loggia, s, and service room, N (sadly, a rainwater head dated 1687 is not original). This was part of a programme that transformed the fenestration of the s (**garden**) **front**. At first-floor level this side contained the principal apartments. These appear to have been built to Thorpe's plan, with a two-storey polygonal central bay to the Great Dining Room, flanked by round and three-sided oriels. Only the shaped gables above and the arcaded Doric loggia (now with modern steel grilles) on either side of the Great Parlour remain after the remodelling, which swept away all the projecting windows and filled in the corners at first-floor level.

The **w front** is of two storeys rather than three, with an enfilade of five rooms on the ground floor, and the gallery running the entire width above. This has a flat roof, and an C18 parapet topped with urns. Behind rises the third storey of the hall block, comprising six shaped gables and a broad central chimneystack. This front has also been conservatively remodelled. The centre is now the tall saloon doorway (the principal entrance in James Watt's time: Bridgens's porch of 1835 was replaced by a great iron and glass conservatory of 1858, removed 1887). The window above is flanked by niches, which until 1958 contained early C17 statues of David and Solomon, originally on the E front.

N front. The service and family wing is the most altered part of the house. The original bay window at the N end of the gallery remains. The next bay E has been extended outwards to the line of the projecting central block, which on the ground floor contained the original kitchen (subsequently servants' hall). The gables here are C18, the five first-floor sash windows of c. 1800. The present single-storey kitchen may be mid C18, and its E extension, formerly containing scullery, icehouse and powder room, is probably a little later. The latter was remodelled for James Watt in 1835.

Interior. Thorpe's drawings, inventories of 1654, 1771 and 1794, sale catalogues of 1817 and 1849, and survey plans of c. 1824 do much to elucidate how the house was used on completion, and from the mid C18. Much of the C17 interior was exuberantly decorated, and several outstanding moulded plaster ceilings survive, together with a richly carved principal staircase, and a fine panelled gallery.

134. Aston Hall, by John Thorpe, begun 1618. Entrance hall

The **entrance hall** [134] – the Great Hall of Sir Thomas Holte's house – was substantially reorganized by the early C18. The ceiling is original and dates from the 1630s, though the frieze of animals was added by James Watt. Round-headed stone archways on the s, w and N (only the first, to the main staircase, in its original position), in walls lined with reused early C17 panelling (that on the E wall is evidently later). Two arches in the panelling on the w wall, flanked by Corinthian columns, contain large paintings of classical landscapes in the manner of *Jacques Rousseau*, while two more arches framed with pilasters on each side wall have grisaille paintings of warriors, also of *c.* 1700 (could these arches have come from the Jacobean screen?). The fireplace was originally on the w wall, but the strapwork overmantel with a panel bearing verses on the merits of service may be from Holte's time. Behind the hall on the w side is the **saloon**, with to the s, the **Best Drawing Room** (C18, but with a fine resited Jacobean fireplace), and a room fitted up as a library *c.* 1800. N of the saloon is the **Small Dining Room**, completed 1771. Its fireplace, and the early C18 panelling in the room beyond (from a house in Old Square, Birmingham), were introduced by Birmingham Museum. Holte's **Great Parlour** lies beyond the main staircase. The room, subsequently the Chapel, retains some C17 panelling, but has lost its fireplace and bay window.

The richly decorated **staircase** is one of the glories of the house. The twenty-two newel posts are carved with masks, scrolls and canopies up to the first floor, with a simpler strapwork design on the upper flights. The string bears a running pattern of wyverns and winged horses. In place of balusters are richly carved panels pierced with flowing strapwork. All this closely resembles a contemporary staircase at Crewe Hall, Cheshire (burnt 1866); a smaller, simpler staircase of the same type is at

Benthall Hall, Shropshire. The staircase was once painted, and on the first-floor landing still exhibits damage said to have been inflicted in a Parliamentarian assault in 1643.

A massive early C17 stone doorway with a strapwork pediment leads into the **Great Dining Room**. The principal state room of Holte's house remained a dining room until 1817, and became the Great Library during James Watt's occupation. It is directly over the Great Parlour, and originally had a large polygonal window on the s wall. The ceiling is the richest in the house, with cherubs' heads in cartouches between the ribs, and grotesque masks, apparently taken from a series designed by Cornelis Floris and engraved by Frans Huys, at the intersections. The frieze of the deep entablature below is decorated with high relief figures of the Nine Worthies, standing in niches. These are taken from C16 Flemish prints published by Philips Galle. The additional figures in the centre of N and s walls are both later. The Jacobean fireplace (decorated with the Holte arms) remains, though the central panel of the overmantel has gone. Bolection-moulded panelling of c. 1700.

To the E is **King Charles Room** (the Best Lodging Chamber in 1654). This has a beaded and jewelled strapwork ceiling and a frieze of real and mythical animals modelled in high relief. Later bed recess, flanked by Gothick columns of c. 1760. On the other side of the Great Dining Room is the **Withdrawing Room** with a fine C17 ceiling and a resited stone, marble and alabaster fireplace. Otherwise the room is as remodelled in the mid C18. It leads into the **gallery**. With its s extension of c. 1700 the gallery is 136 feet (41.5 metres) long. It now lacks the three projecting bays that originally enlivened the w front, but is otherwise largely as built, with an intricate strapwork ceiling, arcaded panelling articulated by fluted Ionic pilasters, and a stone and alabaster fireplace. At its N end the gallery brings one to the family chambers in the N wing and to the secondary staircase (large square newel posts, open well). These rooms are largely C18 in character, and Lady Holte's bedchamber at the E end has a large bed recess added c. 1700. On the second floor, 'Dick's Garret' over the hall chambers, the turret rooms and attic chambers have changed little since the C17.

Much also remains of the original **setting**, and this may be emphasized by forthcoming improvements. To the E, the forecourt walls connect with two square **lodges**, occupied in 1654 by porter and gardener. These are of two storeys topped by an attic with shaped gables. Their projecting E bays, echoing those of the wings behind, originally had ornamental gun-loops rather than windows on the lower floor. The forecourt, originally enclosed by a screen wall and gateway, and later by iron railings and gates, was flanked by a large walled garden, s, and a service court, N. The two-storey rectangular building on the E side of the service court is Sir Thomas Holte's **stable block**, substantially rebuilt in the mid C18, and again 1858–64. Another range of buildings, enclosing the court on the N, was demolished in 1869. At the rear of the site is a **terrace**, nearly 500 feet (150 metres) long, with at its N end the remains of a Jacobean undercroft, perhaps that of the banqueting house listed in the 1654 inventory.

Aston Parish Church (St Peter and St Paul)

A parish church on a grand scale, below the Hall to the E, N of Aston Lane. Its medieval parish included Erdington, Castle Bromwich and Water Orton. The ancient village and the Holte almshouses of 1655–6 have gone.

The fine C15 four-stage tower has square angle buttresses, three-light windows to N, S, and W, and a most unusual bell stage with rows of chamfered, segment-headed recesses containing two tiers of trefoil-headed panels, two on each side forming windows. Tall octagonal spire without broaches, partly rebuilt 1776–7 by *John Cheshire*.

The body of the church was rebuilt from 1879 by *J.A. Chatwin*, largely paid for by John Feeney, owner of the *Birmingham Post*. Chancel and SE (Erdington) chapel were complete by 1883, nave by 1889; the S aisle wall was rebuilt 1893, and the N aisle and S porch were not finished until 1908. The result is Chatwin's finest church, rich, scholarly, eclectic, and wonderfully spacious. The style is mid C14: late Dec, turning Perp. The **exterior** has a magnificent five-sided E apse, its multi-stepped buttresses bristling with pinnacles*, its height emphasized by three-light windows with continuous mullions. The inspiration must be St Michael, Coventry; the material is, appropriately, local sandstone. The chancel side windows have upper transoms, as do those in the nave clerestory, though with more obviously Dec trefoiled heads. Continuous battlements tighten the composition. The aisle and Erdington chapel have *c.* 1300 style Y-tracery, partly to incorporate glass from the previous chancel. Linked NW hall by *K.C. White & Partners*, 1978–9.

The **interior** must also be inspired by Coventry, a single space without a chancel arch, dominated by the apse. The design gains in richness as we go eastward. Seven-bay nave arcades with alternating round and octagonal piers. Decorated capitals with bossy foliage. The walls check in below the clerestory, and the wall shafts break here, and stop just above the labels of the arcade arches, typical Chatwin details, emphasizing the solid character of the design. Opulent two-bay chancel arcades in Lincs. or Notts. Dec, e.g. Hawton. Their ogee arches have rich crocketing, internal cusping embellished with angels, and pinnacles breaking the sills above. The roof has alternating hammerbeams and arch-braced camber-beams. Chancel division marked by hammerbeam trusses. The Erdington Chapel has a wooden barrel vault and a big corbel of a knight. Tall C15 tower arch with four continuous chamfers, alternating plain and hollow. Minimalist C20 N aisle room.

Furnishings. All by *Chatwin*. The grandest set of his characteristic **choir stalls** with scrolled tops to the ends, here carrying Biblical figures.

* Temporarily removed (2005).

– **Pulpit**, 1885, alabaster and grey marble, with Biblical scenes, integral with the low chancel **screen**. – Mosaic **floors** in chancel and Erdington Chapel. – Stone **reredos**. – Simple **pews**. – **Font**, 1881. – **Stained glass**. The climax of the apse is five glorious *Hardman* windows of 1885 representing the Adoration of the Lamb. More *Hardman* windows, of 1883, in the Erdington Chapel. N chapel E, behind the organ, by *Lavers & Barraud, c.* 1860, and good. The N window, by *Francis Eginton*, 1793, is currently in store. S aisle windows from the former church, repositioned. From the E, the second by *Hardman*, 1869; the third by *Alexander Gibbs*, 1862–3; the fifth by *Heaton, Butler & Bayne*, 1893. Tower W by *Lavers, Barraud & Westlake, c.* 1884. Tower N of 1931.

Monuments. A large and important collection; only the best can be described. Chancel. Alabaster effigy of a knight, *c.* 1360, and sandstone effigy of a lady, *c.* 1490, on a stone and alabaster tomb-chest. This is probably Dugdale's 'faire monument of Arden removed from the priorye of Maxstoke'. – Mutilated sandstone effigy of a knight, early C15. – Sir Thomas Erdington d. 1433 and his wife Joan or Anne Harcourt d. 1417, he in armour, she in long skirt and mantle. Alabaster tomb-chest with very linear angels, and shields. Probably made *c.* 1459, when Sir Thomas's son built and endowed a chantry chapel. – Erdington Chapel. Late C15 effigy of a knight, probably Sir William Harcourt. Tomb-chest with finely carved angels. – Sir Edward Devereux d. 1622 and his Lady. A fine altar tomb in alabaster and black marble, under a heavy curved pediment on Corinthian columns. – John Frederick Feeney d. 1899 by *Frampton*. Charming Arts and Crafts plaque in a classical surround. – N aisle, E end. William Holte d. 1518 and wife. Sandstone effigies on a tomb-chest, badly executed. – Sir Thomas Holte d. 1654. Erected after 1679, probably after 1694. Perhaps by *William Stanton*. Corinthian pilasters and weeping putti. All carved with great spirit. – Sir Charles Holte d. 1722, more Baroque, e.g. free-standing columns instead of pilasters. – Sir Lister Holte, by *Westmacott*, 1794. Sarcophagus on lions' feet. – N aisle W, inside room. Edward d. 1592 and Dorothy Holte. Big recess with Corinthian columns. Conventional kneeling figures. – Sir Charles Holte d. 1782. Portrait medallion and mourner. – Henry Charles d. 1700, servant to Sir Charles Holte. Draped tablet – James d. 1821 and Ann Goddington, by *William Hollins*, with typical drooping laurels. – G. Yates d. 1828 by *Seaborne*. Tall tomb-chest. – S aisle, from E. Sir John Bridgeman, d. 1710, erected 1726 and signed by *James Gibbs*. An excellent, strongly architectural piece. – T. and C. Caldecott, d. 1774, 1788. One putto with a Bible, the other a (broken) torch. – Robert and Laetitia Holden d. 1730, 1751, by *Michael Rysbrack*. Simple tablet, but exquisite angels, just heads and wings, in set-backs either side. – E. and S. Brandwood, d. 1731, 1762, by *Eglington Sen*. – Booth family, d. 1673–89. Big oval tablet; segmental pediment.

135. St Peter and St Paul, Aston, by J.A. Chatwin, 1879. Chancel

Soho House and Soho Foundry

Soho Avenue, Handsworth, and Foundry Road, Smethwick
by George Demidowicz

Soho was the brainchild of *Matthew Boulton* (1728–1809), but is better known through the firm of *Boulton & Watt*. In 1775 Boulton entered into an epoch-making partnership with *James Watt* (1736–1819) to provide an improved steam engine, which helped launch the Industrial Revolution. The story of Soho is complex as a result of many other activities (*see* topic box, p. 287), so that in the late C18 it had acquired an international reputation and was much visited from home and abroad: 'Europa's wonder and Britannia's pride.'

The **buildings** divide into four: Soho House, the Soho Manufactory, the Soho Mint and the Soho Foundry. Only the first and the last still stand. The House and the sites of the demolished Manufactory and Mint are grouped together two miles NW from the centre of Birmingham, while the Foundry lies a mile W in Smethwick in the Metropolitan Borough of Sandwell. Soho House has been restored as a branch of Birmingham Museum and Art Gallery. The Foundry, unfortunately derelict and inaccessible, has been the subject of considerable recent study as a basis for restoration and reuse.

Soho House [136], Soho Avenue, is the only surviving building of the Soho Handsworth complex (frequent buses 74, 78 and 79 from Birmingham city centre). The house was acquired by Birmingham City Council in 1990, after many years as a police hostel, and opened as a museum in 1995. It was Matthew Boulton's home from 1766 to his death in 1809.

When Boulton acquired the lease of Soho Mill on Handsworth Heath in 1761, it was not yet five years old. The modest L-shaped house that stood above the mill was still a bare shell, but Boulton quickly fitted out the interior. From 1762 the house was occupied by his business partner, John Fothergill, but the completion of the main Soho Manufactory building in 1766 (*see* below) induced Boulton to move out to Soho. He developed the house piecemeal, as most of his attention and finances were devoted to his countless business activities (*see* topic box, p. 287). These curtailed investment in the house until the late 1790s. Boulton, however, could not resist using his house to experiment with new building materials and ways of making his home life more comfortable.

136. Soho House, south-east façade, probably by Samuel Wyatt, 1798–9

The approach is now from Soho Avenue, dominated by the NW elevation, but this is in fact traditionally the 'back-front'. From here there was a restricted view over the Manufactory, which stood about 150 yards (137 metres) W. The SE elevation, where the main entrance is situated, is now hemmed in by the gardens of C19–early C20 housing, leaving a small area of lawn. This elevation once commanded an extensive view SE over the park and Soho Pool and on towards Birmingham.

The house today is the product of major expansion and formalization in 1796–9, less subsequent demolitions.* Recent research has revealed a rapid turnover of designers in this short period: *James Wyatt*, architect, 1796–7; *William Hollins*, architect, mason and clerk of works, 1797–8; *Samuel Wyatt*, architect and contractor, with his cousin *Benjamin Wyatt* of Sutton Coldfield, 1798–9. In these circumstances it is not easy to distinguish the work of any individual. *James Wyatt*'s grandiose design was only partially implemented, raising the attic storey and adding a two-storey service wing, W (now partly demolished). A frontage block on the SE side was not implemented, so that an intended internal wall soon became the main SE façade. This has seven bays, the central bay framed by giant Ionic pilasters with a Diocletian window in the attic above a tripartite flat-headed window, in turn over a central doorway flanked by narrow windows; the remaining bays have simple sash windows, framed by Ionic pilasters on the corners, which support a plain entablature and heavy cornice. But who designed it? *Hollins* is credited with the first known drawing of the façade as it

*Plans drawn by *Samuel Wyatt* in 1787 and *John Rawstorne* in 1788 were never implemented. The suggestion that *Samuel Wyatt* was involved in work in 1789 has been disproved, and this more likely took place at Heathfield House, designed by the same architect for James Watt.

137. Soho House, dining room, by James Wyatt, 1796–7

appears today (without the porch), but he shows it already constructed and not as a proposal, and may have drawn it as late as 1799. Parallels for the central bay can be seen in *James Wyatt*'s unexecuted design for Badger Hall, Shropshire, but *Samuel Wyatt* submitted a drawing, now lost, of the SE façade to Boulton in June 1798. On balance the evidence favours Samuel, who was almost certainly responsible for encasing the house in slate giving the appearance of finely jointed ashlar (cf. his portico at Shugborough Hall, Staffs.). The stone texture was achieved by adding sand to white lead paint. The present semicircular porch was apparently finished by *Hollins c.* 1804 (rebuilt 1957). Most of the NW elevation belongs to the period 1766–96, including the three-storey canted bay window.

Matthew Boulton made many compromises: the house never attained the desired scale, and illusions of space were introduced where feasible. Two alabaster Doric columns in the **entrance hall** opposite the main entrance frame the doorway into the dining room and cleverly inflate this modest volume. Additional interest is provided by the painted floorcloths, made to the original 1799 pattern during the restoration, when documentary research and meticulous analysis of the fabric provided evidence to reproduce the 1790s appearance. A grand central stair was part of *James Wyatt*'s original design, but this entrance space, forward of the present façade, was never constructed. The '**back stairs**,' reached via a door on the left side of the entrance hall, have since served as the principal route to the first floor. Although unpretentious, the stairs are fascinating for the perforations made in the risers as part an innovative heating system installed throughout. Boulton experimented with various types of 'central' heating in the 1790s, including steam, but his son, *Matthew Robinson Boulton*, appears to have been responsible for the earliest version of the ducted hot-air system in place today. A stove (cockle) can be seen in the cellar from where warm air was fed through a network of ducts emerging through holes in the stair risers and grilles in the hearths.

James Wyatt converted the old kitchen into the **dining room** [137], but needed to expand it at the expense of two neighbouring rooms in order to achieve some scale. Aiding this illusion, four Ionic columns replaced a wall, supporting a shallow groined ceiling spanning to corresponding pilasters opposite. The marbling of columns and pilasters was by the decorative painter *Cornelius Dixon*, who repeated it for the curtains, now remade for the room. The restoration also provided the opportunity for returning many items from Great Tew, Oxon. (Matthew Robinson Boulton's house from 1815) to their original positions, where known. The dining room – or Lunar Room – is one of the most complete in this respect: the mahogany dining table was made by *Benjamin Wyatt* in 1798. It is likely that the meetings of the illustrious Lunar Society took place here. Members included the physician, botanist and zoologist Dr Erasmus Darwin, grandfather of Charles Darwin, Dr William Small, tutor to Thomas Jefferson, William Withering, who developed the medicinal use of digitalis (*see* also p. 232), John Whitehurst, clock and scientific instrument maker, Josiah Wedgwood, the great pottery manufacturer, Dr Joseph Priestley, chemist and polymath scientist – and of course Boulton and Watt.

The **breakfast room**, to the right of the hall, leads directly to the **drawing room**. These rooms form part of the earliest house and now contain the best of the original furniture by *James Newton*. The dominant object in the drawing room is the sidereal clock returned to Soho by an unimpressed Empress Catherine of Russia (case by *Boulton & Fothergill*, pedestal by *Newton, c.* 1771–2). The wallpaper here and in other rooms is a copy of c18 samples found under later schemes. Plated ware, silverware and ormolu made at the nearby Manufactory can be found in many rooms.

Matthew Boulton's **study** and **fossilry** on the ground floor are reached along the narrow stair-corridor. The restored first-floor rooms, spread along an equally tight passageway, include Anne Boulton's **sitting room**, **bedroom** and **powdery** and Matthew Boulton's **bedroom**, formerly a library. Other first-floor rooms contain displays and objects illustrating Boulton's life and ventures. The second floor is used as offices.

As with much that is associated with Matthew Boulton, the house defies categorization. Boulton did not implement the grand plans that would have transformed an overblown villa into a country mansion. He did, however, develop a large landscaped park from the barren heath around the house; unfortunately little of this setting is left. Boulton was

138. Soho Manufactory, by William Wyatt, 1761–7. Engraving, 1795

probably the first industrialist in the country to bring his home and manufactory together on such a scale, and to see Palladianism as a legitimate style for his main working buildings.

The **Soho Manufactory** [138], South Road and St Michael's Hill, was founded in 1761 on the site of a 'feeble' rolling mill on Handsworth Heath; by 1768 Boulton claimed that he had erected 'the largest Hardware Manufactory in the World'. Many travel diaries of the late c18 include a description. Jabez Maud Fisher remarked on the principal building that fronted the works, 'like the stately Palace of some Duke'. Erected 1765–7 to designs by *William Wyatt* as a silver-plate works, but with showrooms, warehousing and living accommodation, this building nearly broke Boulton's bank, (estimate £2,000, cost £10,000: 'a sore grievance to an infant undertaking').

Boulton was an enlightened industrialist and instinctively and practically combined art and industry 'to answer the Dulce as well as the Utile'. No attempt was made to segregate Manufactory from park. Below the front terrace of the principal building, the garden 'canal' returned water to the wheel in the polishing and rolling mill. Taste and technology were fused in 'a Theatre of Business, all conducted like one piece of Mechanism'.

The Manufactory continued to expand until the early c19. The majority of the buildings were constructed in the conventional Birmingham workshop manner; well-lit single- or two-storey brick and timber-truss structures eventually extended around five or six courtyards. In the late 1790s a crescent-shaped building in Palladian style was constructed for the manufacture of 'latchets', springy transferable shoe buckles. Most of the buildings were demolished in the 1850s–60s, the principal building last (1863).

The Soho Enterprises

Matthew Boulton set up a bewildering network of partnerships and firms at Soho, reflecting the vast range of products made: buttons, buckles, boxes, ormolu vases and clock cases, silver and silver-plated candlesticks, tureens and bowls, coins and medals, letter- and drawing-copying machines, and steam engines for pumping, machinery and ships. Personal, mantelpiece and table wares were traditionally known as 'toys' in Birmingham, but Boulton could not rest as an ordinary 'toy' manufacturer. 'He is always inventing, and by the time he has brought the Scheme to Perfection, some new affair offers itself.' (Jabez Maud Fisher, 1776). All this needed premises on a scale that the area had never witnessed before; with an average workforce of *c.* 600, the Soho works ranked among the largest in the country for many decades.

Matthew Boulton forged one of the great partnerships of the industrial revolution with *James Watt*, who was an inventor of genius but a reluctant entrepreneur and factory-builder.

The mystique of steam engines surrounds the Soho enterprises and the first working James Watt engine was installed in 1774 at the Manufactory to pump water back to the rolling and polishing (lapping) mill. Rotary steam engines, developed in the 1780s, were put to work polishing finished goods, running coining machinery and making small steam engine parts. The Soho Foundry at Smethwick followed in 1795–6. The canal location was essential for transporting completed engines to home and foreign markets. By this time the younger Boulton and younger Watt were ready to take on their fathers' inheritance. James Watt Jun. superintended the Soho Foundry, while a little later in 1802–4 Matthew Robinson Boulton expanded the original tiny engine works at the Manufactory. He also developed the coining business and eventually exported machinery for mints across the world (Mexico, India). Boulton assembled other great innovators and engineers around him, in particular William Murdoch, the pioneer of gas lighting. Other names include John Southern, John Rennie and Peter Ewart, some of whom left to develop their own careers. It is not surprising that Soho can boast a number of world firsts: the first steam powered mint, the first gas-lit factory, the first factory producing letter-copying machines, forerunner of the now ubiquitous photocopier.

Deeper in the park Boulton set up the first steam-powered coining presses in the world, at the new **Soho Mint**. With secrecy in mind, this was located within a group of garden buildings including a menagerie, laboratory, tea room and fossil room. For this reason the Soho Mint always presented an unorthodox appearance. When Boulton obtained the contract for the national coinage in 1797 the mint was rebuilt and

William Hollins was asked to design the sensitive elevations facing Soho Pool and the park. The Mint was demolished in the early 1850s, although part was excavated in 1996. The site lies in the rear gardens of houses on the E side of South Road, SW of Soho House.

A mile away to the W in Smethwick, on the Birmingham canal, lies the **Soho Foundry** of *Boulton & Watt* (Foundry Road; no public transport between the two sites). The Foundry was established in 1795–6 by James Watt Jun. (*see* also topic box, p. 287). It was the first purpose-built steam engine manufactory in the world. (Before this engines were sold under licence, and most parts could be made anywhere convenient.)

The Foundry also made coining machinery for the Boulton mint business, much of which was exported. William Murdoch conducted experiments with gas lighting here and in 1798 installed the first fixed gas lighting in a factory. The Foundry was acquired by W. & T. Avery, weighing machine manufacturers, in 1895. Only in the early 1990s was it realized that the early remains are substantial: the only standing buildings at any of the Soho industrial undertakings. The Boulton & Watt buildings and structures, now statutorily listed, lie at the W end of the Avery site. Big classical **front range** and entrance by *Buckland & Haywood*, 1925. Behind, a terrace of **cottages** of 1801–2 and 1809–10. William Murdoch lived in the larger cottage at the W end.

The main **Foundry building** (1795–6, 1801–2, 1895) will never delight the aesthetic senses, but the greater interest here is historic. In the vast and cathedral-like interior, now abandoned, the cylinders and other parts of the *Boulton & Watt* engines were made. The casting pit at its E end leads via 100 yards (91.4 metres) of tunnels built in the rapidly accumulating foundry slag, to the brick vaults of the Pattern Stores, once the repository of thousands of wooden moulds (1799, 1809; upper storey demolished and pattern shops built above *c.* 1898). The **Erecting Shop** immediately N of the main foundry (1847) is another huge space, topped by the original iron roof (made by *H. Smith* of the Vulcan Foundry, West Bromwich). Here the parts of the steam engine were finally assembled. s of the main complex lies the **Soho Foundry Mint** (1860), built by the successor firm, James Watt & Co. (1848–95). Although it has lost its internal walls and its roof is Avery's (*c.* 1896), this is the only standing building in the country that once contained Boulton coining machinery.

In 2004 the Foundry buildings are derelict and dangerous and there is no public access. Plans are developing, however, to restore them.

St Agatha, Sparkbrook

W.H. Bidlake's masterpiece, built in 1899–1901. It is in the free late Gothic Revival, deriving from C14–C15 medieval work, developed by Bodley and G.G. Scott Jun. and continued by J.D. Sedding and Leonard Stokes. Bidlake uses this style with great freedom and invention, especially inside, and the result is one of the finest English churches of its time. The money came from demolishing Christ Church (*see* p. 123) and selling its site. A competition was held for the design, assessed by Sir Arthur Blomfield, who chose Bidlake above *John Douglas*, *Mervyn Macartney* and *Temple Moore*.

The church is built of specially long and thin Staffordshire bricks. On the **exterior** these are reds with some blue burn, with dressings of Bath stone. The w **tower**, facing Stratford Road, is of exceptional quality.* At 120 feet (36.6 metres) it dominates its surroundings. It was heightened from the first scheme, helped by a late donation. It starts with a projecting three-sided baptistery, a Birmingham tradition (cf. Chatwin's SS Mary and Ambrose, Edgbaston, 1897). Then a three-light window, a blank stage with a big niche, and the belfry, its tall windows deeply inset, with massive stone louvres. All is held together firmly by octagonal buttresses, set back near the top, where they gain mullions and stone bands. Finally a pierced parapet, corner pinnacles resembling Sedding's at Holy Trinity, Chelsea, and a slender leaded Hertfordshire-type 'spike'. Flanking porches, gabled N–S, hint at a cross-range through the tower. Relief **tympana** over the entrances: St Peter appearing to St Agatha in prison, left, St Agatha with her persecutor Quintilianus, right. The rest of the exterior is closely surrounded by other buildings. Walls are articulated by triangular piers, a motif used by Stokes and also G.G. Scott Jun. (cf. his St Mark, Milverton, Leamington Spa, 1879). Aisle windows straight-headed, with flowing tracery. Chancel and clerestory windows in the late Dec turning Perp style of e.g. Edington, Wilts., as used by Bodley at St Augustine, Pendlebury.

The **interior** [139] impresses immediately by its height and lightness. Yellow-grey brick with Hollington stone for arches and mouldings. It is an original and remarkable study in angled and chamfered plane surfaces. Bidlake had designed a smaller, simpler interior of this kind at St

*The orientation is reversed, but liturgical directions are used here.

139. St Agatha, Sparkbrook, by W.H. Bidlake, 1899–1901. Nave

Patrick, Salter Street, near Earlswood (1898). The immediate inspiration for both is Leonard Stokes's St Clare, Sefton Park, Liverpool of 1889–90, for which Bidlake drew the interior perspective. The arcade piers are chamfered lozenges narrowing to a front face only 1½ in. (4 cm.) wide, and the side faces run back at an angle which contrasts with both the plane wall above and the differently angled recesses of the clerestory windows. Similar shallow recesses to the aisle windows. The

William Henry Bidlake (1861–1938) was the foremost Birmingham architect of the Arts and Crafts Movement. The son of the prolific Wolverhampton architect George Bidlake, his education marks him as a new kind of architect: Christ's College, Cambridge, followed from 1882 by work in London for R.W. Edis and Bodley & Garner. A fine draughtsman, Bidlake won the RIBA Pugin Travelling Studentship in 1885. In his early years he did perspectives for other architects, including Leonard Stokes. He inaugurated the teaching of architecture at Birmingham School of Art in 1892, and was Head of the School of Architecture 1919–22. He would entertain students by drawing the volutes of the Ionic capital simultaneously with both hands.

Bidlake's finest works show the progressive late c19 Gothic and Domestic Revival approach transformed by an Arts and Crafts simplicity and feel for materials. His most original work begins with St Patrick, Earlswood, Warwicks. (1897–9), where triangular wall-shafts derived from G.G. Scott Jun. and Leonard Stokes articulate the internal elevations. This play of angled planes is developed at his finest church, St Agatha Sparkbrook. Its soaring tower contrasts with that at Bishop Latimer, Winson Green (1902–4), with its dramatically cut-off top. St Andrew, Handsworth (1907–9), modest outside, has an apparently simple nave expanding into passage aisles and tall, wide transepts. Handsworth Cemetery Chapel (1908) has a superbly controlled collegiate interior. Sparkhill URC (1932–3) is round arched.

Bidlake's house designs are concentrated in the period 1895–1901. Hermann Muthesius, in *Das englische Haus* (1904–5), referred to their 'very simple style and the great honesty which they express', and compared him favourably with Lutyens. His finest are his own Woodgate, Four Oaks, Sutton Coldfield (1897); Garth House, Edgbaston Park Road (1901), and Redcroft (now St Winnow), Four Oaks (1901), which dramatically contrasts a bare three-storey tower with a roof sweeping down to the ground-floor windows.

In 1924 Bidlake married an actress over twenty years his junior. Perhaps because of scandal, he retired to Sussex, although he continued in practice into the 1930s.

piers rise up clear to luscious flower corbels supporting the wooden tunnel-vault roof, also derived from Stokes. The arcade arches have a hollow chamfer and a big wave moulding. Their hoodmoulds curve up at the bottom, and appear to pass through the piers, like wires through a block. The angles and planes, the narrow pier fronts, and this kind of detail, create an interior of high nervous tension. N chapel with E vestries; larger s chapel divided into two by an E arcade. The arcade pier has a pensive angel corbel. This planning follows Pearson's St Alban, Bordesley (*see* p. 193), but is reversed from Bidlake's 1899 scheme, where the larger chapel was on the N. The three-bay chancel arcades, with mouldings similar to the nave but enriched by roll mouldings, open into the s chapel and the N vestry passage.

The church was bombed in 1940, when the chancel was badly damaged and the E window destroyed. A temporary wall was built in the chancel arch. In 1959 an arsonist destroyed the nave roof and many furnishings. Repairs and reconstruction, by *Laurence Williams* of *Wood, Kendrick & Williams*, were completed in 1961. The roof is an exact replica. New work at the E end can be distinguished by slightly yellower brick.

Furnishings. The only survivor of *Bidlake*'s is the **pulpit**. Octagonal, with the sacred monogram in tracery on each panel. The stone base has free-standing piers linked to the main block by little arches. – *Laurence Williams*'s forward **altar** of 1964 is in Westmorland green stone. A fashionable type: tapering base and dramatically cantilevered top. – Small marble **font** on a Doric column, of 1865, from Christ Church. A symbolic **stone** from there is set in the baptistery wall. – **Statues** of Virgin and Child, 1922; and St Agatha, *c.* 1930. **Stations of the Cross**, 1931. – **Stained glass.** E window by *L.C. Evetts*, 1961, mildly Expressionist. Some red and blue, and, characteristic of its time, much clear but textured glass.

Next to the church, on Stratford Road, an excellent **board school** by *Martin & Chamberlain*, 1884–5.

St Mary, Pype Hayes

Designed by *Edwin Francis Reynolds* in 1927 and built 1929–30. Douglas
Hickman called Reynolds 'the chief local exponent' of Lethaby's ideas.*
He was Bidlake's assistant during the building of St Agatha Sparkbrook
(*see* p. 289), but much of his career was shaped by Lethaby's concerns.
He won the RIBA Soane Medallion in 1903 with a very Byzantine 'Town
Church' recalling the Sancta Sophia, and from 1909 taught at the
Birmingham School of Architecture as Deputy Director to Lethaby's
friend J.L. Ball. He even played tennis a lot – the game Lethaby saw as
epitomizing progressive behaviour. St Mary is his masterpiece and
arguably the finest building of its time in Birmingham. It also offers
evidence on what Lethaby's ideas meant in practice, and how they relate
to early c20 conceptions of a modern architecture.

The church was built by trustees under an Act which allowed the
demolition of St Mary Whittall Street, off Steelhouse Lane, of 1774. The
sale of its site paid most of the cost of £20,415. The builders were *C.
Bryant & Son*. Reynolds was proposed as architect by the chairman of
the trustees, George Bryson. He was treasurer for the building of A.S.
Dixon's Barnt Green, Worcs., and, as chairman of the city's Licensing
Justices, a great supporter of 'improved' pubs, of which Reynolds
designed several (*see* e.g. the Three Magpies, p. 271, and topic box, p. 25).

St Mary combines a wide nave with passage aisles, and the E part of a
traditional cruciform scheme of chancel, transepts and crossing,
arranged so that every nave seat has an altar view. A N chapel balances
the vestry. The plan is a beautiful thing on paper – by 1927 Reynolds had
absorbed Beaux Arts ideas – and once decided on, everything seems to
fall into place, right down to the vestment cupboards. Lethaby described
complex combinations of plan types in his book on Sancta Sophia, and
Reynolds kept the notes of a lecture he gave in 1918, approvingly quoting
him. He called his approach here 'not traditional in character but frankly
modern', which meant a commonsense application of techniques, traditional or sometimes new, to the needs of the building. Nothing is 'stuck
on', in the phrase both Lethaby and Philip Webb used, and apparently
historic motifs, such as round-headed windows and arches, are chosen
as simple and practical ways of doing the job, not for their associations.

*In 'The Houses of Four Oaks', Victorian Society (Birmingham Group), 1977.

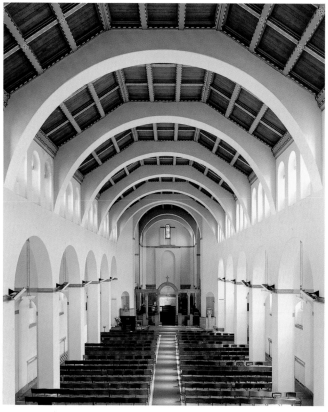

140. St Mary, Pype Hayes, by Edwin F. Reynolds, 1929–30. Interior

The exterior is a long solid block of brick, laid in Reynolds's favourite Flemish stretcher bond, with white Hollington stone details. The massive nave, its effect emphasized by the sloping buttresses of the clerestory derived from Turkish mosques, is well balanced by the projecting transepts. s bell turret, carefully placed where transept meets chancel. On the N side, the modest gabled hall is attached by a cloister.

The interior [140] is plastered. The nave is held in tension, structurally and metaphorically, by great segmental cross-arches (of steel and plaster, though they have the mass of concrete). The Oregon pine roof has painted panels with stencilled patterns. Its purlins run straight through from one end to the other without a break. The cross-arches express the wide nave; the through purlins express the long axis of the traditional cruciform plan. They meet, therefore, with a clash of great underlying power. Details such as the Red Hollington stone caps of the arches are calculated to hold the design together. The same stone is used for the **screen**, with its heavy cornice and central arch, and for the chancel walls, with niches for **sedilia**. The nave cants in to the crossing,

Arts and Crafts Architects and Brick Bonding

Traditional brick walls are two bricks thick. Bonding is the term for the pattern of stretchers – bricks laid lengthways – and headers – bricks laid across the wall to give strength. The best known are English bond, with alternating rows of stretchers and headers, normal until the later C17 and used again by Gothic Revivalists, and Flemish bond, with headers and stretchers alternating in each row, normal during the Georgian period. A simpler variant is English garden wall bond, with several rows of stretchers between each header row.

The Birmingham Arts and Crafts radicals – *A.S. Dixon*, *J.L. Ball* and their followers – followed local traditions of brick construction, even Victorian habits like cornices with cogging (bricks set diagonally for decorative effect). Dixon wanted 'to rebel against this tyranny of bonds' both on constructive and aesthetic grounds. He thought English bond 'ugly' and Flemish 'too mechanically regular', and wanted 'one header to three or four stretchers in each course or one course of alternate headers and stretchers . . . with two or three courses of stretchers.' These are respectively Sussex bond, found occasionally in Birmingham, and Flemish stretcher bond (locally called Flemish garden wall bond), the common bond of local C19 terraced houses.

E.F. Reynolds frequently used Flemish stretcher bond with one row of stretchers between each Flemish row, an arrangement found at Northgate House, Warwick (*c.* 1700), which he altered in the 1920s and which later became his home. *Holland Hobbiss*'s signature is English garden wall bond with three rows of stretchers between each header row. Monk bond, with each row having a pattern of two stretchers, then a header, became fashionable in the 1930s probably because of Edward Maufe's use of it at Guildford Cathedral (begun 1936).

perhaps a hint of Tengbom's Hogalid church at Stockholm. The N chapel has been boxed in, damaging the spatial effect at the E end. Twin **pulpit** and **reading desk**, in niches, flank the chancel arch. The aisle **pavements** are a Reynolds trademark, York stone and green Westmorland slate, in a pattern of squares set diagonally inside larger squares. Original **light fittings** with arched hangers mirroring the screen design, now modified for strip-lights.

When St Mary was completed, Reynolds thanked Bryson and his colleagues 'for giving me a splendid opportunity, and for being ideal clients'. It is not an easy or charming building, but its austere magnificence is compelling. It looks plain compared with the contemporary work of, say, Bernard Miller or F.X. Velarde, and it has nothing to do with contemporary Art Deco or jazz, but it may recall late Sibelius, or the Holst of *Egdon Heath*.

Further Reading

There are few books on **Birmingham's architecture**. Douglas Hickman was the city's leading architectural historian until his untimely death in 1990, but his *Birmingham* (City Buildings Series), 1970, and *Warwickshire* (Shell Guide), 1979, are constrained by format. Bryan Little, *Birmingham Buildings*, 1971, is a general study. P. Leather, *A Guide to the Buildings of Birmingham*, 2002, is strong on rural pre-1800 buildings. Tudor Edwards, *A Birmingham Treasure Chest,* 1955, is poignant in its pleas for buildings since demolished. **Victorian buildings** are splendidly illustrated in J. Whybrow (ed.), *How Does Your Birmingham grow?*, 1972, with descriptions by Douglas Hickman, and in J. Whybrow and R. Waterhouse, *How Birmingham became a Great City,* 1976. Remo Granelli's chapter in Alan Crawford (ed.), *By Hammer and Hand: The Arts and Crafts Movement in Birmingham,* 1984, was the pioneering account of Bidlake, Ball and other local architects, in an equally pioneering book. Roy Hartnell, *Pre-Raphaelite Birmingham,* 1996, has much information. In the 1990s the city's Department of Planning and Architecture published a series of pamphlets on C20 **architecture**: the most substantial is *Architecture and Austerity: Birmingham 1940-1950,* 1995. Liam Kennedy (ed.), *Remaking Birmingham,* 2004, is interesting for current attitudes.

The most important **general history** is the official one by Conrad Gill and Asa Briggs, 1952 (2 vols.), continued for 1939-70 by A. Sutcliffe and R. Smith, 1973. The *Victoria County History* for Warwickshire Vol. VII (Birmingham), 1964, is a mine of information. The best short account of the Chamberlain period is in Asa Briggs, *Victorian Cities,* 1963, supplemented by P.T. Marsh, *Joseph Chamberlain: Entrepreneur in Politics,* 1994. Chris Upton, *A History of Birmingham,* 1993, is lively and concise. Victor Skipp, *A History of Greater Birmingham down to 1830,* 1980, and *Victorian Birmingham,* 1983, have many insights.

The best **planning history** is Gordon Cherry, *Birmingham: a Study in Geography, History and Planning,* 1994. D. Chapman, C. Harridge, J. and G. Harrison and B. Stokes (eds.), *Region and Renaissance,* 2000, updates the story. Official in character but full of helpful information are *Municipal Public Works and Planning in Birmingham 1852-1972* (J.L. Macmorran), 1973, and *Developing Birmingham 1889-1989: 100 Years of City Planning* (Ian Heard), 1989. Sir Frank Price, *Being There,* 2002, is a remarkable autobiography, badly edited.

Eric Hopkins is the leading historian of the city's **industrial development**: *The Rise of the Manufacturing Town*, (1989, rev. 1998), and *Birmingham: The Making of the Second City 1850-1939,* 2001. Ray Shill, *Birmingham's Industrial Heritage 1900-2000,* 2002, is good on specific industries. On canals, Ray Shill, *The Birmingham Canal Navigations,* 2002, is a good introduction. S.R. Broadbridge, *The Birmingham Canal Navigations Vol. 1: 1768-1846,* 1974, was never followed up.

On **building types**, Alan Crawford and Robert Thorne, *Birmingham Pubs 1890-1939* (1975, rev. 1986), is excellent. Allen Eyles, *Odeon Cinemas 1,* 2002, covers work in Birmingham and elsewhere. P. Collins and M. Stratton, *British Car Factories from 1896,* 1993, covers Birmingham's most important c20 industry.

On **architects and artists**, Howard Colvin, *A Biographical Dictionary of British Architects 1660-1840* (3rd. ed. 1995), and Rupert Gunnis, *Dictionary of British Sculptors 1660-1851* (revised ed. 1968), and G.T. Noszlopy, ed. J. Beach, *Public Sculpture of Birmingham* (Public Monuments and Sculpture Association), 1998, are essential. A. Gomme, *Smith of Warwick,* 2000, has much about the area in the early c18. Pugin has a major literature. Phoebe Stanton, *Pugin,* 1971, is a short general study; P. Atterbury and C. Wainwright (eds.), *Pugin: A Gothic Passion*, 1994, is essential for recent scholarship; R. O'Donnell, *The Pugins and the Catholic Midlands,* 2002, covers both A.W.N. and E.W. Pugin. Michael W. Brooks, *John Ruskin and Victorian Architecture*, 1989, has a good account of J.H. Chamberlain. G. Rubens, *William Richard Lethaby,* 1986, is the standard work. For Bidlake *see* Trevor Mitchell's unpublished M. Phil. thesis, University of Manchester, 1994. S. Wildman and J. Christian, *Edward Burne-Jones: Victorian Artist-Dreamer*, 1998, is the best recent account.

On **specific areas and buildings**, Joe Holyoak, *All About Victoria Square*, 1989, and I. Latham and M. Swenarton, *Brindleyplace: A Model for Urban Regeneration,* 1999, are self-explanatory. F. Salmon, *Building on Ruins: The Rediscovery of Rome and English Architecture,* 2000, covers the Town Hall. *By the Gains of Industry: Birmingham Museums and Art Gallery 1885-1985* (Stuart Davies) is a good short account. The Jewellery Quarter is superbly surveyed in J. Cattell, S. Ely and B. Jones, *The Birmingham Jewellery Quarter* (English Heritage), 2002. Its shorter companion is J. Cattell and B. Hawkins's guide of 2000, also for English Heritage. On Edgbaston see T. Slater, *Edgbaston: A History,* 2002. The classic account of the Calthorpe Estate is in David Cannadine, *Lords and Landlords: The Aristocracy and the Towns 1774-1967,* 1980. The Botanical Gardens has Phillada Ballard's excellent history *An Oasis of Delight,* 1983 (rev. 2003). On Bournville, M. Harrison, *Bournville: Model Village to Garden Suburb,* 1999, is strong, while Peter Atkins's chapter in Barbara Tilson (ed.), *Made in Birmingham: Design and Industry 1889-1989*, 1989, closely analyses W.A. Harvey's designs. Oliver Fairclough, *The Grand Old Mansion*, 1984, is the standard account of Aston Hall.

Glossary

Acanthus: *see* [2D].

Acroterion: plinth for a statue on ornament on the apex or ends of a pediment.

Aedicule: architectural surround, usually a pediment on two columns or pilasters.

Ambulatory: aisle around the *sanctuary* of a church.

Anthemion: *see* [2D].

Apse: semicircular or polygonal end, especially in a church.

Arcade: series of arches supported by piers or columns (cf. *colonnade*).

Architrave: *see* [2A]. Also moulded surround to a window or door.

Art Deco: a self-consciously up-to-date interwar style of bold simplified patterns, often derived from non-European art.

Ashlar: large rectangular masonry blocks wrought to even faces.

Atlantes: male figures supporting an *entablature*.

Atrium: a toplit covered court rising through several storeys.

Attic: small top storey within a roof. Also the storey above the main entablature of a classical façade.

Back-to-back houses: with a shared rear or spine wall.

Baldacchino: solid canopy, usually free-standing and over an altar.

Balusters: vertical supports, often of outward-curved profile, for a handrail, etc.; the whole being called a *balustrade*.

Bargeboards: decorative boards fixed beneath the eaves of a gable.

Baroque: bold, free and emphatic European classical style of the C17–C18, revived in the late C19.

Barrel vault: one with a simple arched profile.

Batter: intentional inward inclination of a wall face.

Bay: division of an elevation by regular vertical features such as columns, windows, etc.

Beaux-Arts: a French-derived approach to classical design, at its peak in the later C19–early C20,

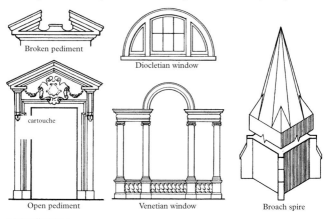

Broken pediment

Diocletian window

cartouche

Open pediment

Venetian window

Broach spire

1. **Miscellaneous**

2. Classical orders and enrichments

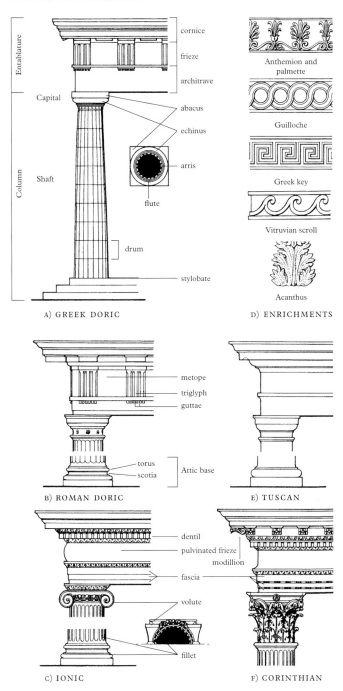

Entablature
- cornice
- frieze
- architrave

Column
- Capital
  - abacus
  - echinus
- Shaft
  - arris
  - flute
- drum
- stylobate

A) GREEK DORIC

Anthemion and palmette

Guilloche

Greek key

Vitruvian scroll

Acanthus

D) ENRICHMENTS

metope
triglyph
guttae

torus
scotia

Attic base

B) ROMAN DORIC

E) TUSCAN

dentil
pulvinated frieze
modillion
fascia

volute

fillet

C) IONIC

F) CORINTHIAN

marked by strong axial planning and the grandiose use of the *orders*.

Billet: ornament of small rectangular blocks.

Blind-back houses: with a windowless rear wall.

Bolection moulding: convex moulding covering the joint between two different planes.

Bressumer: big horizontal beam supporting the wall above, especially in a jettied building; *see* [4C].

Brick: for bond types *see* p. 295.

Broach spire: *see* [1].

Brutalist: used for later 1950s–70s Modernist architecture displaying rough or unfinished concrete, large massive forms, and abrupt juxtapositions.

Cantilever: horizontal projection supported at one end only.

Capital: head feature of a column or pilaster; for classical types *see* [2].

Cartouche: *see* [1].

Castellated: with battlements.

Catslide: a roof continuing down in one plane over a lower projection.

Chancel: the E part or end of a church, where the altar is placed.

Choir: the part of a great church where services are sung.

Clerestory: uppermost storey of an interior, pierced by windows.

Coade stone: ceramic artificial stone, made 1769–*c.* 1840 by Eleanor Coade and associates.

Coffering: decorative arrangement of sunken panels.

Cogging: a decorative course of bricks laid diagonally.

Colonnade: range of columns supporting a flat *lintel* or *entablature* (cf. *arcade*).

Console: bracket of curved outline.

Corbel: projecting block supporting something above.

Composite: classical order with capitals combining Corinthian features (acanthus, *see* [2D]) with Ionic (volutes, *see* [2C]).

Corinthian; cornice: *see* [2A; 2F].

Cove: a broad concave moulding.

Crenellated: with battlements.

Crocket: leafy hooks decorating the edges of Gothic features

Cross-gable: one perpendicular to the main gable(s); on a tower, one of four.

Crucks: pairs of inclined timbers, usually curved, that support the roof timbers; *see* [4B].

Crypt: underground or half-underground area, usually below the E end of a church.

Cupola: a small dome used as a crowning feature.

Cushion capital: of squared form, rounded off below.

Dado: finishing of the lower part of an internal wall.

Decorated (Dec): English Gothic architecture, late C13 to late C14.

Diocletian window: *see* [1].

Doric: *see* [2A, 2B].

Dormer: *see* [3].

Drum: circular or polygonal stage supporting a dome.

Dutch or Flemish gable: *see* [3].

Early English (E.E.): English Gothic architecture, late C12 to late C13.

Electrolier: ornamental fitting for a number of electric lights.

Entablature: *see* [2A].

Faience: moulded *terracotta* that is glazed white or coloured.

Frieze: middle member of a classical *entablature*, *see* [2A, 2C]. Also a horizontal band of ornament.

Geometrical: of *tracery*, a mid-C13–C14 type formed of circles and part-circles, *see* [6].

Giant order: a classical *order* that is two or more storeys high.

Gibbs surround: C18 treatment of an opening with blocked architraves, seen particularly in the work of James Gibbs (1682–1754).

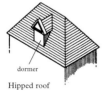

dormer

Hipped roof

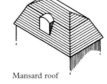

Mansard roof

Flemish or Dutch gable

3. Roofs and gables

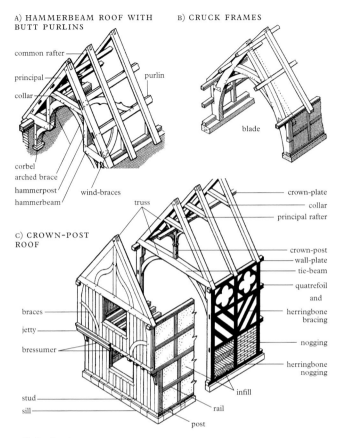

A) HAMMERBEAM ROOF WITH BUTT PURLINS

common rafter

principal

collar

purlin

corbel

arched brace

hammerpost

hammerbeam

wind-braces

B) CRUCK FRAMES

blade

truss

crown-plate

collar

principal rafter

C) CROWN-POST ROOF

crown-post

wall-plate

tie-beam

quatrefoil and herringbone bracing

nogging

herringbone nogging

braces

jetty

bressumer

infill

stud

sill

rail

post

4. Timber framing

Groin vault: one composed of inter-secting *barrel vaults*.

Guilloche: *see* [2D].

Half-timbering: non-structural decorative timberwork.

Hipped roof: *see* [3].

Hoodmould: projecting moulding above an arch or *lintel* to throw off water.

In antis: of columns, set in an opening (properly between simplified pilasters called *antae*).

Ionic: *see* [2C].

Italianate: a classical style derived from the palaces of Renaissance Italy.

Jamb: one of the vertical sides of an opening.

Jettied: with a projecting upper storey, usually timber-framed.

Kingpost roof: one with vertical timbers set centrally on the tie-beams, supporting the ridge.

King-strut: vertical timber placed centrally on a tie-beam, not directly supporting longitudinal timbers.

Lancet: slender, single-light pointed-arched window, *see* [6].

Lantern: a windowed turret crown-ing a roof, tower or dome.

Light: compartment of a window.

Lintel: horizontal beam or stone bridging an opening.

Loggia: open gallery with arches or columns.

Louvre: opening in a roof or wall to allow air to escape.

Lucarne: small gabled opening in a roof or spire.

Lunette: semicircular window or panel.

Mannerist: of classical architecture, with motifs used in deliberate disregard of original conventions or contexts.

Mansard roof: *see* [3].

Mezzanine: low storey between two higher ones.

Moderne: of 1930s design, fashionably streamlined or simplified.

Moulding: shaped ornamental strip of continuous section.

Mullion: vertical member between window lights.

Newel: central or corner post of a staircase.

Norman: the C11–C12 English version of the *Romanesque* style.

Oculus: circular opening.

Œil-de-bœuf: small oval window, set horizontally.

Ogee: of an arch, dome, etc., with double-curved pointed profile.

Orders (classical): for types *see* [2].

Oriel: window projecting above ground level.

Palladian: following the examples and classical principles of Andrea Palladio (1508–80).

Parapet: wall for protection of a sudden drop, e.g. on a bridge, or to conceal a roof.

Passage-entry houses: with side entry from a shared central passage.

Pavilion: ornamental building for occasional use; or a projecting subdivision of a larger building.

Pediment: a formalized gable, derived from that of a classical temple; also used over doors, windows, etc. For types *see* [1].

Pendentive: part-hemispherical surface between arches that meet at an angle to support a drum, dome or vault.

Perpendicular (Perp): English Gothic architecture from the late C14 to early C16.

Piano nobile (Italian): principal floor of a classical building, above a ground floor or basement and with a lesser storey overhead.

Pier: a large masonry or brick support, often for an arch.

Pilaster: flat representation of a classical column in shallow relief.

Pillaret: small pillar or pier.

Pilotis: C20 French term for pillars or stilts that support a building above an open ground floor.

Piscina: basin in a church or chapel for washing mass vessels, usually wall-set.

Platband: flat plain horizontal course or moulding between storeys.

Plinth: projecting courses at the foot of a wall or column, generally chamfered or moulded at the top.

Polychromy: the use of contrasting coloured materials such as bricks as decoration, particularly associated with mid-C19 Gothic styles.

Porte cochère (French): porch large enough to admit wheeled vehicles.

Portico: porch with roof and (frequently) *pediment* supported by a row of columns.

Portland stone: a hard, durable white limestone from the Isle of Portland in Dorset.

Presbytery: a priest's residence.

Pulvinated: of bulging profile; *see* [2c].

Purlin: *see* [4a]. A **ridge purlin** connects the tops of the rafters.

Quatrefoil: opening with four lobes or foils.

Queen Anne: the later Victorian revival of the mid-C17 domestic classical manner, usually in red brick or terracotta.

Queen-post: paired upright timbers on a tie-beam of a roof, supporting purlins.

Quoins: dressed or otherwise emphasized stones at the angles of a building.

Rainwater head: container at a parapet into which rainwater runs from the gutters.

Render: a uniform covering for walls for protection from the weather, usually of cement or *stucco*.

Reredos: painted and/or sculpted screen behind and above an altar.

Rock-faced: masonry cleft to produce a natural, rugged appearance.

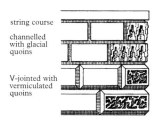

string course

channelled with glacial quoins

V-jointed with vermiculated quoins

5. Rustication

lancet

transom

Geometric   Intersecting   Reticulated

Panel

6. Tracery

Romanesque: round-arched style of the C11 and C12.

Rood: crucifix flanked by the Virgin and St John, carved or painted.

Roughcast: wall plaster mixed with gravel, etc.

Rubble: of masonry, with stones wholly or partly rough and unsquared.

Rustication: exaggerated treatment of masonry to give the effect of strength. For types *see* [5].

Sacristy: room in a church used for sacred vessels and vestments.

Saddleback roof: a pitched roof used on a tower.

Sanctuary: in a church, the area around the main altar.

Scagliola: composition imitating marble.

Sedilia: seats for the priests in the chancel wall of a church or chapel.

Shaped gable: with curved sides, but no pediment (cf. Dutch gable, [3])

Shuttering: temporary framing used for casting concrete.

Spandrel: space between an arch and its framing rectangle, or between adjacent arches.

Stripped classical: with proportions conforming to classical precedent but with the usual decoration implied or removed altogether.

Stucco: durable lime plaster, shaped into ornamental features or used externally as a protective coating.

Terracotta: moulded and fired clay ornament or cladding (cf. *faience*).

Tie-beam: main horizontal transverse timber in a roof structure.

Tile-hanging: overlapping tiled covering on a wall.

Tracery: openwork pattern of masonry or timber in the upper part of an opening; for types *see* [6].

Transept: transverse portion of a church.

Transom: horizontal member between window lights.

Trefoil: with three lobes or foils.

Triforium: middle storey of a church interior treated as an arcaded wall passage or blind arcade.

Truss: braced framework, spanning between supports.

Tumbled-in: of brickwork, laid at right-angles to a slope, usually on a gable.

Tunnel-back houses: terraces with shared open passages for rear access.

Tunnel vault: one with a simple elongated-arched profile.

Tuscan: *see* [2E].

Tympanum: the area enclosed by an arch or pediment.

Undercroft: room(s), usually vaulted, beneath the main space of a building.

Vault: arched stone roof, sometimes imitated in wood or plaster. *See also* Barrel vault.

Venetian window: *see* [1].

Vermiculation: *see* [5].

Vitruvian scroll: *see* [2D].

Volutes: spiral scrolls, especially on Ionic columns (*see* [2C]).

Voussoir: wedge-shaped stones forming an arch.

Wyatt window: large segmental-arched tripartite sash window with narrower side lights, made popular by the Wyatt family of architects in the late C18.

Index
of Artists, Architects and Other Persons Mentioned

Names of artists, architects etc. working in Birmingham are in *italic*; page references including relevant illustrations are in *italic*.

Birmingham (de) family 55, 56
  see also Bermingham
Birmingham Design Services 57, 200
Birmingham Guild 60, 111, 143, 201, 251
Bland, J.G. 12, 166, 168, 269
Bland & Cossins 220
B.L.B. Architects 198
Blee, Anthony 98
Blomfield, Sir Arthur 289
Blomfield, Sir Reginald 142, 145
Bloomer (Harry) & Son 216
Bloxam, M.H. 56
Bloye, William James 64–6, 116, 124,
  126, 128, 137, 143, 144, 229, 230–1,
  246, 252, 253, 258, 260, 265
Blun, John 41
Bodkin, Prof. Thomas 247
Bonham (Paul) Associates 33, 103, 220
Bonham Seager 166
Bonham Seager Associates 134
Boot (Henry) Design and Build 252
Bore, Sir Albert 38
Botham, J.R. 153, 182, 220
Boulton, Matthew 6, 161, 282, 284–8
Boulton, Matthew Robinson 285, 287,
  288
Boulton & Fothergill 285
Boulton (R.L.) & Sons 63
Boulton & Watt 282, 287, 288
Bowyer (Bob) Associates 102
Bradford, Henry 190
Branson, George 221
Bridgeman 224
Bridgeman, Robert 46
Bridgemans 219
Bridgens, Richard 274, 276
Briggs, Samuel 269
Bright, Philip 238
Brindley & Foster 224
Bristow, M.H. 160
*British Railways, London Midland
  Region* 116
Brock, Thomas 123
Broderick, Laurence 87
Bromsgrove Guild 195, 244
Brophy (Frank) Associates 175
Brownhill Hayward Brown 48
Bryant Priest Newman 167, 183
Bryant (C.) & Son 293
Bryson, George 25, 293, 295
Buckland, H.T. 24, 26
Buckland & Haywood 26, 28, 29, 229,
  242, 251, 268n., 288
Buckland & Haywood-Farmer 22, 24,
  26n., 182, 239, 246
Budd, Kenneth 103
Bunce, J.T. 20
Bunce, Kate 195
Bunce, Myra 195

Burchard, Christopher 249
Burdwood & Mitchell 203
Burley, Paul 145
Burlison & Grylls 224
Burn, William 226
Burne-Jones, Edward 21, 41, 45, 55–6
Burnett & Eprile 108
Butler, William 155
Butler, Sir William Waters 25
BVT Architects 258, 268

Cadbury family 257, 258
Cadbury, George 22, 209n., 255–8,
  260, 267
Cadbury, George Jun. 267
Cadbury, Paul 31
Cadbury, Richard 255, 257, 265
Cadbury Bros' Architects' Department
  265
Cadbury-Brown, H.T. 254
Calthorpe family *see below and*
  Gough-Calthorpe family
Calthorpe, 1st Lord 212, 232
Calthorpe, 3rd Lord 10, 212–13, 217,
  227, 235
Calthorpe, 6th Lord 240
Carnegie, Andrew 240
Caröe & Partners 115
Carpenter, Andrew 249
Carpenter, R.C. 9, 235
Carter Green Associates 157
Casson, Sir Hugh 243
Casson (Sir Hugh) & Neville Conder
  242, 245, 253–4
Casson, Conder & Partners 34, 240,
  246, 249, 251
Challen, S.W. 174
Chamberlain, J.H. 11, 13, 14–15, 16, 17,
  20, 60, 68, 69–73, 77, 91, 133, 170,
  180, 214, 222–3, 225, 227, 228
Chamberlain, Joseph 13, 61, 72, 91,
  168, 240, 245
Chamberlain, Neville 26
Chamberlain, Richard 225
Chamberlin, Powell & Bon 34, 240, 252
Chaplin, T. 46
Chapman Taylor 85
Chapman Taylor Partners 108
Charles, F.W.B. 254
Chatwin, Anthony 41, 53–4, 232
Chatwin, J.A. 11, 15, 19, 20, 40, 41–5,
  53, 55, 84, 97, 98, 100, 119, 133, 166,
  174, 178, 183, 195, 214, 221, 223–4,
  231–2, 238, 239, 252, 279–81, 289
Chatwin, John 147, 149
Chatwin, Philip B. 26, 41, 44, 53, 115,
  215, 224
Chatwin, Philip & Anthony 186, 272
Cherrington & Stainton 160, 201

Index

of Localities, Streets and Buildings

Principal references are in **bold** type; page references including relevant illustrations are in *italic*. 'dem.' = 'demolished'

Market Hotel 18, **206**
Market Tavern **193**
Marks & Spencer **108**
Marriott Hotel **215**
Marris & Norton 16, 89, **101**
Marshall and Snelgrove (former)
    114–15
Martineau Galleries **102**
Martineau Street 16
Mary Vale Road 255, 256, **265–6**
Mason College (dem.) 15, 197, 240
Masonic Halls (former):
    Broad Street 27, **142**
    New Street 85, **109–11**
Masshouse 47, **252**
Masshouse Circus (dem.) 38
Medical Institute (former) **130**
Medical Mission (former) **187**
Meriden Street **180**
Messiah, Church of the (dem.) 19
Methodist Central Hall (former) 18,
    22, **106–7**
Methodist Churches:
    Edgbaston (former) **239**
    Selly Oak **267**
Metropolitan House **215–16**
Miall Road **270–2**
Middlemore Emigration Homes
    (dem.) 268n.
Midland and City Arcades 18, *123–4*
Midland Bank, New Street 15, *114*
Midland Educational Co. 89, **101**
Midland Hotel *see* Burlington
    Hotel
Midland Institute (dem.) 77
Midland Land and Investment
    Corporation **98**
Midland Railway 110
Milk Street **182–3**
Millennium Point 37, 179, **190**
Minories 103
Minworth Greaves **261**
Moat Lane 85, **179**
Monument, The (Perrott's Folly)
    220
Monument Road **220**
Moor Street Queensway **84**
Moor Street Station **88**
Moore's Row **183**
Moseley 20
Moseley Road **192–3**
Moseley Street **192**, **193**
Municipal Bank (former):
    Bristol Street **201**
    Broad Street 27, *145–6*
'Municipal Buildings' project 26
Municipal School of Jewellery
    and Silversmithing (former) 158,
    168–9

Museum and Art Gallery *see* Council
    House
Museum of the Jewellery Quarter **177**
Museum of Science and Industry
    (Think Tank) 37, **190**

National Indoor Arena **147**
National Provincial Bank, Waterloo
    Street 10, 28, **127**
National Telephone Co. offices
    (former) 18, *130–1*
National Westminster Bank,
    Colmore Row 33, 34, *95–7*
Navigation Street *207*
Nechells Green 197
Needham's (F.W.) **175**
Needless Alley 89, 113, 118
Nelson monument 6, 8, 85, *86–7*
Neville House:
    Harborne Road 34, *221–2*
    Waterloo Street 28, **126**
New Bartholomew Street **181**
New Canal Street **189–90**
New Cannon Passage **89**
New Hall (dem.) 129
New Hall Coal Co. offices (dem.) 10
New Hall Lane *see* Colmore Row
New Imperial Hotel **123**
New Meeting House (now St
    Michael's) 7, **84**
New Oxford House 28, 65, **126**
New Street 3, 4, 10, 16, 18, 31, 33, 37,
    38, 100, *108–15*, 246
New Street Station 12, 26, 31, 33, *110,*
    116, 196
New Street Station signal box *207*
Newhall Estate 4, 5, 18, *129–40*, 158,
    162
Newhall Street 18, 23, *130–2*, *137–8*,
    160, **165**, 201
Newland House **217**
Newman Brothers' factory (former)
    160
Newton Street 116
Norfolk House 32, **206**
Norfolk Road 214, **239**
North British and Mercantile
    Insurance **93**
North Western Arcade **101–2**
Northampton Parade **168**
Northfield 25
Northfield Road **266–7**
Norwich Union *see* Fire Engine
    House
Novotel **153**

Oak Tree Lane 258, **263–4**
Oakmount **225**
Oasis **102**

Illustration Acknowledgements

Every effort has been made to contact or trace all copyright holders. The publishers will be glad to make good any errors or omissions brought to our attention in future editions.

A special debt of gratitude is owed to English Heritage and its photographer James O. Davies who took the majority of the photographs for this volume. We are grateful to the following for permission to reproduce illustrative material:

Birmingham Central Library (John Whybrow Collection): 24, 46
Birmingham City Archives: 15, 35 (MS1460/7)
Birmingham City Council: 27
Birmingham City Council (City of Hereford Archaeology Unit): 96
Birmingham City Council (Planning Department): 98
Birmingham Museums & Art Gallery: 62, 138

Birmingham Museums & Art Gallery (James O. Davies): 28, 134, 137
Bournville Village Trust, by kind permission : 13
English Heritage (NMR): 2, 4, 5, 6, 7, 8, 9, 10, 11, 12, 16, 17, 19, 20, 21, 22, 23, 25, 26, 29, 30, 31, 34, 36, 37, 38, 39, 40, 42, 43, 44, 45, 47, 48, 49, 50, 51, 52, 53, 54, 55, 56, 57, 58, 59, 60, 61, 63, 64, 65, 66, 67, 68, 69, 70, 71, 73, 74, 75, 76, 77, 78, 80, 81, 83, 84, 85, 86, 87, 88, 89, 90, 92, 93, 94, 95, 97, 99, 101, 102, 103, 104, 105, 106, 107, 108, 109, 110, 111, 112, 113, 114, 115, 116, 117, 118, 121, 122, 123, 124, 126, 127, 128, 129, 131, 132, 133, 135, 136, 139, 140
Arthur Lockwood (donated to the Birmingham Museums & Art Gallery): 14
John Madin: 32
Touchmedia: 1, 33, 61, 72, 79, 82, 91, 100, 119, 125, 130
Victorian Society (Birmingham and West Midlands Group): 41